MW01120654

Studies in International Performance
Published in association with the International Federation of Theatre Research

General Editors: **Janelle Reinelt** and **Brian Singleton**

Culture and performance cross borders constantly, and not just the borders that define nations. In this new series, scholars of performance produce interactions between and among nations and cultures as well as genres, identities and imaginations.

Inter-national in the largest sense, the books collected in the *Studies in International Performance* series display a range of historical, theoretical and critical approaches to the panoply of performances that make up the global surround. The series embraces 'Culture' which is institutional as well as improvised, underground or alternate, and treats 'Performance' as either intercultural or transnational as well as intracultural within nations.

Titles include:

Khalid Amine and Marvin Carlson
THE THEATRES OF MOROCCO, ALGERIA AND TUNISIA
Performance Traditions of the Maghreb

Patrick Anderson and Jisha Menon (*editors*)
VIOLENCE PERFORMED
Local Roots and Global Routes of Conflict

Elaine Aston and Sue-Ellen Case
STAGING INTERNATIONAL FEMINISMS

Matthew Isaac Cohen
PERFORMING OTHERNESS
Java and Bali on International Stages, 1905–1952

Susan Leigh Foster (*editor*)
WORLDING DANCE

Helen Gilbert and Jacqueline Lo
PERFORMANCE AND COSMOPOLITICS
Cross-Cultural Transactions in Australasia

Milija Gluhovic
PERFORMING EUROPEAN MEMORIES
Trauma, Ethics, Politics

Helena Grehan
PERFORMANCE, ETHICS AND SPECTATORSHIP IN A GLOBAL AGE

Susan C. Haedicke
CONTEMPORARY STREET ARTS IN EUROPE
Aesthetics and Politics

James Harding and Cindy Rosenthal (*editors*)
THE RISE OF PERFORMANCE STUDIES
Rethinking Richard Schechner's Broad Spectrum

Silvija Jestrovic and Yana Meerzon (*editors*)
PERFORMANCE, EXILE AND 'AMERICA'

Silvija Jestrovic
PERFORMANCE, SPACE, UTOPIA

Ola Johansson
COMMUNITY THEATRE AND AIDS

Ketu Katrak
CONTEMPORARY INDIAN DANCE
New Creative Choreography in India and the Diaspora

Sonja Arsham Kuftinec
THEATRE, FACILITATION, AND NATION FORMATION IN THE
BALKANS AND MIDDLE EAST

Daphne P. Lei
ALTERNATIVE CHINESE OPERA IN THE AGE OF GLOBALIZATION
Performing Zero

Carol Martin (*editor*)
THE DRAMATURGY OF THE REAL ON THE WORLD STAGE

Carol Martin
THEATRE OF THE REAL

Yana Meerzon
PERFORMING EXILE, PERFORMING SELF
Drama, Theatre, Film

Lara D. Nielson and Patricia Ybarra (*editors*)
NEOLIBERALISM AND GLOBAL THEATRES
Performance Permutations

Alan Read
THEATRE, INTIMACY & ENGAGEMENT
The Last Human Venue

Shannon Steen
RACIAL GEOMETRIES OF THE BLACK ATLANTIC,
ASIAN PACIFIC AND AMERICAN THEATRE

Marcus Tan
ACOUSTIC INTERCULTURALISM
Listening to Performance

Maurya Wickstrom
PERFORMANCE IN THE BLOCKADES OF NEOLIBERALISM
Thinking the Political Anew

S.E. Wilmer
NATIONAL THEATRES IN A CHANGING EUROPE

Evan Darwin Winet
INDONESIAN POSTCOLONIAL THEATRE
Spectral Genealogies and Absent Faces

Forthcoming titles:

Adrian Kear
THEATRE AND EVENT

Studies in International Performance
Series Standing Order ISBN 978–1–403–94456–6 (hardback)
978–1–403–94457–3 (paperback)
(*outside North America only*)

You can receive future titles in this series as they are published by placing a standing
order. Please contact your bookseller or, in case of difficulty, write to us at the address
below with your name and address, the title of the series and the ISBN quoted above.

Customer Services Department, Macmillan Distribution Ltd, Houndmills, Basingstoke,
Hampshire RG21 6XS, England

Performing European Memories

Trauma, Ethics, Politics

Milija Gluhovic

School of Theatre, Performance, and Cultural Policy Studies
University of Warwick, UK

First published 2013 by
PALGRAVE MACMILLAN

Palgrave Macmillan in the UK is an imprint of Macmillan Publishers Limited, registered in England, company number 785998, of Houndmills, Basingstoke, Hampshire RG21 6XS.

Palgrave Macmillan in the US is a division of St Martin's Press LLC, 175 Fifth Avenue, New York, NY 10010.

Palgrave Macmillan is the global academic imprint of the above companies and has companies and representatives throughout the world.

Palgrave® and Macmillan® are registered trademarks in the United States, the United Kingdom, Europe and other countries.

ISBN 978–0–230–29790–6

This book is printed on paper suitable for recycling and made from fully managed and sustained forest sources. Logging, pulping and manufacturing processes are expected to conform to the environmental regulations of the country of origin.

A catalogue record for this book is available from the British Library.

A catalog record for this book is available from the Library of Congress.

To the memory of my grandparents:
Neđo and Ljeposava Gluhović
Danilo and Savka Lažetić

Contents

List of Illustrations

Acknowledgements

I am greatly indebted to the many friends, teachers, and colleagues who have provided me with encouragement, advice, and support over the years.

At the University of Toronto, I thank first and foremost Tamara Trojanowska for her unrelenting support, encouragement, and thoughtful guidance. Her sharp critical insights and commitment to scholarship have been an inspiration for me. I owe a special debt of appreciation to John H. Astington, whose witty advice, kindness, and unfailing encouragement were indispensable, as well as to Jörg Bochow for his many useful insights, especially into the German aspects of my work. I am also grateful to Rebecca Comay, who helped me think through the field of memory studies, Frederick J. Marker for useful suggestions on Pinter, as well as to Nancy Copeland, Pia Kleber, Alan L. Ackerman Jr., Veronika Ambros, Thomas Lahusen, and Linda Hutcheon for the various forms of support and insight they offered. My warmest thanks are also due to my former Drama Centre colleagues, faculty, and staff for their friendship, intellectual companionship, and assistance over the years I spent among them.

The School of Theatre, Performance, and Cultural Policy Studies at the University of Warwick provided an excellent environment for my research and teaching over the past six years. My special thanks go to my current and former Warwick colleagues Janelle Reinelt, Silvija Jestrović, Jim Davis, Nadine Holdsworth, Yvette Hutchison, Tim White, Gurminder Bhambra, Nobuko Anan, and Claire Bishop, all of whom have been amazing intellectual and personal resources. The Erasmus Mundus MA in International Performance Research has also provided an important venue for feedback. Colleagues from Amsterdam, Tampere, Helsinki, Belgrade, Warwick, and many international scholars and students that have taken part in the MAIPR programme since 2008 have helped me to articulate the pan-European and internationalist aspects of this project in more detail. The University of Warwick generously granted me study leave in the autumn terms of 2009–10 and 2012–13 for which I am grateful.

I am deeply grateful, moreover, to Andrew Busza, Ira B. Nadel, John Xiros Cooper, Sneja Gunew, and Errol Durbach from the University of British Columbia in Vancouver, where I started my graduate career, for helping me frame the first questions for this project; I owe many thanks also to Ross Chambers from the University of Michigan, who was the first to introduce me to testimonial writing through his guest course at UBC; this intellectual encounter has been formative for my thinking about forms of collective violence and other traumatic experiences.

There are also those whom I would like to acknowledge for their implicit and explicit forms of solidarity and inspiration, which have meant a great deal to me: Agnieszka Polakowska, Karen Fricker, Katrin Sieg, Leslie Katz, Justyna Sempruch, Natalie Alvarez, and Olivera Jokić, who read the whole or substantial parts of this manuscript at its various stages and offered valuable comments; Michal Kobialka for commenting on my chapter on Kantor, sharing generously his unpublished work and translations of Kantor's work, as well as for inspiring conversations about this artist's theatre while teaching at Warwick in 2012; Freddie Rokem and Pirkko Koski for sending me their essays and offering crucial advice; Joachim Fiebach for sharing his knowledge of Müller's work; Dragana Varagić for many inspiring conversations over the years, which moved my thinking in too many ways to recount; Joanna Falck, Kim Solga, Barbara Orel, Lisa Fitzpatrick, Eszter Jagica, Olga Ponichtera, Jesenka Karamehmedović, the late Aleksandra Đajić Horvath, Lejla Hasanbegović, Nihad Kreševljaković, Nataša Glišić, and Lisa Skwirblies.

Many thanks go out to the late Harold Pinter for his kindness in allowing me to access the drafts of his plays in the Pinter Archive at the British Library. I am also grateful to the staff of the following libraries and archives: the University of Warwick Library; the Libraries of the University of Toronto; the Harold Pinter Archive at the British Library and the Royal National Theatre Archive in London; the Centre for the Documentation of the Art of Tadeusz Kantor (Cricoteka) in Cracow; the Berliner Ensemble Archive and the Archives of the Academy of Arts in Berlin. Furthermore, I would like to express my gratitude to the Humanities Research Centre at Warwick; the Graduate Centre for Study of Drama, the Munk Centre for International Studies and the School of Graduate Studies at the University of Toronto, as well as to the Social Sciences and Humanities Research Council of Canada and the Ministry of Education and Training, Provincial Government of Ontario, for the various fellowships and travel grants that made this research possible. I would also like to thank my current and former students at Warwick and in Toronto and Vancouver for their curiosity about memory issues, theatre, and critical theory, which has proved both addictive and sustaining.

I owe many heartfelt thanks to Janelle Reinelt and Brian Singleton, who brought this project on board through their series Studies in International Performance, for their enthusiastic encouragement and incisive advice throughout the project. To Janelle, whose scholarship I have long admired and who remains an invaluable interlocutor, I owe an inestimable debt. She has been a model senior scholar since I have known her, as well as a dear colleague and friend. I would also like to extend my gratitude to Paula Kennedy and the staff at Palgrave Macmillan for their expert production work. Thanks also to the *Toronto Slavic Quarterly*, *Polish Theatre Perspectives*, and the Polish Institute of Arts and Sciences of America, for allowing me to reproduce segments from earlier versions of Chapter 3 as well as all the editors and editorial staff concerned.

Many thanks as well to Brigitte Maria Mayer, Inka Ihmels of the Aufbau Verlag, and Manuel Quirin of Suhrkamp Verlag for permissions to include poems by Inge and Heiner Müller in my book. For their generous assistance with obtaining photographs of Kantor's work and permissions to include them here, I am very grateful to Duncan Jamieson, Adela Karsznia, Małgorzata Paluch-Cybulska, and Tomasz Tomaszewski.

With devotion, I thank my families on both sides of the Atlantic, especially my parents Borika and Miladin Gluhović.

Most of all, for his love and support and for seeing me through this project, my heartfelt thanks to Brent Fowler.

Series Editors' Preface

The "Studies in International Performance" series was initiated in 2004 on behalf of the International Federation for Theatre Research, by Janelle Reinelt and Brian Singleton, successive Presidents of the Federation. Their aim was, and still is, to call on performance scholars to expand their disciplinary horizons to include the comparative study of performances across national, cultural, social, and political borders. This is necessary not only in order to avoid the homogenizing tendency of national paradigms in performance scholarship, but also in order to engage in creating new performance scholarship that takes account of and embraces the complexities of transnational cultural production, the new media, and the economic and social consequences of increasingly international forms of artistic expression. Comparative studies (especially when conceived across more than two terms) can value both the specifically local and the broadly conceived global forms of performance practices, histories, and social formations. Comparative aesthetics can challenge the limitations of national orthodoxies of art criticism and current artistic knowledges. In formalizing the work of the Federation's members through rigorous and innovative scholarship this Series aims to make a significant contribution to an ever-changing project of knowledge creation.

Janelle Reinelt and Brian Singleton
International Federation for Theatre Research
Fédération Internationale pour la Recherche Théâtrale

1
Introduction: Theorising Europe and Recollection

Discussing the ways in which memories of the Second World War have shaped the imagined geography of Europe, the French historian Henry Rousso quotes with approval the Dutch specialist on sites of memory, Pim den Boer, who argues that Europe "needs sites of memory: not as a mnemonic technique merely to identify mutilated bodies, but in order to make people understand, forgive, and forget" (Rousso, 2007: 28). To Rousso, this means that "European memory must be conceived within a horizon of expectation rather than within a space of experience, and is therefore something that has yet to be built rather than something to be exhumed" (2007: 28). I share these authors' concerns over the role memory has come to play in the reorganisation of the European political landscape in the wake of *perestroika* and the Iron Curtain's collapse. In *Performing European Memories*, I examine the part played by cultures of remembrance in shoring up the borders of emerging postwar national or supranational ("western European," "Warsaw pact," "pan-European") identities. At the same time, however, through my analysis of the works by Heiner Müller, Tadeusz Kantor, Harold Pinter, Andrzej Wajda, Artur Żmijewski, and several others, I also seek to point to the simultaneous difficulty and necessity of confronting bodies from the past, bodies which retain the marks of politics, history, and reverence.

Often positioned within a specific memory discourse in which they intervene – from Western debates (and oblivions) of the slave trade and the colonies, via the Holocaust to the recent debates of the Soviet crimes in Central and Eastern Europe and the Allied bombing raids of German cities during the Second World War – these works insist on unfinished business: guilt and reparation remain the dominant themes. Forcing their audiences to become excavators of these repressed pasts, these artworks challenge their audiences' historical imagination and renew their affective engagement with Europe's past. As I argue here, the main ethical impetus behind their engagement with the past arises from their need to bear witness and to mourn. The work of mourning may never dissolve all melancholy or heal all wounds, but it is to be hoped that it may disclose unrealised possibilities within the past and create new openings for the future.

While *Performing European Memories* attempts to present a multidimensional geographical perspective, it does not presume to be a comprehensive, narrative history of twentieth- and twenty-first-century European theatre and performance engaging with the themes of European memory and history. However, I hope that it adds an important dimension to the already existing research in the field, showing that there are many perspectives within Europe itself, depending on from which concrete memories the present situation is considered: a more Western European perspective or a more Eastern one. The devastation of the world wars and the Holocaust legacy have been widely rehearsed on European stages, especially in Western Europe. Many studies have been devoted to still fraught issues of the Holocaust's representation and the way it has been embedded in the official memory cultures of European nation states (Schumacher, 1998; Rokem, 2000; Plunka, 2009). In addition to the artists I discuss in this book, some of the most important voices of twentieth-century European theatre and performance such as Thomas Bernhard and Elfriede Jelinek in Austria, Gorge Tabori in Germany, Charlotte Delbo in France, and Jerzy Grotowski and Tadeusz Różewicz in Poland, to name but a few, have written politically situated memory-plays, often taking an activist stance against the distortion and repression of the past enacted in the official discourses in their native countries. Still very little work has addressed the processes of imperialism, colonialism, and slavery that, if largely unacknowledged, are an integral part of European history and identity. In the east of the continent, the complex legacy of the communist past is still being actively negotiated. For instance, the current social science scholarship is grappling with a nostalgic turn across the former Soviet bloc, which resulted from widespread disillusionment (all across Eastern Europe) with the social and especially the economic changes that ensued in the post-communist era (Todorova, 2010; Todorova and Gille, 2010). As scholars of Eastern European theatre and performance point out, East European arts, especially in Russia, are also engaged in opposing new post-communist governments exploitation of post-communist nostalgia in the service of strategic repression and calculated misrepresentation of the memory of the past (Meerzon, 2011). Similar kinds of contestation take place in other social arenas across the east of the continent as well, as recent official commemorations of the Great Famine that decimated the population of Ukraine in 1932–33 show. The official narrative of the event as a genocide is still widely contested in Ukraine, while it also represents a stumbling block in Ukrainian-Russian relations (Zhurzhenko, 2010). On the other hand, Israeli director Yael Bartana's 2007 film *Nightmares* (*Mary Koszmary*), featuring a scene with a young Polish politician, who delivers a resounding speech at an empty sporting arena in Warsaw, appealing to three million Jews to return to Poland to live with Poles again, testifies compellingly to the complexity of Jewish-Polish relations up to the present day, but also reminds us that "similar dynamics to those Bartana has identified in Poland exist throughout the region" (Underhill, 2011: 581). The case of the Roma and their continued discrimination and marginalisation across the continent is also of interest for the study of European memory. As Ioana Szeman notes in her analysis of Romani artist Tibor Balogh's installation "Rain of Tears" in the *Hidden Holocaust* exhibition displayed in Budapest and Venice in 2004 and 2007 respectively, there is a lack of historical awareness about the Romani Holocaust in most European countries.

The north and south of Europe may not seem to have as traumatic a recent history as the east and west of the continent have, but as controversy that erupted in Finland after the staging of *The Unknown Soldier* at the Finnish National Theatre in Helsinki in 2009 indicates, the memory of the Second World War is still a politically loaded subject in Finland. Based on the classic Finnish novel by Väinö Linna and directed by Kristian Smeds, the performance included screened close-ups of the actors playing Finnish soldiers from the Second World War, on whose faces an image was projected of "the raped and killed bodies of Soviet female soldiers, images which were not revealed until decades after the war had ended" (Koski, 2010, n.p.) Beyond Finland, an international conference entitled "The Past Is

Still to Change: Performing History from 1945 to the Present," held in 2009 at the Vytautas Magnus University in Kaunas, Lithuania, offered a range of perspectives on the ways in which theatre and performance artists in Eastern Europe and the Baltic region in particular have engaged the legacy of the Second World War and the Cold War. In the south of the continent, scholars have addressed theatrical representations of the memories of war and violence, specifically in the context of the Spanish Civil War (see, for instance, Orozco, 2007; Buffery, 2007; Duprey-Colon, 2010). Finally, "the *ultimate* act in the century-long European drama – or, rather, tragedy – of exterminations, expulsions and exchanges (of populations, that is)," the wars in Yugoslavia in the 1990s also revived painful memories of the Second World War (Müller, 2012: 237). While a couple of decades may be "insufficient time for a meaningful historicisation process to have occurred" (Stone, 2013: 25), theatre and performance studies scholars who have written on this topic show that the disintegration of Yugoslavia continues to be an arena of contestation, both in politics and the arts, which will hopefully give rise to justice, reconciliation, and peaceful cohabitation in the region (Jakovljević, 2008; Lukić, 2009; Jestrović, 2012).

The concept of memory is complex and seldom invoked in precisely the same sense, hence the ramifications, traditions, and histories, which are conflated in their current usages, need to be unpacked and evaluated. In this introduction, I thus discuss three aspects of memory discourse: the historical (relation between historiography and individual/collective memory), psychological (trauma, mourning, and melancholia), and philosophical (subjectivity), as well as how they can be brought to bear on my subsequent discussion of different layers of the European (theatrical) imagination during a time of great change. The three notions in the book's subtitle – trauma, ethics, politics – aim to describe this complexity, pointing at a narrative dimension leading from trauma (intended as a plural containing the numerous catastrophes designed by humans), to a consideration of their ethical dimensions through witnessing and mourning, and ending with the perspective of a reintegrated Europe which in spite of the remarkable progress made, is still/again facing xenophobia, racism, and inequality. But this book is also written in an attempt to face the challenges this "new" Europe is itself facing as it is looks back at its own histories of trauma, confronting the ethical dimensions of the past.[1]

Much of this book is in dialogue with the burgeoning debates on the politics of memory in Europe, especially in the fields of historiography (for instance, Jarausch and Lindenberger, 2007; Passerini, 2007; Pakier and Stråth, 2010), political science (for instance, Jan-Werner Müller, 2002), sociology (Olick, 2003), and international relations (for instance, Mälksoo, 2009; Berg and Ehin, 2009), which have come to play a crucial role in the developing discourse on common European identity, especially as regards the process of European integration. As Jan-Werner Müller notes, "In recent years a number of politicians and intellectuals have openly expressed the wish to see the formation of a kind of 'Europeansiation' of collective memory or even a clearly discernable 'supranational European memory'" (2010: 25). In this context many have argued that the commemoration of the Holocaust is increasingly becoming the core of a unifying European memory, thus giving constitution building in Europe the necessary symbolic foundation (see, for instance, Beck, 2003; Levy and Sznaider, 2002). The arguments put forward by these authors are in many respects reasonable and persuasive, particularly in highlighting that the Holocaust has become a matter of universal concern, and that more and more countries in Europe seek to come to terms with the heritage of the Holocaust and their moral and historical guilt or even their involvement with the Holocaust. Yet this wish for "oneness" of memory is fraught with its own problems, such as the suspicion that "a pan-European focus on Nazism and the Holocaust might actually be an attempt to redistribute German guilt across the European Union" (Jan-Werner Müller, 2010: 25). Furthermore, the Holocaust is differently embedded in the political culture of European countries (and the US). Although recent historiography has deepened our understanding of the Holocaust as a transnational phenomenon involving almost every country in Europe, we know more about the murder of the Jews in Western Europe than in Eastern Europe. For instance, even though immediately after the Second World War many Jewish survivors and in particular professional historians in Poland, set the foundations for Holocaust research in general (Aleksiun, 2004), scholars in the West remained largely indifferent to the scholarship produced in Eastern Europe: that half of the continent "remained a largely uncharted territory for the most prominent historians of the Holocaust" (Bartov, 2008: 559). Yet, as Timothy Snyder argues, the Holocaust was "an east European event" in several respects:

> The vast majority of European Jews were east European Jews, from Poland or the Soviet Union. The death camps were all located in German-occupied Poland. Half of the Jews who died in the Holocaust perished in death pits rather than in death camps; almost all of the major shooting actions took place in Ukraine, Belarus, Russia, and Poland. (2009: 9)

The relatively slow development of research on the Holocaust in Eastern Europe stemmed from a combination of many factors. As Wendy Lower notes, the field of Holocaust studies first addressed other issues such as "the highest decision-making levels of the Third Reich" and the killing centres such as Auschwitz-Birkenau (2008: 5). Furthermore, the geopolitical division of the continent during the Cold War era made it difficult for scholars to access the archives located behind the Iron Curtain and to integrate the acts of political violence that took place in regions such as present-day Ukraine, Belarus, Lithuania, Estonia or Moldova into a general account of European history.

To be sure, the historical reception of the Holocaust in the countries of the former Soviet Bloc was marked by its own set of specific problems and denials, as I show, for instance, in my discussion of the painful Polish self-interrogation over the massacre at Jedwabne in my chapter on Kantor. Several decades of communism that controlled public space in Eastern European countries, limited access to archives, and the Eastern European governments' manipulation and censorship on representation of the experience of the last war deeply influenced the ways in which the Holocaust has been remembered – and not remembered in Eastern European official narratives and a wider public sphere. Even though the Holocaust changed the cultural landscape of Eastern Europe in unprecedented ways, "the communist narrative of the war left no room for the unique fate of the Jews during the Nazi occupation, instead folding it into the general narrative of 'fascist' crimes and the victimization of the nation's citizens" (Bartov 2008: 562). Furthermore, because so many non-Jewish Eastern Europeans were killed by the Germans, the Soviet position that murdered Jews were simply murdered citizens was more or less acceptable in Soviet-dominated Eastern Europe (2009: 11). Furthermore, throughout the Cold War east European countries remained reluctant to examine their role in the complex matrix of continent-wide genocide.

Moreover, the idea that a new mode of solidarity beyond the nation-state and a common European identity might be based on the shared experiences of the Second World War (Habermas, 2001) is hampered by the fact that the much longer and much more diverse Communist episode (Stalinism, Soviet occupation, and many other forms of oppression) are at the core of the national memories of most Eastern European states that claimed political independence after the collapse of Communism. Many in Eastern Europe perceive the states of Western Europe and those of NATO as having betrayed them by accepting Europe's postwar division and the occupation of the eastern half of the continent by the colonising power of the Soviet Union. As Charles Turner asserts, "The wound inflicted more than a half a century ago at Yalta is still felt" and is slow to heal (2004: 303). Moreover, the suffering experienced by the many millions of victims of the Soviet regime, deported to Gulags, tortured, exploited as forced labourers and murdered, has not yet become an integral part of a pan-European memory landscape (Blaive, Gerbel, and Lindenberger, 2011; Stone, 2012). As I show in my discussion of Kantor's and Wajda's representations of the Katyń massacre, while all sorts of cultural and historical remembrances evoke Nazi crimes, comparable markers of specific national and regional suffering under Communism are much fewer. However, in recent years Poland and the Baltic states, especially their political elites, have been at the forefront of a new European commemorative politics demanding a pan-European acknowledgement of their distinct historical experiences of the Second World War (Mälksoo, 2009), though often forgetful of their own role in the extermination of the local Jewish populations.

As my arguments show, re-telling the past may be a powerful mechanism for generating a collective sense of identity in a complex society such as Europe. However, this process needs to involve the diverging memories of Eastern and Western Europe, which would allow the peoples of the continent to take a reflexive view of themselves in light of others' experiences. It is these memories that can contribute to create an increasingly complex collective identity of Europeans involving strong bonds, and, hopefully, a common

European cultural space. However, I am also mindful that the experience of some countries on the southern boundaries of Europe such as Greece, Portugal, and (especially) Spain cannot be easily aligned with "mythic narratives of resistance, Allied solidarity, and democratic renewal," which dominated nation-building in post-1945 Western Europe (Stone, 2012: 717).

The Cold War division of Europe caused the Western Allies to support Southern European dictatorships with past "Nazi links or empathies," which were able to persist as dictatorial and authoritarian regimes into the 1970s (Graham and Quroga, 2012: 504). A particularly interesting case is Spain, where the post-1975 transition to democracy "was negotiated by reformist Francoists and the democratic opposition on the basis of a consensus that the civil war was a 'tragedy' over which a veil of silence should be drawn, a strategy aided by the 1977 Amnesty Law" (Stone, 2012: 722). The painful process of coming to terms with the traumatic legacy of Francoist repression started on the fringes of civil society in the early 1980s, gaining momentum with the dramatic opening of mass graves from the civil war in 2000, and continuing with the passing of the Law of Historical Memory in 2007 – an important attempt at the institutional level to engender a public debate on the violence and repression that took place during the war and Dictatorship (see Labanyi, 2009; Renshaw, 2011). This change in social sensitivity toward memory that occurred in the Spanish public sphere at the start of the twenty-first century, which also led to a greater interest in the Holocaust in that country, can thus be seen as part of the wider European debate about history, memory, and culture.

I also argue that a European incorporation of the dark sides of Europe's past should also include histories and memories of European colonialism and imperialism, which still profoundly shape the present. While the project of European integration provided a significant avenue for former colonial powers to "adjust to the changing political and economic circumstances brought about by decolonization," scholars have paid little attention to the relationship between colonialism, the processes of decolonisation (not yet completed), and notions of European identity (Hansen, 2002: 493). Given that colonialism is arguably integral to the story of European integration, there is a curious omission of European dependencies and protectorates located across the world in official discourses of the EU and its territorial representations. For instance, in the French Overseas

Departments of Réunion, Guyana, Martinique, and Guadeloupe, as well as in the Spanish possessions in North Africa, Melilla, and Ceuta, "payments are made in euros and the inhabitants are 'citizens of the EU,'" while the inhabitants of several French, Dutch, Danish, and British Overseas Countries and Territories (OCTS) also carry EU passport (Hansen, 2004: 55). And yet these putatively European territories and citizens figure little in conceptions of contemporary Europe. As Peo Hansen remarks, the EU's disinclination to acknowledge that its borders stretch into Africa, the Caribbean, South America, the Pacific, and the Indian Ocean also reflects its reluctance "to deal with the history and legacy of colonialism" (2004: 57). This disavowal of Europe's colonial past and present continues to have implications for the inclusion and exclusion of minorities and migrants in relation to the European Union today.

Stressing the colonial past, I contend, is also a useful check on Eurocentrism and Europe's universalist pretensions in the present. Laying claim to a European identity articulated around peace, democracy, and human rights, Europe sees itself predestined for a key role in twenty-first-century global politics. While this position becomes increasingly common in academic studies of Europe, it was perhaps most forcefully articulated in an essay written by Jürgen Habermas, co-signed by Jacques Derrida, and published simultaneously in German and French in 2003, as part of a concentrated action of European intellectuals to show their solidarity with Europe-wide protests against the Iraq war. They suggested that "The simultaneity of these overwhelming demonstrations – the largest since the end of the Second World War – may well, in hindsight, go down in history as a sign of the birth of a European public sphere" (Habermas and Derrida, 2005: 4). They traced this achievement directly to the French Revolution, assuming that the concept of universal human rights is a quintessentially European achievement. This assertion conveniently forgets that revolutionary France never ceased to be actively imperial, and that it actively sought to suppress the black liberation struggle in the Caribbean that sought to put in practice the promise of the French revolution. I engage with these issues at more length in the following chapter, where I analyse Müller's play *The Task*. The play stages the problematic relationship between history and memory in a context that reaches beyond European boundaries to raise the question of the suppression and disavowal of revolutionary antislavery in the

Caribbean and to challenge certain accounts of the historical origins of modernity. As Susan Buck-Morss argues in her recent study of Hegel and Haiti, "Present realities demand such historical remappings as an alternative to the fantasies of clashing civilizations and exclusionary redemptions" (2009: 73). Much of my analysis of Müller's complex text, which involved drawing a map around the silences and gaps that punctuate the elite historical and cultural records in regard to the only revolution that centred on the issue of racial equality – the Haitian Revolution (1791–1804) – would not be possible without the painstaking work done by the historians of slavery, slave resistance, and the particular revolution.

Interest in the relationship between history and memory has been an important aspect of European historiography since the 1980s.[2] The issue of how history is remembered gained in urgency with the volatile political developments since 1989, and the return of memories that could not be articulated in the public sphere during the Cold War. As I pointed out earlier, the memory boom since the end of the Cold War, and especially in the new millennium, with its various narratives concerning the Second World War, the Holocaust, the history of communism, and the legacy of colonialism has brought about new challenges to European politics. And while European integration is seen by some as "the most important political experiment undertaken anywhere in the last half century" (Calhoun, 2009: 637), and the "European memory" currently debated has been constructed as pivotal for fostering a collective sense of European identity in the EU, its nation-states remain primary arenas for democratic public life and provide the contexts of everyday solidarities (as the Eurozone crisis well demonstrates), while the focus on national histories continues to inform twenty-first century "postnational" discourses. Outside the EU, the collapse of the Soviet Union as well as the demise of Yugoslavia and the series of wars that engulfed it (a topic I discuss at some length in the final chapter) appeared to spell the conclusive triumph of the nation-state. As we shall also see in the examples of Germany, Poland, and France, the shaping and negotiating of issues of memory, identity, and cultural values within the bounds of the nation-state is often both problematic and highly charged.

The decade after the unification of the two Germanies witnessed a series of discussions and debates surrounding Holocaust-centred

memory: the rearticulation of Berlin's memory landscape, epitomised by the memorial to the murdered Jews of Europe; the Daniel
Goldhagen controversy of the guilt of average Germans; the *Wermach-
tausstellung* about the crimes of the army; and the Walser-Bubis affair
and compensation for slave labourers, to mention only the most
prominent (see Langenbacher, 2010). At the beginning of the third
millennium, however, for the first time in years, public discussions
shifted from the suffering Germans inflicted on others to the suffering Germans themselves experienced during the Third Reich and its
immediate aftermath, especially as regards the expulsion of Germans
from then-Eastern Germany and Eastern Europe after the war and
the Allied bombing raids of German cities. Although these discussions are not entirely new, given evidence of a widespread confrontation with these events in the earlier postwar decades, the return to
the memory of German suffering certainly marks an important shift
in German memory regimes, which may augment and relativise the
dominance of Holocaust memory (Langenbacher, 2003). I discuss
this phenomenon in the course of my analysis of Müller's *Explosion
of a Memory /Description of a Picture* and its 2001 staging at the
Berliner Ensemble, which coincided with this latest memory debate.
Since the dialectics between victim and victimiser is at the centre of
the play's story, I argue that the performance served as a vehicle for
complex audience responses, and intervened directly in the contemporary discourse of national remembrance in Germany.

If many ordinary men and women in Eastern Europe – and not just
intellectuals and political leaders – believed in state socialism and
the fully Communist society it promised, then the toppling of massive statues of heroes of communist regimes at the end of the 1980s
and early 1990s announced the end of that belief. Spelling the end
of Marxism as a global language of opposition (if not the end of the
European and global Left and Marxism as a theory), this destruction
also produced its own nostalgia for lost historical possibilities which
are for some of us still associated with this political experiment:
equality, genuine inclusion in a political community, and justice. The
replacement of a statue of Karl Marx with that of Theodore Mommsen
in front of Humboldt University partly inspired Müller's *Mommsen's
Block*, another text by Müller discussed in the next chapter, although
the question of what the statue of Marx meant to the population of
Berlin is never explicitly addressed by Müller. Rather, the play serves

as a testament to a stalemate position in which public intellectuals from the former German Democratic Republic (GDR), such as Müller and Christa Wolf, found themselves after the unification. The last play by Müller that I analyse here, *The Task*, as I mentioned earlier, stages the expansion of French revolutionary ideals by Europe's enslaved, colonised subjects in the Caribbean in the aftermath of the French revolution, inviting reflection on the excision of the Haitian revolution from standard accounts of the age of revolutions.

However, we do not need to leave Europe in order to find signs of both the violence of colonialism and the silence imposed upon it. As we know today, the Nazi racialisation of Jews as non-white and procedures such as concentration camps, slavery, and extermination used against Jews, Roma, Slavs, and others are practices drawn from the colonial periphery of the modern European world and used by other European powers in that context. Camps and extermination were also employed by the Soviets against the Polish people in the course of the Second World War in preparation for a permanent takeover of the country. Working from symptomatic fragments, keeping track of what is said, and especially what is not said, in my third chapter I analyse Kantor's performance *Let the Artist Die*, which resurrected the memory of the Katyń massacre. In 1940, under Stalin's orders, the NKVD executed almost twenty-two thousand Polish officers at Katyń, Kalinin, Starobelsk, and other secret locations. Although the majority of the Polish population had never accepted the Soviet blame of the Germans for the massacre, during the postwar period in which Poland was subjugated by Russia the issue of Katyń was suppressed in the official discourse of national remembrance, and the Polish Communist line on the subject concurred with the Soviet one. A clear instantiation of how public and official memories do not always coincide, the issue was officially still taboo in 1986 when Kantor staged his performance.

Let us also remember at this point that a long period of silence accompanied the issue of the Holocaust in the West: debate over its historical significance and its place in the heritage of the West developed very slowly. The importance of Hannah Arendt's *The Burden of Our Time*, written in 1951, which made it clear that understanding genocide is a burden that our century has imposed upon us, was recognised only in the 1970s. In fact this burden was accepted by very few for a very long time. In the aftermath of the war, Polish writers such as Tadeusz Borowski, Zofia Nałkowska, Julian Stryjkowski, and many others responded to this challenge and produced some of the most significant Holocaust texts. Similarly, the Polish historiography of the Holocaust produced in the years immediately after the Second World War (1945–48) constitutes the roots of Holocaust scholarship in general (Aleksiun 2004). However, in the 1970s, when Kantor began his work on a cycle of performances called "The Theatre of Death" cycle of performances, the issue of the Holocaust and the so-called "Jewish Question" was conspicuously suppressed in Polish public discourse. In my discussion of Kantor's *Wielopole, Wielopole*, I address this issue, as well as the significance of Kantor's mnemonic intervention in this regard.

Many plays and performances analysed in the following chapters engage in various ways with the pathologies of trauma. Some works foreground traumatic suffering of an individual – such is the case with Józef Tarnawa in Żmijewski's video work *80064* – and the repercussions of that suffering in later life. Others address more directly the collective suffering caused by massive historic fractures, such as that introduced by the Holocaust and the transatlantic slave trade as invoked in Kantor's *Wielopole, Wielopole* and Müller's *The Task* respectively. Associated with this is the suffering of those who witnessed traumatogenic events, and those who identify with them. Sometimes the source of trauma exceeds the boundaries of any particular shock or discrete event, as is the case with the specific damages produced in relation to everyday forms of violence experienced by people living under authoritarian regimes as portrayed in Wajda's *Katyń*. While I criticise some of the prevailing assertions about the operations of trauma (and the theoretically unreflective embrace of memory), trauma theory also offers an indispensable framework for my analysis here. My goal is not so much to associate the impact of trauma registered in the works of artists I analyse with particular conceptualisations of trauma (for example, Leys, 2000; Radstone, 2007a) – though to some extent this might be inevitable – but to demonstrate that their plays and performances can be regarded as engendering specific languages of trauma that proceed from its lived experience. Furthermore, if the unspeakable or the unwitnessable makes its incognisible mark on the mind as a traumatic memory, or in the body, as embodied memory, as a dominant strand of trauma theory has it (Caruth, 1995; 1996), leaving traces that can only be

read (if at all) through belated witnessing, then, I argue, overextending
the scope of the argument and rash claims of traumatisation or unrep-
resentability without paying attention to its cultural and social contin-
gence might result in an inadequate account of the psychic suffering
in question.[3] In order to avoid this trap, in the following chapters,
especially when I analyse Kantor's and Müller's works, I explore in
as much detail as possible not only where and when the "trauma"
actually emerged, but also why certain events were not assimilable.
I ask why certain histories of suffering have been neglected, supressed,
or disavowed, why and by whom; and what role theatre and cultural
production played in this process.

Furthermore, I argue that if our conceptual framework is marked
out by "memory" alone, we will find it difficult to understand
how the historical gaps and silences problematised, for instance, in
Müller's *The Task* or Kantor's *Let the Artists Die* ever came into being.
An audience uninitiated in Polish history will be at loss to organise
a discursive overload, and to respond to a range of memory triggers
that inform Kantor's play. Similarly, the intricate historical issues
and ideological battles that are acted out in *The Task* become visible only if we have some understanding of the conflicts surrounding colonial slavery during the French Revolution. Furthermore, in
regards to *The Task*, I focus strategically on the Haitian Revolution
and the transatlantic slave trade as historical formations rather than
metaphors for German domestic troubles, with an intention to avoid
the Eurocentric tendencies of much work in memory studies, often
markedly restricted by an almost exclusive interest in the Holocaust
as a conceptual limit case. Although I engage the Nazi genocide at
length in the following chapters, I also argue for the extension of
the discussion of historical trauma, memory, and forgetting to other
non-Western regions and nations across the globe that are often
preoccupied with historical tragedies they themselves experienced.
At the same time, my analysis remains attentive to the resonances
and connections between various international contexts of traumatic
transfer.

In recent years Memory Studies has emerged as a truly transnational field of inquiry, moving beyond its early focus on Euro-
American events and experiences. Scholars in the field of theatre and
performance studies have been at the forefront of this transformation, resituating a study of memory within an international arena

and decentring the pattern of Western memory, where unwelcome knowledge, histories, and traumas have been expunged or sanitised. Diana Taylor's *The Archive and the Repertoire: Performing Cultural Memory in the Americas* (2003), Ana Elena Puga's *Memory, Allegory, and Testimony in South American Theater: Upstaging Dictatorship* (2008), and Jean Graham-Jones's *Exorcising History: Argentine Theater under Dictatorship* (2000), for instance, have explored valences of traumatic memory in the Latin American context, particularly the legacies of centuries of social trauma undergone by many populations in the Americas – from the onset of the colonial conquest to the twentieth-century dictatorships in Uruguay, Chile, Argentina, and other South American countries. Loren Kruger's *Post-Imperial Brecht: Politics and Performance, East and South*, Catherine Cole's *Performing South Africa's Truth Commission: Stages of Transition* (2010), and Yvette Hutchison's *South African Performance and the Archives of Memory* (2013) have engaged the difficult legacy of the decades of systematic traumatisation of black people by white rulers in South Africa and the social, political, historical, and ethical significance of the Truth and Reconciliation Commission. Emily Roxworthy's *The Spectacle of Japanese American Trauma: Racial Performativity and World War II* (2008) has brought to light the US government's internment policies during the Second World War and their impact on the postwar lives of many Japanese Americans, while one of the chapters in *Performance and Cosmopolitics: Cross-Cultural Transactions in Australasia*, co-authored by Helen Gilbert and Jacqueline Lo, examines a variety of artistic and political responses in the Australian context to traumas of the most abject of cosmopolitan subjects – refugees and forced migrants. More so than questions of asylum, in the last two decades the traumas of Australia's "stolen generations," the survivors and offspring of Indigenous children taken by force from their families in the 1930s through the 1970s, and placed in "white families," have received the attention of theatre and performance scholars (and mainstream representations, including films *Rabbit-Proof Fence* (2002) and *Australia* (2008) directed by Phillip Noyce and Baz Luhrmann respectively), while research on the Truth and Reconciliation Commission of Canada, whose mandate is to learn the truth about what happened in the residential schools across the country, where First Nations, Métis, and Inuit children were placed from 1870s until 1996, often against their parents' wishes, is already gaining momentum.

Cathy Caruth has suggested that "trauma itself may provide the very link between cultures" (1995: 11), promising cross-cultural listening, and even this cursory look at some recent outputs in the field of theatre and performance studies dealing with historical traumas, violence, and witnessing seems to fulfil this promise. These works show that the interdisciplinary field of theatre and performance studies, involving methodologies from anthropology, history, visual cultures, and critical theory as well as a number of performing arts disciplines such as dance, theatre, and performance art, could be seen as one of the exemplary sites where memory research is productively practised within academic disciplines. Along with theories of testimony and witnessing, trauma theory has become one of the key modes within which performance and other scholars analyse the transmission of experiences of extreme suffering and violence (and is central to this evolving field of transnational memory studies). However, as Susannah Radstone, one of the leading trauma scholars in the humanities today, argues "without careful disciplinary embedding and testing, concepts such as trauma may appear to explain more than they actually can" (2008: 35). Furthermore, some of trauma theory's early speculations about processes of memory risk uncritical reception and applications (such as Caruth's formulation of traumatic ordeal as "a break in the mind's experience of time" that is characterised by "the structure of its experience or reception: the event is not assimilated or experienced fully at the time, but only belatedly, in its repeated possession of the one who experiences it" [Caruth, 1996: 61; 1995: 4]). Radstone also warns that trauma theory "pays little attention to the question of the fit, or lack of fit between the cultural, local, regional and national knowledges and repertoires of testifier and witness, and neither does it address the differentials of power embedded within any such differences" (2011: 117). In a similar vein, in her important book *The Era of The Witness*, the French historian Annete Wieviorka has compellingly argued that to understand how testimony functions in a public sphere, it is necessary to examine the "circumstances surrounding the act of bearing witness" and the "larger story" of which it is part (2006: xiv–xv). While engaging critically an aspect of trauma theory, which asserts that language or representation fails in the face of trauma, in *Performing European Memories* I argue for the importance of attention to specific articulations of trauma, the range of contexts in which they emerge, and the ways in which cultural differences and regimes of memory in place in particular European settings have affected the manner in which they have been expressed and communicated until today.

Ongoing research on the impact of the Holocaust not only on individuals but also on entire communities constitutes one of the most influential strands of research within memory studies. The most influential writings on the traumatic legacies of the Holocaust and challenges it poses for witnessing emerged in the 1980s in the United States. As will be discussed ahead, certain core assumptions informing these conceptions of trauma have not gone uncontested. In her book *Holocaust and Memory* (*Zagłada i pamięć*, 2001 [1994]), the Polish sociologist Barbara Engelking explores, among other subjects, the psychological consequences of wartime experiences for Jewish Holocaust survivors still living in Poland, questioning what she sees as hardening orthodoxies of memory studies. Engelking writes:

> It would seem that the [Anglo-Saxon] researchers take a position similar to that of wartime witnesses to the Holocaust: in discerning only the medical, pathological consequences of these experiences, they place the experiences themselves beyond the bounds of the understandable, interpretable world. They close them up in a great cupboard with a notice reading "Dysfunction" or "Psychopathology," which provides an alibi for not taking part in other people's suffering . . . Researches into wartime experiences therefore join, willy nilly, the "conspiracy of silence" [that] . . . really began with absence of reaction on the part of the world to the Holocaust during the war, and it goes on until today. (2001: 267)

According to Engelking, knowledge about traumatic experiences and their consequences, "which was built up mainly on the basis of American research, took insufficient notice of cultural differences between pre- and postwar communities of survivors, and the influence of these differences on their psychological well-being" (267). The survivors who found themselves in the United States after the war could not communicate their traumas to the society that had not shared their wartime experiences.

> And apart from wartime experiences, their baggage contained value systems shaped in the pre-war world. This could mean that

the survivors themselves had difficulty in adapting to the new universal cultural and moral values that were so different from the ones they had lost. From this point of view, some of their problems could be seen as a research artefact which resulted to a great extent not from the very essence of the experience of war, but from a confrontation between these experiences and the postwar world which did not understand them and was not understood by them, and had a different civilisational and cultural existence. (268)

Engelking also alludes to the difficulties survivors experienced in rendering their experiences in foreign languages, which they had learnt only after the war. So while the stand of trauma theory that dominates the Humanities today was largely informed by the experiences of the Holocaust survivors who found themselves in the United States after the war, Engelking believes that "accounts by Polish survivors in Polish are more reliable, closer to the inner truth, than accounts given in other languages" (Engelking, 2001: 269).[4]

While Engelking emphasises how important it is to pay attention to aspects of the location in which memories are transmitted, in an essay on Soviet memories, Catherine Merridale questions the universalisation of trauma theory and its applicability to the traumatic legacies of the Soviet era. After conducting an oral history project with Gulag survivors and Red Army veterans from the Second World War in Russia in the 1990s, this historian concluded that:

the classic story of trauma's legacy, the medical diagnosis of post-traumatic stress disorder (PTSD) now so universally accepted, simply misses the point in the Soviet case. It is irrelevant because it is an import to the Soviet situation, a discovery that suggests that, while suffering is universal, the reactions to it, especially at the social level, are culturally specific. (2010: 379–80)

Merridale's contention that there is a misfit between globalising trauma theory and localised social realities related to the Soviet case as well as her implicit claim that trauma homogenises all victims and obliterates experience are true to a point, but also could be more nuanced. While her stance is not universally shared among scholars writing on the cultural memory of the Soviet terror (see, for instance, Etkind, 2009; Baraban, 2007), it gestures to a crucial linkage between the individual and the social in the context of human suffering. The devastating experiences of the Second World War and the Gulags that gave rise to trauma, pain, and other disorders, could be seen as principally psychological or medical, and hence, individual; yet, they are also social, political, and cultural matters. Something gets lost, argues Merridale, when the local idioms of victims are translated into the universal language of trauma, thereby remaking the experiences of suffering.

Merridale's reservations about the usefulness of existing conceptions of trauma for analysing the traumatic disruptions peculiar to twentieth-century Soviet history spring also from other concerns, which she shares with some postcolonial scholars (for instance, Glissant, 1989; Khanna, 2003). For one, trauma theory's insistence on the individual psyche fails to account not only for the collective nature of the trauma in the Soviet case, but also its long duress. As some critics note – especially those that consider "postcolonial" trauma's place in contemporary trauma theory – "there is a need to expand our understanding of trauma from sudden, unexpected catastrophic events" in order "to encompass ongoing, everyday forms of violence and oppression affecting subordinate groups" (Craps: 2010: 54). They advocate a model of trauma that would reflect the experience of subaltern groups by bringing to light their "chronic psychic suffering" endured through "[e]xposure to acts or threats of physical and psychological violence" (Craps, 2010: 55). Rather than being a break from the norm, an interruption of the existing sense of the self as anchored in a decipherable past, then, trauma can be endured over a long period of time. Edouard Glissant's analogy between the individual psyche and the collective neurosis that sheds light on the relation between structural and historical traumas brought on by slavery, the destruction of aboriginal communities, and genocide, imperialistic, and postimperialistic oppression in the Antilles is apt here. He asks:

> Would it be ridiculous to consider our lived history as a steadily advancing neurosis? To see the Slave Trade as a traumatic shock, our relocation (in the new land) as a repressive phase, slavery as the period of latency, "emancipation" in 1848 as reactivation, our everyday fantasies as symptoms, and even our horror of "returning to those things of the past" as possible manifestation of the neurotic's fear of his past? (1989: 65–6)

As we shall see in the following chapter, gesturing to this Caribbean context, Müller makes similar observations about the Haitian trauma, pointing to its collective nature and its long unfolding, from the time of slavery, to the Haitian Revolution and its aftermath. Both Glissant and Müller suggest that in the contexts where colonialism, racism, and cultural assimilation are the norm, merely recovering the capacity to narrate or represent the story may be insufficient to enable healing and the restoration of agency.[5]

The works that I consider in *Performing European Memories* were produced by the artists who – except for Żmijewski – were themselves primary witnesses or survivors of historical trauma. As Jeanette Malkin observes, "Müller's two major (political and personal) traumas were German fascism and East German communism" (1999: 73). In a prose text entitled "The Father," written in the late 1950s, Müller remembers how his father, a minor functionary of the Social Democratic Party of Germany, was taken away by the Nazis in 1933, while he was pretending to be asleep. In 1945, at the age of 16, Heiner Müller was drafted into the German Labour Force and sent to the front. Soon after came the partitioning of Germany, which made him an East German, while by the end of his life, he witnessed the unification, an event which, if less hurtful than the others he experienced in his lifetime, left him deeply resigned.

For Kantor and Wajda too, the Second World War and communism left behind a set of ineradicable memories, images, and sense impressions. "It is impossible to speak about my theatre without conveying the image of that inhuman epoch," Kantor said in one of his last interviews. "World War, murderer-gods, death camps, slavery, genocide, as the principal political idea, and then a half century when power was exercised with utter primitivism by people bearing the untouchable title of 'First Secretary,' while the whole civilised world looked on with absolute indifference" (qtd. in Pleśniarowicz, 1994a: 12). To this list we should add the execution of his father in Auschwitz in 1942. For most of the war Kantor was in hiding, except when he worked as a "decoration painter" in one of Cracow's theatres between 5 April 1942 and 30 September 1943. In this period he also engaged in illegal artistic activities – as Germans banned Poles from presenting "serious performances" – staging with his Independent Theatre (founded around 1942) several performances, notably *The Return of Odysseus* by Stanisław Wyspiański (Pleśniarowicz, 1994a: 12).

And while Kantor's father died at the hands of the Nazis, Wajda's was executed by the Soviet secret police in the Katyń massacre in Russia in 1940, along with thousands of other Polish prisoners of war. This is a wound Wajda carried with him from a young age, and which served as a strong personal impetus for his film *Katyń* (2007) I address later in the third chapter.

Pinter was nine when the Second World War broke out. Although he was twice evacuated from London, first in 1939 to Cornwall, and then in 1941 to Reading, he spent most of the war in the East End, which, as he recalls, underwent "sporadic but pretty intense bombardment" (qtd. in Billington, 1996: 8). In a late interview Pinter stated: "I was fifteen when the War ended; I could listen and hear and add two and two, so these images of horror and man's inhumanity to man were very strong in my mind as a young man. They've been with me all my life, really" (qtd. in Merritt, 2000: 75).

Żmijewski is here the only representative of a younger generation of artists, born much later after the Second World War, whose relationship to historical experience of the previous generation is by necessity mediated by temporal distance and cultural memory – encounters with historical, documentary, and fictional accounts of the Holocaust as well as familial and/or collective repository of violent imagery related to the event transmitted from one generation to another. However, the anxiety about transmission persists for those who survive the survivors of cataclysmic events and their stories. The workings of inter- and transgenerational transmission of trauma bring to the fore a related yet distinct set of issues for the children of survivors and those of their generation born in the aftermath of histories of violence such as war, slavery, and expulsion, who connect so deeply to the past they have never directly experienced that they insist on the term "memory" to describe that connection. Marianne Hirsch, a US-based literary critic, has named this phenomenon "postmemory": "identification with the victim or witness of trauma, modulated by an admission of an unbridgeable distance separating the participant from the one born after" (1999: 8). Postmemory also entails reaching across lines of difference to the experience of others to whom one is not related by blood, a kind of connective memory work that could engender "transnational interconnections and intersections in a global space of remembrance" (Hirsch, 2012: 247).

The performances of memory among Eastern European Jews and their descendants who still feel and seek a connection to their roots through the layered and fragmented memory left to them represent one such postmemorial landscape. Since the fall of the Berlin Wall, and the transformation of the Eastern bloc, many such individuals have travelled to their ancestral sites in Eastern Europe, which – as their travelogues confirm – still constitute an integral part of their identity. *Ghosts of Home: The Afterlife of Czernowitz in Jewish Memory* (2010), written collaboratively by Hirsch and the historian Leo Spitzer, is an excellent example here. It offers a rich account of Czernowitz, a multicultural, tolerant place in the former Austro-Hungarian Empire, whose heir, the city of Chernivtsi, emerged after the Second World War and the Holocaust as an almost homogeneous Ukrainian city. Hirsch and Spitzer's project involved heritage trips to this city in the south-western part of Ukraine, together with Hirsch's parents, Holocaust survivors who came from Czernowitz. Drawing on personal interviews, published memoirs by German-Jewish Czernowitzers, and their own second-generation experiences and inherited memories, Hirsch and Spitzer draw a fascinating portrait of Czernowitz, accounting for its many ethnic and cultural transformations: from the Habsburg era, when German-Jewish culture flourished in the city, to the contemporary period. Hirsh explains her reasons for going to Chernivtsi early on in the book. "I grew up in 1950s Bucharest, Romania, within a community of fellow German-speaking exiles from Czernowitz whose tastes, attitudes, behaviours, and stories about a world that had long ceased to exist shaped me profoundly," she writes. "My desire to visit Czernowitz originated with these encounters and grew in intensity over many years" (Hirsch and Spitzer, 2010: 9). After she and her parents moved to Austria in 1961 and then to the US in 1962, for Hirsch her "parents' city of origin acquired an even more distant, mythic aura" (Hirsch and Spitzer, 2009:10).

Examples of journeys to Eastern Europe with similar goals and itineraries abound. In the US version of the popular TV series *Who Do You Think You Are?* (originally developed by the BBC), the Hollywood star Lisa Kudrow undertook a similar "roots trip" to Ilya in Belarus, to find out what happened to her great-grandmother Mera Mordejovich. Featuring her visits to archives in Belarus, personal interviews with the locals, and visits to the site where most of the local Jews were killed by Nazi murder squads, the programme offers a moving look at a rich local culture erased by persecution, deportation, extermination, and exile. Also motivated by personal connections to Eastern Europe, Omer Bartov's *Erased: Vanished Traces of Jewish Galicia in Present-Day Ukraine* (2007), explores the Holocaust and the disappearing memory of a Jewish presence in Western Ukraine. Written in a travelogue style to appeal to the broadest possible audience, but also in a more provocative and polemical tone, this scholarly study mourns the disappearance of the material traces of the Jewish presence in Ukraine, while demonstrating that the appeal of Ukraine (or other Eastern European nations) as a site of ancestral beginnings for many remains strong.[6]

These cultural responses to the traumatic effects of political violence constitute acts of witnessing in their own right, enacted within layered contexts of embodiment: collective, intersubjective, individual. And while in her writings Hirsch puts an emphasis on the social and potentially ethical dimensions of postmemorial witnessing, she also points to the dangers involved in such witnessing, such as the conflation of distinct subject positions through the confusion of empathy with identification with someone else's suffering. In *Ghosts of Home*, she also notes how visits with her parents, relatives, and friends to several former Jewish ghettos, camps, and memorial sites in Transnistria, a region where many of Jews from Czernowitz were deported, "activated deep, embodied trauma" (2010: 282) in the survivors and emphasised the power of these memories to wound. As memory studies scholars know well, all too regularly, those engaged in the retrieval of traumatic images are inattentive to how the transformations they induce contribute to the suffering they seek to bring into the light of day and thus remedy. Merridale, for instance records how in her travels around western Ukraine in 1998, she encountered local survivors of the Holocaust, shortly after a team of researchers who had conducted interviews with them had left the area. Giving testimony and reliving the traumatic past left many of these survivors in a vulnerable state. "Apart from the sheer stress of recollection," notes Merridale, "the problem was that elderly people had been left without support, comfort, or companionship as the interviewers drove away" (2010: 379). I engage some of these ethical issues at length in the fourth chapter, where I examine the space of an encounter between firsthand and postmemorial witnesses. In this chapter, in addition to analysing Pinter's *Ashes to Ashes*,

I also analyse Żmijewski's video piece *80064*, where witnessing comes with no ethical guarantees. While in Pinter's play postmemorial repetition seems to be motivated by a sympathetic identification with the survivor, witnessing and humiliation of a Holocaust survivor in *80064* comes to us as a result of coercion employed to recover "hidden emotions" from the time of mass extermination, rendered more valuable to Żmijewski by the unbridgeable distance between that time and the present.

Throughout *Performing European Memories*, I pervasively and systematically address loss, something that has come to interest many of us in the present, when loss, trauma, and aggression seem to be of great concern. If trauma "always makes itself felt viscerally in the here and now" (Taylor, 2006: 1675), such traumatic fusing of past and present is also characteristic of melancholy. As Kathleen Biddick's argues, drawing on Freud: "To unfuse past, present, and future, to return to the narrative relation of temporality, requires the work of mourning. Mourning does not find the lost object; it acknowledges its loss, thus allowing the lost object to be lost while maintaining a narrative connection to it" (1998: 10). Memory as mourning and melancholy is central to many plays, performances, and screen works I discuss in *Performing European Memories*, as well as to the sense of loss that pervades them. While many of these works have prompted massive interest on the part of critics, the elementary structures of mourning and melancholia within these works have yet to be closely examined. My analysis of mourning and melancholia thematised in these works such as Müller's "left melancholia" in *Mommsen's Block*, Kantor's belated grieving of his father who perished in Auschwitz in *I Shall Never Return* or the melancholic identification of Rebecca with other people's traumatic past in Pinter's *Ashes to Ashes* moves on ground contested in many urgent, simultaneous debates in historiography (for instance, LaCapra, 2004; 2009), psychoanalysis and philosophy (for instance, Butler, 2004; 2009; Oliver, 2001; 2007) and theatre and performance studies. Its epistemological and interpretative value derives from its willingness to join them and to show their relations and relevance for their works.

Freud's writings on mourning and melancholia consist primarily of the well-known essay entitled "Mourning and Melancholia" (1917 [1957]), and "On Transience" (1916). In the previous, which has defined the study of loss for much of the last century, he seeks to explain the distinction between a normal and pathological affect occasioned by the death of an object of love (be it a beloved person or an abstract ideal). For Freud, mourning is the attenuated detachment of the libido from the object that had been charged or cathected by the ego. Although mourning is invariably difficult in that "libido clings to its objects and will not [willingly] renounce those that are lost even when a substitute lies ready to hand" (1957: 306–7), the resolution of grief is nonetheless complete when the ego succeeds in detaching itself from the past through either the replacement of a cherished object with a new one or the temporary return of libido to the ego. Thus, Freud argues, a successful work of mourning constitutes an articulated reaction to loss: the loss is recognised by the subject and separated from the body through the recognition of what has been lost. What is "recognised" is both separated from the body and simultaneously interiorised within the body through a kind of psychic assimilation.

In contrast to mourning, melancholia is characterised by the inability of the subject to separate itself from the object (that is, by the ego's identification with the lost object) and an essential misrecognition of what has been lost. As Freud puts it, "melancholia is in some way related to an object-loss which is withdrawn from consciousness, in contradistinction to mourning, in which there is nothing about the loss that is unconscious" (1957: 245). In other words, the difference between a "normal" and "pathological" affect here is that in mourning the lost object is always perceived as distinct and existing outside of the ego, while in melancholia that what has been lost constitutes an enigma. And while in both mourning and melancholia the subject dwells on the past, the melancholic appears unable to leave the past behind – grief does not end.

Ultimately, Freud's initial confidence in the possibility of successful mourning without residue appears to waver. Although in "Mourning and Melancholia" he posits the resolution of grief through the withdrawal of libidinal energy from an object, in "The Ego and the Id" (1923) he comes to view mourning and melancholia as processes that instead deepen the relation to the object, allowing the very formation of identification (1955: 28–9). In other words, while in the initial essay Freud regards identification as being exclusively the preserve of the melancholic ego, he later comes to regard it as a necessary component of the functioning of the psyche.

In *The Psychic Life of Power*, Judith Butler expands upon Freud's findings from *The Ego and the Id*, where he comes to see the ego as a precipitate of lost attachments, as well as upon Nicolas Abraham's and Maria Torok's insights into the structures of incorporative melancholia (on which I will expend below). Butler argues that melancholia is "precisely what interiorises the psyche, that is, makes it possible to refer to the psyche through such topographical tropes. The turn from object to ego is the movement that makes the distinction between them possible, that marks the division, the separation or loss, that forms the ego to begin with" (1997a: 170). Like Butler, Julia Kristeva describes melancholia as a condition for the constitution of the subject. In *Black Sun: Depression and Melancholia* (1989), Kristeva reiterates and reworks the classic psychoanalytic conception of melancholy (Abraham, Freud, Melanie Klein) that detects in it intolerance for object loss; she comes to present melancholy as a formative loss that is prior to object love, ultimately associated with the maternal body.[7] The special focus of *Black Sun* is what befalls the primitive self in respect to the archaic and incomplete parting from the mother: the shadow cast on the fragile self by the impact of primal loss. The depressed person is not the prisoner and guardian of a lost object, but the prisoner and guardian of an affect recording immemorial loss. Thus, both Kristeva and Butler extend classic psychoanalytic theory of melancholy in the same direction when they suggest that melancholia is an essential prerequisite for the subject and object formation.[8]

In his writings, Freud often presented introjection and incorporation, two crucial analytical concepts for an exploration of the concepts of mourning and melancholia, as synonymous. Nicolas Abraham and Maria Torok (1986; 1994) have enriched our understanding of these phenomena through their insistence on the distinction between introjection (successful morning) and incorporation (pathological forms and variations of morning), and by proposing the notion of a "psychic crypt." Such a space, they suggest, is often generated by the trauma of object loss and an impossible mourning it effects; the lost object is kept inside the self unconsciously, as though buried alive. And while in mourning, psychic pain can gain access to symbolisation, in melancholia there is an inability to symbolise due to the encryptment of the death of the other. Abraham and Torok further explain this phenomenon by introducing a concept of a "supplemental topography" (1994: 135) entombed in the psyche so that the need to acknowledge the loss of a love object and the need to mourn it need never be avowed. In an effort to preserve itself from the demands of reality that threatens to cause the change, the subject stands divided against itself, while the distinctions between inside and outside, subject and object, active and passive become blurred. As Abraham and Torok write:

> To state that endocryptic identification is the work of fantasy alone means that its content amounts to maintaining the illusion of the topographical *status quo*, as it had not been prior to the covert transformation. As for the *inclusion* itself, it is not fantasy. Inclusion attests to a painful reality, forever denied: the "gaping wound" of topography. (1994: 142; original emphasis)

The authors further explain that against the gradual and possibly long-drawn libidinal reinvestment which the recognition and acceptance of what has been lost entail, "the magical 'cure' by incorporation exempts the subject from the painful process of reorganisation. When in the form of imaginary or real nourishment, we ingest the love-object we miss, this means that we refuse to mourn and thus we shun the consequences of mourning even though our psyche is fully bereaved" (1994: 127). Against the backdrop of this theory of mourning and melancholia, I analyse Kantor's performance *I Shall Never Return*, which commemorates the death of his father, who perished in Auschwitz, as well as Andrzej Wajda's film *Katyń* that commemorates the killing of thousands of Polish POWs and citizens by the Soviets in the Katyń forest in 1940. I argue that for most of his lifetime, Kantor was unable to grieve his father, while the wound or psychic trace left by this loss, effected an encystation, incorporation of the lost object. The performance in turn, stages an attempt to come to terms with this loss and "decorporation" of the cryptic object. In Wajda's film, on the other hand, the staging of long and mute pain associated with Polish losses at Katyń, I contend, also masks the disavowal of Polish-Jewish losses suffered there.

As I mentioned earlier, in "Mourning and Melancholia" Freud writes that "mourning is regularly the reaction to the loss of a loved person, or to the loss of some abstraction which has taken place of one, such as one's country, liberty, an ideal, and so on" (157, 243).

In *Symbolic Loss* (2000), Peter Homans elaborates this idea that one can lose and mourn an attachment to an abstraction. He defines symbolic loss as "the loss of an attachment to a political ideology or religious creed, or to some aspect or fragment of one, and to the inner work of coming to terms with this kind of loss. In this sense it resembles mourning" (20). However, as Homans further observes, "in the case of symbolic loss the object that is lost is, ordinarily, sociohistorical, cognitive, and collective. The lost object is a symbol or rather a system of symbols not a person" (20). I approach this kind of loss in my analysis of Müller's *Mommsen's Block*, his first longer text written after the unification of the two Germanies. The work is permeated by a deep sense of loss – the loss of a creed, a country, and a way of living. There is grief in its sentences. But these lines also betray the struggle to lay this loss to rest – to come to terms with the past – still in progress. The piece is rich in resentment and derision, as well as in the sense of loss and sadness. The kind of resentment exhibited in *Mommsen's Block* commonly occurs when the realisation that a loss has taken place is accompanied by a reluctance or an inability to let go of what has been lost. This is the inability to mourn that eventuates in resignation.

Ultimately, I contend, as an aesthetic phenomenon, the articulations of mourning and melancholia in the works by Müller, Kantor, Pinter, Wajda, and Żmijewski can be understood as the works' memorialising of the cultural and emotional losses of our past. They suggest that while Europe's past "resounds with catastrophic losses of bodies, spaces, and ideals," a continuous engagement with these losses and their remains might inspire solidarity and perhaps a quest for global justice (Eng and Kazanjian, 2003: 5). Exploring the productive possibilities of melancholic consciousness, I argue, along with David Eng and David Kazanjian, that "avowals of and attachments to loss can produce a world of remains as a world of new representations and new meanings," and allow us to gain new perspectives on and new understanding of the lost objects (2003: 5). Furthermore, here I also engage the idea that the vocabulary of grievance, as the social and legal articulation of grief (Cheng, 2001) and the attendant belief in its efficacy in redressing grief that permeates political discourses in Europe (and elsewhere) today have ironically deflected attention away from the more immaterial, unquantifiable repository of public and private grief that is part of the dark pages of European history.

Overall, I argue that while they stand for a network of concerns, a range of responses to the complex overlapping between the present and the past, the individual and the collective, the psychic and the social, and the aesthetic and the political, the artists whose works I engage here show that how we think about the culture of the past cannot really be separated from how we act in the present. In the face of trauma, they neither give us justice nor assert the redemptive value of bearing witness. Instead, they make us acknowledge that which can never leave us. Their texts and performances engage the work of mourning in order not to disavow the past; they constantly demand that both their producers and their audiences work their own lifelines into recent European history, and so connect past with present, and future.

2
History, Memory, and Trauma in Heiner Müller's Theatre

Modernity disavowed: memory of a revolution in Müller's *The Task*

In *On Revolution*, Hannah Arendt offers an analysis of the vicissitudes of the French and American Revolutions, mourning what she calls the "lost treasure" of the revolutionary tradition (1963: 284). According to Arendt, the revolutionary spirit is not available to our discussions of possible futures. Neither in the French Revolution nor in the American revolutions did that spirit – the promise of a better world – find an appropriate institutional form. While the lost treasure of revolution may never be found, it could be partially compensated through memory and recollection: "What saves the affairs of mortal men from their inherent futility is nothing but this incessant talk about them, which in turn remains futile unless certain concepts, certain guideposts for future remembrance, and even for sheer reference, arise out of it" (1963: 222). Since it is our poets who save the memory of past actions from oblivion and ravages of time and make them a source of inspiration for political action in the present and future, it is to them, according to Arendt, that we must turn "in order to find an approximate articulation of the actual content of our lost treasure" (1963: 284).

Like many others before and after her, Arendt takes the French and American Revolutions as landmarks in the emergence of political modernity and fails to mention, much less to analyse, the case of Haiti (along with any other nonmetropolitan revolution). Therefore, it is very ironic that she is so critical of the nineteenth- and twentieth-century thinkers who have "proceeded as though there never had occurred a revolution in the New World and as though there never had been any American notions and experiences in the realm of politics and government worth thinking about" (1963: 218); while she is careful to address the American Revolution, and even briefly alludes to slavery (1963: 90), she herself remains oblivious to the third great revolution of the eighteenth century. Her failure to deal with this event is puzzling considering, for instance, that she was among few (white) American and European thinkers who have drawn attention to the importance of the colonial experience for understanding of European fascism.[1] As David Scott, in his *Conscripts of Modernity*, observes, her oversight is all the more ironic, "because what she is lamenting in *On Revolution* is precisely the failure of memory; she is in fact urging the importance of 'remembrance' to sustaining the spirit of the revolutionary tradition" (2004: 218).

Coming from a different register, Heiner Müller's play *The Task* (*Der Auftrag*, 1979), subtitled *Memory of a Revolution* (*Erinnerung an eine Revolution*), avoids the suppression and disavowal of revolutionary antislavery and attendant movements in the Caribbean that mark Arendt's narrative on revolution. Remembering and forgetting form the thematic kernel of *The Task*. Müller based the play on a true historical event that took place in the Caribbean in the aftermath of the Haitian revolution and on its retelling in Anna Seghers's short story "The Light on the Gallows" ("Das Licht auf dem Galgen," 1961) from her cycle *Caribbean Tales* (*Karibische Geschichten*, 1962).[2] The tale is split by Müller and interspersed with complex intertextual references (to Brecht, Büchner, Beckett, Genet, Kafka, and others) and memory fragments that broaden the context to include past and present, the first (former), second, and the developing worlds, the French and socialist revolutions. Its collage structure is reminiscent of other plays Müller wrote in this period, such as *Hamletmachine* (1977), *Quartet* (*Quartett*, 1981), *Despoiled Shore Medeamaterial Landscape with Argonauts* (*Verkommenes Ufer Medeamaterial Landschaft mit Argonauten*, 1982), *Explosion of a Memory/Description of a Picture* (*Bildbeschreibung*, 1984), and *Volokolamsk Highway* (*Wolokolamsker Chaussee*, 1984–87), among others. However, as Müller put it, in this case "the devia-tion from some dramaturgical norm is especially extreme since so many historical periods are mixed" (Müller, 1984: 83). Reaching diachronically from the Age of Revolution (1791–1848) to the present, *The Task* presents an explosive synthesis that explores the relation – or apparent nonrelation – between the events in the Caribbean and the metropolitan discourse of modernity, exposing the many ways in which those aspects of "modernity's project" represented by the potential of radical antislavery have been misunderstood, ignored, and disavowed.

The short prologue section of the play begins in post-Revolutionary France with a voice reading a letter:

> Galloudec to Antoine. I am writing this letter on my deathbed. I am writing in my own name and in the name of Citizen Sasportas who has been hanged at Port Royal. I am herewith informing you that we have to give back the task with which the Assembly asked your person to entrust us since we were unable to fulfil it. Maybe others will do better. You won't hear from Debuisson anymore, he is fine. It seems that traitors have a good time when the people walk in blood. That is the way the world is designed and it is not good. Excuse my handwriting, they have amputated one of my legs and I am writing in fever. I hope the letter will find you in good health, and I remain with Republican greetings. (Müller, 1984: 85)

Written at the time of Galloudec's imminent death, the letter is a testimony to death and betrayal, with which Galloudec takes leave of Antoine and bequeaths an inheritance of memory. The letter has a force of a summons: it is addressed to "you" in the singular, which implies an address reserved for a determinable subject, Antoine, but the postal relay of the performance enacts a repetition of that address. Read on stage, the letter is an open letter in which the personal pronoun *you* refers to you, the spectator of the performance, as well. If it is genuinely received, the letter will live on in its spectators just as Galloudec hopes it will live on in Antoine. When we watch *The Task*, we intercept an address destined for Galloudec. Our manner of receiving his letter is therefore patterned on this address. In order to understand what happens when we receive this legacy, we need to understand how the position we occupy as spectators is marked by Antoine. What characterises Antoine? Antoine is a former revolutionary official, who had presented three French revolutionaries: Galloudec, Sasportas, and Debuisson with a mission of fomenting a slave insurrection on Jamaica in 1799 – which was later aborted – but is now living incognito and in fear for his life in Bonapartist Paris. The letter alone is not enough to elicit Antoine's acknowledgement of the history that he would rather not remember. "I do not know of any Galloudec," he initially responds to the Sailor (85). Only the evocative force of the Sailor's words, which transmit the agony of Galloudec's death, are able to finally break through Antoine's wall of denial: "he howled and that was the pain. It came in waves. And it took long enough – until he was through with dying. . . . first they cut off one of his legs up to the knee, then the rest of it" (86). The Sailor also tells Antoine of Sasportas's death. He was hanged at Port Royal, at the gallows on a cliff, as a horrific deterrent to others: "When they're dead they're cut down to drop into the sea below. The sharks take care of the rest" (86). This testimony causes Antoine, one of the leaders of the Revolution, to reveal himself: "I am the Antoine you've been looking for." He admits that, "I was there when the people stormed the Bastille. I was there when the head of the last of the Bourbons dropped into the basket. We have reaped the heads of the aristocrats. We have reaped the heads of the traitors" (86). At the end of the opening scene the Sailor departs, leaving Antoine to confront the ghosts from the crypt of his mind – Galloudec and Sasportas: "What do you want of me. . . . Go. Go away. Get lost. You tell them, woman. Tell them they should go away, I don't want to see them anymore. Are you still here. Your letter has arrived, Galloudec. This is it" (87).

Where Galloudec remained faithful to the revolutionary cause, Antoine betrayed it. Galloudec's address to Antoine is complicated by this fact. I want to argue that this complication carries over to the performative action of *The Task*. *The Task* can be seen as Müller's address to us who live in oblivion of the events that transpired in the Caribbean in the Age of Revolution, and – despite their distance from the revolutionary "centres" – profoundly shaped our modernity. Legacies traverse such distances. *The Task* is at once an illustration and a demonstration of that fact: the play stages and enacts something of this legacy to the Western world – even though this relay is not free of ambivalence. As Andrzej Wirth put it: "the *restoration* period is '*then*' and '*now*'" (1993: 64; original emphasis). *The Task* makes political and ethical demands on its spectators: its objective is to elicit acknowledgement, which is analogous to recognition.

Furthermore, as Jeanette Malkin suggests in her excellent book *Memory-Theater and Postmodern Drama*, the play's collage structure and postdramatic features further indicate that Antoine cannot be seen as the sole locus of recall in the text, thus prompting the audiences "to see the memory as belonging to, and aimed at, a larger collective" (1999: 87).

For Walter Benjamin, as for Müller, memory is the central category of an historical consciousness. In his "Thesis on the Philosophy of History" (completed in 1940), Benjamin offers a view of a historical/ redemptive methodology based on grasping and working with the fragments of the past that break through into a present where they become provisionally available – a view that is highly evocative of Müller's *The Task*. "To articulate the past historically," writes Benjamin, "does not mean to recognize it 'the way it really was.' It means to seize hold of a memory as it flashes up at a moment of danger" (1968: 255). Benjamin admonishes the historicist for seeking to grasp and to hold on to the past, to cease its motion and fix a genuine historical image for all eternity. In his "Thesis," he calls on us to seize hold of elusive histories that have been obscured by the historicist's genuine image, not in order to fix those histories and establish new genuine images or new eternal truths, but rather to allow the (repressed, often marginalised) past to step into the light of a present moment of danger and reorient the politics of the present into the future of justice.

Memories flash up "at a moment of danger," Benjamin writes. These memories belong to the context of their remembrance – a historical, cultural and psychical context that mediates memories at the point of their redemption. How, then, do the meditations of our present historical, cultural, and psychical context bear upon the memories invoked in Müller's *The Task*? How, that is, do our present "dangers" shape our understanding of Müller's text today? Furthermore, if we are to practice remembrance in the Benjaminian sense and be truthful to his injunction "to blast open the continuum of history" (1968: 262) another set of important questions needs to be asked: Where do the memories recalled in Müller's *The Task* come from? In other words, what exactly is the historical context of their origin? What does remembrance articulate? The task of illuminating this context, including the historical enigma of the Jamaica episode of the play, has not often been taken up by scholars. We may speculate that the author himself in part influenced the interpretative paths taken by scholars who have written about this play when he stated:

> The French Revolution . . . didn't interest me as much as a historical event, however it did as "theatre," as a revolutionary model that had an especially large arsenal of theatrical forms, among other reasons there was the relatively wide discrepancy between the intentions of the protagonists and the real mechanism, the real objectives . . . It is, of course, the only model for revolutions in Europe, or the – now as ever – classic model from which we can "read" fairly accurately the progression and the wrong moves of other, subsequent revolutions. (1984: 83)

The fact that most of the existing critiques of the play read it as an allegory for the failed socialist revolutions is certainly also due to the historical and socio-cultural context in which it was originally produced.[3] It is also telling of the ways in which Germany's colonial past has been dealt with in both West and East Germany as well as in the unified Germany – a subject I would like to address briefly before moving on with my discussion of *The Task*.

Scattered across Southwest Africa, East Africa, Togo, Cameroon, and several smaller holdings in the Pacific, including Samoa, the formal German empire lasted just a little over three decades: from 24 April 1884, when Germany declared Southwest Africa a protectorate, to the First World War. But, as George Steinmetz reminds us, Germans also participated in "European exploration, colonialism, and slaving, often in the service of another flag," for centuries (2006: 3). Many scholars have argued that Germany's thirty-year colonial endeavour and its profound effects on the peoples of Africa and Oceania as well as Germany's role in a wider pan-European colonial enterprise has been largely lost to memory. Whereas other Europeans after 1945 were engaged with often violent processes of decolonisation, the argument goes, "Germans believed that they had nothing to do with the colonial exploitation of large parts of Africa, Asia or South America" (Perraudin and Zimmerer, 2011: 1). As Germany's colonial culpability receded into oblivion, public historical debates focused on Nazism, Communism, and the Holocaust (Steinmetz and Hell, 2006: 150). Other scholars sought to offer a more nuanced view of colonialism's continued relevance for Germans after the

Second World War, arguing that Germans never really experienced a postcolonial amnesia (Albrecht, 2011). Jason Verber, for instance, argues that "German politicians, bureaucrats, businessmen, and workers dealt with colonialism, its decline, and its aftermath on a regular basis" (2010: 1). As this author shows, European colonies and, increasingly, former European colonies "were objects of foreign policy-making," while "decolonization provided an important context for political and economic developments within, between, and beyond both German states" (2010: 1). However, while West Germany's membership in the European Economic Community created a variety of opportunities for West German business and individuals who established extensive commercial and non-commercial economic ties with the colonial and postcolonial countries, committing the Federal Republic to certain colonial projects, the German Democratic Republic (GDR), sought to radically distance itself from any manifestations of European colonialism. Along with the Soviet Union and other socialist states, the GDR took an active part in a worldwide anti-imperialist movement, encouraging decolonisation efforts in Africa, Asia, and the rest of the world as part of its concerted effort to gain international legitimacy, enhance its global stature, and win allies. East Germany's solidarity with and support of liberation movements in Africa, and its branding West Germany and its chief ally, the United States, as neo-colonialist, could be also seen as a concerted effort to distance itself from colonial guilt and responsibility, while seeking to relegate West Germany to that past (see, Verber, 2010; Conrad, 2011; Madureira, 2011). Supporting this view, Luis Madureira for instance cites Erich Honecker's address at an international conference held in East Berlin in 1980, where he boldly asserted that, having established friendly relations with many colonial, decolonising, and postcolonial countries in Africa and the rest of the world, "the German Democratic Republic has broken with the German imperialist past once and for all" (qtd. in Madureira, 2011: 283). But, according to Madureira, despite "the reassuring rhetoric about solidarity" the GDR's military, economic, and humanitarian interventions in Africa produced forms of domination not so different from West German neo-colonialism.[4]

As Honecker's speech and some other examples show, German politicians and major media outlets in the post-1945 era were well aware of the history of colonialism but chose "to prioritize contemporary events over the issue of coming to terms with the past" (Albrecht, 2011). Hence, Germany's colonial atrocities and imperialism's horrific legacy were largely relegated to the margins of public discourse, and little effort was made to address the injustices that were committed. Even in the aftermath of Reunification, this chapter of German history does not figure significantly in the German collective memory. As Sebastian Conrad notes, "To date, no official critical remembrances of the colonial era, such as monuments or museums, have been created, and even local attempts to have streets with colonialist names re-designated have met with little success" (2011: 196). One of the few events that brought the problems of public postcolonial memory to the fore was a lawsuit launched by the Herero People's Reparation Corporation in September 2001 demanding reparation by the German government and a number of private companies that profited from the forced labour of prisoners taken in the Herero war (1904–08). Described by the United Nations-commissioned "Whitaker Report" from the mid-1980s as "the first genocide of the twentieth century" (Melber, 2011: 251), the genocide of the Hereros in German Southwest Africa (now Namibia) received a high-profile acknowledgement in August 2004, the anniversary of the war, when the German government issued a formal apology for the events of 1904. To some critics this public reckoning with the difficult past "showed that Germany had finally arrived at a postcolonial European normality" (Perraudin and Zimmerer, 2011: 2), while some even argued that Germany has here set an example that could be emulated by other former colonial powers. But, as Dominik Schaller points out, the Herero "were not at all convinced, since the German government refused to pay retrospective compensation" (2011: 266).

Colonialism's continued relevance for Germans (and, indeed, the continued relevance of Germans in Europe's waning overseas empires) as well as the socio-historical changes that occurred in Europe in the last two decades make it both possible and necessary to bring to the fore a broader global perspective that is generated in the play. To be sure, there is a body of work that analyses the play in the context of the developing world (especially Teraoka, 1985; Fiebach, 1990). However, even these critics do not address substantially the full implications of the fact that there is another revolution lurking behind others invoked in Müller's text: the successful revolution in Haiti. This should not come as much of a surprise, since, as Sibylle Fischer writes: "To this day, most accounts of the period that shaped Western modernity and placed notions of liberty and equality at the centre of political thought fail to mention the only revolution that centred around the issue of racial equality" (2004: ix). Why this curious "silencing" – as Michel-Rolph Trouillot (1995) would call it – of the Haitian Revolution, an (almost) complete elision of it and its place in the story of the revolutionary tradition and its legacy? As I tried to answer these questions, it became clear that the incomplete, partial, fragmentary truth of the revolutionary tradition and many lacunae of Muller's text can begin to show their significance only against the background of the histories of the Revolutionary age in and around the Caribbean Basin as well as in Europe.

The play's central narrative makes use of motifs from Anna Seghers's short story, itself based on a true but little known incident that transpired in 1799 in the Caribbean. The betrayal of the Caribbean revolution by Bonapartism and a French attempt to raise a slave revolt in Jamaica are dramatised in Müller's text in four sections, which are framed by Antoine's initial act of forced recall, and the final section of Debuisson's embrace of oblivion. In each of these sections Müller employs very different theatrical languages and constantly borrows and varies motifs from other plays inspired by revolutionary traditions. The first section is rendered in a realistic dialogue highly evocative of Brecht's *The Measures Taken*.[5] It shows Debuisson, the prodigal son of Jamaican slave-owners turned revolutionary, Galloudec, a Breton peasant, and Sasportas, an ex-slave, arriving in Jamaica "where our task is to stir up a rebellion of the slaves against the rule of the British Crown in the name of Republic of France" (87). Just as Brecht's revolutionaries assume conspiratorial masks and identities, "Debuisson Galloudec Sasportas" adopt false identities that will allow them to form a revolutionary "cell" and foment the insurrection. "Fleeing from the successful black revolution in Haiti, I attached myself to Master Debuisson since God has created me for slavery," we hear Sasportas rehearse his role, while Galloudec feigns his faith in "the holy order of monarchy and church" (89). While scholars generally acknowledge the fact that the story told here is based on a (forgotten) historical accident that took place in Jamaica in 1799 (Teraoka, 1985; Eke, 1989; Malkin, 1999), they never move beyond the plot presented in Seghers's story which inspired Müller. My concern here lies with the historical truth behind the accident, and the broader historical context in which it unravelled. Although I am going to take a circuitous route in pursuing my goal, the apparent detour is in fact part of the argument itself.

While the space here does not allow for a comprehensive analysis of the impact of the interrelated French and Haitian Revolutions on colonies within and encircling the Caribbean, it is important to mention that there existed an important relationship between events in Europe and corresponding legal, social, and political developments in the Caribbean slave colonies. As Susan Buck-Morss writes, there are "fundamental contradictions" between the political changes in France wrought by the French Revolution and its aftermath and the emergence of the slave revolution in Saint Domingue (nowadays Haiti) and neighbouring slave colonies (2009: 36). "It took years of bloodshed before slavery – really-existing slavery, not merely its metaphorical analogy – was abolished in the French colonies, and even then the gains were only temporary" (Buck-Morss, 2009: 36). And while Buck-Morss is right that neither the French Revolution's multivalent discourses of liberty and equality nor "the revolutionary actions of the French" did abolish slavery (2009: 36), they catalysed local traditions of resistance in the region – the most explosive of which was the slave revolution of Saint Domingue, better known as the Haitian Revolution. At the same time, struggles over slavery and citizenship in the Caribbean transformed the political culture of Europe and the Americas (Gaspar and Geggus, 1997).[6]

Two years of demands by white planters for representation and greater autonomy and by free persons of colour for full equality (for themselves, not slaves) were followed by the self-determined, massive slave rebellion in 1791. While the centre of this conflagration was the wealthy sugar colony of Saint Domingue, *gens de couleur* and slaves in Guadeloupe and Martinique also began using the language of rights in pursuit of equality and freedom.[7] The struggle by the black army under the leadership of Toussaint Louverture for the unconditional and universal abolition of slavery ended in victory. On 4 February 1794 the National Assembly had formalised a local decision made in Saint Domingue in 1793, abolishing slavery throughout the French Empire. By driving France to abolish slavery, the revolution produced a powerful alliance of former slaves and the French Republic across the region that quickly reversed Britain's otherwise seemingly inevitable takeover of French Caribbean territories. This struggle "strengthened the Abolitionist movement within Britain, setting the stage for the British suspension of the slave trade in 1807" (Buck-Morss, 2009: 37).

In late 1799, a new government, the Consulate, came to power in France, with Napoleon Bonaparte as the First Consul. Breaking with the colonial project of the previous years, Bonaparte developed a new colonial policy introducing broad changes in colonial governance. Bonaparte sent two missions to re-establish slavery in the Caribbean islands. In February 1802 he sent General Leclerc with ten thousand troops to invade Saint Domingue, and two months later he dispatched the Richepance expedition with more than three thousand troops to Guadeloupe. As Bonaparte's government sought to restore racial hierarchy and slavery, "men and women in the Antilles began to seek alternatives, both through projects to gain national independence and through individual efforts to maintain freedom" (Dubois, 2004b: 12). Ultimately, these former slaves took the struggle for liberty into their own hands prepared to die for a slavery-free society. In May 1803, the French military government brutally repressed opposition and officially reinstated slavery in Guadeloupe. Meanwhile, across the water, the arrival in June of news of the restoration of slavery in Guadeloupe further reinvigorated the black struggle against the French in Saint Domingue, which ultimately led to the creation of the Republic of Haiti in 1804. These events, leading to universal emancipation from slave labour, were unprecedented. As David Richardson writes: "Never before had a slave society successfully overthrown its ruling class" (1985: 114).

The profound social, political, and economic changes that occurred in the Caribbean during the 1790s, which also left a deep mark on metropolitan France, launched the global process of decolonisation that continues unfinished today. However, this radical antislavery – its ideologies, politics, and practices – have not been incorporated into the standard historical accounts of the emergence of the "West" as a distinctively modern, liberal, and democratic part of the world.[8] In her compelling book titled *Modernity Disavowed: Haiti and the Cultures of Slavery in the Age of Revolution*, Sibylle Fischer is primarily concerned with this curious silencing of the only revolution that centred on racial equality. To understand how the radical antislavery of the Haitian Revolution was suppressed and made to vanish from hegemonic conceptions of egalitarian modernity in Europe and

North America, Fischer deploys the concept of disavowal, which is understood "both in its everyday sense as 'refusal to acknowledge,' 'repudiation,' and 'denial' (OED) and in its more technical meaning in psychoanalytical theory as a 'refusal to recognize the reality of a traumatic perception'" (2004: 37–8). Disavowal is a statement of recognition, argues Fischer, and the silencing of the Haitian Revolution is a testament to its importance. I will return to the centrality of Haitian revolution for the formation and understanding of Western modernity later in this chapter.

The late twentieth and the beginning of the twenty-first century, however, have seen increasing popular and academic attention given to Atlantic slavery, abolition, and resistance, as activists and writers have increasingly sought to reconstruct and revive this past as part of an effort to challenge and transform understandings of the geographies and histories of modernity. This is also the past in the context of which unravels the Jamaican episode of Müller's *The Task*. By combining some existing historical sources with invented ones (as presented in Müller's *The Task*), my intention here is to confront the silences and gaps in the current scholarship on this play that pertain to the historical events which transpired in the Caribbean in the late eighteenth century (as evoked in the play) – the events that, if they are impossible to fully recover, are nonetheless necessary to remember.

What exactly is the historical truth behind the French Mission to Jamaica invoked in Müller's *The Task*? In 1798 the French government and its representatives in Saint Domingue started making plans for a military expedition against Jamaica. Since Toussaint Louverture, a black freedman and the central figure in the Haitian Revolution, had opposed the invasion, the French General Hedouville entrusted Philippe Roume, the official French agent in Saint Domingue, to carry out the operation. Early in November 1799, Roume sent his spies to Kingston headed by Sasportas, a Jew, and Debuisson, an emigrant French Officer, "to prepare the ground by gaining support among the French community there and also among the Blue Mountain Maroons" (Geggus, 1987: 287). However, Louverture refused to allow the Executive Directory to stage the invasion of Jamaica from Saint Domingue. He revealed the plan to the British, as he needed to secure their assistance in making Saint Domingue independent of France. Martial law was instantly proclaimed on Jamaica, and the spies were arrested soon upon their arrival to the island. A close observer of these events, the American Consul to Saint Domingue, Edward Stevens, explains cogently the rationale behind this French operation in a letter from September of 1799:

> It is not difficult to penetrate the Motives which have induced the Directory to urge the Invasion of Jamaica at the present Moment. Either T——t and his Army will succeed or not if they make the Attempt. Success would forever separate from Great Britain one of her most valuable Colonies and diminish her Resources. Should they fail they will fall Victims to their Rashness and Presumption or like Buonaparte and *his* Army cease to be Objects of Dread or Jealousy to the Government of France. The old System might then be restored in St: Domingo and Slavery reestablished. (Stevens, 1910: 84; original emphasis)[9]

Louverture knew that only his armies, not French goodwill, ultimately protected freedom in Saint Domingue. His discreet betrayal of a French attempt shows him as a pragmatic politician ready to forego political solidarity with slaves of Jamaica (and widespread liberation around the Atlantic basin) in order to preserve working relations with the powerful British naval forces and the hard-won gains of his people. Granted, as Stevens's letter indicates, if successful, the French invasion would have resulted in black liberation on the island of Jamaica; however, the Executive Directory's motivation was to weaken the ability of Britain to make war. This historical evidence also dispels the illusion that there was ever a French-led humanitarian mission (invoked by Müller and Seghers) in the first place (see, also, Dubois, 2004a: 225). Why is it of more than arcane interest to bear witness to this revolutionary sequence, the truth of which has managed to slip away from us? After all, Müller never makes any pretensions to present the historical truth of the events he narrates in his play. There are many possible answers, but in a world of systemic and direct violence that we inhabit one is surely to insist on the radical openness of the past as a resource for crafting alternative visions of social justice, human rights and freedom, and of politics of the global.

After initiating us into the task of "Debuisson Galloudec Sasportas," the task that – taking the historical facts into account, was flawed from its inception – the scene changes to the slave plantation of

Debuisson's parents. This setting functions like a theatrical backdrop against which the scenario entitled "the return of the prodigal son" is played out in the idiom of Genet's *The Blacks* (*Les Nègres*, 1958), and Peter Weiss's *Marat/Sade* (1964).[10] In this scene, Müller makes FirstLove – the woman associated with the joys of colonial privilege, previously abandoned by Debuisson for the "second love" of revolution – into the spokesmen of a conservative stance in regards to the liberation of slaves:

> Slavery is a law of nature as old as mankind. Why should it end before. Look at my slaves and yours, our property. All their lives they've been animals. Why should they be humans because it is written on a piece of paper in France. Barely readable because of so much more blood than has ever been spilled for slavery here in your and my beautiful Jamaica. I'll tell you a story: In Barbados, a plantation-owner was slain two months after the abolition of slavery. His liberated slaves came to him. They walked on their knees like in church. And do you know what they wanted. To return to the protection of slavery. That is man: his first home is his mother, a prison. (91)

It is ironic that FirstLove speaks these words, having in mind that in the period of Atlantic revolution white women, caught in the unrelenting chains of male domination in both Europe and the United States, used the comparison between their situations and the institution of colonial slavery to champion for the causes of abolition, antislavery, and women's rights (see, for instance, Sklar and Stewart, 2007; Clapp and Jeffrey, 2011). Yet, FirstLove's monologue also reminds us that at this time there were important parallels between the justifications used for the political exclusion of women in the metropole (and the colonies) and those used against the people of African descent in the colonies. In metropolitan France, for instance, eloquent voices arguing in favour of granting citizenship to women were drowned out by those who asserted that women did not have the capacity for political participation.[11]

In demanding rights, both women and the enslaved revolutionaries similarly sought to deploy and expand the universalist language of rights wielded by those who excluded them. In winning their freedom, France's "slaves-turned-citizens" exposed the tensions and contradictions embedded in the Declaration of the Rights of Man and Citizen between the natural rights of the Enlightenment and the property rights inherent in individual liberty, pushing metropolitan revolutionaries further and further on questions of rights and citizenship (Dubois, 2004b: 2). As Laurent Dubois shows in his study of Atlantic slave emancipation, aptly titled *A Colony of Citizens*, the struggles that slave insurgents and their Republican allies waged in the French Caribbean led to a new colonial order, "one in which the principles of universalism were put into effect through regimes that applied the same constitution in the metropole and the colony and granted all the people within the French Empire the same rights" (Dubois, 2004b: 2).

Yet, struggling to contain the damage to their plantation economies, white authorities on both sides of the Atlantic charged with implementing the colonial post-emancipation regimes undermined its universalism in favour of continuing plantation-based colonialism, coerced labour, and the denial of full citizenship rights to the newly emancipated on racialist grounds. As a result, France's dilemma of justifying republicanism and colonial imperialism, liberty and plantation labour, equality and racial differentiation resulted in a peculiar kind of policy that Dubois defines as "Republican racism" (2004b: 3). Thus, even as the colonial state seemed steadfast in its support of revolutionary emancipation, colonial administrators in the revolutionary French Caribbean argued – deploying the false logic that characterises FirstLove's tale – "that the majority of the colonised did not have the cultural and intellectual capacities necessary to responsibly exercise political rights" (Dubois, 2004b: 4).

It is also worth remembering here that in 1825 Haiti was compelled to pay France an "indemnity" of some one hundred and fifty million francs to compensate former plantation owners for losses (including the losses of their slaves) sustained during the revolutionary period, which was an amount roughly equal to the French annual budget at the time. By paying this amount (using loans from France), a condition of political recognition of Haiti's independence, the Haitian government hoped to put an end to France's attempts to reacquire its former colony. Though the indemnity was eventually renegotiated down to ninety million francs, "by the end of the nineteenth century Haiti's payments to France still consumed around eighty percent of its national budget" (Hallward, 2007: 12). The repayment, for which France received the last instalment in 1947, crippled the Haitian economy and became one of the primary causes of its economic underdevelopment. As Peter Hallward writes in his important study *Damning the Flood: Haiti, Aristide, and the Politics of Containment*, which examines the post-Duvalier era in Haitian politics: "Haitians have thus had to pay their original oppressors three times over – through the slaves' initial labour, through compensation for the French loss of this labour, and then in interest on the payment of this compensation" (2007: 12). In 2004, the then Haitian president Jean-Bertrand Aristide demanded reparations from France for the nineteenth-century payments Haiti had made; however, after the coup d'état of March 2004 ended his presidency, the new president Boniface Alexandre dropped the demand for payback.

In the following trial scene entitled "The Theatre of Revolution," Galloudec and Sasportas are costumed in Danton and Robespierre puppet heads, while Debuisson takes his position on the throne with FirstLove acting as his footstool. A number of "classical" plays about the French Revolution are invoked. The revolution "devoid of sex," as Sasportas puts it (93), stands accused of transforming its own initial desire for reform into bloody acts of violence, echoing Sade's words from Peter Weiss's *Marat/Sade*: "It had become mechanical / It was inhuman it was dull / and curiously technocratic" (1966: 49). In a mock version of the rational debate scenes from Büchner's *Danton's Death* (*Dantons Tod*, 1835), "SasportasRobespierre" and "GalloudecDanton" abuse each other with vulgar insults and ridicule, and then, by way of illustrating what happened when the Revolution turned against itself and became the tool of its own destruction, they behead each other. Finally, in a manner reminiscent of the clownery from Brecht's *Baden Learning Play on Acceptance* (*Badener Lehrstück vom Einverständnis*, 1926), they proceed by playing with each other's false heads.

While twentieth-century historiography gradually abandoned the practice of organising historical narratives around dominating figures, the scene here indicates that the popularised images of both Danton and Robespierre continue to haunt the historical imagination. In *A Critical Dictionary of the French Revolution*, Mona Ozouf acknowledges the powerful couple formed by Danton and Robespierre: "Robespierre has been compared to Danton as virtue to vice, incorruptibility to venality, industriousness to indolence, faith to cynicism" (1989: 213–14). Ozouf contributes in turn the following vision: "But, one might equally well contrast the two men as sickly to strong, suspicious to generous, feminine to masculine (or more accurately, female to male), abstract to concrete, written to oral, deadly systematiser to lively improviser – such is the Dantonist version" (214). I contend that in this scene Müller draws on these popularised images of the two revolutionaries. Note for example the following exchange of insults:

SASPORTASROBESPIERRE: Parasite Syphilitic Aristocrat's flunkey.
GALLOUDECDANTON: Hypocrite Eunuch Lackey of Wall Street (93)

In this respect it is also useful to notice that there is a strong affinity between the figures of Debuisson and Danton as represented in Müller's *The Task*. While early on in the plot Debuisson is represented as a progressive revolutionary who later becomes disillusioned with the revolutionary cause (and many critics read him as a disenchanted progressive intellectual), it is important to note that he is also, like Danton, a privileged white capitalist. Debuisson, the text tells us, is a son of plantation and slave owners in Jamaica. A brief historical reminder of his social and economic status may be instructive here. At the height of their powers in the second half of the eighteenth century, the West Indian sugar planters were "celebrated as the most successful agricultural entrepreneur[s] of the time" and hailed as "the leaders of Atlantic modernity" (Beckles, 1997: 778). The global scale of their operations was unprecedented: they established a highly profitable system of slave management in which they successfully manipulated complex agro-industrial technology, a complicated integrated trade network, linking Africa and Europe with the Caribbean, and, most importantly, a brutal system of labour exploitation that had never been seen in the metropolis. Furthermore, as Hilary Beckles points out, taking advantage of their economic privilege, "they lobbied and bought their way into metropolitan Parliaments and Imperial Courts in an effort to protect and promote the world they had made" (Beckles, 1997: 778).

This in mind, Debuisson's quick "change of heart" upon the arrival of the letter ordering that the mission be put to an end should not come to us all that surprising. This is Debuisson:

Our company has been struck from the commercial register. It is bankrupt. The merchandise we are offering for sale, payable in the standard currency TearsSweatBlood, isn't traded anymore in this world. *Tears the paper.* I free us of our task. You, Galloudec, the peasant from Brittany. You, Sasportas, the son of slavery. Me, Debuisson.

SASPORTAS: (softly.) The son of slaveholders. (97)

After "The Theatre of the Revolution" scene, Müller suddenly inserts the "Man in the Elevator" section, disrupting the Jamaican narrative, while at the same time broadening the context of the *Memory of a Revolution* to include the present in which the play was written. This Kafkaesque monologue is spoken by a man riding in an old elevator attempting to reach Number One's office:

> I am standing among men who are strangers to me, in an old ele-vator with a metal cage that rattles during the ascent. I am dressed like an office clerk or a worker on a Sunday. I have even put on a tie, my collar rubs against my neck, I am sweating. When I move my head, the collar constricts my throat. I have been summoned to the boss (in my thoughts I call him Number One), his office is on the fourth floor or was it the twentieth; as soon as I think about it I am not sure anymore. The message of my appointment with the Boss (whom I call Number One in my thoughts) reached me in the basement, an expansive space with empty concrete cubicles and direction signs for air raid precautions. I suppose it concerns a task that is to be assigned to me. (94)

In the rest of the monologue, the man's anxiety grows as the time passes with an increasing speed, while the elevator travels more and more slowly, and finally comes to a halt. The once so important "task" becomes "NOT OPERATIVE," ending "ON FILE where no one will check any more" (95), as the man finally steps out of the elevator onto a destitute street in Peru. Having never received the task to fulfil, the man keeps "walking into the landscape that has no other work but to wait for the disappearance of man" (96). As we shall see, the end of the scene prefigures Debuisson's final embrace of denial and oblivion at the end of the play.

Malkin speaks for many of Müller's critics when she maintains that this is the part of the play that is most unambiguously "linked to the East German reality within which Müller was writing, and whose ideological corruptions he now explicitly laments and assails" (1999: 91). In a similar vein, Teraoka writes that "The predicament of the official is in part that of the (Marxist) intellectual in a post-Stalinist era" (1985: 154). However, the proliferation of an amorphous bureaucracy and the failure of the originary revolutionary impetus to improve the world – the "forgetting" of the task – that are thematised in this section, could be of course traced back to the time of the Revolution, or more precisely, the moment the Constitution of 1791 made very clear that the nation could exercise its authority only by delegation. In other words, the elevator monologue implicitly evokes the issue of political representation during and after the French Revolution, to maintain that alienation is the real form of power.

In his study that explores the intermingling of theatre and politics during the French Revolution, Paul Friedland defines "political modernity" as a theory and practice of representation that "sang the praises of democracy" even as it required "the exclusion from active political power of the very people in whose name their representative government claims to rule" (2002: 11). As he notes, the French Revolution "that was enacted in the name of the public effectively excluded the public from the process of national representation" (2002: 89). Therefore, we may find surprising "the willingness with which the political audience so quickly resumed their seats after taking the political stage and suspended their disbelief while the National Assembly or a Committee of Public Safety (or Napoleon for that matter) acted in their place, with virtually no tangible input on their part" (Friedland, 2002: 89). For all their differences, from 1789 until 1815 the various regimes of the revolutionary period continued to pay lip service to the ideals of transparency and popular sovereignty, while they sought to relegate their constituents behind a political fourth wall. Thus, Friedland argues, the general trend over time, in France as elsewhere in the modern world – in both capitalist and socialist orders – has been to relegate constituents to the role of spectators, without their meaningful participation. Instead, it is the political actors – represented in Müller's text by the head official "Number One" – who make up the representative body, betraying the inherently undemocratic nature of this form of representation. While both Friedland and Müller display an anxiety that is, to a large extent, an inevitable consequence of the particular system of government instituted more than two hundred years ago – which still dominates, for better or worse, the Western world – they perhaps overstate the case for the permanent silencing of the people. As the slave revolution of 1791 to 1804 in the Caribbean, the momentous events of 1989 in Eastern Europe, and, most recently, the Arab Spring of 2011 all show, popular resistance has remained, of course, an almost constant feature of both modern history and our time, continually interrupting any and all scripts.

The last section of the play, which stages an ideological debate between the intellectual/aristocrat/capitalist Debuisson, and the black ex-slave, Sasportas, raises many important questions, both historical and philosophical. How to gauge the relations between the political changes in the metropole and the emergence of slave revolution in the Caribbean? Were the ideas of the French Revolution a central motor to the events, or was the Haitian Revolution an event in its own right, as Aimé Césaire (1960) argued? How did the libertarian ideals of the French Revolution intersect with traditions of slave resistance and visions of freedom crafted out of the colonial world? And what did the principles guiding the French Revolution, the universalist principles of liberty and equality really mean, and what did they mean to whom? As we shall see now, these issues are adjudicated in different ways, both in *The Task* and in the current scholarly debates, with some scholars basing their judgements on socio-economic conditions and others on ideological and cultural features.

Debuisson hands Sasportas and Galloudec a paper conveying the news of the Revolution's failure in Paris: "The General Bonaparte has dissolved the Directorate. France is called Napoleon. The world will be what it was, a home for masters and slaves" (96). To Debuisson this means the end of their task: "we need our time now to call off the black revolution we prepared so thoroughly in the name of a future that already has become the past like the others before it" (99). All Debuisson – "the master of four hundred slaves" – wants now is his "piece of the cake of the world" which he will cut himself "from the hunger of the world" (99). Speaking from a historical point of view, ever since the decree of 1794, which formally granted all slaves immediate and unconditional liberty throughout the French Empire, "the administrators sent to colonies were given a difficult task: to apply universal emancipation while containing its economic, social, and political effects" (Dubois, 2004b: 183). Likewise, for the planters, that is, the enslaving bourgeoisie – liberty and equality were not only political matters, but ones that would also ensure the unhampered continuation of trade and commerce. Though they were the members of the revolutionary bourgeoisie, their interests were tied nonetheless to the maintenance of forms of labour and modes of production of plantations slavery. Here, liberty was seen in economic terms. As Galloudec quickly infers, it seems Debuisson was "just waiting for this General Bonaparte" (97).

It was a different case, of course, with slaves, for whom liberty was a question of outright freedom from slavery and ultimately of the right to define in their own ways the material conditions that should accompany it. To Sasportas, the task is still the universal human imperative. The ideas about liberty and equality, which were circulating so profusely once revolution broke out in France, no doubt served as a catalytic force in impelling the revolts that occurred in each of the indigenous sectors of Saint Domingue's colonial society. But revolutionary ideas alone could not have produced the unfolding of events in the colony. As Sasportas says, in their fight for freedom, the slaves drew their strength from their experience of racial subordination and genocide as well as the memory of their dead: "When the living can no longer fight, the dead will" (100).

In his study *Slavery and the Spirits of the Dead*, Vincent Brown demonstrates the extent to which relations between the living and the dead shaped political life in a New World slave society, particularly on Jamaica. In colonial Jamaica, which by 1774 had become both the richest and the deadliest colony in the entire British Empire, the dead were too plentiful, too powerful, and too useful to ever rest in peace. Brown writes that slaves used their beliefs and cultural practices associated with death such as "witchcraft and spirit veneration to signify and enhance their own limited powers" (2003: 7). At times, the relations with the deceased girded conflicts and rebellions against the plantocracy. As Brown informs us: "Occult rituals fuelled a major slave rebellion in 1760. Thereafter, Jamaican law punished by death or exile 'any Negro who shall pretend to any Supernatural Power,' and the aggressive persecution of black shamans remained a pre-eminent concern in the slave court trials of the late eighteenth and the early nineteenth centuries" (2003: 7).[12]

The moment of Debuisson's betrayal of the revolutionary cause is also a moment of recognition for black Sasportas: "What's a general's coup in Paris got to do with our task, the liberation of slaves in Jamaica. . . . What is Paris to these men [slaves], a distant stone pile that was for as short time the metropolis of their hope" (97). The insight of the Caribbean writer Aimé Césaire, who identifies the specificity of the Haitian Revolution in its transformation from one of many upheavals and insurrections that disrupted the entrenched patterns of colonialism and slavery in the region into a revolution that led inexorably to truly global repercussions, is illuminating here:

> To have awaited the abolition of slavery as a spontaneous gesture of the French bourgeoisie, under the pretext that abolition was a logical conclusion of the Declaration of the Rights of Man, would have been . . . to ignore that the bourgeois revolution's own historical task was only carried out when they were pushed on by the people with a sword at their back. What is astonishing is that the black masses so quickly understood that they should expect nothing form Paris and that they would only definitively achieve what they would have the courage to conquer for themselves. (qtd. in Nesbitt, 2004: 28)

He continues: "As soon as Toussaint joined in, [the rebellion (*l'émeute*)] became a revolution. And this meant . . . becoming conscious of one thing: that, beyond individuals, it was a system that had to be destroyed. The goal, the only valid goal, could be none other than freedom, universal freedom" (qtd. in Nesbitt, 2004: 29). Thus, in his view, the Haitian Revolution, which brought about the localised destruction of plantation slavery and the world historical invention and institution of a political system of undivided human rights, "was fundamentally a *transformation in consciousness*, consciousness of universal freedom as a categorical imperative" (Nesbitt, 2004: 29; original emphasis).

In her seminal essay "Hegel and Haiti", Susan Buck-Morss usefully points out that Hegel too "insists that freedom cannot be granted to slaves from above" (2009: 55). She quotes Hegel's defining statement on the dialectic of lordship and bondage from *The Phenomenology of Mind* that only in staking one's life in struggle does one become "a person," which would seem to reflect Sasportas's conviction that death is in every way preferable to slavery. Thus, Hegel writes: "And it is solely by risking life that freedom is obtained. . . . The individual, who has not staked his life, may, no doubt, be recognised as a Person; but he has not attained the truth of this recognition as an independent self-consciousness" (qtd. in Buck-Morss, 2009: 55–6).[13] This striking image of the "'struggle to death' between master and slave," Buck-Morss argues, in fact echoed "the final struggle for independence" of Haiti led by Louverture under "the banner Liberty of Death" (2009: 48, 42). Offering the most pertinent example of this struggle for recognition, and the violent assertion of the self-freeing self, "the Haitian Revolution was the crucible, the trial by fire for the ideals of the French Enlightenment" (2009: 42).

However, this does not mean that the Haitian Revolution was "a mere tropical echo of its better-known French and American cousins," which is an idea that still inflects the dominant Euro-American accounts of the Age of Revolution (Nesbitt, 2005: 22). Writing about the dynamics of oppression and resistance, historian Eugene Genovese for instance argues that the 1791 slave revolution in Saint Domingue marked the integration of slave revolts into the Age of Democratic Revolution. Black revolts in the New World in the eighteenth and the early nineteenth century followed a parallel trajectory with revolt in Europe, and, like the latter, shifted from a particularist and restorationist model to a universalist and progressive one after 1789. Thus, the Haitian Revolution signals the incorporation of Afro-American resistance into the world-bourgeois democratic mainstream. "When the [the slave revolts] did become revolutionary and raise the banner of abolition, they did so within the context of the bourgeois-democratic revolutionary wave, with bourgeois democratic slogans and demands and with a commitment to bourgeois property relations" (1979: xxi–xxii). From this point on, Genovese claims, slaves no longer sought to simply secede from slavery, but to abolish it – in the name of the Jacobin ideals drawn from the radical wing of the bourgeois-democratic view. While he rightly notes that this was the most significant case in which a black slave revolution became clearly interwoven with European domestic upheaval and recognises the Haitian Revolution as a profoundly modern event on the cutting edge of world history, he still presses New World movements into Continental European patterns.

In the process, he erases the significance of "those vital social, economic, and cultural realities of the ex-slaves whose independent relationship to the land, African in outlook, formed the foundation of their vision of freedom . . . " (Fick, 1990: 250). Furthermore, as Nick Nesbitt aptly puts it, the revolutionary process that took place in Haiti from 1791–1804 was no mere "passive mimicry" of European Enlightenment thought, but rather "one in which the slaves of Saint Domingue actively restructured contemporary debate on universal human rights" (2008: 61). For Nesbitt, former slaves on Saint Domingue borrowed from, shaped, challenged, and remade Enlightenment philosophies to achieve universal emancipation. Critically engaging with Jürgen Habermas's conceptualisation of the public sphere and redefining it for postcolonial contexts, Nesbitt demonstrates the existence of what he terms a "Black Atlantic public sphere" (2008: 65) that not only included the former slaves such as Toussaint Louverture familiar with the ideas of the French Revolution, but also all those former slaves who asserted their rights through violence and forced the Convention to abolish slavery in 1794.

In *Avengers of the New World*, Dubois offers an exhaustive account of upheavals that transformed Saint Domingue into Haiti, recounting in much detail the manner in which enslaved men and women of the colony rose up in August of 1791 and battled against their masters and the French colonial state. His captivating retelling of an episode that took place a few weeks into the insurrection summarises effectively the diversity of black revolutionary inspiration: from the ideology of the French Revolution to insurgents' experiences of enslavement and memories of Africa. Dubois narrates the story of an insurgent, captured and killed by a troop of white soldiers, who was found in possession of pamphlets about the Rights of Man, a packet of tinder, phosphate, and lime, and a sack of herbs, bone, and hair (a Haitian Vodou fetish). Dubois comments: "The law of liberty, ingredients for firing a gun, and a powerful amulet to call on the help of the gods: clearly, a potent combination" (2004a: 102–3).

"I will go with you, Sasportas," says Galloudec at the end of this scene, which stages an ideological duel between Debuisson and Sasportas. "All of us must die, Debuisson. And that's the only thing we still have in common. After the massacre in Guadeloupe, they found in the midst of a pile of corpses, all of them black, one white man who was just as dead. However, that can't happen to you anymore, Debuisson. You are out of this" (100). Galloudec speaks here about some kind of atrocity – what exactly did happen in Guadeloupe about two centuries ago? Galloudec's speech stands as a reminder that struggles for emancipation and equality in the context of the revolutionary Atlantic were never limited to Saint Domingue but also took in neighbouring Santo Domingo, as well as Martinique, Guiana, Guadeloupe, Jamaica, and other parts of the circum-Caribbean. Unlike the nearby Haitians, who achieved independence from France in 1804, the people of Guadeloupe remained under French rule; they experienced emancipation in 1794, only to be returned to slavery nine years later. In *A Colony of Citizens*, Dubois reconstructs in rich detail the 1802 insurgency by former slaves and free coloureds in Guadeloupe aimed at staving off the reestablishment of slavery that Bonaparte was determined to institute. He chronicles the struggle waged by insurgent forces led by Louis Delgrès against the French forces. In May 1802, the insurgents found themselves overwhelmed by French troops commanded by Richepance. Trapped in a plantation near the town of Matouba, they placed barrels of gunpowder around the plantation house, refusing to surrender. Dubois narrates: "As the enemy closed in, the insurgents, holding each other by the hand, yelled, 'No Slavery! Long live Death!' And when the advance guard of the French troops arrived on the porch, a massive explosion consumed the building, leaving 'a vast pyre whose flames were devouring more than five hundred corpses, among which were women and children'" (2004b: 400). In the end, the insurrection in Guadeloupe was savagely repressed, leading directly to ten thousand deaths and deportations and another forty-five years of slavery. The slaves and free coloureds of Guadeloupe did not win their independence from France to forge an autonomous black-ruled nation as did their Haitian counterparts – Guadeloupe remains an overseas department of France. However, as Müller's text suggests (through Galloudec's example), this tragic moment of history needs to be juxtaposed to the ones in which the consciousness of (white) individuals surpassed the confines of present constellations of power: "the French soldiers sent by Napoleon to the colony who, upon hearing these former slaves singing the 'Marseillaise,' wondered aloud if they were not fighting the wrong side" (Buck-Morss, 2009: 75) and the embittered and disillusioned Polish legionaries sent by Napoleon to crush the revolution, known also as "the white negros of Europe" (Pochoński and

Wilson, 1986: 213), "who disobeyed orders and refused to drown six hundred captured Saint-Dominguans" (Buck-Morss, 2009: 75).[14]

At the end of *The Task* Galloudec and Sasportas leave Debuisson, who in the final act of betrayal embraces "his first love who was Treason" (100). The play closes with an unattributed block of prose conveying Debuisson's surrender to forgetting:

> Treason danced. Debuisson pressed his hands against his eyes. He heard his heart beating the rhythm of the dance steps. . . . He opened his eyes. Treason smiling showed her breasts and silently spread her legs wide open, her beauty hit Debuisson like an axe. He forgot the storm of the Bastille, the Hungermarch of the Eighty-thousand, the end of Gironde, the Last Supper, a corpse at the banquet, Saint Just, the Black Angel, Danton, the voice of Revolution, Marat hunched over the dagger, Robespierre's broken jaw, his scream when the executioner ripped off the bandage, his last pitying look at the exultant mob. Debuisson clutched at the last memory that hadn't left him yet . . . rubbed the sand from his eyes, covered his ears against the song of the crickets. Then Treason threw herself upon him like a heaven, the bliss of the labia a dawn. (100–1)

The scene mirrors the closing moments of the play's opening scene, which tells of Antoine's copulation with the Woman/Angel of Despair who promised him "ecstasy, numbness, oblivion, the lust and the torment of bodies" (87). The promise has now been fulfilled as "the bliss of the labia" replaces memory (101). Debuisson's final recollection is thus an act of disavowal, a refusal to acknowledge the traumatic reality (Laplanche and Pontalis, 1973). As Freud writes in *An Outline of Psychoanalysis*, acts of disavowal always "turn out to be half-measures, incomplete attempts at detachment from reality. The disavowal is always supplemented by an acknowledgement" (1966: 204). Just as in his encounter with the Sailor, Antoine briefly returns to the site of a traumatic memory which he has long since repressed, only to disavow his traumatic loss. In these final moments of the play, we are one more time reminded of the historical past that Debuisson casts off in his passionate embrace of oblivion. If Müller presents us here with Debuisson's state of mind, this is also a strategy on his part in that it brings forth the past being obliterated: the

Bastille, the Hungermarch, the Gironde, Saint-Just, Danton, Marat, Robespierre.

Thus in the play's ending, Müller once again emphasises (before the onset of forgetting) the centrality of the trauma of the Revolutionary Terror (1793–94) for any elaboration of the French Revolution. Historians have always been fascinated by the role of violence in Revolutionary France trying to explain the death of idealism, and the descent from the Declaration of the Rights of Man and the ideal of citizenship into terror in 1793. Nineteenth-century historians saw the Terror as a means of defending the Republic against its external enemies and all those who worked against or interfered with the central government's efforts to meet the military and economic emergency. Hippolyte Taine and his followers, on the other hand, saw the Terror as a kind of class war, energised by the desire for inflicting pain and suffering on past oppressors (Greer, 1935: 5–7). And while today some revisionist scholars see in the Terror "an antechamber to the horrors of the 20th century" (Livesey, 2009: 65), on the other end of the scholarly spectrum, as Jean Baudrillard notes, "the Bicentennial's revisionist historians offered a perfectly pious *vision* of the Revolution, cast in terms of the Rights of Man. Not even a nostalgic vision, but one recycled in the terms of postmodern intellectual comfort. A vision which allows us to eliminate Saint-Just from the *Dictionnaire de la Révolution*. 'Overrated rhetoric,' says François Furet, perfect historian of the repentance of the Terror and of glory" (1994: 23–4, original emphasis).

Rejecting the usual economic, political, and social explanations, Marie-Hélène Huet provides another relevant insight to our undiminished anxiety about the violence of the guillotine. Huet contends that the undoing of the revolutionary idea was inherent in the ideal itself: "That Terror may be an unavoidable component of the democratic process, that the origin of the modern state should be tainted with bloodshed that would be part and parcel of Revolution itself, is a question all historians – of all political stripes – have laboured to elude" (1997: 172). In her view, "Anxiety about an origin necessarily founded in violence may in turn account for the necessity historians have felt, either to ascribe the origin of such violence to outside factors (the war, the effects of European coalition against France), or to put the blame for the terror on an extra-ordinary individual" (1997: 172; original emphasis).

Müller avoids this trap. While flooding the audience's memory with a list of traumatic events from the revolutionary period, Müller's play dissolves the chronological boundaries of the terror.

THE REVOLUTION IS THE MASK OF DEATH DEATH IS THE MASK OF REVOLUTION THE REVOLUTION IS THE MASK OF DEATH DEATH IS THE MASK OF REVOLUTION . . . (90)

For Müller the revolution is a block, as the image of block letters on the page suggests. As Rebecca Comay asserts, in Hegel's analysis of the French Revolution as well "the revolution is a block: the terror cannot be surgically excised as a local anomaly, deformation, or betrayal of its founding principles, the revolution does not splinter into essential and inessential, structural and incidental" (2004: 386–7). Thus, Comay continues:

> For Hegel . . . the terror proper begins not with the law of 22 Prairial, not with the law of suspects, not with the regicide in January 1793, not with the king's arrest and trial, not with the September massacres of 1792, not with the riots at the Tuileries on August 10, 1792, not with the suspensive veto of the 1791 Constitution, and not with the storming of the Bastille. Hegel backdates the terror to the very onset of the revolution, if not before – June 17, 1789, the day the États Généraux spontaneously and virtually unanimously recreated itself as the Assemblée Nationale as sole agent and embodiment of the nation's will. (2004: 386–7)

However, as Comay points out, while he identifies terror with the commencement of political modernity, Hegel still labours to explain it "as inevitable, comprehensible, and infinitely productive" (2004: 388).[15] The second half of Müller's slogan ("DEATH IS THE MASK OF REVOLUTION") also points, if circuitously, in this affirmative direction. We may remember here that it was in Saint Domingue, not Paris, that violence reached unimagined heights of brutality on both sides, that "an entire society was literally reduced to ashes by 1804, in the name of a single imperative: universal emancipation" (Nesbitt, 2004: 11). As Antoine says to the Sailor early on in the play: "We now feed the people in Haiti their own soil. That was the Negro Republic for you"

(86). But we should also be mindful of the fact that the events in this former French colony marked a watershed: some two hundred years ago before the time of this writing, on 1 January 1804, the slaves of the Caribbean island of Saint Domingue struck a mighty blow against slavery, defeated the most powerful army in the world (Napoleon's), and established the first state in the world to be founded on the rejection of slavery and citizenship for all. In the years that followed, the very existence of Haiti emboldened the embattled ranks of abolitionists in all those parts of the Americas where slavery could be found to reach for freedom and eventually to vanquish slavery in the New World (Hunt, 1988).

Teraoka wrote that with Debuisson's betrayal at the end of *The Task* – a mirror image of Antoine's betrayal at its beginning – the play comes full circle and "dissolves at the end into *forgetfulness*" (1985: 165; her emphasis). Throughout this chapter, however, I have argued that at the core of *The Task*, we encounter the dialectical relationship between the disavowal and the work of memory. Memory opposes disavowal, but not in the simple sense by which memory "completes" our view of the past by filling in the blind spots that mar the picture. Memory can no longer discern the discontinuities that are constitutive of the history of the black Atlantic and the French Revolution, and thus of Western modernity. If our conceptual framework is marked out by "memory" alone, we will find it difficult to understand how the gaps and silences in hegemonic concepts of modernity ever came into being. As I have tried to demonstrate, the intricate historical issues that are acted out in this play become visible only if we have some understanding of the conflicts surrounding the issues of colonial slavery during the French Revolution.

The disavowal of revolutionary antislavery thematised in the play, as we have seen, has also become an ingredient in hegemonic conceptions of modernity. Two centuries later, Haiti is oft-cited as the poorest country in the Western Hemisphere and one of the poorest countries in the world. The devastating 2010 earthquake that destroyed Port-au-Prince and much of its environs, has exacerbated an already dire political and economic situation on the island underscoring the utter incapacity of the state and government to address the very basic human needs of the people in the aftermath of the catastrophe. But as Erica Caple James writes, what is often rendered opaque in news reports and studies about Haiti is "the way in which international and national political and economic powers have contributed to its dire state" and the systemic destruction of Haitian democracy (2011: 8). In light of such knowledge, there can be no simple coming to terms with the Haitian past. Müller's *The Task* reminds us of the unresolved antagonisms and the past that has been obliterated, as the contemporary Haitians, the descendants of the former slaves who accomplished one of "the most remarkable and important transactions of the day" (Rainsford, 1805: 364), strive to defend their human rights and dignity against the "New World Order" of the day.

On *Description of a Picture / Explosion of a Memory*

> Here is the bridge
> And I see you walking
> Over the wooden planks
> And three are missing in the middle
> I give you my hand
> And you do not see it
> You see the water underneath
> And the wind, that is strong
> My hand shakes
> In the middle between water
> And wind
> And here is the bridge
>
> Inge Müller (1954)

> In the water I saw
> Your eyes, that were searching for me. There
> I found myself. And I ceased to be afraid
> Of the wind. It carried us
> Those who hold each other's hands.
>
> Heiner Müller (1954)[16]

As Joachim Fiebach reminds us: "Since the mid-1970s, Müller structured his texts for the theatre mostly as prose narratives, particularly with an 'I' at the centre. He presented individuals' or 'characters'' perspectives on the events dealt with, thus dramatizing self-reflexivity – in *Wolokolamsk Highway*, *Landscape with Argonauts*,

Description of a Landscape, The Task/ Der Auftrag" (2003: 172).[17] Taking the cue from Fiebach, in the following part of this chapter I will offer a reading of Müller's *Explosion of A Memory/Description of a Picture (Bildbeschreibung,* 1984). My argument will also be structured around few other lyrical and prose pieces by Müller, which feature an "I" in the centre and are clearly autobiographical in character, and which are thematically related to *Explosion of A Memory/Description of a Picture.* I contend that all of these texts, however circuitously, mourn the death of his wife, Inge Müller. Inge Müller's poems will be also invoked here. These poems, I believe, offer some new ways of understanding this dense and complex play; they also bring into the picture a broader historical horizon – a horizon on which both repressed and obsessed-about historical traumas from a not so distant German past assume a concrete shape. Clearly, I am aware that to identify any art as being "about" something risks the danger of "reduc[ing] work to a singular defining subject matter in a fashion that is often anathema to artists, who construe the operations of their work as exceeding any single signifying function" (Bennett, 2005: 3). There is also "a certain hubris in colonising [private] experience" in this kind of undertaking (Bennett, 2005: 3). However, I believe that reading this text in an autobiographical mode creates new insights that go beyond the personal matters of the authors involved. This will become more clear in the second half of this section where I discuss a staging of the play at the Berliner Ensemble in 2001 in the context of the memory of German suffering during the Second World War and in its immediate aftermath, which has resurfaced in German public consciousness during the last decade.

The Description of a Picture, a text that is actually a single eight-page long sentence, starts in a straightforward manner:

> A landscape neither quite steppe nor savannah, the sky a Prussian blue, two colossal clouds float in it as though held together by wires, or some other structure that can't be determined, the larger one on the left might be an inflated rubber animal from an amusement park that has broken away from its mooring, or a chunk of Antarctica flying home . . . (Müller, 1989: 97)[18]

Gradually a picture emerges: two clouds in the sky, a mountain range in the background, three trees to the right. In the foreground are a house, a fruit tree, a table beneath the tree with a bowl of fruit, and a toppled wine glass. There are three figures in the scene: a man in the doorway, a bird in the in the branches of the fruit tree, and a woman filling the right side of the picture. Early on in the narration, the authorial eye focuses on the woman:

> . . . her head splitting the mountain range in two, the face is gentle, very young, the nose too long, with a swelling at its root, perhaps a fist hit her, her gaze directed on the ground as though there were an image she cannot forget and/or another she refuses to see, her hair long and wispy, blond or whitish-grey, the harsh light makes no distinction, her clothing a moth-eaten fur coat, tailored for broader shoulders, flung over a threadbare flimsy shirt, likely of linen, from whose right sleeve, too wide and badly frayed at one spot, a fragile forearm lifts a hand to heart level, i.e. the left breast, a defensive gesture or from the language of deaf-mutes, the defence is meant against familiar terror, the blow shove stab has happened, the shot has been fired, the wound no longer bleeds, the repetition hits a void where there is no room left for fear, the woman's face becomes readable if the second assumption is right, a rat's face, an angel of the rodents, the jaws grinding word carcasses and language debris, the left coat sleeve hanging in tatters as after an accident or an assault by some ganged beast or machine . . . (97–8)

The woman, as becomes clear, has been subjected to some kind of violence. The "second assumption" that the onlooker makes suggests that she is dead. But then immediately the onlooker wishes another possibility:

> . . . peculiar that the arm isn't injured, or are the brown stains on the sleeve dried blood, the gesture of the long-fingered right hand, is it meant for a pain in the left shoulder, is the arm hanging limply in its sleeve broken or disabled by a flash wound, the arm is cropped at the wrist by the picture's edge, the hand might be a claw, a stump (encrusted with blood perhaps) or a hook . . . (98)

To the hypothetical violence undergone by the woman is added that performed by the painting that frames the woman: " . . . up to even above her knees the woman stands in a void, amputated by the picture's edge . . . " (98). The narrator wonders, "is she growing from the ground as the man steps from the house and will disappear into the ground again as the man into the house . . . ," thus invoking the motif of the resurrection of the dead, or a return of memory. The description proceeds with the authorial I offering various scenarios for what may have happened before the moment that is captured by the painting, as well as for what might happen in the future. In a mode reminiscent of an obsessive traumatic recall, the narrator imagines a number of possibilities, all which have in common the murder of the woman by the man. But if the man kills the woman repeatedly, it is because she always comes back. The job that the man performs, it follows, represents "perhaps daily murder of the perhaps daily resurrected woman" (100).

In the endnote to his text Müller writes:

> DESCRIPTION OF A PICTURE may be read as an overpainting of Euripides' ALCESTIS which quotes the Noh play KUMASAKA, the Eleventh Canto of the ODYSSEY, and Hitchcock's THE BIRDS. The text describes a landscape beyond death. The action is optional since its consequences are past, explosion of a memory in an extinct dramatic structure. (102)

In Teraoka's view, "Three main themes hold this open set of very disparate texts together: resurrection, the revolt of nature against man, and the release or redemption of the dead" (1992: 182–3). What interest me here most, however, is the motif of a dead woman coming back to the world of the living, which constitutes the basic plot of Euripides's *Alcestis* – a tragedy about mourning. Admetus is allowed to escape death only if he finds someone who will take his place. He asks his father and mother, but they refuse; his wife Alcestis, however, agrees to replace him, and is on the verge of death as the play opens. Admetus bemoans her passing with extravagant and excruciating lamentation, and his grief is a focal point of the play's action. I will return to this play later in my analysis. This motif also pervades much of Müller's work. For instance, a dead woman "returns" to the world of the living in his *Hamletmachine*: "I am Ophelia. The one the river didn't keep. The woman dangling from the rope. The woman with her arteries cut open. The woman with the overdose. SNOW ON HER LIPS. The woman with her head in the gas stove. Yesterday I stopped killing myself" (Müller, 1984: 54–5). Then there are two versions of *Obituary* in which the author evokes the moment of finding his wife dead upon returning home late one night. Finally, in the poem "Yesterday on a Sunny Afternoon," the lyrical "I" states his wish to excavate the corpse of his late wife. As I suggested earlier, I contend that behind all these images of the dead woman lurks the image of Müller's first wife Inge Müller, who committed suicide in 1966.

Inge Müller (1925–1966) was a poet. She married Heiner Müller in 1953, and they lived together for thirteen years until her death. Towards the end of the war, during the bombing of Berlin, Inge was buried alive under the rubble for three days. Both of her parents perished in the same accident. This traumatic experience left an indelible mark on her; much of her poetry speaks directly of this horrific experience.[19] In her poem "Under the Rubble" ("Unterm Schutt") she writes:

> And then all at once the sky gave way
> I laughed and was blind
> And was again the childish kind
> In the womb wild with nothing to say
> With arms and legs which thrust untaught
> And grabbed and walked.
> Images all around
> No floor no roof
> What is – vanished
> I am before I was
> One breath hours
> The others! A second bright like in the sea
> A knock from somebody –
> Give the globe to me!

> (1997: 117)

In the last eight years of her life, Inge attempted to commit suicide several times, but each time Müller had been present and able to stop her suicide attempts. In his poem "Self-Portrait Two A.M." from 1959, Müller writes of this experience:

> Yesterday she tried to hang herself. Tomorrow
> She'll cut open her arteries or whatdoIknow.

At least she has a goal to look for.
That she'll attain, one way or another
And the heart is a spacious graveyard.

(2001: 49–50)

In his autobiography entitled *War without Battle* (*Krieg Ohne Schlacht*) Müller recalls that his work was beginning to suffer as a result of his wife's depression, and how, one evening, when he came home after a lengthy conversation with Adolf Dresen about the future, or lack of it, of Marxism, he found her dead (1992: 209). In *Obituary* (*Todesanzeige*), first published in 1975 under the title *Wüsten der Liebe*, Müller deals directly with the memory of this event:

> She was lying on the kitchen floor, half on her stomach, half on her side, one leg folded inward as if in sleep, the head close to the door. I crouched down, turned her face out of its profile and said the name I called her by when we were alone. I had the feeling I was acting. I saw myself, leaning in the doorway, half bored, half amused, watching a man who had come home about three o'clock in the morning, crouched down on his kitchen floor, bent over a woman perhaps unconscious perhaps dead, holding up her head in his hands, talking to her as if to a puppet for no other audience than myself. (1995: 24)[20]

Inge, who had gassed herself in the oven, had not left any note, which made some suspicious that Müller was somehow involved in her death: "WHERE IS THE NOTE WHAT NOTE DID SHE NOT LEAVE A NOTE WHERE WERE YOU FROM WHEN TILL WHEN" (25).

Obituary is written in three sections. It comprises a description of Müller's thought, actions, and feeling after discovering his wife's dead body, a phantasmagorical segment in which the speaking subject murders three times a figure referred to only as "CHICKEN FACE" (Hühnergesicht), and a final section entitled "DREAM," where the "I" encounters a hanged naked body of a woman, ultimately sexually penetrating her. The "I" at the centre of the *Obituary* connects the three narratives, leading the reader to associate murder and a rape depicted in the second and the third sections with Heiner Müller himself in the first section. Furthermore, in the piece, Müller describes how upon encountering his wife's lifeless body he had the feeling that he "was acting" (in the theatre), but, as Aled Griffiths notes, "the shift from the third person on the theatrical stage back to the writing and speaking subject in the first person is only effected by the identification of himself as a murderer and abuser" (2000: 42). Finally, the connection between these three sections and their narrator(s) is further emphasized through repetition:

> Going into the room next door (three times), to look at the dead woman ONE MORE TIME (three times), she is naked under the sheets. . . . He has no place in my dreams any more since I killed him (three times). . . . Above me the monstrous thighs, opened pit like a pair of scissors, which I walk further into with every step. (25–6)

The parallels here between *Obituary* and *Description of a Picture* are, I think, quite overt. In both cases, by representing Inge's suicide as murder and rape, Müller is clearly not attempting to evade responsibility for Inge's death.

Like a Freudian melancholic, Müller is self-absorbed, observing himself. He is a "self-critical" (Freud, 1957: 254) narcissist, who experiences the death of his wife in the form of "obsessional self-reproaches" (267), which are often "heightened into philosophical introspection" (255). In the central passage of "Mourning and Melancholia" Freud writes:

> the melancholic's disorder affords the view of the constitution of the human ego. We see how in him one part of the ego sets itself over against the other, judges it critically, and as it were, takes it as its object. Our suspicion that the critical agency which is here split off from the ego might also show its independence in other circumstances will be confirmed by ever further observation. We shall really find grounds for distinguishing this agency from the rest of the ego. What we are here becoming acquainted with is the agency commonly called "conscience." . . . In the clinical picture of melancholia, dissatisfaction with the ego on moral grounds is the most outstanding feature. (256)

The inexorable march of melancholia, which Freud captures here, resembles strongly the radical solipsism of pain that infuses Müller's *Obituary*. There the melancholic subject, excessively and morbidly self-observing in the face of shock, refuses to "kill the dead" a second time, prolonging her existence (246). For Müller, a relentless melancholic, his wife keeps on living, then, but as a ghost haunting his psyche. Such is the force of melancholia, of the interminable and inconclusive work of mourning: "[T]he law of mourning . . . would have to fail in order to succeed. In order to succeed, it would have to fail, to fail well" (Derrida, 1996: 173).

We recall that, in Freud, mourning is a regular and normal psychic "reaction to the loss of a loved one/object" (1957: 252). The successful work of mourning implies a painful and sometimes extended process of libidinal disinvestment from the object of our sorrowful loss by the end of which we are able to restore our psychic equilibrium. In other words, what we do when in mourning is to gradually overcome the loss of the beloved, either through accepting the test of reality or by "moving on" with our life and letting go of the deceased in order to invest in the new (246). With this, Freud claims, the work of mourning can be "completed." In melancholia, however, the attachment to the lost object supersedes any desire to recover from this loss. Furthermore, Freud reminds us of the second singular feature of melancholia: the melancholic "knows whom he has lost (as the mourner does) but not what he has lost in him" (254):

> In mourning we found that the inhibition and loss of interest are fully accounted for by the work of mourning in which the ego is absorbed. In melancholia, the unknown loss will result in a similar internal work and will therefore be responsible for the melancholic inhibition. The difference is that the inhibition of the melancholic seems puzzling to us because we cannot see what is that is absorbing him so entirely. (254)

Walter Benjamin is also attuned to this kind of melancholic investment. In *The Origin of German Tragic Drama*, he argues that the melancholic gets invested in things, imbuing knowledge itself with a thing-like quality: "In its tenacious self-absorption [melancholy] embraces dead objects in its contemplation" (1977: 157). As Wendy Brown has remarked, Benjamin's melancholy suggests "a certain logic of fetishism – with all the conservatism of withdrawal from human relations that fetishistic desire implies – contained within the melancholic logic" (1999: 21). And just as the narrator in *Description of a Picture* resurrects the woman, so in a poem entitled "Yesterday on a Sunny Afternoon" from 1969, the lyrical "I" expresses a desire to exhume the corpse of his wife:

> And to see what's left of her
> Bones I never saw
> To hold her skull in my hands
> And to imagine what her face was like
> Behind the masks she wore
> Through the dead city of Berlin and other cities
> When I was still dressed in her flesh.
>
> I did not give in to my desire
> For fear of the police and the gossip of my friends.
>
> (2001: 21)

Similarly, in Euripides's *Alcestis* Admetus, unable to let go of Alcestis, remains attached to the deceased. "Alcestis, everything has gone with you," he wails (1999: 22). Other women only remind him of her. Refusing to accept the test of reality and free himself from the prolonged existence of the lost object of love, he describes the statue that he will have made of her:

> What shall I do,
> Have a sculptor make a model of you?
> Stretch out with it, on our bed,
> Call it Alcestis, whisper to it?
> Tell it all I would have told you?
> Embrace it – horrible! – stroke it!
> Knowing it can never be you.
> Horrible! To dream you have come back
> Alive, happy, full of love as ever –
> Then to wake up!
>
> (22)

"To dream you have come back alive" marks a libidinal cathexis to his dead wife, his inability to sublimate and reincorporate the lost object into the ego. Fantasising about lying with her in the coffin "together forever" (23), his only desire is for death itself. It is only at the end of the play that his depressive position is resolved, after Heracles, thankful for Admetus's hospitality, goes down to the underworld and wrestles Alcestis away from death.

In a response to Müller's first version of *Obituary* (and perhaps to his poem "Yesterday on a Sunny Afternoon"), Ginka Tscholakowa, who was married to Heiner Müller from 1967 to 1986, wrote a short piece of prose entitled "The Mask of Silence" ("Die Maske des Schweigens"). Writing "on behalf of" the dead woman who cannot speak – ventriloquising her – she offers a scathing critique of Müller's text:

> Sooner or later he will be sitting in front of an empty piece of paper in the typing machine and he will have no desire to do anything. Then I will return to the tile floor in the kitchen, he would want to make coffee for himself and see me lying there. My dentures next to me about which I never told him. And he will realise that he missed the chance to be through with me. He can talk to me quietly and suggestively, but I won't listen to him anymore. And then he will return to the machine and write down his justification. As all poets he believes that words can undo deeds. He will write how often I tried to commit suicide. He will be terrified through this writing, and he will enjoy it at the same time, to see me dead. And if he gives a reason for it, it will be my childhood, the bombs, the war, Germany. The struggle of gestures against the stiffness of words, my own world, me, the Other behind the mask of loud silence he will not mention. (1999: 40)[21]

Contra Tscholakova, however, I believe that Müller, a knowing melancholic, is aware all the way that, as Ross Chambers aptly puts it, "the law of the aftermath is that of the irreparable" (Chambers, 2004: 265). In his study titled *Untimely Interventions*, Chambers explores a cultural history of "aftermath" – how a culture can be haunted by its own history. Engaging a broad cross-section of collective disasters: the AIDS crisis, the First World War, and the Holocaust, he shows how in a writing of aftermath – characteristically the work of a surviving friend, lover, or relative – the initial traumatic event and its aftermath are in some sense co-constitutive. At the same time, he shows that the losses these works often address do not necessarily signify a straightforward annihilation of prior relationships even if the form of these relationships changes significantly. Going back to

Figure 2.1 Inge and Heiner Müller on the Lehnitzer Lake, circa 1958; photograph courtesy of the Academy of Arts in Berlin, Heiner Müller Archive

Müller's works, I contend that whereas both poems quoted in the epigraph above: Inge Müller's "Here is the bridge" and Heiner Müller's "In the water I saw" emphasise the closeness of the bonds of love (Figure 2.1), even as they acknowledge their fragility or inadequacy in the face of death (that is, Inge's attempted suicides), both versions of *Obituary* as well as *Description of a Picture* agree in identifying the death of the other as a premortem failure – a failure on the part of the survivor to love, extend generosity, or show care for an object of love that is now irrevocably lost. A first division, the gradual estrangement of the husband and wife during their life together ("why doesn't he come" . . . "why doesn't he come"), foreshadows the irreparable distance that will come between them after Inge's death, a distance aggravated by the survivor's awareness that all his attempts to repair the initial disaster are bound to fail (Müller, 1995: 41).

In *Description of a Picture*, the survivor is attempting vainly to repair the two initial breaks through his writing:

> . . . wanted: the gap in the process, the Other in the recurrence of the Same, the stammer in the speechless text, the hole in eternity,

the possibly redeeming ERROR: the distracted gaze of the killer with the edge of the knife, at the bird in the tree, into the emptiness of the landscape, hesitating before the incision, a closing of the eyes, before the gush of blood, the woman's laughter, one glimpse long loosening the stranglehold, making tremble the hand with the knife, the bird dive-bombing at the blade's gleam, the lending on the man's skull, the beak's slashes, one right, one left, reeling and roaring of the blinded, blood spraying in the tempest's whirl, who gropes for the woman, fear that the blunder will be made while he's squinting, that the peephole into Time will open between one glimpse and the next, hope lives on the edge of the knife that rotates ever faster, with increasing attention that equals fatigue, insecurity lightening the certainty of the ultimate horror . . . (101)

In the aftermath of Inge's death, then, the weight of continued responsibility is added to that of remorse, the knowledge not only of the failure of his generosity under the test of Inge's attempted suicides, but also that the damage done (Inge's death) cannot be repaired or forgotten. Mourning of his wife cannot be brought to term because the severe pain of loss persists. Inge persists in memory; she has, in other words, become spectral. And her spectrality signifies in turn his own hauntedness – his inability to pull back from the departed one. (To be haunted, we know, is the sign of the impossibility of mourning.) Providing a fitting metaphor for the intricate correlations between death, mourning, and memory thematised in the playwright's works, this hauntedness – Inge Müller's enduring, ghostly presence – also affects a crucial linkage between the writer, the reader, and the dead.

In *Black Sun*, Kristeva draws a connection between art and agency, arguing that creative aesthetic practice – the sublimatory translation of semiotic drive energies into symbolic patterns of signification – is one of the few effective means of coming to terms with loss, particularly the sense of primordial alienation that haunts us from the very inception of subjectivity. Sublimation thus allows the subject to translate its internal void into external fullness in an effort to contain the bitterness of loss: beauty, as "the royal way through which humanity transcends the grief of being apart," comes to envelope the subject's lack so as to empower it to continue living despite the fact that it always, inevitably and inexorably, carries within itself an imprint of archaic loss as the very condition of being (1989: 99–100). "The imaginative capacity of Western man," Kristeva concludes, "is the ability to transfer meaning to the very place where it was lost in death and/or nonmeaning. This is survival of idealisation . . . a self-illusion, nothing but dreams and words, words, words. . . . It affirms the almightiness of temporal subjectivity – the one who knows enough to speak until death comes" (1989: 103). But Müller's *Description of a Picture*, fractured and unable to achieve narrative coherence, stands more for an imitation of his own ghostlike state rather than holding the promise of his own creative overcoming of melancholia. As in the case of the constellation of testimonials analysed by Chambers in *Untimely Meditations*, writing here is "the defining activity of survival" (Chambers, 2004: 166). It signals "both the character of survival as degraded repetition, and the failure of repetition to mend the impact of the previous fall(s)" (166). Thus, as the domain of the communicable imprint of affective reality, *Description of a Picture* presents not only a powerful exploration of the promises and limitations of melancholia, but it also offers a fundamental insight that the present can never entirely redeem the past.

In her study on affect, trauma, and contemporary art, Jill Bennett explores the ways in which some artworks register traumatic memory and open it up to an audience. Theorising the affective transaction between the spectator and the artwork, she contends that though "art cannot communicate the essence of a memory that is 'owned' by a subject, it may nevertheless envisage a form of memory for more than one subject, inhabited in different modalities by different people" (2005: 11). Focusing on the kind of artworks that she sees as "fundamentally relational rather than expressive in the traditional (communicative) sense of the term," she aims to show how "by realising a way of seeing and feeling, this art makes a particular kind of contribution to thought and to politics specifically: how certain conjunctions of affective and critical operations might constitute the basis for something we can call "emphatic vision" (2005: 12; 21). Discussing his *Description of a Picture* in terms congenial to Bennett's, Müller explains how he sees the affective transaction between the spectator and this artwork, and how this encounter could engender a manner of thinking:

As far as *Description of a Picture* is concerned, everybody can do it [i.e., describing the picture] more or less well and everybody in a different way. The most advanced art is the most *democratic*; every human being can describe a picture and the description produces new images if people write down what comes to mind while describing. It is a *model for play* (*Spielmodell*), which is at the disposal of anybody who can see and write. (qtd. in Vaßen, 1995: 178; original emphasis)

This "model for play" as further "painting over" of *Description of a Picture* by active participants implies, in contrast to a discursive analysis, one's own creative activity, an aesthetic productivity. In this respect, the play may also be termed, in the words of Elinor Fuchs, "spectator's response theatre: we write our own script out of the 'pieces of culture' offered" (1996: 111).

Müller's claims were put to the test in the spring of 2001 at the Berliner Ensemble, where the text was explored as a "model for a play." Directed by Philip Tiedemann, and featuring Krista Birkner, Margarita Broich, Detlef Lutz, and Steffen Schroeder, this was the first production of any Müller's text at that theatre since his death in 1995. Upon entering the space of the Berliner Ensemble's *Probebühne* in late June 2001, I realised that the director took the title of the play quite literally. The first thing the audience immediately notices is a big golden frame, perhaps four metres wide and four metres high, "hanging" on a black wall. The frame in this production, we realise, is the stage within which the performance takes place. Inside the frame is a platform covered with a white sheet that has an appearance of a lifeless, sterile horizon. The production starts with resurrection: a soil-smeared hand emerges on the horizon; it moves, stretches, and touches the white surface. Every touch, it seems, generates or provokes a cheerful, playful organ sound. Then the second hand appears, and then slowly a whole human figure emerges. Gradually, three more human figures come into view as well (Figure 2.2).

What we hear first is not "A landscape between steppe and savannah" (the opening line of *Bildbeschreibung*), but the phrases found later in the text. "I TOLD YOU YOU SHOULDN'T COME BACK," says one man directly into the audience. "DEAD IS DEAD," says a woman. "ALIEN IN YOUR OWN BODY," utters the second man. "HAVING SEEN IT ALL" ("ALLES GESEHEN") says the second woman. The stage figures (the awakened "dead") look from the frame in our direction as if into some distant horizon, and start describing their mutual impressions. Gradually, we

Figure 2.2   Scene from Heiner Müller's *Bildbeschreibung*, dir. Philip Tiedemann, the Berliner Ensemble, 2001; photo courtesy of Monika Rittershaus

(the audience) realise that it is not we who are looking at the picture, but that it is the picture, or rather the "dead", who are staring at us. We can only witness the act of describing. Since the picture is indeterminate, the spectator/listener must mentally "construct" his or her own images in the course of listening; the largely mental theatrical action consists of the collision between that construction process and the speakers' creative journey. Müller's emphasis on audience coproduction is clearly called upon here. "Are we faced with a group therapy?", asked Julia Michelis in her review of the performance for *Die Welt* newspaper – a question pertinent to both Tiedemann's *mise en scène* and its audience reception (2001: n.p.). In the programme for the performance, the dramaturg Henrik Adler wrote that the central question which Müller's *Description of a Picture* poses is: "Who is the victim, who is the perpetrator?" This question, regarding Germany's past, suggests Adler, was often posed in different media and modes of discourse in Berlin in the spring of 2001. Tiedemann's staging of the play, it follows, depended largely on the audience's capacity to filter a literary text through historical memory, thus allowing Müller's text to reverberate anew. In what follows I elaborate on the larger German memory discourse in which this performance intervened. As we shall see, this discourse shares much in common with the memory issues raised in my analysis of this Müller text in the preceding pages.

Since the beginning of the twenty-first century Germany has witnessed the resurgence of memories of German suffering during the Third Reich and its immediate aftermath, which were long absent from public consciousness and from discourse: the expulsion (*Vertreibung*) of 10–14 million Germans from then-Eastern Germany and Eastern Europe after the war, in the course of which more than two million Germans were killed (Naimark, 1995); the allied bombing raids of German cities that left 600,000 civilians dead (in the bombing of Dresden more than a hundred thousand died in a single night); and the mass rape of German women (estimates range from tens of thousands to two million) by members of the Red Army and Eastern European partisans. While it is unlikely that these German-centred memories will entirely replace the ongoing cultural preoccupation with the Holocaust, their recent revitalisation certainly signals an important political-cultural event. Television documentaries, eyewitness accounts, autobiographies, and other visual and literary representations of the past have flooded the cultural landscape of the united Germany. Several books and an amplifying media response have fuelled the current debate about German victimisation. Günther Grass's novella, *Im Krebsgang* (2002), translated into English in 2003 as *Crabwalk*, deals with the sinking of the *Wilhelm Gustloff* in January 1945, a boat filled primarily with refugees fleeing the East Prussian front that was torpedoed and sunk by a Red Army submarine. Published in the same year, Jörg Friedrich's *Der Brand: Deutschland im Bombenkreig, 1940–1945* (*The Fire: Germany Under Bombardment, 1940–1945*) describes the bombing of German cities during the Second World War. Another history, Anthony Beevor's *The Fall of Berlin 1945* (2002), recently translated into German, details the mass rapes and other war crimes committed against the German people by the Red Army as it captured Berlin. Finally, the Allied air attacks, and specifically the presumed failure of German literature to represent them, are the subjects of the first part of W. G. Sebald's *On the Natural History of Destruction* (2003).

In order to explain the current explosion of memories of German victimhood, some authors assert that Germans had collectively supressed the national traumas of expulsion, the air war, and the rapes, and that only recently they finally realised that they need to workthrough this difficult past. The lack of engagement with the Allied air raids, which W. G. Sebald first attacked in a series of lectures "Air War and Literature" (*Luftkrieg und Literatur*) he gave at the University of Zurich in the fall of 1997, has been seen as emblematic of a taboo on the discussion of German suffering during the war. By the end of the 1990s, the idea that the topic was a taboo had become widespread.[22]

Speaking about the bombing campaign against German cities conducted by British and American forces between 1940–45, Sebald writes:

> The destruction, on a scale without historical precedent, entered the annals of the nation only in the form of vague generalisations as Germany set about rebuilding itself. It seems to have left scarcely a trace of pain behind in the collective consciousness, it has been largely obliterated from the retrospective understanding of those affected, and it never played an appreciable part in discussion of the internal constitution of our country. (2003: 4)

According to Sebald, the great majority of Germans were complicit in this repression: "There was a tacit agreement, equally binding on everyone, that the true state of material and moral ruin in which the country found itself was not to be described . . . a kind of taboo like a shameful family secret, a secret that perhaps could not even be privately acknowledged" (2003: 10). In his view, it is quite understandable why Germans did not articulate the experiences of the bombings adequately immediately after the war: "The need to know was at odds with the desire to close down the senses . . . there were true stories that exceeded anyone's capacity to grasp them" (2003: 23). Furthermore, to Sebald, "it is impossible to gauge the depths of the trauma suffered by those who came away from the epicentres of the catastrophe. The right to silence claimed by the majority of these people is as inviolable as that of the survivors of Hiroshima" (2003: 89).[23] Along with Grass, Friedrich, and others, Sebald asserts that the needs of the present necessarily overwhelmed all other concerns. A comprehensive "cordoning" of traumatic German-centred memories, intertwined with a silent collective refusal to engage with the responsibility for the Nazi past, may have been necessary for the manic reconstruction of the country in the war aftermath.

However, much recent scholarship shows that Sebald's argument about the alleged silence about the Nazi past and German suffering – presented first by scholars like Theodor Adorno and Alexander and Margarete Mitscherlich in the 1950s and 1960s – is largely incorrect.[24] Robert Moeller, for instance, argues that both East and West Germany "devoted considerable energy to assessing the losses and incorporating victim status into public memory, . . . in the political arena and forms of commemoration, stories of German loss and suffering were ubiquitous" (2006: 27–8; see also Moeller, 2001). Immediate postwar West Germany was dominated not by silence, but by a carefully manipulated representation of the past that was moulded with one goal in mind: to downplay German culpability in Nazi crimes by focusing on their own victimisation first by a distant Nazi regime and then, even more, by the Soviet Union. He explains that "by telling stories of the enormity of their loses" Germans "could talk about the end of the Third Reich without assuming responsibility for its origins" (2001: 3). Moeller concludes that these postwar notions of German victimisation played a major integrative and legitimising role for the young republic.[25]

Furthermore, it should be made clear that in the German Democratic Republic the repression of German suffering was clearly structured differently. It is therefore important to distinguish between memory discourses in the two Germanys as well as between different aspects of suffering, which were represented or silenced in different ways. As Laurel Cohen-Pfister and Dagmar Wienroeder-Skinner remind us, in East Germany, antifascist legitimation, which placed victimisation followed by heroic resistance and victorious redemption at the core of national consciousness, "allowed for mourning the devastation caused by the air war carried out by the Western, capitalist Anglo-American powers" (2006: 6). However, they add that other aspects of suffering such as expulsions and the mass rapes that were "politically sensitive subjects for the communists, East Block-aligned GDR" were avoided (2006: 6–7).

Events such as the civil wars in the former Yugoslavia in the 1990s, especially German involvement in the Kosovo crisis, as well as the projected enlargement of the European Union (much discussed in early 2000s) to include Eastern European countries from which many Germans were expelled after 1945 may have spurred collective remembrance of German suffering. Furthermore, according to Eric Langenbacher, one of the key factors behind this new preoccupation with German victims is that "the left has belatedly confronted these memories" and is now coming to terms with them (2003: 62). As he notes, "almost all of the protagonists in these discussions and debates have been leftists, including Grass, Fischer, Vollmer, Friedrich, and Schneider; many others like Habermas have been conspicuous in their silence" (2003: 62). Ultimately, to Langenbacher the coexistence of the Holocaust memory and a reappropriated German-centred memory could be harnessed for progressive political ends. For those concerned with the future of the Holocaust-centred memory in Germany since unification, he concludes that the dominance of this memory "was never in doubt and remains *the* ethical imperative for German political culture" (2010: 35; original emphasis).

In his study of German memories of the Second World War after 1945, Gilad Margalit offers a view that differs from this overtly celebratory portrayal of the postwar German history of memory. He argues that in the 1950s both German successor states to the Third Reich created essentially apologetic narratives of the Second World War, which never completely disappeared from public consciousness. This discourse, "one that grants the Germans the status of victims," continued to exist "in families and the semi-public space," only to resurface with a vengeance in the aftermath of German unification (2010: 249; 291). This Israeli historian ends his study with an alarmist view that "the previous consensus about the fundamental difference between the experiences of the Nazis' victims and those of the Germans – a matter of common wisdom in the political culture of the Bonn republic for thirty years – has weakened in recent years" (2010: 249). In support of his argument, Margalit cites Bill Niven's critical assessment of contemporary German commemorative culture. If collective memory prioritises the Holocaust and Nazi crimes, while the private remembering of families focuses on suffering of family members in the war, then, argues Niven, "the current explosion of memory of German victimhood in the public realm might represent the triumph of the private over the public, of emotion over enlightenment, and of uncritical empathy over pedagogy" (qtd. in Margalit, 2010: 294).

I contend that it is only against this larger discourse on German memory that we can begin to "read" the numerous transitions and transformations that turned Müller's play into both an individual and a collective act of recall and recrimination for its Berliner Ensemble audience at the beginning of the third millennium. At the end of this production of *Description of a Picture*, the fragmentation of the narrator that Müller's text describes (starting with the phrase "ALIEN IN YOUR OWN BODY") is enacted in the performance through the dismemberment of the actors' own bodies. With the line "rock slides triggered by the wanderings of the dead, underground, the secret pulse of the planet which the picture is meant to represent," the stage becomes darker, and the white fabric starts sinking into holes in the platform, taking with it the figures on the stage. Through the holes on the black surface (under "the stage") the actors stick out their hands, arms, heads, a mouth, thus creating a pile of body parts. The performance ends when the description runs out. The final tableau freezes on a mouth wide open. Then darkness fills the golden frame.

If the production has served as a vehicle for evolving German perceptions of familial and national guilt and pain, if it has reminded us of the not-so-distant German past, it has also hopefully prompted audiences to think through the interconnectedness of different forms of violence, which are too often compartmentalised and remembered in isolation from one another. I state this because, as Cohen-Pfister and Wienroeder-Skinner warn us, even as the complex interconnectedness of world cultures under the current regimes of globalisation and "multiculturalism diffuse an ethnocentric self-understanding of what it means to be German today, the emergence of 1945 in cultural memory as a collective national trauma moves German national identity in a Germano-centric direction" (2006: 9). Now that Germany has become multicultural, it is essential to overcome portraying it as an autonomous entity untouched by race matters and unchanged by its contact with various Others (for instance, Jews, Africans, Muslims, Roma, and Sinti) and the legacies of racism, colonialism, and the post-Second World War migrations.

Michael Rothberg's *Multidirectional Memory*, which explores the relations between Holocaust memory and decolonisation struggles, is perhaps instructive here. Emphasising memory's multidirectional potential, Rothberg provides a model of memory whereby one cannot draw sharp boundaries between identities and traumatic histories, as they overlap in our attempt to recollect and understand them. He insists that collective memories cannot simply be associated with discrete identities, nor can they be formed in isolation from one another. Furthermore, producing a critique of the "conception of competitive memory," the widely held view that different collective memories compete for public attention in the public sphere and marginalise one another, Rothberg focuses on memory's "jagged" borders, providing a model of transcultural remembrance that allows us to understand how we can imagine different sites of violence together without reducing them to either the same type of suffering or to utterly separate events (2009: 5). Arguing that we ought to recognise the power of this memory to move us beyond a logic of competitive memory, he shows, for instance, how disparate occasions of political violence such as Nazism and decolonisation can actually serve as vehicles of remembrance for each other. Such an effort can build bridges between different discourses and regimes of memory in mutually productive ways and lead towards new forms of solidarity among traumatised groups and new visions of justice.

In this respect, the acknowledgement of the power of the felt history and emotions expressed and passed on within families to shape the individual picture of German history, which I have mentioned above, need not necessarily be regarded pessimistically. As Daniel Becker writes, the current proliferation of sympathetic accounts acknowledging German victimhood does not necessarily relativise the atrocities perpetrated by the Germans. Rather, historical consciousness in unified Germany may be seen as "reflect[ing] the manifold social and cultural changes the country has undergone in the decades since the end of World War II" (2006: 355). Furthermore, now that the German society has become "more heterogeneous, now encompassing children of children who have not only no temporal but also no ethnic and no cultural connection" to the deeds, suffering, and memories of "the eyewitnesses, the survivors, the victims and the perpetrators," German historical memories are becoming increasingly particularised and fragmented (2006: 355). It is perhaps for this very reason that the Berliner Ensemble's staging of Müller's *Description of a Picture* – a postdramatic text that does not locate the violence it recalls in any particular history – enabled its audiences to make mnemonic connections between different traumatic pasts (the Holocaust, the bombings of German cities, slavery, colonialism) in Berlin in 2001. Focusing on perpetration as much as on suffering, while emphasising memory's multidirectional potential, it allowed for yet another personal and collective rapprochement to the dead, always to be revised, never-ending.

Mommsen's Block and Left melancholia

"Between city and city / After the wall the abyss" (Müller, 2001: 57). So begins Müller's poem "Hapless Angel 2" ("Glückloser Engel 2"), written in 1991. With the fall of the Berlin Wall, perhaps the most symbolic event of the collapse of "real-existing socialism" in Eastern Europe, a paradigm that had informed most of Müller's work crumbled. This resulted in the author's creative crisis, which was thematised in *Mommsen's Block*, the first longer text that Müller wrote in the post-unification period.[26] In it, Müller reflects on the then current historical situation and his position as an author after the collapse of socialism. As I will argue, the text also evokes a certain kind of melancholy, which derives from Müller's disappointment with the outcome of the *Wende*, or postcommunist turn, and the changes brought about by unification. Müller seems keenly aware that "something was lost in Europe's transition from a divided continent to a single market" (Scribner, 2003: 118). But what has been lost? Hope and the belief in utopia? The promise of well-being, progress, and equality? The possibility of dissidence? The belief in the idea of radical change, no longer imaginable? Humanity? A future?

As I mentioned earlier in this chapter, already in his 1917 essay "Mourning and Melancholia," Freud acknowledges that while the cause of melancholia is frequently readily discernible, in some instances "one cannot see clearly what it is that has been lost" (1957: 245). To Freud, "This would suggest that melancholia is in some way related to an object-loss which is withdrawn from consciousness, in contradistinction to mourning, in which there is nothing about the loss that is unconscious" (245). In other words, melancholia lends silent expression to a loss that is often unavowed and unavowable. I suggest that the difficulty Müller faces in articulating this loss can be seen as a symptom of the collective woundedness and posthistorical melancholia that accompanied the passing of communism in Eastern Europe at the end of the twentieth century. Devoted to the fate of the "communist idea" throughout the twentieth century, François Furet's *The Passing of an Illusion*, for instance, ends with a melancholy conclusion: "Once again, history has become a tunnel that we enter in darkness, not knowing where our actions will lead, uncertain of our destiny, stripped of the illusory security of a science of what to do" (1999: 502). In *Mommsen's Block* too, history is no longer seen to have a telos: it has simply become a routine part of consumer society, a necessity without goal. Hence the author's writer's block.

Reflecting upon the perceptions of posthistorical loss, Müller participates in a wider cultural formation – the memory crisis that has fixated the gaze of many Europeans onto recent history. While mourning the passing of the "real existing socialism" has released much artistic reflection (see, for instance, Scribner, 2003; Lužina, 2007; O'Driscoll, 2011), recent years have also seen an increased volume of scholarly publications on communism and its legacies in Eastern Europe. Yet, according to Maria Todorova, inadequate state support and lack of other serious sources of funding in Eastern Europe and the former Soviet Republics means that the cultural heritage and memories of the (former) Second World are threatened with obsolescence and forgetting. There is a pressing need "to rescue from oblivion the artefacts, but especially the thoughts, about this past" (Todorova, 2010a: 14).

While Todorova acknowledges that there is much ambivalence towards the communist past across Europe due to its past record of violence, she contends that it would be also instructive to look at "the communist legacy in education, culture in general, healthcare, and welfare" (Todorova, 2010a: 13). "While this legacy is not to be idealised," adds this Bulgarian historian, "it would be difficult to dismiss it" (2010a: 13). In a similar vein, *Post-Communist Nostalgia*, a collection of essays Todorova co-edited with Zsuzsa Gille, addresses the complex interplay between remembering and knowledge making in the post-communist world. It shows, for instance, how difficult it is to pin down what post-communist nostalgia really expresses. The object of longing here ranges from "the collective unity of the past" and "one's country and shared way of life that disappeared overnight" (Gilles, 2010: 278) – as was the case with the former Yugoslavia – to "a very specific form of sociability" and "a desire among those who lived through communism, even when they have opposed it or were indifferent to its ideology, to invest their lives with meaning and dignity, not to be thought of, remembered, or bemoaned as losers or 'slaves'" (Todorova, 2010b: 7). In light of this growing interest in the process of remembering communism as well as a renewed interest in leftist politics – which I address briefly at the end of this chapter – a surge in melancholy sentiment that permeates Müller's *Mommsen's Block* need not spell out the end of a critical stance. Rather, as I elaborate at the end of this chapter, it suggests that loss may be the condition of possibility of recovery.

According to Carl Weber, two events in particular inspired *Mommsen's Block*: the replacement of a statue of Karl Marx with one of the historian Theodor Mommsen (1817–1903) at the entrance to Berlin's Humboldt University, and the publication in 1992 of two collections of notes based on Mommsen's lectures on Imperial Rome, which were discovered in a Nuremberg antiquarian shop by the Berlin historian Alexander Demandt in 1980 (Weber, 2001: 123). Mommsen was one of the most distinguished historians of the nineteenth century. In 1902, he became the first German awarded the Nobel Prize for Literature. The award was granted to him for the first three volumes (books 1–5) of *The History of Rome* published between 1854 and 1856. The last volume of this series ends with the victory of Caesar at Thapsus in Africa on 6 April 46 BC. Volume V, *The Provinces of the Roman Empire from Caesar to Diocletian*, appeared three decades later, in 1885. Mommsen also envisaged writing volume IV, an account of the imperial history up to the collapse of the Empire in the period of great migrations (books 6 and 7), and raised public expectations in this respect on several occasions. Although he lectured on this chapter of ancient Rome's history, he never completed the project. The title of the Müller text can thus have a double connotation. Besides referring to the block on which the statue of Mommsen used to stand, it can also refer to Mommsen's own writer's block, his inability or lack of inspiration to write about Imperial Rome.

Müller's *Mommsen's Block* starts with the question asked by many: why did this great historian not write the long expected fourth volume of his *History of Rome* on the age of emperors? The narrator of Müller's text offers a number of possible reasons. As we shall soon establish, many of these are derived from Alexander Demandt's introduction to the two collections of notes taken of Mommsen's lectures on Imperial Rome, which were published in the same year as Müller wrote his text. In *Mommsen's Block*, Müller refers implicitly to reading this material: "Yesterday while eating in a four-star restaurant / In the once more resurrected capital Berlin / I leafed through the notes of your lectures / On the Roman age of Caesars fresh from the book market" (2001: 128). Following Demandt, Müller writes that one of the reasons for Mommsen's inability to write this chapter of ancient Rome history might have been "The lack of inscriptions," that is, the absence of materials that would have the status of archival evidence, and which would serve as a control on the narratives of historical writers from this period, such as Livy and Appian. In a letter to James Bryce, quoted in the epigraph of *Mommsen's Block*, Mommsen complains that the narrative sources from this period report mostly about the Emperor and his court: "What authorities are there beyond Court tittle-tattle" (124). As it is well known, one of the reasons why Mommsen could put forward many original views about some hitherto unquestioned problems of Roman history was that his historical research was based mostly on primary sources (for example, numismatics and epigraphy) rather than records of analysts. Next, Müller writes of the fact that "he [Mommsen] didn't like them those Caesars of the late empire" (124). He continues:

> He'd had enough of the peerless Julius
> Whom he liked as much as his own tombstone
> Even TO WRITE ABOUT CEASAR'S DEATH he had
> When he was asked about the still missing
> Fourth volume NOT ENOUGH PASSION LEFT
> And THE PUTRESCENT CENTURIES after him
> GRAY IN GRAY BLACK UPON BLACK   For whom
> The epitaph
>
> (124)

"Tombstone" and "epitaph" are extrapolated here from Demandt's introduction, in which he quotes the opinion of Anglophone scholars who "believed that Mommsen suffered from 'agonising political neurosis' that the present era was witnessing late antiquity over again, and that he therefore wanted to spare his contemporaries this 'terrifying funeral epitaph' . . . " (1992: 8). Müller further elaborates on this insight: "That the midwife Bismarck / Was as well the gravedigger of the empire / That afterbirth of a counterfeit dispatch / could be concluded from the third volume" (124). As is well known, Mommsen was an opponent of Bismarck, the creator of the Imperial Third Reich, who was also instrumental in triggering the outbreak of World War I through his insistence on annexing Alsace-Lorraine from France.

Müller also refers to a letter from Dilthey to Count Yorck from 1884,[27] who suggests another reason for Mommsen's inability to write on the age of emperors:

> BUT HE IS TIRED AND QUITE DUSTY
> The pious Dilthey wrote to Count York
> FROM TREADING THE BACKROADS OF PHILOLOGY
> INSCRIPTIONS AND PARTY POLITICS
> HIS MIND ISN'T HOMESICK FOR THE IN-
> VISIBLE EMPIRE . . .

(125)

Dilthey writes in the letter: "it is hard to imagine how anyone could write about the age of early Christianity without any religious feeling, or indeed without any spiritual yearning for the invisible Kingdom. I do not regard him as capable of writing an account even of the early history of the German tribes" (qtd. in Demandt, 1996: 2). However, Dilthey's letter to Yorck was provoked by a rumour that circulated at the time that Mommsen was working on his fourth volume of the *History of Rome*. Indeed, in his reply to Dilthey, Count Yorck writes: "Mommsen really is writing on imperial history and is reading – critical studies of early Christianity!" (qtd. in Demandt, 1996: 2).

In the next passage, Müller then suggests that the ebbing of creative energy, and the lack of arrogance – an attribute of the young – may have been responsible for Mommsen's "writer's block:"

> In a letter to one of his daughters Mrs. Wilamowitz
> He dreams of a villa near Naples
> Not so he'd learn how to die Comes time comes death
> . . .
> the dream of Italy is a dream of writing
> The stimulant of moonlight on ruins
> With the divine arrogance of MY YOUNG YEARS
> THE YOUNGER ONES AT LEAST YOUNG I NEVER WAS
> What remains is the DIVINE BLUNTNESS – A POOR
> SUBSTITUTE . . .

(125)

Here Müller draws again from Demandt's "Introduction" to Mommsen's *History of Rome under the Emperors*, which quotes Mommsen's letter to his daughter Marie Wilamowitz, written in April 1882 from a villa at Naples. In the letter, Mommsen conveys his dream of spending six to eight months in such a villa to give himself a chance to see if he "can still write something that people would want to read" (qtd. in Demandt, 1996: 5). However, his scepticism is quick to follow: "actually I don't believe I could – not that I feel enfeebled by age, but the sacred self-deception of youth is gone. I know now, alas, how little I know, and the divine arrogance has deserted me. The divine bloody-mindedness in which I would still be able to achieve something is a poor substitute" (qtd. in Demandt, 1996: 5). Italy is also referred to in a letter written to Mommsen by his son-in-law Wilamowitz on 27 October 1883. While encouraging Mommsen to persist in his aspiration to write a historical account of the age of emperors, Wilamowitz also mocks his romantic sentiments: "You will have no need of moonlight or devastation to spur you on to a new 'history of the fall and decline of the Roman Empire:' but even without sentimentality Rome would be the best location from which to dare to compete with Gibbon" (qtd. in Demandt, 1996: 24).

To the list of speculations why Mommsen's fifth volume of the *History of Rome* was never published in his lifetime, Müller adds the fire that broke out at Mommsen's home at no. 6 Marchstrasse in the Berlin neighbourhood of Charlottenburg on 12 July 1880:

> A fire in the Mommsen's house caused
> Not by the Christian zeal against libraries
> As two thousand years earlier in Alexandria
> But by a gas explosion at Number eight March Street[28]
> Gave rise to the horrible hope
> The great scholar might have written after all
> The fourth volume the long-awaited one
> About the age of emperors
> And the text had been burnt
> With the rest of the library for instance
> Forty thousand volumes plus manuscripts

> (126)

Demandt finds this speculation unsubstantiated: "Neither the newspaper reports nor Mommsen himself referred to the loss of the

History of the Roman Emperors" (1992: 23). However, as Müller informs us further, "Rescued was the Academy Fragment / Seven pages of a draft framed by the fire / IN POINTED BRACKETS THE SCORCHED WORDS / OF MOMMSEN as the editors write / One hundred and twelve years after the fire" (126). On 5 March 1991, while conducting research in the Academy of Sciences in former East Berlin, Demandt discovered a file entitled "A Further MS on the History of Rome." Among other documents which survived the fire at Mommsen's house, the file contained a ten-page introduction to the history of emperors, suggesting that by 1880 Mommsen had already started writing the manuscript (Demandt, 1992: 23). While Demandt finds it unlikely that Mommsen had written more on the subject than these ten pages, the possibility that "the text had been burnt" still haunts many people's imagination today as it did in the time of Mommsen.

In a letter to Peter Gast, quoted at length by both Demandt and Müller, Nietzsche wrote: "Have you heard of the fire at Mommsen's / house?" (Müller, 2001: 126). He then refers to Mommsen's desperate attempts to salvage his library until he had to be restrained after sustaining burn injuries. He continues: "When / I heard the story it truly wrung my heart / and even now I am in physical distress when I / think of it is this compassion? But what is / Mommsen to me? I am not at all fond of him" (127). "The fear of solitude is hidden in the question mark," Müller comments, and uses this cue to interpolate his own persona in the remaining narrative: "He who writes into the void has no use of punctuation / Permit me to speak of myself Mommsen Professor" (127).

From this point in the text on, Müller engages in an imaginary dialogue with Mommsen, referring directly to the historical and political reality of the moment in which he writes:

> The bombs of World War II You know they
> Did not spare March Street Nor
> Was spared your Academy of Sciences
> From the fall of the Asiatic despotism Product
> Of an erroneous reading and falsely called
> Socialism after the great historian
> Of capital Whom you didn't notice
> A worker in a different quarry
> Until his monument stood on your pedestal

For the duration of one state The pedestal is yours again
Before the university that was named after Humboldt
By the rulers of an illusion

(127–8)

The replacement of the bust of Marx by the one of Mommsen is part
of a much larger culture of architectural memory that has preoccupied
Germany since unification. The fall of the Berlin Wall is only the most
obvious example of the urban change in the post-turn years; Berliners
have also witnessed the debates over Peter Eisenman's Holocaust
memorial, Sir Norman Foster's renovated Reichstag, Daniel Libeskind's
Jewish Museum, the reconstruction of the Berlin *Stadtschloss*, the
changing of many street names, and the destruction of some munici-
pal buildings, among other substantial transformations. Many symbols of GDR history have been effaced.[29] In her book *The Detachment*
(*Die Entfernung* 1996), Sophie Calle, one of the most prominent figures
in contemporary art in France, records the disappearance of socialist
realist objects and architecture in the Berlin area. Calle opens the text
by citing from an announcement made by the Berlin Senate in 1992:
"Whenever a system of rule dissolves or is overthrown, the justification for its monuments – at least those which served to legitimise and
foster its rule – no longer exists" (6). The verdicts of the senate commission differ from case to case: "Preserve as is." "Add information
board." "Dismantle." "Cover with earth; also usable as embankment
material; definitely no reconstruction" (Calle, 1996: 1). As she worked
on the project, Calle not only photographed the sites of disappearance, but also asked passers-by to describe the objects which had once
filled these empty spaces. While most of the statues and other symbols
of the GDR socialist past had been removed by the time Calle started
her project, the passers-by accounts that she includes in her book testify that the collective memory of some East Berliners still retains the
impressions of disappeared socialist realist urban space.

The replacement of the bust of Marx with the bust of Mommsen,
however, does not prompt Müller to ask larger questions about the
spatial and material dimensions of collective memory.[30] Instead, he
offers a sort of a summation of the October Revolution.

THE GREAT OCTOBER OF THE WORKING CLASS – extolled
Voluntarily with hope or in a twofold stranglehold

By too many and even after their throats had been cut –
Was a summer storm in the World Bank's shadow
A dance of gnats above the graves of Tartars
WHERE THE DEAD ONES WAIT
FOR THE EARTHQUAKES TO COME

(128)

As Horst Domdey comments, "the deceased waiting for salvation, for the day of revenge, pictured as an earthquake, a time of revolutionary upheavals" is a metaphor that frequently punctuates Müller's work (1995: 238). To Domdey, what Müller suggests in this passage is that all "mankind needs in order to be saved . . . is one, final decisive battle," which will then be followed by rebirth (238). Thus, in this author's view: "Müller conceives the basic Dionysian model of 'tearing apart and rebirth,' of 'dying and becoming' on a world scale, an unadulterated philosophy of history" (238). Domdey's statement needs further qualification. It is my contention that what is invoked in this cryptic statement (that calls for the resurrection of the dead) bears a resemblance to a particular mixture of the messianic impulse and radical-utopian thought popular with left-wing European intelligentsia especially during the early twentieth century, exemplified for instance by the writings of Walter Benjamin and the Marxist philosopher Georg Lukács.

Messianism is generally understood as a doctrine that envisions a fundamental break between the present and the messianic future, delivering humankind from the corrupted nature of present-day social existence and inaugurating a completely new era. In its radical secular variant, messianism posed a profound challenge to many of the central assumptions of modernity, rejecting the Enlightenment and Marxist faith in infinite progression toward the best possible world. In his *Redemption and Utopia*, Michael Löwy demonstrates the complex interplay that existed between the Jewish tradition of historical messianism and radical secular utopianism that emerged in central Europe in the early twentieth century. The convergence between redemptive religious messianic thought and libertarian utopianism solidified particularly around the vision of revolution as a redemptive interruption of the continuity of history. To Gershom Scholem, one of the key Jewish intellectuals of this period and Benjamin's close friend, "Messianism in our age proves its immense force precisely in this form of the revolutionary apocalypse, and no longer in that of the rational utopia (if one can call it that) of eternal progress as the Enlightenment's surrogate for Redemption" (qtd. in Lowy: 1992: 18). And as Susan Buck-Morss has suggested in her book on Benjamin's uncompleted "Arcades Project," in such a fusion of utopia and messianism, "utopian desire can and must be trusted as the motivation of political action – can, because every experience of happiness or despair that was ours teaches us that the present course of events does not exhaust reality's potential, and must, because revolution is understood as a Messianic break from history's course and not its culmination" (1989: 243).

Domdey argues that in some ways *Mommsen's Block* resembles a "prophetic speech," but he also notes that there is "no mention of the Messiah who will cause earthquakes which will be followed by a New Jerusalem, free from utilisation of capital, production of goods and a world market" (1995: 239). While in the past Müller had invoked the historical subject that would carry the banner of the revolution, such as the proletariat (*Wound Woyzeck*), terrorists (*Hamletmachine*), or the Third World (*The Task*), here it is reduced to "a John of the Drug scene, who talks big and pretends there is a Saviour who will free the world from capitalism" (Domdey, 1995: 239). Müller's disillusionment with the direction history was taking during the *Wende* period is best exemplified in the way he portrayed Fortinbras in his 1989/1990 production of *Hamlet/Hamletmachine* at the *Deutsches Theater* in Berlin. As Jörg Bochow informs us, during his work on the production "Müller hesitated to decide the final question about 'who was Fortinbras?'" (2005: 7). In the end, Müller decided that Hamlet becomes Fortinbras: "Hamlet is made into Fortinbras by the ghost, who is of course not any more the ghost of Stalin, but the ghost of the Deutsche Bank (German Bank)" (qtd. in Bochow, 2005: 7).

Despite its quasi-religious faith in a revolutionary redemption, the messianic generation of central European Jewish intellectuals did not abandon the rationalist principles of the Enlightenment, nor did they aspire to simply recapture the premodern past. It is only when belief in the automatic and irresistible march of reason has been undermined, that the redemptive narrative of eternal progress was transformed into a grand narrative of catastrophic decline. This is the pathology of the modern society that Jean-François Lyotard spells out in *The Postmodern Condition* (1984) – a deep cultural malaise that manifests itself in the collapse or implosion of any concept of power, revolution, repression, or desire. As Seidman writes: "The great modernist stories of progress and decadence almost always operate with one-dimensional, virtually mythic notions of dominance and liberation. These grand narratives frame history and social conflicts in grossly simplifying or apocalyptical images. They utterly fail to grasp the multifaceted, heterogeneous, morally ambiguous social currents and strains that make up the life of any society" (191: 140). Müller's text, it seems, comes dangerously close to embodying this paradigm.

In the next section of *Mommsen's Block*, for instance, the narrator quotes a conversation between new German "money changers and dealers" that he overheard in an expensive restaurant:

> "This four million / Must come our way at once //But that won't work // But that won't be conspicuous at all // If you haven't mastered the rules of this game // You're lost . . . We have to bag him for the Deutsche Bank // We'll haul him in for ourselves / As soon as I put the screws on / I'll teach him a lesson Then he'll make / Serious money." (129)

He reacts with disgusts and loathing, and for the first time understands the nature of Mommsen's "writer's block." A clear parallel is established between Mommsen's inability to write about the time of Roman emperors, and Müller's inability to write about the victory of capitalism in 1989/1990. Furthermore, while the re-united Germany stands for the declining Roman Empire, the GDR is implicitly identified with the Roman Republic. Müller writes:

> Who would write that down
> With passion Hate is a waste Contempt an empty exercise
> For the first time I understood your writer's block
> Comrade Professor facing the Roman age of Caesars
> The as we know happy times of Nero's reign
> Knowing the unwritten text is a wound
> Oozing blood that no posthumous fame will staunch
> And the yawning gap in your Roman history
> Was a pain in my – how long still? – breathing body

(129)

Müller's melancholic stance brings to mind Benjamin's 1931 essay, "Left-Wing Melancholy." In this essay Benjamin criticises the writings of Eric Kästner, a member of the circle of critics and writers associated with the *Neue Sachlichkeit* (New Objectivity), in order to offer a broader social critique of a form of political resignation and quietism hiding under the banner of leftist moral indignation, which appeared predominant among left-oriented intellectuals in the 1930s. While Benjamin never offers a precise formulation of "left melancholia," he finds it a fitting term to describe what held many of his contemporaries in its grip, frozen in their sullen contemplation of better times, feeling aimless and without horizon for action. In the critique of Kästner's poems, Benjamin characterises the Left melancholic as one who "takes as much pride in the traces in the former spiritual goods as the bourgeois do in their material goods" (Benjamin, 1994: 305). In Benjamin's insistence on "the time of the Now" (*Jeztzeit*), the register of time infused with both messianic and revolutionary potential, Left melancholia represents not only the inability of those identified with that decade to connect with the present in any meaningful way, but it also signifies a narcissistic identification with past beliefs and structures of feeling, standing in the way of an emancipatory desire, political mobilisation, or transformation. As Wendy Brown writes, "Left melancholia, in short, is Benjamin's name for a mournful, conservative, backward-looking attachment to a feeling, analysis, or relationship that has been rendered thinglike and frozen in the heart of the putative Leftist" (1999: 21–2).

Benjamin's indictment of Kästner's writing could be launched against Müller's predilection for melancholia, his tired contemplation of the lost objects of modernity, and hollow irony. In *Mommsen's Block*, on some level Müller acknowledges and accepts that the GDR and the rest of the Soviet bloc were doomed to extinguish themselves in the near future ("THE GREAT OCTOBER OF THE WORKING CLASS/ . . . Was a summer storm in the World Bank's shadow"). Elsewhere, he pronounced that to him it was "obvious already in 1953" that the GDR could not exist for a longer period: "The GDR had never existed, it was always only an extension of the Soviet Union" (qtd. in Bochow, 2005: 5). Yet despite this recognition and the fact that the impossibility of remaking the GDR became obvious within weeks of the opening of the Berlin Wall, he attaches himself to this lost object all the more. Feeling adrift, aimless, and "burned out," Müller is perhaps unable to truly mourn the demise of a revolutionary telos that once inspired the socialist project. Disaffected with the present, he remains incapable of offering a radical critique of the status quo or igniting political passion. If there is any rebellion at work in this melancholic detachment it is a passive one. Convinced that all avenues toward effective action have been closed off, the melancholic writer recedes into a resigned interiority, brooding over the very conditions of the impossibility of actions themselves. With the apparent absence of real alternatives to the existing order of things, the subject at the centre of *Mommsen's Block* is closed off from meaningful avenues for active self-expression. The melancholic paralysis – *acedia* – manifests then in the form of writer's block, "a wound / oozing blood that no posthumous fame will staunch" (Müller, 2001: 129).

Put in a broader perspective, we might say that the wound narrated here could also stand for, to use Agnes Heller's phrase, "a wound of the consciousness of contingency" (1999: 6) that characterises our postmodernity. In her book *A Theory of Modernity* Heller contends: "Understanding the future as being-open – that is, keeping the wound of contingency bare without applying the medicines that knowledge and/or faith offer – and taking responsibility for the present and the future, are difficult positions to assume" (1999: 6–7). In what immediately follows, I will make use of some of Heller's insights in regards to (post)modernity as these seem to offer a much needed antidote to Müller's (posthistorical) melancholic stance.

Born into a middle-class Jewish family in Budapest in 1929, Heller directly experienced the brutalities of German occupation (her father perished in Auschwitz) and authoritarian state socialism, the dissolution of reform communism, and political dissidence in Eastern Europe. With her husband and frequent collaborator, philosopher Ferenc Fehér, she spent almost ten years in Australia (1978–86), before moving to the United States, where she spent fifteen years teaching at the New School, until her return to Hungary after the fall of Communism (Beilharz, 2003: 110). Having completed her doctoral studies under the supervision of Georg Lukács, Heller has been seriously engaging the topic of modernity from the late 1970s; hence, her *A Theory of Modernity* could be seen as a summation of the last twenty years of her reflections on the theme, with a particular emphasis on the experience of modernity and its core value of contingency.

As Heller herself puts it, her book is a theory of modernity from a postmodern perspective. She argues that because of the challenges and difficulties involved with assuming the position of what she terms as "reflected postmodernity," reflected postmodern thinking is accompanied by two forms of unreflected postmodern thinking: fundamentalism and cynicism. The former is the position of those who "need the drugs of the future certainties" while the latter is characteristic of those who "reject, or fail to take, responsibility" (1999: 7). "In order to take responsibility in the consciousness of contingency," writes Heller, "one needs to think in terms of an 'absolute present tense'" (7). To illustrate her point, Heller provides the metaphor of the railway station: "In the modernist view, the present is like a railway station where the denizens of the modern world need to catch one of the fast trains that run through, or stop in this location only for a few moments. Those trains will carry us to the future. Settling in the railway station would have meant stagnation – for them" (7). In Heller's view both the liberal and the Marxist kind of modernist imagination marginalised the present to the expense of the project, and projection, of an infinite future:

> The liberal kind envisioned the future in the model of infinite progression toward the best possible world. The Marxian and socialist kinds envisioned it as a development with a turning-point, where the best possible world appears at a stroke. The conflicts between those two images appeared in the juxtaposition of "reform/revolution" or "evolution/revolution." . . . Both versions, however, shared the faith in the progression; both based their faith on scientific knowledge, and both claimed absolute certainty for their predictions. (7–8)

In other words, both the progressivist-liberal view and the Marxian/socialist view (in their many versions) were teleological in their nature.

As Heller usefully reminds us, this logic at work in "high modernism" is no longer legitimate in our present. While the revolutionary paradigm collapsed with the historical events of 1989, the evolutionary paradigm has been slowly eroding. In other words, as Heller ironically puts it, the teleological narrative of modernity was realised: "the fast trains ran toward their final destination – and the names of the terminal railways stations were Auschwitz and the Gulag – the stations of extermination" (8). To these two twentieth century events that had largely devastated the Enlightenment promise we may add others: the continuous exploitation of the Third World by the First, the onslaught of global capitalism and neoliberal economic policies that increase the precariousness of growing numbers of people, the recent rise of violent ethnonationalism, environmental spoilage, human trafficking, AIDS and so on.

In an interview with Jan Hoet during Documenta IX, an international exhibition of contemporary art held at Kassel, Germany, in the wake of the GDR's dissolution, Müller also employed the metaphor of a railway waiting room to articulate his experience of reality in the former GDR.

> Here everything was in a constant state of anticipation. It was like being in a waiting-room. There would be an announcement: "The train will arrive at 18.15 and depart at 18.20" – and it never did arrive at 18.15. Then came the next announcement: "The train will arrive at 20.10." And so on. You went on sitting there in the waiting-room, thinking, "It's bound to come at 21.05." That was the situation. Basically, a state of Messianic anticipation. There are constant announcements of the Messiah's independent arrival, and you know perfectly well that he won't be coming. And yet, somehow, it's good to hear him announced all over again. (1992: 96–7)

Reminiscing over the former life in the East, Müller still finds in it something affirmative. In spite of its depressing reality, the East nonetheless embodied a utopian imaginary. Müller values state socialism for enabling a certain kind of experience that was also the opening of a possibility to think and live differently. "This whole waiting-room mentality, the whole situation," states Müller, "gives you a lot more contact with the earth on which the waiting-room is built, because there is no acceleration. Acceleration can prevent and destroy experiences. When you are rooted to one spot, you experience that place; you learn all about the strata, both geological and historical" (1992: 97). Living in the GDR still allowed for a felt possibility of a more just, free, and egalitarian order. For him, everyday life under Socialism still constituted the crucial terrain for the development of emancipatory tendencies and unseen but profound transformations. In truth, the GDR only symbolised a particular kind of futurity that was never fully realised. In the West, however, Müller claims that the imperative to travel forward destroyed any such potential: "Travelling destroys experiences, and waiting to travel actually accumulates them" (97).

During the momentous events of 1989, Müller could still claim: "The communists' loss of power, now globally underway, is also an opportunity. The opportunity to win back the idea of utopia, which has until now been monopolised by the terrorists" (Müller, 1990: 245).[31] In the same vein, many West German intellectuals thought it was imperative to reaffirm socialist principles at the very point when "actually existing socialism" was swept away in Eastern Europe. In a similar vein, as Andreas Huyssen writes, "East German intellectuals such as Wolf, Heym, Müller as well as many in the *Bürgerbewegung* (citizens' movement) invested the emerging forms of a *Basisdemokratie* (grass roots democracy) with the hopes for a reform of the socialist project" (1995: 47). He continues: "The old dream of realising socialism with a human face was revived at a time when, as Frank Hörnigk has argued, this project could no longer be saved" (47). Indeed, there was little that could have been done by East German intellectuals at this point in order to prevent the collapse of the state. What happened to "real existing socialism" in East Germany (and elsewhere in Europe) is by now well-known. As Wendy Brown put it, "State socialism is economically unviable in a capitalist world order – inefficient, uncompetitive, impoverished. Nor does it emancipate: work is no less alienating, no more under the control of the worker, no more organised, no more engaging of human creativity, no less dreary than under any other regime" (2005: 105). But, under these circumstances, what are the alternatives?[32]

In the last years of his life, the period in which *Mommsen's Block* was written, Müller does not envision any alternative. This may to do in part with the fact that the unique East German circumstances after unification – "an abrupt and painful, but complete, absorption and institutional break with the former legacy" – is compared to "a much more gradual adjustment with institutional and personal continuities" that marked social and political transformations in Eastern Europe in the 1990s, and that are still ongoing (Todorova, 2010a: 12). The statement he made in 1994 is in accord with the sense of loss and disillusionment that pervades *Mommsen's Block*: "Germany has become a market among many others, one devoid of background or metaphysical reserves. . . . Now there are only markets, and through this an immense emptiness is created" (qtd. in Herzinger, 1995: 113). His poem from 1994 entitled "Empty Time" betrays the same melancholic predicament. Here, the lyrical subject of the poem is condemned to live life marked by the awareness that destiny is often completed before death: "No wind from the sea / Waiting for nothing" (2001: 237).[33]

Once again, Benjamin's critique of Eric Kästner, the subject of his "Left-Wing Melancholy" essay, seems strangely relevant here, and may be extended to Müller. Benjamin writes: "This poet is dissatisfied, indeed heavy-hearted. But this heaviness of heart derives from routine. For to be in a routine means to have sacrificed one's idiosyncrasies, to have fortified the gift of distaste. And this makes one heavy-hearted" (1994: 305). What is entailed in discarding the narcissistic orthodoxy of the traditional Left, to enliven it with the visions of new forms of democracy, new forms of relationship between the state and civil society? "How might we draw creative sustenance from socialist ideals of dignity, equality, and freedom, while recognising that these ideals were conjured from historical conditions and prospects that are not those of the present" (Brown, 1999: 26–7). In other words, could loss be seen as the condition of possibility of recovery? If so, how could we mobilise our attachments to left projects in order to uncover the hidden potentialities of the present?

For Heller, the substitutive object of the modernist Left, is the postmodernist view. As she reminds us, while in Hegel's system world history legitimates the modern age, and in the theory of universal progression it is the future that legitimates the present along with all its trappings and sufferings, neither of these options is available to the postmoderns. To this philosopher, the postmodern is not a project but a condition. "The postmoderns," writes Heller, "accept the life on the railway station. That is, they accept living in an absolute present" (1999: 9). The way Heller sees it, since "[a]ll final destinations are unmasked as harbouring disaster . . . the postmoderns claim ignorance in the matters of final destination; they accept the 'provisory state,' the here and now, as the final stage – for them" (1999: 9–10). For Heller, the future is ever unknown. This does not mean that Heller sides with recent calls for the "end" of history or the "death of the subject" made by the thinkers such as Jean Baudrillard and Michel Foucault, which are indicative of a certain postmodernist stance of hopelessness and apathy – the position that Müller comes close to in his last works. Nor does she associate utopian pursuits with the modernist grand narratives. As she asserts in her *A Philosophy of History in Fragments*, utopias "are not mere figments of human imagination. They draw their strength from actuality; they exist, insofar as they exist, in the present. Utopia is lived, practised, maintained by men and women as a form of life" (1993: 58). As Heller points out, the "establishment" postmodernists would like us to accept the prevailing social and historical predicament as inescapable, failing to interrogate the horizon of the possibilities within the contemporary world. Challenging the rhetoric of catastrophe employed by certain postmodern thinkers, Heller would rather hold modernity to its promise of democracy and freedom. Advocating responsibility for the present, rather than the abstract commitment to the distant future of utopia or dystopia, she privileges an ethics of responsibility to that of ultimate ends. In doing so, Heller argues that we must identify human practices that resist commodification and alienation within the life-world as it currently exists. As I mentioned above, contingency is central to Heller's thinking, so it is no surprise that in her theory of modernity she focuses on the everyday as a central domain of ideological contestation and "utopic" resistances, while seeing much potential in art, philosophy, and love because of their capacity to make us see differently reified social practices and attitudes (see Gardiner, 2000).

Heller's *A Theory of Modernity* was written in the aftermath of the Left's defeat and despair of the 1990s. Only a decade into the twenty-first century, the European and global political, social, and economic landscape looks very different. According to Costas Douzinas and Slavoj Žižek, "the triumphalist 'end of history,' the unipolar world of American hegemony – are fast becoming old news" (2010: vii). In their view, "If 1989 was the inaugural year of the new world order, 2001 announced its decline, and the collapse of banking systems in 2008 marked the beginning of a return to full-blown history" (2010: vii–viii). In 2009, these two scholars, along with some leading political philosophers and critical theorists of the Left such as Alain Badiou, Susan Buck-Morss, Terry Eagleton, Jean-Luc Nancy, and Jacques

Rancière, took part in the conference "The Idea of Communism," organised by the Birkbeck Institute for the Humanities. The conference was intended to consider how the philosophical idea of communism might be revitalised and made useful in the twenty-first century within a world marked by economic, military, and ecological crisis. In the introduction to the conference proceedings, Douzinas and Žižek take the enormous participation and interest that the conference generated (more than one thousand people attended) as a sign that "the period of guilt is over" and that "the Left can finally leave behind the introspection, contrition and penance that followed the fall of the Soviet Union" (2010: viii). As evidence of the "return of history" the authors invoke "new forms of radical militancy and mobilization" across the globe such as "the different new Lefts in Bolivia, Venezuela and Brazil [that] are developing unprecedented and imaginative national paths to socialism" and new forms of social activism in India, China, and Africa (2010: viii). To these progressive social movements, we could also add the regime changes in the Arab world after massive popular mobilisation.

Concerned with what he terms "the structural violence of the economy," Etienne Balibar, another prominent critical theorist of the Left, is less optimistic about the capacities of "the collective subject" for "*making difference* in the structures of power, and *sustaining that difference* over a period sufficient to produce a transformation" (2012: 16; original emphasis). As he notes, "The economy is more violent than ever, and the state is not disarmed, but it is disseminated and 'privatized' in a way that renders the ideological protocols of 'mass politics' highly indeterminate" (2012: 16). Balibar is even less optimistic about the prospects of the European Left – an association of democratic socialist and communist political parties in the European Union and other European countries active since 2004 – which in his view "has lost every capacity to express social struggles or launch emancipatory movements" (2010a: n.p.). The parties that represent it have not been able to offer a democratically elaborated political action against the crisis at the European level. They have remained passive in the face of the recent finance capital meltdown, recession, and state fiscal crisis, passive in the face of the IMF's implementation of its plan in Greece, and "passive again when it was proposed to 'rescue the Euro' at the expense of wage labourers and ordinary consumers" (2010a: n.p.). Powerless spectators of the devastating impact these transformations are having on jobs, welfare provisions, access to healthcare, education, and housing, they "proved unable to launch a public debate on the possibility and the means of a Europe of solidarity" (2010a: n.a.). For, as Balibar further argues, the IMF's programme for Greece now means that "the Eurozone, which was meant to become a zone of complementarity and solidarity among national economies in Europe, is now decidedly a zone of fierce and wide competition among its own members" (2010b: 309).

Now that Europe urgently needs some sort of radical re-envisioning of both its economic policy and its social model, the onus is also on progressive intellectuals to engage in public debates on the most desirable political action against the European crisis. And, indeed, in a letter to the *Guardian* of 8 June 2012, Balibar and several other leading critical theorists of the Left expressed their support for "the ideals embodied by the Greek Left (report, 1 June) in the election of 17 June, which articulate the need for social and economic democracy under neoliberalism" (Balibar et al., 2012: 37). In the letter, signed also by Wendy Brown, Judith Butler, Gayatri Chakravorty Spivak, Costas Douzinas, Jacqueline Rose, Joanna Bourke, Jacques Rancière, Drucilla Cornell, Slavoj Žižek, and Jean-Luc Nancy, these public intellectuals argued that the Greek Left is struggling to revive democracy in the European space and create a new foundation for Europe, resisting the colonisation by an unprecedented plutocracy through organisation and manipulation in finance capital.

As the signatories of this letter suggest, now that the survival of democracy in Greece and Europe is at stake, we are in need of radical and urgent solutions and visions. It would seem that there is no room for melancholy politics here. Yet, if the present cannot be understood without the past, and communism for our time requires re-articulation, as the key participants in the Birkbeck conference argued, then in order to reinvigorate the European Left with a new kind of transformative politics would also entail the rescue and critical re-examination of the Left intellectual tradition and the now bruised ideals that we have inherited. Benjamin's thesis on the politically progressive uses of historical memory in "Thesis on the Philosophy of History" might be still useful for our attempts to articulate the current European predicament. As Eng and Kazanjian write, "Benjamin proffers a continuous double take on loss – one version moves and creates, the other slackens and lingers . . . Indeed, the politics of mourning might be described as that creative process mediating a hopeful or hopeless relationship between loss and history" (2003: 2). Thus, engaging Benjamin's work, these two authors argue that melancholia can be critical, creative, and enabling for an ethics or politics. Here I have examined some of the ways in which the predicament of the European left in the late 1980s and the early 1990s was felt and reflected on by Müller. In doing so, my hope is that – to quote from Isaac Balbus's *Mourning and Modernity* – I have "engag[ed] our reparative impulses and remind[ed] us just how much we still love what we have lost" (2005: 89). I have also gestured at the current ideological and programmatic impasses and hopes of the European and global Left. It is, of course, too early to predict whether the European Left will come up with viable alternatives to the current financial and ideological deadlock. The answers are in the future.

3
Contested Pasts and the Ethics of Remembrance in Tadeusz Kantor's "Theatre of Death"

The mnemonics of Kantor's *Wielopole, Wielopole*

"To say of Kantor that he is among Poland's most outstanding artists of the second half of the twentieth century is to say very little," states Jaroslaw Suchan, curator of the exhibition "Tadeusz Kantor – Impossible" (qtd. in Kitowska-Lysiak, 2002: 3). "Kantor is to Polish art what Joseph Beuys was to German art, what Andy Warhol was to American art," continues Suchan. "He created a unique strain of theatre, was an active participant in the revolutions of the neo-avant-garde, a highly original theoretician, an innovator strongly grounded in tradition, an anti-painterly painter, a happener-heretic, and an ironic conceptualist. These are only a few of his many incarnations" (ibid.: 3).[1] While he was certainly one of Poland's foremost theatre artists of the second half of the twentieth century, as Suchan's praise suggests, Kantor theatrical oeuvre also undoubtedly left a deep and lasting imprint on theatre and performance arts in Europe and wider.

Kantor studied at the Academy of Fine Arts in Cracow, where his work as a painter and stage designer evolved in a constant dialogue with the dominant avant-garde movements such as constructivism, dadaism, and surrealism in the 1920s and 1930s. He survived the Second World War working as a decoration painter in the Słowacki Theatre in Cracow. During the war he also engaged in clandestine theatre activities, famously staging Juliusz Słowacki's *Balladyna* (1839) and Stanisław Wyspiański's *The Return of Odysseus* (*Powrót Odysa*, 1907), the latter of which he would revisit toward the end of his career. As Michal Kobialka elaborates in his masterful study *Further on, Nothing: Tadeusz Kantor's Theatre* (2009), in the postwar decades, when socialist realism flourished as the official aesthetics in Poland and other countries of Eastern Europe, Kantor still managed to take part in the major artistic currents of Western avant-garde by conducting his own "provocations" and experiments with Informel Art, Emballages, and Happenings, all the while incessantly questioning the very idea of representation. Together with his Cricot 2 theatre company, founded in 1955, he also presented many radical stagings of Stanisław Ignacy Witkiewicz (1885–1939, pen name Witkacy), which brought these works much critical acclaim at theatre festivals in France, Italy, and the UK in the late 1960s and early 1970s.

In the mid-seventies, however, Kantor moved into a new territory: the cycle of performances that he entitled the "Theatre of Death" (1975–90) marked the beginning of his sustained, almost obsessive engagement with historical trauma, memory, and forgetting. For Kantor, who can be seen as one of the most significant figures among the many Polish artists and scholars who have tried to engage the traumatic experiences of the twentieth century, especially the Holocaust, the stakes of memory are enormous.[2] His memory-theatre constitutes a platform of interventionist cultural and political engagement, a form of repair and redress. Having directly experienced the Holocaust and the Second World War in Poland, he sought to represent and commemorate those staggering losses in the hope of a better future. Keenly aware of power as a central factor in mediating the public appearance of collective memories in communist Poland, in his performances Kantor constantly challenged the frames of intelligibility. That is, concerned with epistemological and ontological problems that were more than incidental, he exposed and critiqued the dominant structures of recognition and knowledge that shaped the representation of the Second World War in the communist East of Europe, circumscribed the war's meaning, and effaced violence's affect – certain forms of grief and mourning that could not be openly expressed in Poland of the day. In so doing, he allowed for heretofore silenced, suppressed, and disavowed experiences of his audiences to emerge. Challenging their historical imagination of the two world wars, his performances aimed at renewing his audiences' affective engagement with the dark sides of Europe's past.

The Dead Class (*Umarła klasa*, 1975), acclaimed by many critics as Kantor's masterpiece, brought him and Cricot 2 international recognition and fame. In this piece Kantor works with closely intertwined material of personal memories and intertextual references to the works of Polish modernists (Bruno Schultz, Witold Gombrowicz, and Witkacy), while pursuing an obsessive reflection on the nature of time and human memory. As in his previous stagings of Witkacy's plays, Kantor does away here with the primacy of the text and the narrative character of theatrical representation, emphasising instead a sensory overload of visual, oral, aural, and other elements, and questioning any firm boundaries between theatre and performance art. *The Dead Class* and the rest of his performances from the "Theatre of Death," which I discuss below, exhibit a distinct kind of postdramatic theatre, now widely recognisable for its potent visual images, masterful theatricality, and strong emotional grip on its audiences. According to the central theorist of this genre, Hans Thies Lehmann, Kantor could be seen – along with Robert Wilson, Heiner Müller, and several other artists and theatre collectives that came to prominence in the late 1980s and 1990s, such as the Wooster Group, Jan Fabre, Jan Lauwers, Reza Abdoh, and the Societas Raffaello Sanzio – as one of its main protagonists. As Christopher Balme summarises Lehmann's key arguments, postdramatic theatre is marked by "a preference for the visual image over the written word, collage and montage instead of linear structure, a reliance on metonymic rather than metaphoric representation, and a redefinition of the performer's function in terms of being and materiality rather than appearance and mimetic imitation" (2004: 1). Balme's observation about the way performers function in postdramatic theatre cannot be more true than in the case of *The Dead Class*. As in his more explicitly autobiographical pieces that would follow, Kantor was physically present on stage, playing simultaneously the role of a silent witness and re-creator of the events represented: the bygone school days, the vanished world of a pre-war Poland, and catastrophic events that marked the twentieth century.

In this chapter, I will analyse three performances from Kantor's "Theatre of Death" that were created during the last decade of Kantor's life. I focus my attention first on the now equally famous *Wielopole, Wielopole* (1980), the first major work Kantor and his Cricot 2 company produced after *The Dead Class*. Here I examine the ways in which *Wielopole, Wielopole* "remembers," taking into consideration both its theatrical strategies and the ethical implications of recall. In other words, I will explore some of the ways in which memory functions within this performance, as well as the means by which this performance and the theoretical texts that Kantor produced while working on it function within memory – the ways in which they reflect and respond to different "versions" or modes of memory within the Western tradition.[3] By way of situating my discussion of these themes in a specific historical context, and establishing the ethical stakes of this performance for Kantor, I will also refer to the public discourses of national remembrance in Poland (especially the repression of the disturbing memories of the Holocaust, which the official culture occluded for so many years), and Jewish-Polish relations in the aftermath of the Holocaust (1945 to the present).[4] It is this historical background that informs my discussion of both the stakes of the mnemonic in *Wielopole, Wielopole*, and of the deep difficulties involved in directly confronting the dilemma of witnessing the destruction of Jews in Poland.

In the following segments of this chapter, I will examine two subsequent performances from "The Theatre of Death" – *Let the Artists Die* (*Niech sczezną artyści*, 1985) and *I Shall Never Return* (*Nigdy tu już nie powrócę*, 1988). Engaging with the burgeoning historiography of the Katyń massacre, here I show the ways in which *Let the Artist Die* engaged the silenced and repressed Polish collective memories of this national tragedy, thus enabling their transmission and circulation in the public sphere. I discuss *Let the Artists Die* alongside of Andrzej Wajda's film *Katyń*, which provides an excellent intertext for Kantor's piece. Much more discursive than Kantor's almost hermetic work, Wajda's film also cites archival film footage of German and Soviet forensic exhumations to investigate the deaths of Polish prisoners of war murdered by the Soviets in spring 1940. Nowadays, in countries such as Bosnia and Herzegovina, Spain, Rwanda, and several South and Central American states, exhumation and human identification play an important role in processes of postconflict mourning, reconciliation, and reconstruction (see Renshaw, 2011); these documentaries, however, highlight the extremes of instrumentalisation of these processes during the Second World War for propaganda purposes. While they were widely distributed across Europe during the war years, they also remind us of the silence and disavowal that surrounded the Katyń question in Europe during the postwar years, when the Katyń dead constituted – to use Judith Butler's term – "ungrievable" casualties (Butler, 2004: 2009) not only in Poland, but also in the rest of Europe, both east and west of the Iron Curtain. And while the Soviet atrocities perpetrated against Poles at the beginning of the Second World War constitute the immediate historical reference for my analyses in this part of the chapter, my aim here is to contribute an insight applicable to broader debates about theatre, violence, and the human condition.

If the two world wars' destructiveness had a compelling gravity that attracted and challenged Kantor, then the personal aspect of Kantor's obsession with this thematics is best revealed in the last piece I analyse here, and the penultimate piece from "The Theatre of Death" – *I Shall Never Return*. This is perhaps one of Kantor's most intimate pieces, which broaches the death of his father, a secular Jew who was killed by the Nazis at the beginning of the Second World War. Identifying a wide array of emotions that inflect this piece, from melancholy, grief, alienation, and trauma to self-irony and self-mockery, I show how in this work, just as in other performances from Kantor's "late style" cycle, mourning can be considered a practice of countermemory that attends to that which has been negated, deemed unrepresentable on account of its traumatic nature, or silenced.

The "Wielopole" of the title invokes the author's birthplace, a small town near Cracow where he was born in 1915 (Figure 3.1). "On the square," remembers Kantor, "stood a chapel with some saints for the Catholic faithful and a well where, usually at the full moon, Jewish weddings were held. On one side there was a church with a presbytery and a cemetery; on the other side, a synagogue, a few crowded Jewish lanes, and a different cemetery. Both sides lived in an agreeable symbiosis" (qtd. in Pleśniarowicz, 1994a: 9). As Kantor further relates on another occasion, "During the last war half of the town was destroyed, many houses were burnt down and the Jews deported" (qtd. in Thibaudat, 2003: 184). Today, no trace exists of the eighty-seven Jewish families that lived here. Jean-Pierre Thibaudat, who visited the town in 1989, notes that even "the Jewish cemetery on the outskirts of Wielopole does not exist any more, its ruins lost, buried under clods of earth, where grass grows lush" (2003: 184). In his "Theatre of Death" Kantor both bemoans the forgotten past, and combats this amnesia by theatrically "exhuming" the forgotten past and people. Like in old days, the Jews and Catholics appear together

Figure 3.1   Wielopole Skrzyńskie, main square, circa 1910; foreground, from the left: Stanisław Berger, and Helena and Marian Kantor; courtesy of the Cricoteka Archive

in Kantor's performances. This is not solely an issue of memory, as it is often said, but also of hospitality, which includes hospitality extended to memory. For this past is not strictly speaking unknown to his audience, but rather unacknowledged, relegated to the margins of consciousness: the position of that which – because it is traumatic, supressed, or silenced – has to be both known and at the same time unrecognised.

The invention of mnemotechnics (the *ars memoriae*) is credited to the Greek poet Simonides of Keos (sixth century BCE). In Quintilian's version of the legend:

> [Simonides] had written an ode of the kind that was usually composed in honour of victorious athletes, to celebrate the achievement of one who had gained the crown for boxing. Part of the sum for which he had contracted was refused him on the ground that, following the common practice of poets, he had introduced a digression in praise of Castor and Pollux, and he was told that, in view of what he had done, he had best ask for the rest of the

sum due from those whose deeds he had extolled. And according to the story they paid their debt. For when a great banquet was given in honour of the boxer's success, Simonides was summoned forth from the feast, to which he had been invited, by a message to the effect that two youths who had ridden to the door urgently desired his presence. He found no trace of them, but what followed proved to him that the gods have shown their gratitude. For he had scarcely crossed the threshold on his way out, when the banqueting hall fell in upon the heads of the guests and wrought such havoc among them that the relatives of the dead who came to seek the bodies for burial were unable to distinguish not merely the faces but even the limbs of the dead. Then it is said, Simonides, who remembered the order in which the guests had been sitting, succeeded in restoring to each man his own dead. (Quintilian, *Institutio oratoria*, XI, 2.11–13)

According to the Simonides legend, the first memory theatre consists of mutilated corpses. "The finding of absent images heals what has been destroyed: the art of *memoria* restores shape to the mutilated victims and makes them recognisable by establishing their place and seat in life. . . . A survivor – the poet as a bearer of cultural memory – is necessary to inscribe the representatives of the unrecognisable, absent primary signs in the syntax of place" (Lachmann, 1997: 6, 9). Only after they have been linked with the place where they sat do they become identifiable and regain their names, through a second act of naming, an act of memory. Quintilian's narrative suggests that this process of identifying through naming should be understood as a vicarious supplying of images.

At the beginning of *memoria* as art, therefore, stands the effort to technologise the work of mourning. The recollection of order mobilises a work of reconstruction to counter the destruction, even as this destruction marks the beginning of re-membering. In addition, as Jody Enders points out in her study *The Medieval Theater of Cruelty*, the Simonides legend problematises some key dramatic features of mnemotechnics: "that the object of remembrance must first die in order to be brought back to life; that the metaphorically encrypted and subsequently resurrected dead are moving, talking images or simulacra; that mnemotechnics renders present those who are absent or dead; and that it does so by repainting their picture and by giving them voice"

(1999: 72). As we shall see, the authentic act of remembering, which closes the drama of the catastrophe and opens that of the burial, "inaugurates a commemorative model that establishes fascinating parallels between theatre and birth, death, and resurrection" (Enders, 1997: 72) – a model echoed by Kantor's "Theatre of Death."

The performance text of *Wielopole, Wielopole* also starts with an act of naming, through which Kantor introduces his dead relatives, the protagonists of this memory séance:

> Here is my Grandmother, my
> mother's mother, Katarzyna.
> And that's her brother, the
> Priest.
> Some used to call him uncle.
> He will die shortly.
> My father sits over there.
> The first from the left.
> On the reverse of this
> photograph he sends his -
> greetings.
> Date: 12th September 1914.
> Mother Helka will be here any
> minute.
> The rest are Uncles and Aunts.
> They went the way of all flesh,
> somewhere in the world.
> Now they are in the room,
> imprinted as memories:
> Uncle Karol, Uncle Olek,
> Auntie Mańka, Auntie Józka.
> From this moment on, their
> fortunes begin to change
> passing through a series of
> radical alterations,
> often quite embarrassing, such
> as they would have been unable
> to face, had they been among
> the living.
>
> (Kantor, 1990a: 17) [5]

This act of naming the dead was absent from the beginning of this memory séance.[6] Instead, the audience saw Kantor's solitary figure walking around the performance space as if in search for the remnants of his life. His were the first gestures of summoning up the memory of his childhood, gestures strongly reminiscent of the underlying principles of the ancient mnemonics. According to the ancients, the would-be memory artist remembered (or imagined) an organised space – houses or theatres were commonly suggested. Within this space he distributed at regular intervals images that would serve as prompts to the memory. Later, when the user wished to remember something, he would, in an act of literal re-collection, mentally retrieve the images in any order he desired. In a similar vein, at the beginning of the séance, Kantor moved around the performance space – a simple wooden platform – empty except for a few pieces of furniture. He opened and closed the wardrobe, arranged the chairs, moved the bed with the mannequin of the priest on it out of the way. After this initial procedure of "furnishing" the room of memory, a signal was given, and the sliding doors at the back of the room were opened. From this anteroom area of history, memory, and loss, two groups of actors appeared on stage: Kantor's family, whose bodies were scattered around, and a group of soldiers who positioned themselves in a corner, as if posing for a camera.

The process of furnishing the room of memory was then continued by two identically looking stage figures, Kantor's uncles Karol and Olek, played by the Janicki twins. Through the stage presence of the twins, Kantor explicitly evoked the figure of doubling, which is the basic figure of the work of memory. As Renate Lachmann reminds us, the Simonides legend assigns a central role to the Dioscuri in the development of mnemotechnics:

The twins who, as thanks for his song of praise, call Simonides outside across the threshold of the door and of time without revealing themselves to him, thereby saving him from catastrophe, appear as the personification of doubling. Personification in absentia is already in itself a kind of doubling: those absent are represented by the meaning ascribed to them in the context of the legend. The twin gods present a *Doppelgänger* pair, each of whom undergoes a further doubling process: the boxer with his opponent (as in a duel), the horse tamer with his animal (suggesting the symbiosis of horse and rider). This prototypical duo, in acting out the *Doppelgänger* relations between mortal body and immortal soul, death and life, portrays synchronically the metamorphosis from life to death, a metamorphosis that takes place in the conclave following a temporal linearity, and in the course of which the corpses become the *Doppelgänger* of the banqueters. (1997: 8)

Immediately the twins in Kantor's performance recognised that everything on the stage was out of place. Since memories could not be induced or brought forth until things had been put in order, the uncles – following a lot of double talk – set to work. After moving things about in a slapstick manner, they finally agreed on the rightful places in which the body of the dead priest, the chairs, the window, and other pieces of furniture should be set. The performance got underway only after everything was satisfactorily put in place; a hymn played over the loudspeakers, and Grandma, who up until then has been lying on the floor in silence, got up to speak.

The process of physically *imaging* memory and memory process on stage as presented in *Wielopole, Wielopole* is well encapsulated in Kantor's prose piece "The Room. Maybe a New Phase" (1980):

It is difficult to define the spatial dimension of memory.
Here, this is a room of my childhood,
with all its inhabitants.
This is the room that I keep reconstructing again and again
and that keeps dying again and again.
Its inhabitants are the members of my family.
They continuously repeat all their movements and activities
as if they were imprinted on a film negative shown interminably.
They will keep repeating those banal,
elementary, and aimless activities
with the same expression on their faces,
concentrating on the same gesture,
until boredom strikes.

Those trivial activities
that stubbornly and oppressively preoccupy us
fill up our lives. . . .
These DEAD FAÇADES

come to life, become real and important
through this stubborn REPETITION OF ACTION.
Maybe this stubborn repetition of action,
this pulsating rhythm
that lasts for life,
that ends in n o t h i n g n e s s ,
which is futile,
is an inherent part of MEMORY.

(1993: 142–3)

In *Wielopole, Wielopole,* memory is imaged as a room, which means memory is localised within a concrete, material form.[7] Here, as in Samuel Beckett's *Krapp's Last Tape*, where it is imaged as a tape recorder, "memory seems self-contained, redeemable, and very present, rather than diffuse and elusive"; it depends for its "use" on a proper configuration of the mnemonic field that would in turn induce memories (Malkin, 1999: 44). The theatricalisation of memory function and human subjectivity in these two pieces highlights "the dualism of rememberer and memory, where memory is imagined as objectified 'other' that cannot be completely controlled" (ibid.: 44). Thus both Kantor and Beckett present us "not only with the act of remembering a life, but with a dialogue between living and remembrance, present and past: Man and his Memory" (ibid.: 45).

Clearly there are vestiges of ancient mnemotechnics at work in Kantor's *Wielopole, Wielopole*. We are reminded of the rhetorical origins of Kantor's "room of memory" even though Kantor does not explicitly acknowledge this.[8] Ancient and medieval writers on memory recognised, as we do now, the dual aspects of storage and recollection involved in remembering. Their most common model for human memory likened it to a tablet or a parchment page upon which a person writes. Re-collection was essentially a task of composition, literally bringing together matters found in their various storage places, and reassembling them in a new place. Furthermore, one of two major metaphors used in ancient and medieval times for the educated memory was that of *thesaurus*, "storage-room," and later "strong-box." Whereas the metaphor of the seal-in-wax or written tablets was a model for the process of making the memorial phantasm and storing it in a place in memory, the storage-room metaphor refers both to the contents of such a memory and to its internal organisation. A version of the storage room metaphor occurs in Plato's *Theaetetus*, when Socrates, explaining how one is able to recall particular pieces of information, likens things stored in memory to pigeons housed in a pigeon-coop. This occurrence attests to the antiquity of the idea; indeed, both metaphors, equally visual, equally spatial, seem to be equally ancient as well.[9]

The childhood room, this living heart of memory, situated at the core of *Wielopole, Wielopole* (like the nursery in Chekhov's *Three Sisters*), is a system of backgrounds, a support, or a scene that induces images. Around it, as though summoned, induced by it, is established and radiates all the imagery, the entire thematics of *Wielopole, Wielopole*: the return, the sorrowful experience, age, lost time, and absence. In the course of the performance, the audience witnesses the death of Uncle Józef-Priest; Grandmother-Katarzyna's carrying out the last rites for him; the three "dead photographs" of the Priest, the Family, and a group of soldiers – including Kantor's father Marian – before they went to battle; Father Marian and Mother-Helka's wedding ceremony; Aunt Mańka's apocalyptic prophecies; the rape of Helka by the soldiers; Adaś's mobilisation and his departure/funeral in a cattle wagon with a group of conscripts; the funeral of the Priest; the Rabbi's repeated execution by the soldiers; the last gathering of the family interrupted by yet another invasion of the soldiers; and the last group photograph. A constant repetition of the music themes employed in the performance further amplified the theme of memory: Chopin's "Scherzo" would emerge every now and then from Uncle Stasio's violin case; a Psalm was sung at the Priest's deathbed; a Polish military march, "The Grey Infantry," constantly accompanied the soldiers' presence on stage; the Rabbi sang an old Yiddish song.

From the everyday perspective, what once existed but exists no longer (or at least not in the same way) belongs to the past, a past that is irrecoverable, unchangeable. Events from the past cannot be lived in the manner of firstness, but only as grey replicas of what they once were. At best they can be relived in memory. Conventional wisdom suggests that one may remember and restore the past, or forget and deny it, but one concedes that what was has passed away. That which has gone by cannot be brought back materially. I have suggested that the past, the "not" expressed as the irrecoverability of what has gone by, is experienced by Kantor as retained, as imprinted or stored, kept as image and word. Memory is not something apart from the ongoing experience of retrieval, but the process of bringing back that which was previously encoded.

Kantor expresses this idea well in a performance text for his "cricotage" *Silent Night* (1990), in a section entitled "Imprints:"

> From the dim recesses,
> as if from the abyss of Hell,
> there started to emerge
> people who had died long time ago
> and memories of events
> that, as in a dream,
> had no explanation,
> no beginning, no end,
> no cause or effect.
> They would emerge
> and keep returning stubbornly,
> as if waiting for my permission to let them enter.
> I gave them my consent.
> I understood their nature.
> I understood where they were coming from.
> The i m p r i n t s
> impressed deeply
> in the immemorial past.

(1993: 180)

This idea can be traced back to the early stages of his "Theatre of Death" – including *Wielopole, Wielopole* – and, indeed, to the classical practice of mnemotechnics, as we shall see now.

In the second book of Cicero's *De oratore*, the work of memory requires the sketching of an inner image, an *effigies*. This inner image must designate (*notare*) the *res* that is to be remembered, which is invisible and no longer present. In the process, the image becomes a visible sign that inscribes itself in the memory place. The images are registered in the memory tablet – just as letters are incised into a writing tablet. If the *simulacra* function like letters (*De Oratore*, II, 353), it is because they belong to a different order of signs from the objects they are supposed to fix; they note these objects as marks and abbreviations.[10] The mnemotechnical animation and personification of the memory images (*imagines agentes*) thus mean that the images, as personae, are masks – masks of those things that are deposited in the memory theatre. The conception of persona or mask also has the connotation of dissimulation, or of a phantom. The translation of that which is to be remembered into a mnemonic image is already a disfiguring, beginning with the representation of one sign by another, given that the representing sign does not participate in the primary sign but merely takes possession of it through a relation of similarity (*similitudo*). This *similitudo* does not guarantee a faithful copy of the primal image; rather, it is itself *simulatio*.

As the *Rhetorica ad Herennium* author in his own lengthy treatment of the artificial memory writes, "an image is, as it were, a figure, mark, or a *simulacrum* of the object we wish to remember" (*Rhetorica ad Herennium*, iii: 29). Similarly, in his discussion of personification, this author clarifies that simulacra are created dramatically through voicing and imaginary behaviours. *Conformatio*, he writes, "*consists in representing an absent person as present*, or in making a *mute thing* or one lacking form articulate, and attributing to it a definite form and a language or a certain behaviour appropriate to its character" (*Rhetorica ad Herennium*, IV: 66, emphasis mine). The presence of memory thus depends on the absence of things past, and on the resurrected presence of the dead who may be brought back to life so that they might speak again.

In a section from *Wielopole, Wielopole* entitled "Agency for the hiring the dear departed" Kantor acknowledges this paradox:

In memories
truthful and magnanimous people do not exist.
Let's say it quite openly: the process of evoking memories
is suspect and none too clean.
It is simply a hiring agency.
The memory makes use of "hired" characters.
They are sinister individuals, mediocre and suspect creatures
waiting to be "hired" like home helps "by the hour."
Almost crumpled, dirty, badly dressed, sickly,
bastardised, acting out badly the parts of people often
near and dear to us.
This ambiguous character is disguised as a recruit, pretending to be
my father.

Mother is evidently played by a street walker,
my uncles are mere ragamuffins.
The daringly widow of our town's esteemed photographer,
who keeps up the name of the photography shop,
"The Memory," is usually a foul cleaning woman
in the parish morgue.
As for the priest, better not mention him.
His sister is a simple scullery maid.
And again Uncle Stasio, the lugubrious figure of a Deportee,
Wandering beggar with a barrel-organ.

(Kantor, n.d.a: n.pag.)

In *Wielopole, Wielopole*, anamnesic activity does not lead to a presence grasped on stage. Kantor, who no longer resides in the childhood house, must resort to the artifice of memory in order to reanimate fantasy and reactivate images, to piece together the simulacrum of a place haunted by absence. This dwelling is not the Edenic microcosm, a welcoming cavity of images. The sort of invention it induces is not as euphoric as it might first seem: abundance is eaten away and neutralised by an irreparable loss. As Ugo Volli observed:

By watching Kantor, we were witnessing rather than penetrating, the appearance of memory. The representation of memory is not memory, but a new fact, affected by weaknesses and perversion of memory and not by its authenticity. To witness is to betray. Presented to others, interiority becomes exteriority and necessarily false. But the artist *must* witness. The artist is obliged to betray. Expression is desired because it is the means toward exteriority. The stage is the site of this necessary betrayal. (1995: 247).

Remembrance is, in a sense, an inherently dualistic activity. One part of the mind recalls, brings up the past, while the other watches, listens, is reminded, reacts, sometimes refuses the memory brought up and rejects it. The process of memory retrieval, writes St Augustine:

brings me out onto the lawns and spacious structures of memory, where treasure is stored, all the representations conveyed there by any of my senses . . . Some things, summoned, are instantly delivered up, though others require a longer search, to be drawn from recesses less penetrable. And all the while, jumbled memories flirt out on their own, interrupting the search for what I want, pestering: Wasn't it us you were seeking? My heart's hand strenuously waves these things away from my memory's gaze, until the dim thing sought arrives at last, fresh from depths. Yet other things are brought up easily, in proper sequence from beginning to end, and laid back in the same order, recallable at will – which happens whenever I recite a literary passage by heart. (2002: 49)

The passage offers us a glimpse into the process of gathering memories perfected in medieval monastic meditation, but it also illustrates an instant of mnemotechnical distraction, when the mnemonic pathways leak from one associational network to another. "The great vice of *memoria is* not forgetting but disorder," writes Marry Carruthers in *The Craft of Thought*, a study of memory in medieval culture (1998: 82). "Image 'crowding'" or *curiositas* was considered "a mnemotechnical vice, because crowding images together blurs them, blocks them, and thus dissipates their effectiveness" (Carruthers, 1998: 82). As Carruthers further notes, John Cassian, a medieval mnemonist, categorised this phenomenon as "a form of mental fornication," "*wandering* against *having a way* or *a route*" (1998: 83, her emphasis). Although Kantor, like Augustine, can (after "a longer search") retrieve his buried past, as the performance progresses, it become clear that the room of his memory could never be organised. For Augustine, the will ("I") is lord, its ability to "wave away" and presumably dis-place, with an effort, mnemonic intrusions into an unfrequented corridor of memory is no longer the working assumption. The performance sequences in *Wielopole, Wielopole*, were constantly disrupted by the intrusions of *phantasmata* from behind the doors – the anteroom of history – where "a storm and inferno rage, / and the waters of the flood rise" (Kantor, 1993: 142). Kantor begins by wanting to recollect the past; but memory flooding the stage will prove stronger than his own will. This merging of past and present creates a sense of simultaneity, as in traumatised recall. The insufficiency of voluntary memory – the illusion that the "storehouse" of images can be locked, unlocked, and used at will – becomes obvious in the following scene.

In the last section of the performance, Kantor stages a scene in which a rabbi joins a funeral cortege of his deceased friend, a

Catholic priest, and starts singing a Jewish popular song. Kantor describes the scene as follows:

> From behind the scenes, the little Rabbi darts out unexpectedly, a marionette-like figure in synagogue garments. Running up to this weird procession, he catches up with the Priest who follows the Coffin-Cross. Wringing his hands in despair he sings his music-hall "funeral" song.
>
> THE RABBI: "Sha sha de rebe / gite / sha sha sha de rebe / shite . . . "
>
> In the end the soldiers have had enough. They take aim in a flash. The firing squad do their work. The wretched Little Rabbi falls down (the full significance of this image will only emerge later.) The Priest lifts the Little Rabbi. The Little Rabbi takes up his song again. Another volley, the Little Rabbi collapses, *and so it goes on, a number of times*, repeated as things are in my theatre. Then the Rabbi leaves forever. (1990a: 86–7; my emphasis)

The death of the rabbi is the central and the most obsessive image of remembering in Kantor's *Wielopole, Wielopole*. In this scene, Kantor insists on the suddenness of perception, and describes the shock-image in evident analogy to the temporal structure of instantaneous photography: the scene underlines both the flashlike character of the visual impression, and the instantaneousness of the exposure. It recalls Simmel's description of war-trauma: "the lightning flash of horror leaves a photographically exact impression" (qtd. in Schäffner, 1991: 34). The moment of the rabbi's death, his dancing and singing of "Rebecca" against machine-guns, becomes a frozen image of shock which clings to the memory. If we read this image literally, along with other stagings of violence in *Wielopole, Wielopole* (Adaś's death; the rape of Helka by the soldiers), then the scene can be read as an attempt to present the traumatic war-memory as a fixation on the shock image – the image that forces itself upon the protagonist in its quasi-photographic nature again and again, as well as an endless retroactive attempt to master the shock. As Caruth elaborates, traumatic memory is a memory of an event which "is not assimilated or experienced fully at the time, but only belat-edly, in its repeated *possession* of the one who experiences it. To be traumatised is precisely to be possessed by an image or an event." The "enigmatic core" of the trauma consists, therefore, in the fact that an event that was not really experienced as such returns repeatedly as a literal memory, a memory that remains "absolutely *true* to the event." Thus, "[t]he traumatised . . . carry an impossible history within them, or they become themselves the symptom of a history that they cannot entirely possess" but which instead possesses them (Caruth, 1995: 4–5).

Others oppose this mimetic version of trauma, prevalent in the Anglo-American community of trauma discourse. In her essay "The Traumatic Paradox," Janet Walker shows how the accounts given by those who have suffered cultural, political, or psychological violence can operate in different registers of truth at the same time. According to her, "traumatic events can and do result in the very amnesias and mistakes in memory that are generally considered, outside the theory of traumatic memory, to undermine their claim to veracity" (2003: 106). She suggests, however, that memory makes these mistakes because of the wound. Amnesias, exaggerations, mistakes all bear witness to the ways in which survivors of traumatic events negotiate a path between the historic and psychoanalytic, the constative and performative aspects of witnessing. When a witness's story proves historically incorrect or exaggerated, then we must hear what is being witnessed in this account. According to Walker, "these very mistakes and amnesiac elements are actually a feature of traumatic experience itself," testifying to the difficulties involved working through the mnemonic and affective residue of trauma (2003: 106). Memories correspond to experience, but not literally; this for Walker is the "traumatic paradox" (2003: 107).

While Caruth's account of trauma seems to correspond closer to the image presented on the stage, as we shall see Walker's non-mimetic account of trauma is also relevant here. Namely, some biographical elements of this condensed historical image can be traced back to an event in Kantor's early childhood. After his father went to the front in the First World War, Kantor's mother and her two children found a refuge in the house of the priest from Wielopole, Kantor's uncle Józef Radoniewicz, who passed away in 1921. Kantor remembers:

> Numerous priests from the whole neighbourhood came to the funeral. And suddenly, already not far from the cemetery, they all

scattered, running across the field, like in Buñuel's film. We were left alone: my mother, sister, me, Uncle Olek and the coffin. Mother said to me: "Look!" The whole Jewish commune of Wielopole was walking to meet us, carrying the tablets of the Decalogue – it was wonderful. This exactly was the reason for the priests' dispersal. A huge scandal broke out. (qtd. in Thibaudat, 2003: 184)

This anecdote suggests that in the scene of the rabbi's death Kantor has collapsed and telescoped an early recollection from his childhood into another, informed by his memory of the events that transpired during the Second World War. Rather than a veridical memory of an event experienced first hand by Kantor, the scene seems to be a dynamic reconstruction and representation of a collective trauma.

As we have seen, throughout the performance, Kantor reproduces two opposed routes of recall: the critical faculty that tries to control the "room of memory" by shaping the form of its enunciation, and the involuntary incursion of traumatic memory as repetitive text that, as Cathy Caruth put it, "possesses" the victim of loss (1995: 5). In the final scene of the performance, one more time the memories burst on stage without order, causality, direction, or coherence. The scene is entitled "The Last Supper," after the famous work of Leonardo da Vinci, and it represents the last gathering of the family before their final "departure" (Figure 3.2). "You can feel that they are arriving for the last time," writes Kantor in the stage directions (1990a: 90). In the final tableau, an immaculately white, ceremonially starched cloth with sharp-ironed folds is laid over the muddy, sand-and-lime coated boards. Kantor's family, seated at the table "persist with their hoary arguments, resentments and retrospection, as if they have little time to lose" (94). Behind them are naked dummies standing like condemned men, behind the dummies a forest of crosses, still further off – the Army. Rifles point up, with fixed bayonets. "The massive sound of a Psalm imposes a religious dimension on it all" (94). But as the Psalm and "The Grey Infantry" begin to merge, the dummies – the naked corpses "of those killed in action" – start pushing everything forward (96). Finally, the Army, "deluded, frenzied, push everything to the edge of the stage, dangerously close to the audience – the wardrobe, the table, the chairs, the window, the bed – a monstrous pulp of wreckage" (96). Next, we hear a machine gun, "the soldiers fall, swearing, screaming, bodies and objects pile up, then freeze. The participants of

Figure 3.2 Scene from Kantor's *Wielopole, Wielopole*, preparations for the "Last Supper," photographer unknown, image courtesy of the Cricoteka Archive

the Last Supper have frozen as well, around the table, caught in their emotional gesticulations" (96).

"Memory does not possess a silent gallery of variable paintings," writes Giovanni Ciampoli (1589–1643), poet and friend of Galileo. "They are not printed there; they are not fixed there. It is a population of living *simulacra*; they live there noisily, untamed, in constant uproar" (qtd. in Bolzoni, 2001: 258). This polemic is directed against an Aristotelian tradition that he sees still operating in the mentality of his contemporaries; the idea of memory as a wax upon which seals can be impressed has generated the image of the mind as a gallery of paintings. He prefers a distinction between a theatre and a prison-house of memory. In the prison-house perceptible images are amassed and deposited; but in the small space of the theatre of memory they are called forth by the mind to reanimate themselves:

> On first entering, the watchful mind sees that they are peaceful; then new troops of foreign *phantasmata* arrive; the former ones,

once they have had their audience, retire to the cells of memory in which they rest unseen, waiting for their turn to be led back to the operations of the theatre. (qtd. in Bolzoni, 2001: 258)

But the borders between the confused mass in the prison and the illuminated scene of the theatre are not always clear-cut and under control:

But during slumber, when the guards are sleeping, they boldly burst out. What commotion is made by these unguarded phantoms inside our head without our consent? They sing, they sigh, they dance, they war, they plunder the altars, they violate the gods, without distinction, without law, recklessly, unregulated, furiously, surprising the works of nature with the inventions of dreams; they show us a world gone mad with the impossibilities of disproportion. (qtd. in Bolzoni, 2001: 258)

Ciampoli, like Kantor after him, distances himself from the Aristotelian tradition by placing its topical images (theatre, prison-house, gallery) in a new context. As we know now, psychoanalysis came to confirm this insight made by Ciampoli; the "possession" delivered by this figuration of memory is double edged, for the autonomy of the subject "balances only precariously upon its own 'primitive' and/or infantile substratum – a substratum that could rise up and 'possess' its possessor" (Radstone and Hodgkin, 2003: 4). Clearly, Ciampoli's insight into the workings of memory, echoed by the final scene of *Wielopole, Wielopole*, also closely matches Freud's description of the physiology of trauma from his *Beyond the Pleasure Principle*. According to Freud, psychic trauma, like physical trauma, breaks through the subject's protective shield so that there is an influx of excitation which cannot be mastered or tolerated (1953–74a: 29–30).

The nearly final image of the performance – the tableaux with the participants of the Last Supper – is of petrification and death, of silence, perhaps even closure. But this is not the end – or the closure – Kantor has in mind. In the final moments of the performance, Kantor disrupts this stasis by suddenly inserting a new gesture that radically shifts the play's imagery. As the actors slowly retreat from the stage accompanied by the tunes of a Christmas carol, one body remains – that of the Priest. "Then, from the hall the Little Rabbi in his synagogue garments approaches the priest, helps him up and leads him away" (Kantor, 1990a: 98). Only then does Kantor go up to the table, fold the table-cloth, and leave the stage.[11]

Wielopole, Wielopole is clearly a performance of mourning, in a Freudian sense, "working through" the trauma of loss by remembering, repeating, and re-experiencing that loss (Freud, 1953–74b: 244–5). This, however, does not imply a cathartic interpretation of the performance. Despite the mourning and "re-experiencing," I find the performance, and especially the scene with the rabbi, far more political than such interpretation would allow. If longing for the lost past is the performance's overt theme, fighting forgetting and repression is its underlying impetus. This impetus is inscribed into the performance most powerfully in the scene of rabbi's death – a character that signifies the Jewish people and its experience during the Second World War – through a structure of repetition. This self-reflective exhortation to tell and repeat, to hold onto the past and onto the death by "calling" it through cultural practice, is both a call to active intervention in the discourse of the national remembrance, and a mark of Kantor's aesthetics. Every time Kantor replays this violent death on stage, he is doing more than merely returning to a traumatic moment. This procedure – repetitive and obsessive – might be also seen as a way of inducing anxiety, of forcing the spectator to re-experience the (traumatic) explosion of an irreparable past in a way that impedes emotional indifference. These insistent repetitions suggest a hope that, if often enough "rehearsed" and replayed, the death of the rabbi – this "memory" so integral to culture and yet only diffusively "present" within the culture – might also become a collective trauma to be remembered and mourned.

* * *

In recent years there has been a great increase of interest in the Holocaust in Poland, where the topic of Polish-Jewish relations before and during the Second World War remains controversial. For more than four decades after the Holocaust, Poles and Jews remained strongly divided over the events that transpired during the German occupation. On the one hand, Jewish perceptions during this period were to a large extent shaped by survivor testimonies that often spoke of widespread Polish antisemitism and indifference to the fate of Jews during the Holocaust; on the other hand, Polish historio-graphical consensus reflected the views most common among the Polish public, which emphasised shared Polish-Jewish suffering and Polish aid extended to Jews.

Since the late 1970s, however, there has been a revival of interest in the Polish-Jewish past in Poland. Antony Polonsky sees this phenomenon as a result of several factors: nostalgia of "the largely mono-ethnic and mono-religious Poland of today . . . for the more diverse Poland of the past"; "a growing awareness that it is impossible to provide a coherent account of Polish history and culture without taking into account the contributions of national minorities and in particular the Jews"; and, most importantly, the morally motivated willingness to come to terms with some of the less attractive features of the Polish past, principally chauvinism and anti-Semitism (Polonsky, 1992: 69). Several developments in the 1980s led to a shift in Polish perceptions of Jews, Judaism, and Jewish culture. The role of the Solidarity movement that emerged in this period, and its ultimately successful challenge to the communist system, cannot be overestimated. The experience of the Solidarity years enabled the Poles to begin to restore the broken connection to tradition, and to rediscover (or acknowledge) the history that has been silenced, which in turn allowed for a reckoning with the less admirable aspects of the Polish past. A succession of international conferences on Polish-Jewish studies, the appearance of scholarly journals devoted to the subject, the production of new studies by Polish scholars, and a series of public debates on wartime Polish-Jewish relations, has led to a reassessment of the history of the Holocaust in Poland among some scholars and segments of Polish society.

The first in a series of public debates on wartime Polish-Jewish relations, which according to Joshua D. Zimmerman posed "the first public challenge to the dominant Polish narrative of heroism and martyrology" (2003: 5), was initiated by Jan Błoński's essay "The Poor Poles Look at the Ghetto," which was published in the Polish Catholic weekly *Tygodnik Powszechny* in January 1987. The essay was occasioned by Czesław Miłosz's poem "A Poor Christian Looks at the Ghetto," published in the same journal in the same month. Written in 1943, the poem expresses the horror of witnessing genocide as a passive bystander, and the fear of being counted among the "helpers of death" (qtd. in Błoński, 1990: 51). To Błoński, the poem made palpable the heritage of guilt born of witnessing the Holocaust in the context of the unique history of Polish-Jewish relations, which, in his view has become part of the Polish psyche, "buried" and "muffled" under the strata of rationalisation and denial (Błoński, 1990: 41). Błoński writes: "We must stop haggling, trying to defend and justify ourselves. We must stop arguing about the things which were beyond our power to do, during the occupation and before-hand. Nor must we place blame on political, social and economic conditions. We must say first of all – Yes, we are guilty" (1990: 44). To him, "This is the moral revolution which is imperative when consid-ering the Polish-Jewish past" (1990: 45). The article provoked a fierce nationwide debate in Poland on wartime Jewish-Polish relations, revealing the depth of difficulties involved in attempts at a direct confrontation with the dilemma of witnessing the destruction of Jews on Polish soil. However, the issue of actual Polish collaboration in this destruction remained largely untouched until the publication of Jan Tomasz Gross' book *Neighbors: The Destruction of the Jewish Community in Jedwabne, Poland* (Polish edition 2000, English edition 2001), in which the author discussed the murders of several hundred Jews by their Polish neighbours on 10 July 1941, in the town of Jedwabne in northeastern Poland.

While some Polish historians and members of the public continue to deny that Poles were substantially involved in the massacre, most have come to terms with the 2002 findings of the Institute of National Remembrance that "the Polish population played a decisive role in the execution of the criminal plan" and that "the perpetrators of the crime *sensu stricto* were Polish inhabitants of Jedwabne and its environs" (qtd. in Polonsky and Michlic, 2004: 134–5). Gross's book and subsequent studies by scholars in Poland about other incidents of anti-Jewish violence by non-Jewish Poles at that time, depicting wartime events in which Poles were not only bystanders, victims, or resisters but also perpetrators, challenged dominant public percep-tions and memories of this past in Polish society. *Neighbors* seeks to understand what generated genocide at this particular point in time in a region where Jews and Gentiles had coexisted for centu-ries and how anti-semitism could be activated and radicalised at a certain moment. Furthermore, rather than presenting the massacre as the result of random acts of a few "bad apples" or assigning col-lective responsibility for the massacre, Gross's study "presents a case of individual choices mediated by ethnic and religious identities, strongly felt and linked to material sources of power" (Holc, 2002: 455). Gross's re-narration of this specific historical moment and the whole of the Jedwabne discussion that followed have served to integrate the Polish-Jewish debate in a new way into the larger history of European totalitarianism and modernity, suggesting to some observers that it is possible "to move beyond strongly held, competing, and incompatible narratives of the past and to reach some consensus that will be acceptable to all people of goodwill" (Polonsky and Michlic, 2004: 43).

In the wake of the Jedwabne controversy and in the light of the burgeoning research into the motivation, nature, and extent of involvement of local populations in the Holocaust in Eastern Europe, scepticism is inevitably aroused when shtetl residents recall peace rather than pogroms. How can we reconcile memory of the peaceful symbiosis of the shtetl with memory of the Holocaust? Yet, as Rosa Lehmann writes in her book *Symbiosis and Ambivalence: Poles and Jews in a Small Galician Town*, "Recent studies have come to address the issue of coexistence between Jews and Poles and conclude that, while it is true that Jews and Poles periodically found themselves in confrontation, most of the time they lived in cooperative symbiosis" (2001: xxi). For instance, in her book *Shtetl*, Eva Hoffman weaves together literary sources, historiographical sources, and present day testimonies to reconstruct the history of the Jewish community of Bransk, Poland. She seeks to shows the extent to which the historical, difficult, ordinary, everyday coexistence of Jews and Poles was a mixture of intimacy and distance, friendly neighbourliness and religious and ethnic antagonism. As we shall see, there are numerous resonances between Kantor's recollections of Wielopole that I mentioned earlier and Hoffman's account of life in a prewar shtetl:

> Morally and spiritually, the two societies remained resolutely separate, by choice on both sides. Yet they lived in close proximity and, willy-nilly, familiarity. . . . This was where both prejudices and bonds were most palpably enacted – where a Polish peasant might develop a genuine affection for his Jewish neighbour despite negative stereotypes and, conversely, where an act of unfairness or betrayal could be most wounding because it came from a familiar.

As an example of Polish-Jewish relations during World War II, the shtetl offered the most extreme scenario. The villages and small towns were where Jews and Poles were at their most exposed and vulnerable, and where ongoing political conflicts were at their sharpest. This was where Jewish inhabitants experienced acts of the most unmediated cruelty from their neighbours – and also of most immediate generosity. In the dark years of the Holocaust, the shtetl became a study in ordinary morality tested, and sometimes warped, by inhuman circumstances. (1998: 12–13)

Like many other studies on thousands of provincial towns in Eastern Europe commonly called *shtetlekh* (the plural of *shtetl*, Yiddish for "small town"), where many Jews cohabited with local populations before the Second World War, Hoffman's narrative shows that despite their ethnic, cultural, linguistic, and religious differences, the everyday coexistence of Jews and Poles was not a coexistence of those who were merely other to each other in an absolute, mutually exclusive sense; rather, there were permanent and constant exchanges between them. Even in Gross's book, we are confronted with an interpretation of life in Jedwabne as a shared experience. As Gross points out, the Jewish and Polish residents of Jedwabne, like many residents of similar towns throughout Poland, were indeed neighbours.

The Jedwabne-born social historian Marta Kurkowska-Budzan, who carried out research in her home town before the controversy over *Neighbors* became common knowledge in Jedwabne and elsewhere, found out that even sixty years later some elderly residents, when prompted, could still remember the names of their Jewish neighbours, their everyday coexistence, and the tragic events that happened there in 1941. Natalia G., who was born in 1926, remembered playing together and going to school with the seven children of her Jewish neighbour Sholimowa. When the author asked her whether she remembered any Jewish words she responded in the negative. Yet, the following day, when recollecting the wedding day of her neighbour's daughter, she broke into Yiddish song. "She was deeply moved, and I had the impression that she was transported into the past," writes Kurkowska-Budzan (2004: 203). That was the moment when the historian realises that her interviewees "had in a sense lost part of their lives. This lost world used to be their world too, in the broad meaning of this notion – their reality. They told me without needing to be asked, that they missed 'something'" . . . (2004: 204). The interview goes to show that the Jews, in fact, pertained to a kind of ordinary, everyday otherness, and that such otherness was not alien to the affirmation of a certain kind of cohabitation.

Drawing from Jewish tradition, shaped by the historical experience of displacement, exile, and living among those who are not the same, in her recent essay Judith Butler reanimates an idea of cohabitation as an alternative or supplement to that of integrative multiculturalism – an idea akin to the modes of cohabitation invoked by Lehmann and Hoffman in their reflection on Eastern European *shtetlekh* I mentioned earlier. "To co-habit the earth is prior to any possible community or nation or neighbourhood," she writes (2011a: 84). "We might choose where to live, and who to live by, but we cannot choose with whom to co-habit the earth" (2011a: 84). To seek to decide with whom to cohabit, then, is to seek to pre-empt a basic condition of social and political existence. Rather, Butler argues, we must actively seek to preserve "the non-chosen character of inclusive and plural co-habitation" (2011a: 83).

Interpreting the Jedwabne episode in the wider context of Polish antisemitism, Zylinska proposes that by their resistance to "domestication into the monoreligious Catholic landscape," the Jewish neighbours of Jedwabne posed "a challenge to the idea of neighbourliness seen as consolidation of identity devoid of difference, the identity of the self-same" (2007: 287). To Zylinska, then, "The death of the Jedwabne Jews in a neighbour's barn . . . can perhaps be interpreted as an attempt to 'enclose' alterity, to put an end to it" (2007: 286–7). The main shortcoming in this engaging argument regards generalisation concerning the agency of Jewish erasure (in Jedwabne). The terms such as "Pole's dislike of Jews" and "Polish antisemitism" (2007: 284; 287) are too broad; they create an image of amorphous, homogenous "Poland" set on destroying its Jews in the course of the Second Word War. Zylinska's psychohistorical diagnosis here seems to subsume the historical and assimilate it, as it were, into the family romance of psychoanalysis. Certainly, psychoanalytic thinking, as a sustained body of work that mediates on the complex nature of the psyche could be vital to historical understanding or a historical treatment of problems. However, Zylinska's symptomatic reading of how it came to pass, that in one particular time and place, Poles behaved toward Jews precisely as they did requires a larger body of empirical evidence than she mobilises in order to compel acceptance. I find the Jedwabne case so compelling not because it offers an opportunity to revisit the issue of collective national responsibility or guilt, but rather because "it stands at the nexus of the questions of modernity, revolution, and totalitarianism" (Shore, 2005: 373). As Janine Holc writes, "*Neighbors* does not deliver any kind of 'victory' to the so-called Jewish side or the Polish side, but invites us to develop a more nuanced understanding of the dynamic between individual decision and social identity in a time of trauma" (2002: 458). Furthermore, in a world plagued with nationalistic, ethnic, and religious wars and other forms of violence in which civilians are sacrificed daily in the name of ethnic or religious ideals or fictions, or the political struggle for power, this historical event invites us to ponder the question of how to forge an ethical relation to the other.

The last two decades have seen the appearance of a rich body of cultural, scholarly, and historical work by Polish academics and cultural workers in regard to the history and culture of Polish Jewry in general, and on the subject of the Holocaust in particular. This new body of historical material has led to a gradual reinterpretation of twentieth-century Polish-Jewish relations, especially of the war years. It is also gradually bringing concrete knowledge of Jewish history and culture into the wider public sphere. The efforts to recover Poland's Jewish heritage and culture taking place in universities, publishing houses, cultural centres, museum exhibits, documentaries, and festivals such as the annual Jewish cultural week in Cracow are part of the process of forging the nation's post-Communist identity also under way in other countries from the former Eastern Bloc.

The expansion of Jewish memory-work in Poland including Holocaust-related commemorative activity also went hand in hand with the country's integration into the European Union. The European Union has enshrined Holocaust memory in its mission, which is clearly visible in the in the political statements of the Stockholm International Forum on the Holocaust. Hence, many countries of eastern Europe also "promote the Holocaust memory as a way of proving that they are on board with the mainstream European understanding of the past" (Stone, 2010: 33). However, the last few years have also seen the change of emphasis in the Polish war narrative from the German to the Soviet occupation and the subsequent Soviet hegemony. Undoubtedly the 1940 Katyń massacre, which was systematically threatened by state-sanctioned erasure for fifty years, has a special place here, as we shall see in the next part of this chapter.

Exhumations: the return of the dead in Tadeusz Kantor's *Let the Artists Die* and Andrzej Wajda's *Katyń*

In this part of the chapter I focus on Tadeusz Kantor's performance *Let the Artists Die* and Andrzej Wajda's film *Katyń* (2007), two works that evoke the Second World War massacre of Polish prisoners of war in Katyń Forest. Albeit that the manner in which these two works reference this historic event is very different, both Kantor's theatrical ghosts and Wajda's cinematic images carry the traces of the absent, the disappeared, the dead, revealing a history that hurts. As I will argue, both Kantor's performance and Wajda's film perform the redressive work actualised by remembrance. For Kantor, a need to mourn the Katyń massacre was augmented by the disallowance of an official space of mourning within Poland in the postwar decades. Kantor's seizing hold of the past enabled the aggrieved to recount the history that was "forgotten," excluded, rendered unthinkable or made marginal. *Let the Artists Die*, as well as the other performances from his "Theatre of Death" cycle (1975–90), aim to rescue the unnamed and the still unaccounted-for from obscurity and oblivion, and thus to counter the disavowals constitutive of public discourse of national remembrance in Poland until the late 1980s. Wajda's *Katyń* can also be seen as part of a pattern, since it marks a return to issues of the Second World War, various aspects of which Wajda already explored in films such as *A Generation* (*Pokolenie*, 1955), *Kanal* (*Kanał*, 1957), *Ashes and Diamonds* (*Popiół i diament*, 1958), *Landscape after Battle* (*Krajobraz po bitwie*, 1970), *Korczak* (*Korczak*, 1990), and *Holy Week* (*Wielki Tydzień*, 1995). Like Kantor's performance, Wajda's film can also be seen as an instance of counter-memory, although it was created at a significantly different historical juncture, and responds to different needs now that the previously inadmissible experience has entered a fractured ecology of truth. The film transmits the national trauma of Katyń much more explicitly than Kantor's work, while making an attempt at integrating this event into collective consciousness by remembering and repeating it symbolically. Finally, while both works constitute a return to a traumatic past, they are also infused with melancholia, but of a different kind. While *Let the Artists Die* acts as a site of resistance in an instance of officially instituted melancholia, a socially instituted foreclosure of mourning, the melancholia that manifests on Wajda's screen is of a regressive, narcissistic kind, which could be understood as a symptom of an "exclusive preoccupation with one's own wounds" (Plonowska Ziarek, 2007: 319), a kind of disavowal that does not enable witnessing of the other's trauma.

The name Katyń now stands not only for the best-known execution site, but for other execution sites where agents of the Soviet NKVD (People's Commissariat for Internal Affairs) murdered some 14,522 Polish citizens in spring 1940, including the prisoners of war from three special camps in the Soviet Union – Kozelsk (southeast of Smolensk), Ostashkov (west of Kalinin/Tver), and Starobelsk (southeast of Kharkov). They were shot and buried at Katyń, Kalinin/Tver, and Kharkov. This number of casualties also includes 7,305 prisoners of war executed in NKVD prisons in western Belorussia and in Ukraine at the time (Cienciala et al., 2008: 122; 332). These men had been taken prisoner by the Red Army after 17 September 1939, following the Soviet Union's invasion and occupation of eastern Poland, which was then annexed under the terms of the Molotov–Ribbentrop Pact.[12]

On 13 April 1943, the German army announced their discovery of the mass graves in Katyń (Figure 3.3). German forces in the area had interrogated local inhabitants, who told them that the NKVD had carried out the killings in the spring of 1940. Three on-site investigations of the Katyń graves were conducted: by a German Inquiry Commission, an International Medical Commission, and a Polish Red Cross Technical Commission from German-occupied Poland. All three concluded that the crime must have been committed in 1940; that is, when the territory was under Soviet control (Cienciala et al., 2008: 222; Zaslavsky, 2008: 55–6). The Soviet side responded with a counter-attack, blaming the Germans and breaking off diplomatic relations with Poland. In January 1944, an official Soviet investigative commission headed by Nikolai N. Burdenko concluded that Germans committed the murders in autumn 1941. When the subject of Katyń came up in June 1946 during the Nuremberg War Crime Trials, it was dismissed for lack of sufficient evidence. In 1952, a US congressional committee of investigation announced its findings in regard to Katyń, which proved that the Soviet NKVD had committed

Figure 3.3 Katyń, opening of the mass graves, April 1943; *Bild* 183-J21201; photograph courtesy of the *Bundesarchiv*

the massacre (Zaslavsky, 2008: 66–7). Soviet authorities continued to insist on German responsibility for the crime until 1990.[13] Although the huge majority of the Polish population had never accepted the Soviet explanations for the massacre, the subordinate regime in Poland had nevertheless kept the issue of Katyń suppressed for half a century.

In 1985, when Kantor staged *Let the Artists Die*, the Katyń massacre was still an absolutely forbidden topic in Poland.[14] I will argue that by making use of a generic catachresis during the course of the performance, Kantor adapts autobiography into a form of what Ross Chambers, in his book *Untimely Interventions* (2004) terms "dual" or "collective" autobiography. Depriviliging his own voice and emphasising the experience of the Katyń dead – through appropriation of the aesthetics of autobiography – Kantor continues his project of cultural witnessing that he initiated with *The Dead Class* and *Wielopole, Wielopole*. Once again, references to ghosts and other apparitions of the dead return with *Let the Artists Die*. Kantor attends to their command to remember, showing that we cannot fully avoid and repress the past, for the spirits that plague us have their own mnemic authority and will not rest until mourning is complete, until the guilt and fear clustered around the memories of their deaths have been dissipated or dispelled. Thus, it should not come as a surprise that images of burial and exhumation abound in *Let the Artists Die*, serving as metaphors for both the repression of disturbing memories, and the inevitable way in which such memories perpetually return to consciousness.

Let the Artists Die opens in the cemetery storeroom of Kantor's memory. The childhood room of memory – previously the operative metaphor for the process of recollection in *Wielopole, Wielopole* – is transformed here into a mortuary space. As will soon become clear, this change is more strategic than substantial, a matter of emphasis in the service of certain dramaturgical goals – especially if we recall both the crypt-like and cryptic quality of the room of memory from *Wielopole, Wielopole*. In *Let the Artists Die*, Kantor also makes strategic use of photography because, as he explains, "PHOTO-NEGATIVES OF MEMORY are near the regions of / DEATH / They can be easily found / in a CEMETERY STOREROOM" (qtd. in Lawson, 1995: 42).[15] The visual mode of memory that dominates Kantor's performances is so closely related to an experience of disintegration and rupture, which enacts what one could refer to as an aesthetics of shock, often associated with the photographic medium, that it is no surprise that in his writings Kantor also continually reflects on photography. It is easy to see how photography can serve as a metaphor for memory: the process of remembering and the subsequent inscription of the memory, both essential to the autobiographical act, find a perfect image in the photograph. It is therefore also not surprising that, following the discovery of photography, its metaphorical potential has often been utilised by authors in their autobiographies (see, for instance, Rugg, 2007). In Kantor's largely autobiographical cycle "The Theatre of Death", photography plays an important role as well. Not only does the author animate certain photographs on stage, as happens in *Wielopole, Wielopole*, *Let the Artists Die*, and *Today Is My Birthday* (1990), he also conceives visual experience in reference to the medium: memories can at any moment take the quality of the photographic image.[16]

Just like Walter Benjamin, who in an early version of his autobiography *The Berlin Chronicle* (1979 [1932]) describes human memory as a photographic plate, in a piece of poetic prose entitled "Memory Plates" ("Klisze") Kantor writes:

> In our "warehouse" of the memory there exist "catalogues"
> of photographic plates, registered by our senses.
> These are for the most part seamlessly meaningless details,
> pitiful ones, scrapes, clippings of a kind. . .
> and they are IMMOBILE!
> And, what is more important: TRANSPARENT, like
> photographic negatives.
> They can be placed on top of each other.
> And that's why one should not be surprised if, for instance,
> distant events link up with those of today,
> personages get mixed up, and we have serious problems
> with history, morality, and all sorts of
> conventions.
> The waves of memory, now bright and peaceful, are suddenly
> stirred up,
> the elements are unleashed,
> HELL . . .
>
> (n.d.b: 231)[17]

Once memory (both individual and historical) is equated with photographic flashes, an altered form of narration suggests itself, one consonant with the photographic experience of the past. In Kantor's *Let the Artists Die*, the operative metaphor of photography as memory plays a role in determining the fragmentary form of the performance. In a fragment entitled "MIEJSCE AKCJI" ("THE PLACE OF ACTION"), Kantor explains:

> You won't find it on this stage.
> Nor is there any action.
> There is, rather, a j o u r n e y
> into the past, into the abyss of m e m o r y,
> into the p a s t   t e n s e, which has flowed on,
> yet which continually attracts us;
> the time which c o m e s   i n t o   c o n t a c t somewhere
> with the regions of D R E A M, I N F E R N U M,
> T H E   W O R L D   O F   T H E   D E A D

A N D E T E R N I T Y
and becomes one with them!
This is why the present day is found there too,
despite the fact that we don't intend to describe it whatsoever . . .

This is a world and a time where everything happens A T O N C E,
where to our pragmatic QUOTIDIANITY
everything appears to be s e n s e l e s s
a i m l e s s,
somehow f a c e t i o u s,
lost in contradictions,
balanced between dignity and the ridiculous,
between heaven and hell,
prayer and blasphemy,
valour and cowardice . . . .
A black hole – INFERNUM.

M y p o o r l i t t l e r o o m
o f t h e i m a g i n a t i o n
s a n s w a l l s, c e i l i n g, a n d f l o o r!

(n.d.b: 231)

Kantor *images* the setting for the performance as an ever-shifting chronotope, with memory photo-negatives overlaying one another. While the stage action starts in a cemetery storeroom, a memory photo-negative of a poor room overlaid with that of a cemetery, subsequent places evoked on stage are the result of further overlays of memory photo-negatives that are read through one another. Furthermore, while the stage action begins at a specific moment in time – midnight, the time when the dead "rise up" to commingle with the living – the subsequent moments of the performance stretch both backward to embrace a specific moment of Kantor's childhood, and forward to the imagined moment of his death. To this end Kantor employs several characters: Kantor-remembered at the age of six (I-when I was Six); Kantor-himself, in the present time of the performance, who sits at the side of the room (I-the Real Me); Kantor-imagined, just before his moment of death (I-Dying); and I-Dying's Author (who shows up as the *Doppelgänger* of I-Dying), who describes, through him, his own death.

The performance begins with the entrance, the dressing for burial, and the departure of an unnamed dead man; when the owner of the cemetery storeroom of Kantor's memory enters, the room becomes his cemetery storeroom haunted by the spectre of Kantor's mother; it then becomes a sickroom when both I-Dying and his Author enter, get into bed, and cough themselves to death; when mother's little boy enters on his tricycle the sickroom becomes a playroom; soon after it becomes killing fields, or perhaps an execution site of You-Know-Who's soldiers and, at the end of Act I, a parade route for the travelling actors who come to town. At the beginning of Act II, the room becomes a hangout in which the travelling actors run their handful of lines over and over again. As *Let the Artists Die* continues, this hangout becomes the base from which other scenes and characters will journey and return. First it turns into a roadside camp where travelling actors meet up with another traveller: You-Know-Who[18] on his skeleton horse, who sings a mournful song; then a hangout; then the Actors are again at the roadside camp for another song by You-Know-Who, and then on to I-Dying's sickroom; then the hangout again; pillories are subsequently brought in and the room becomes a prison cell for a secret agent (who is supposed to be the medieval artist Wit Stwosz (Veit Stoss), incarnated as a *fin de siècle* Decadent) to torture the actors to death; then back to the hangout; then the secret agent has a barricade built out of everything that happened in the performance; and the finale sees everyone circle the barricade for a curtain call and parade out of town.

As in *Wielopole, Wielopole*, only vestiges of recollections are present in this crypt of Kantor's memory: a few chairs, a door hung in its frame, several wooden grave-crosses, and a hospital sickbed. The owner of the cemetery storeroom of memory enters this room announcing that it is after midnight. Soon the dead will arrive, but before the spectres can be summoned the room has to be "tidied," just as happened in *Wielopole, Wielopole*. Crosses and chairs scattered around the room have to be set right, and a dishevelled bed has to be made up. The owner quickly moves around putting everything in order. Like the Twins in *Wielopole, Wielopole*, in cleaning up the room its owner acts on Kantor's behalf; he knows the contents of the author's memory, as well as where and how to place them in order to effect memories. When the last piece is in place, the owner sits on his chair to rest. Soon steps – the first of many imaginings and memories to come – sound over the loudspeakers.

After the entrance of a group of travelling actors ("Those leading someone to his eternal rest"), "He, to whom they bid farewell" enters slowly, dressed in a black overcoat and hat. The rest of the actors (the "Inhabitants of the Cemetery Shed") enter, and "he" (the dead man) suddenly stiffens. The inhabitants pick him up, undress him, wash him ceremoniously, and then dress him up again ceremoniously, as in preparation for a burial. Downstage right, the owner stands to attention ceremoniously. The dead man leaves the stage slowly, mechanically, to the accompaniment of the old march *My, Pierwsza Brygada* (We of the First Brigade) played at such a slow tempo that it loses all of its military pomp, becoming instead a mournful funerary march. As we shall see, this scene – as its title "overture" suggests – stands as a *mise en abyme* for the rest of the performance, which proceeds by raising and appeasing the (war) dead.

In the next segment of the performance, there follows a presentation of Kantor's memory of his mother overlaid with memories of her death, which in turn prompts Kantor's imaginings of his own death. The cemetery storeroom opens on its own, and in comes the figure of an I-Dying. Kantor's imaginings of himself dying (I-Dying) are accompanied by remembrances of the slow, inexorable death about which the Polish author Zbigniew Uniłowski wrote in his novel *A Shared Room* (*Wspólny pokój*, 1932). These remembrances take the form of an Author who enters right on I-Dying's heels. Imaginings of death and remembrances of Uniłowski's novel so overlay one another that they become one and the same; comically played by the Janicki twins, I-Dying and his Author are identical and interchangeable.

In a lecture on memory and imagining the past, Benjamin speaks of the proto-photographic strip of images from life that is said to go through the heads of the dying. The intimation is that something closely resembling a celluloid self lies buried in our unconscious. Memories are imagined as "involuntarily summoned strips of montaged images, flashing past in rapid succession" at the moment of death (Leslie, 2003: 177). In his *partytura* (score) for *Let the Artists Die*, Kantor evokes this memory topos when he writes: "The hour of one's death always evokes an image of one's childhood" (n.d.b: 242). This statement introduces the following scene in which his dying self suddenly calls for his *wózeczek* (tricycle) from the time when he was six years old.[19]

The owner opens the door, a funeral dirge plays over the loud-speakers, and in comes Kantor as a boy (I-When I was Six). Dressed in a uniform worn by the soldiers of Poland's First Brigade, he slowly rolls forward on a tricycle, but remains only for a moment, soon slipping backward through the door and into the dim, dark reaches that lie far beyond Kantor's memory storeroom. The owner slowly closes the door. Everything is still and silent. Struggling to remember, I-Dying plaintively calls out, "Wózeczek!" again and again. This redoubled effort to remember brings a rush of memories. The little boy on a tricycle comes in again, followed by a general dressed in the same uniform as the little boy, who is listed in the program as You-Know-Who, and The Man Whose Name Shall Not Be Mentioned. It is presumably Marshal Piłsudski, a boyhood model of manly glory and liberating power. But the boy's dream-double is riding on the skeleton of a horse. The general, played by Maria Kantor, begins to sing a haunting melancholy song, which gradually transforms into a powerful lament.[20]

The general is followed by soldiers, You-Know-Who's Generals, who look as if risen from the grave. Once they have found their way into a line that stretched across the stage, they keep march-ing mechanically to the droning, dirge version of "We, of the First Brigade" (Figure 3.4). As Gitta Honegger has put it, in this scene, "The vision of death becomes a child's play; but the boy tries in vain to push the soldiers to the ground – he can't manipulate them, control them as only the 'real' artist, Kantor, the unrelenting director, can do, just as the dying man can't put them out of his memory" (1986: 59). It all gets too much for Kantor, who rises from his chair and steps into the room to banish all of the invaders with a swiping wave of his hand. Kantor clears everything out of his memory storeroom as if trying once again to have a clear remembrance of his mother and lost childhood. However, the effort is a futile one. Memory entails inva-sions. We watch Kantor head back to his chair as the owner closes the door after the last soldier leaves the room. Kantor comments on this scene as follows:

> But one cannot evoke the TIME
> of one's childhood, THE PAST, with i m p u n i t y.
> For suddenly, the figures of the DEAD
> appear, spectral, demanding, contorted in pain,

with wax faces and empty eye sockets.
The happy little SOLDIER is followed by
his retinue and his dreams,
THE T H E A T R E O F D E A T H,
THE MORTUARY GLORY
OF HIM, WHOSE NAME WILL NOT BE MENTIONED,
A PAINFUL FIGURE TRAMPING STEP BY STEP
AFTER THE LITTLE SOLDIER,
HIS FAITHFUL GENERALS
OF TIN, DEAD.
Nothing but uniforms. SILVER.
And thus, for the first time, my little room of memory
becomes painfully wounded!

(n.d.b: 243)

The issue here is explicitly the tension between the personal and the social. We have seen that in the earlier sections of the

Figure 3.4 Scene from Kantor's *Let the Artists Die* (The Parade); photograph: Leszek Dziedzic, courtesy of the Cricoteka Archives

performance, personal subjectivity, the individual perspective controlling depiction, obviously dominates the representation of the past by the present. This mode expresses itself in the familiar (and familial) strains of remembrance (Kantor's memories of his mother, his childhood and so on). But in the scene with the soldiers, history menacingly usurps contemporaneity. Under such conditions, individual subjectivity is overwhelmed by the persistence of the past, and comes to seem dominated, indeed possessed by it. The past appears as an ineradicable inscription that, when read in the present, displaces the immediacy of experience and co-opts contemporaneity. Kantor's representation of memory therefore seems to turn on locating the power of our history to dominate and even to shatter our present. As in *Wielopole, Wielopole*, the past in *Let the Artists Die* is thus conceived in the image of a trauma.

In 1985 the condensed image of the parading soldiers brought painful memories and associations. Referring to this scene Kantor writes: "It is impossible to say whether this is a victory parade or a funeral procession of the nation's glory" (n.d.b: 246). According to Krzysztof Miklaszewski, one of the Cricot 2 actors, "'Although Kantor cleverly masked it, the inspiration for this piece is clearly Marshal Józef Piłsudski, the acclaimed leader who brought about the rebirth of Poland following the First World War and was officially branded an Enemy of Communism by the Government of People's Poland, 1946–1989" (2002: 248). Krzysztof Pleśniarowicz adds that for this scene Kantor "drew his inspiration from a pre-war photograph of Piłsudski's funeral: Polish generals carrying the open coffin with the body of the dead Marshal," but he also crucially indicates that these revenants on Kantor's stage suggest "both the leaden soldiers of childhood playtime, and the pictures of the exhumation of thousands of Polish officers murdered by the NKVD at Katyń in 1940" (1994: 248).[21] Michal Kobialka also references Katyń, acknowledging that this "episode" in Polish history served as an impetus behind the creation of *Let the Artists Die* (2009: 301). While both critics offer illuminating accounts of the performance (Pleśniarowicz by focusing on the avant-garde techniques employed by Kantor and offering an existential reading of the piece, Kobialka by foregrounding the "nonrepresentational, nonillustrative" aspects of the artist's encounter with history, absence, and death [2009: 301]), neither engages at any length with a historiography of Katyń. It is my contention that we miss something important in our analysis of Kantor's work if we do not keep a keen eye on the Polish context in which it evolved. While the innovative theatrical form, as well as the spirit of Kantor's performances, has proven successful with international audiences, the particulars of their ostensibly Polish subject matter have often escaped them. But Kantor's art is saturated in memory – historical, literary, ideological, as well as personal. For him, the stakes of memory are enormous. *Let the Artists Die*, like other performances from his "Theatre of Death" cycle, carries the indelible traces of the past shaped as specifically historical, and positioned within a concrete memory discourse. Their goal is "local" and immediate, often aimed at filling the "blank spots" of history and representing on stage what could not be openly said in other public forums, although their appeal has been much more far-reaching.

In his *Untimely Interventions*, Ross Chambers puts forward a hypothesis that "events and experiences that are traumatic, whether collectively or to individuals, and become the object of witnessing practices have the cultural status of the obscene" (2004: 23). Chambers defines the obscene as "the 'offstage' or 'backstage' space that delimits, and is simultaneously inseparable from, a scene of activity on which attention is focused. The cultural obscene is 'obscured' or 'covered' with respect to a scene of culture, but without being discontinuous with it" (2004: 23). The author relates this concept to the cultural practice of witnessing. He argues that witnessing has its place in culture as a genre, but that "it also disturbs social 'rules' because it is 'about' – more accurately, it *signposts* – the obscene" (2004: 25). Thus, it is precisely as a generic anomaly that it functions within culture as an infringement of social expectations. In Chambers' view, witnessing entails the appropriation of pre-existing genres, those that are by definition not dedicated to the kind of subject matter a given culture may classify as obscene, but which become appropriated for special purposes, such as that of witnessing. "Culturally speaking," writes Chambers, "witnessing is thus a genre of writing that is constitutively parasitic on other genres" (2004: 25). Chambers illustrates his point by using the following example:

> Because living and dying, for example, are closely identified (they are proximate phenomena and they resemble each other), the genre of autobiography or life writing can readily be adapted

catachrestically to become an account of one's dying, an autothanatography. Because dying can scarcely be dissociated from different ways of dying, certain ways of dying regarded as obscene (dying in an extermination camp, dying of AIDS) can become smuggled into the form of autothanatography. (2004: 30)

In other words, a catachresis of genre disturbs some basic cultural assumptions, expectations, and indeed certainties. I contend that *Let the Artists Die* represents a tangible example of this practice. It appears to espouse a familiar genre – (Kantor's) autobiography – but it feels like an error or an infraction. This error, however, is deliberate, designed to express the ethical concerns and issues that could not be invoked more directly in 1980s Poland. The performance's task – its vocation – resides, therefore, in bringing the culturally obscene (the anxiogenic and haunting memories of the repressed past) into the Polish public sphere. Teresa Krzemień's moving review of the performance, worth quoting at length, is telling of its effect on its Polish audiences:

Sequences of quotations, distinguishable pains – human and Polish – everything cut, torn, recalled senselessly, accidentally, in disorder. Suddenly, horribly logical, all this creates symbolical scenes with precise meanings, strung like beads onto a thread – one after the other, whole layers of meaning, an endless pit. And now we can name each single one; with every recognition it becomes more painful – even more horrible. The result, resumé? None! – a theatre of death is a theatre of death, only Kantor is alive, the rest is the action of opening the graves – but from the graves ghosts crawl out, their lives turn out to be eternal. (1986: 12)

As Krzemień's reflections suggest, the cultural haunting at work in *Let the Artists Die* is neither metaphysical in nature, nor confined to the perception of individuals, but historical and collective. In his *Ghostly Matters*, the sociologist Avery Gordon writes compellingly about this phenomenon:

Haunting is a constituent element of social life. It is neither a premodern superstition nor individual psychosis; it is a generalisable social phenomenon of great import. . . . The ghost is not simply a dead or missing person, but a social figure, and investigating it can lead to that dense site where history and subjectivity make social life. . . . Being haunted draws us affectively, sometimes against our will and always a bit magically, into the structure of feeling of a reality we come to experience, not as cold knowledge, but as transformative recognition. (1997: 7–8)

Through its indexical character, *Let the Artists Die* could be seen in this context as a vehicle of the return of what was occluded for so many years by the official culture in Poland. The performance demonstrates that the survival of memory – by which I mean the ability of the culture's obscenities to return, and to return in a striking guise that haunts the mind; that is, our susceptibility to be reminded of what the official culture would prefers us to forget – depends on an art of witnessing.

Wajda's film *Katyń*, which premiered in Warsaw on 17 September 2007, the sixty-eighth anniversary of the Soviet invasion of Poland, is based on Andrzej Mularczyk's novel *Post Mortem* (2005) and the letters and diaries by many of the victims that were unearthed when the Nazis first came across the mass graves in 1943. The film opens with a scene showing two groups of Polish refugees crossing a bridge in opposite directions: it is 17 September 1939, and one group escaping German troops runs head-on into a second group fleeing the Red Army from the other side of the river. "People, where are you going? Turn back!" the two groups shout to one another. Standing out among the stranded and bewildered crowd is a young Polish mother with her daughter. The film then switches to a Catholic priest giving the last rites to a number of Polish soldiers who fell fighting the Red Army earlier in the day, and then to a group of Polish officers who have been taken prisoner by Soviet troops and are awaiting transportation. Next we see the woman pleading with her husband to flee with her and their child before the train arrives to transport the officers to the Soviet Union. He responds by reminding her of the vow he took to Poland. Soon after, Wajda shows a group of Soviet soldiers tearing a Polish flag to transform it into a red Soviet banner, and German officers in a friendly conversation with the Soviets along the new German-Soviet border. These initial scenes already contain some key tropes of Polish suffering during the war: the loss of sovereignty and domination by foreign powers, the killings, and the dramatic decimation of traditional values and binding communal norms. The film continues by alternating between scenes among the Polish prisoners of war (depicting their deportation, internment, and execution) and scenes among the families left behind and their struggles with the Germans, the Soviets, and especially the postwar Polish government that forbade any public reference to Katyń as a Soviet crime.

By weaving together the stories of several families of the Polish officers taken prisoner by the Soviets, and depicting the pain of their separation and bereavement, Wajda shows that the violence was not simply inflicted upon the bodies of the individuals who were taken away, but also on the body of the nation and the families and communities that were torn apart (as made dramatically visible by the opening scene at the bridge). Katyń was of course only one of many grave injuries inflicted on Poland during the Second World War with which the nation is still coming to terms, including the near-complete annihilation of the Polish Jewry, the uprisings of the Warsaw Ghetto in 1943, and of the city itself in 1944, and the tragic fates of many Polish citizens arrested and deported to the far reaches of the Soviet Union, many of whom never returned. To these traumatic events we must add the daily traumas that characterised almost fifty years of political, social, and economic domination of Poland by the Soviet Union.

In *Beyond the Pleasure Principle* (1920), Freud defines trauma as a breach in the protective shield of consciousness, the mental projection of the body's surface that normally filters out excessive stimuli. According to Freud, the shock of something unexpected that suddenly attacks the subject from outside tears this filter; the subject is unable to master the excess of affect produced by the impact – and flooding results (1953–74a: 29–30). But Freud's figuration of psychic trauma as an internal foreign body and its associate imagery of a defensive position in war cannot be seen as merely metaphorical. As Peng Cheah has argued, "the security of an *individual* psyche's interiority in its interaction with the external world and its management of external excitations is the template for historical forms of sociality and political community" (2008: 194). In a similar vein, Kai Erikson has argued that the social tissue of a community can be damaged in ways similar to the tissues of mind and body. Collective trauma ruptures social bonds, undermines communality, and destroys previous sources of support (1995: 185–8). As Freud and others have argued (see, for example, Caruth 1995; Leys, 2000), in cases of trauma the repressed memory of the affect becomes engraved within the psyche and continues to act long after the passing of the event that brought about traumatisation. Until this trace or mnemonic residue of the traumatic event has been recuperated and worked though, the trauma will continue to live in us as a past that refuses to go away.

In the process of translating and imaging the loss and the traumatic shock of Katyń in his film, Wajda relies crucially on the archival footage taken by Germans and Soviets at Katyń during the war, which represent the first cinematic witnessing of the atrocity, as well as the subsequent encounters with these images and his own graphic reconstruction of the massacre itself. In my analysis of these different figurations of trauma, I will propose that Wajda is primarily concerned with searching for a filmic language capable of efficiently communicating a set of historical facts to a mass audience so that the trauma of Katyń might be recognised, negotiated, and reconfigured.[22] The past is never wholly accessible, nor is it ever really past. But Wajda's film suggests that in the process of coming to terms with what was we may move from trauma to witnessing, to mourning and perhaps even reconciliation.

Wajda uses the archival footage of German and then Soviet exhumations at Katyń to show the role of these films in making the atrocities public during the war years, and how they shaped the history – as well as Polish memories – of the massacre. In *Katyń*, both documentaries are mediated through the eyes of Róza, the wife of a Polish general who perished at Katyń. In Wajda's view, this dramaturgical device was meant to aid his audiences "to see the Katyń lie as plain as daylight" (2008: 80). In April 1943, Róza is summoned into the offices of the German propaganda department in Cracow, where she learns about the fate of her husband and other officers. The Germans express their condolences, and then ask her to read a denunciation of the USSR for their radio broadcast. After she refuses, she is forced to watch a German film with the images of the open mass graves in Katyń.[23] From the first week of May 1943, this German newsreel (*Auslandstonwoche* issue 609), featuring the discovery, exhumation, forensic investigation and identification of the corpses of the Polish prisoners was distributed throughout the occupied territories and countries allied with Germany (Winkel, 2004: 10). In December 1943, the documentary short *Im Wald von Katyn* (*In Katyń Forest*, 1943), was also released for foreign use.[24] We know less about the Soviet propaganda film *Tragediia v Katyńskom lesu* (*Tragedy in the Katyń Wood*), directed by Irina Setkina, watched by Róża and others in Cracow's main square in winter 1945. As I mentioned earlier, in 1944 the Burdenko Commission blamed the massacre on the Germans, distorting and burying uncomfortable facts and ordering fake autopsy reports. After the war, a commission was established in Moscow that was responsible for the preparation of the evidentiary materials on Katyń to be used in Nuremberg in 1946, where the Soviet delegation hoped to settle definitively the question of responsibility for the Katyń massacre. The Chair of the commission, the notorious former prosecutor General Andrey Vyshinsky, personally oversaw the preparation of a documentary film on Katyń (Zaslavsky, 2008: 61–2). In all likelihood, both films (the one intended for Nuremberg and the one screened for the Polish public in Cracow in 1945) were based on the film footage taken by the Soviets in 1944.

Both the German and Soviet propaganda documentaries cited in Wajda's film feature the excavations of the victims and evoke the connections between bodies of evidence and the uses to which they are put. Both present evidence, beginning with the most irrefutable "fact" of all – the body, while offering differing explanations of what happened. The narration they employ does not simply strengthen the verisimilitude of the images or authenticate what is being seen, but also produces an interpretative matrix for what is seen. The German narrator explains that the footage was taken in the Katyń forest near Smolensk and that the exhumed bodies belong to Polish prisoners of war. With a rhetorical flourish common to wartime documentaries, he reveals that the German and Polish forensic teams "ascertained the typically Bolshevik way of murdering by a shot in the back of the head" and "proved evidently that all those Polish officers were murdered in the spring of 1940" (qtd. in Wajda, 2008: 82). In the Soviet version of the narrative, the narrator concurs that the Poles were killed by a shot in the back of the head, but only to instruct his audience that this was "the favourite way of killing of Gestapo murderers," and, crucially, that the Soviet forensic team determined that the victims "were murdered not earlier than in the fall of 1941" (qtd. in Wajda, 2008: 100).

Perhaps in order to pre-empt possible doubts about the veracity of their images, both documentaries supply witnesses to corroborate the truth of their representations. The German film shows the exhumation of uniformed corpses, as well as footage of the Polish Red Cross and the international press examining the mass grave at Katyń, and scenes from Vinnytsia that portray local civilians attempting to identify decomposed corpses. At both sites the bodies were then reburied with religious pomp. The Soviet film also features a priest, a delegation of the First Polish Corps in the Soviet Union that came under Soviet orders to pay honour to their compatriots, as well as a group of Western reporters for whose benefit the show was staged (see, for example, Tolczyk, 2008: 12). Both films feature the reburial of the excavated bodies. They also both *hail* the viewer, thanks to their power of interpellation (in the Althusserian sense), to witness these deaths as evidence of atrocity, with the assumption that this will discredit the enemy in the eyes of the local population and elicit concern, outrage, perhaps action of the international community. They were also meant to serve, perhaps, at some point in the future, as exhibits to be admitted in the historical trial. As in newsreel-type documentaries made by several Allied nations at the end of the war, the gaze of the spectator in these films is "positioned as forensic: objective, knowledgeable, authoritative" (Hirsch, 2004: 34). Both films present the masses of the dead bodies at Katyń "as a historical spectacle that poses little difficulty for the conventional cinematic, historical, and forensic discourses" (Hirsch, 2004: 34) by which their respective audiences could attempt to comprehend this atrocity, while glossing over the epistemological, moral, or psychological problems of the act of bearing witness. Thus in these first cinematic representations of Katyń the trauma was effectively contained and assimilated into the respective German and Soviet master-narratives of the Second World War.

On another level, the "forensic gaze" that these cinematic images instate is also meant to prevent us from going beneath the surface, seeing what these images both expose and foreclose. The filmic evidence of atrocities from Katyń and Vinnytsia (because and in spite of the referentiality inherent in every photographic medium) cannot fully account for what is shown in the images. When we look at this footage, we are dealing with the pictures that assert the evidence of what they show but do not allow us to gain any further insights. In spite of its apparentness, its evidence, what is depicted can be made to speak only by the addition of the discursive anchoring, such as

witnesses' accounts, historical sources, juridical and medical discourses, etc. Only these allow us to place them in a wider interpretative context and narrow the decisive rift between the substratum of
compiled visual facts and the gaze that rests on them.

Some recent research suggests that in their Criminal Investigation
Report on the Vinnytsia massacre as well as their film footage from
Vinnytsia, the Germans conducted what Irina Paperno calls "ethnic
cleansing of evidence" (2001: 108). While the German investigation
into the ethnicity of the victims established that "of the 679 identified bodies, 490 were Ukrainians, 28 Poles, and 161 of 'unknown
nationality,'" later testimonies revealed that Germans deliberately
obfuscated the evidence by failing to acknowledge that Jews and
Russians (including NKVD officers) were among those identified
(Paperno, 2001: 95). On the other hand, they emphasised the
Jewishness of the NKVD personnel who committed the crime, when
this was evident, as well as the Jewishness of their informants. The
images of the disfigured and putrefying corpses from Katyń and
Vinnytsia were meant to serve "as proof of the 'Judeo-Bolshevik'
(and Judeo-Russian) terror aimed against the Ukrainian population"
(Paperno, 2001: 96),[25] as well as to intimidate the entire continent
by showing its people "what fate awaited all European nations from
the Bolshevik murderous plague" (qtd. in Wajda, 2008: 82), as the
voiceover accompanying the documentary footage tells us. They
were also meant to justify the extermination of the Jews in the occupied territories. By the time Germans were busy recording the extent
and the brutality of the Soviet crimes, they had largely completed
the extermination of the Jews from Vinnytsia (Paperno, 2001: 96–7).
Thus, in the German documentary, these deaths – those killed by the
NKVD and Nazis, function in different registers of materiality and
recognition, where the materiality of one is the absence of the other,
where the recognition of one requires the negation of the other.
We can see the cinematic frame within which these representations
appear, then, "as active, as jettisoning and presenting, and as doing
both at once, in silence, without a visible sign of its operation and
yet effectively" (Butler, 2007: 953).

We know very little about the potential traumatic impact these
films may have had on their respective audiences across Europe when
they first encountered their images. Crucial to their traumatic potential is the prior absence of such images: although the destructiveness

of the First World War was unprecedented and modern memory has since been haunted by its experience, "the images associated with it remained predominantly archaic images of individual suffering and heroism" (Hüppauf, 1993: 51) that negated the modernity of the war. On the other hand, many critics have claimed that the moment the West first encountered the photographs and newsreel films taken by the British and American armies during the liberation of the Nazi concentration camps in 1945 – the images of the bulldozer moving corpses into enormous mass graves at Bergen-Belsen, wagons full of corpses at Dachau, half-dead and sick survivors in the camp at Buchenwald – constituted "a major epistemological shift in modern Western history" (Hirsch, 2004: 14). In Deborah Staines' words, the corpses that appeared here "in a new formation – 'the masses'", "re-articulated the way modern bodies could be made visible" (2002: 18). Reproduced over and over again, these images of the liberation have long become part of the West's collective visual memory. As Marianne Hirsch, along with many others has argued, these "tropes of Holocaust memory" have also become "tropes for photography" (2001: 16); latently present in our cultural imaginary, they structure our view of contemporary atrocities. However, even though the Nazi and Soviet Katyń films were widely disseminated during the war, from 1943 onwards (and even though they predated the photographic documentation of the liberation of the camps), this did not ensure their visibility after the war; today, the images of the pits at Katyń and Vinnytsia are not immediately recognisable. Furthermore, while the documentary film *Nazi Concentration Camps* by George Stevens, based on the documentary footage taken by the Allies during the liberation of the camps, was used as trial evidence at the International Military Tribunal in Nuremberg in 1945, as well as at the trial of Adolf Eichmann in Jerusalem in 1961 (Douglas, 1995), the documentary footage of the Katyń atrocities was not employed in the Nuremberg proceedings. In his memoirs, Churchill wrote that: "It was decided by the victorious Governments concerned that the issue should be avoided, and the crime of Katyń was never probed in detail" (qtd. in Zaslavsky, 2008: 63). Following Nuremberg, the West maintained an agonising silence in the face of the Soviet Union's falsehoods surrounding the Katyń case for half a century. These inclusions and exclusions constitute an essential part of the European "regimes of memory" (Radstone and Hodgkin, 2003) in the second half of the twentieth century, a point to which I will return shortly.

At the end of Wajda's film we see the Polish officers at the camp at Kozelsk in 1940 being led in groups outside the camp's gate, as if to freedom. The sequence is accompanied by the mournful return of memory and history through a voiceover commentary based on an authentic testimony found in the diary of Major Solski, unearthed by the Polish Red Cross at Katyń in 1943. Facing imminent death, Solski wrote:

> Five in the morning. The day started peculiarly. The prison vans departed. We were taken to the forest, something like a summer camp. We were searched carefully. They asked about my wedding ring, which they didn't find. They confiscated my belt, army knife. They also took my watch; it is 8:30, 6:30 Polish time. What will happen to us? (qtd. in Wajda, 2008: 184)

These were his last words. The film ends with a brutal, almost unwatchable, depiction of systematic murder. Echoing written descriptions of eyewitnesses from the Polish Red Cross commission, it shows how some of the prisoners were shot indoors individually, by surprise, and their bodies subsequently transported. Such was the fate of the prisoners at the Ostashkov and Starobelsk camps. Others were shot in Katyń forest, fully aware of their fate, at the edge of enormous burial ditches. Those who struggled were hooded before being shot at the back of the head; others went to their deaths quietly. The bulldozers then pushed dirt onto the mass graves. The final words of the film come from composer Krzysztof Penderecki's oratorio *"Requiem aeternam dona eis"* – "Eternal rest grant unto them!"

Wajda's depiction raises numerous questions. In the end, given the irreparable nature of this event, of what use is this itinerary of terror? Does it do more than provide evidence of what we cannot change, or quell the uncertainty and doubt regarding the identity of the perpetrators of the crime? Does a trauma like Katyń, which was characterised by silence and denial for half a century, require this extraordinary degree of repetition? Does this ending point to an ethical duty to keep impressions of the dead alive in the aftermath of their violent death? Was Wajda, in his anxious quest for the most effective form of transmitting this memory to younger generations, following Nietzsche's insight that pain is key in fashioning memory? ("If something is to stay in the memory," writes Nietzsche, "it must be burned in: only that which never ceases to hurt stays in the memory" [1989: 61].) Is the will to remember here counterposed and in opposition to the active need to forget – that mode of forgetfulness, perhaps necessary for robust health, which enables subjects to ingest and incorporate experience but also to digest and expel it? Or is the symbolic repetition of trauma a necessary aspect of working through loss and of "letting go" of the lost object? In other words, is the return to the scene of a crime that cries out to be remembered a necessary step, as Wajda's film suggests, in the process of letting go of past traumas?

Asked in an interview about the impact he thought the film would have in Poland Wajda stated: "If my film has an impact I hope it's going to be atoning, soothing, because for the first time the crime – the lie – has been shown on the screen."[26] Pressed to answer whether he thought that the film may change the way people thought about the massacre and Poland's relations with Russia, he responded: "I wanted this film to be a farewell, an end to the subject. What I didn't want was for it to cause any political problems, any conflicts. I just wanted it to end the subject."[27] On one hand, it would seem that Wajda's emphasis on remembering and working through the past injury exposes an insatiable desire for curatives, for healing. However, on the other hand – to return to one of my earlier questions – if the purported goal of the film was "atoning," as the director states here, then why does his film end with such a stark, perhaps even accusatory, portrayal of the executions? It seems to me that his ambiguous mention of "atoning" (for who is to do the work of atoning here?), despite his claims to the contrary, suggests an inability to "get over" the past.

The Katyń trauma seems to remain an open wound deeply engraved into the Polish collective memory. As Ewa Thompson notes, "Of all the murders of Poles by the Soviets this one is best remembered" (2005: 8). We could even argue that the Katyń tragedy could be seen as an instance of "chosen trauma," which Vamik Volkan defines as "the transgenerational transmission of . . . a shared traumatic event . . . linked to the past generation's inability to mourn losses of people, land or prestige," which "indicates the large group's failure to reverse narcissistic injury and humiliation inflicted by another large group, usually a neighbour" (2001: 87). According to

Volkan, the term "reflects a large group's unconscious 'choice' to add a past generation's mental representation of an event to its own identity, and the fact that, while groups may have experienced any number of traumas in their history, only certain ones remain alive over centuries" (Volkan, 2001: 88). The reasons for an inability of Poles to gain a sense of closure and move beyond this past seem both political and psychological. On one hand, it took a long time for the truth about Katyń to emerge and gain recognition. But on the other, it would seem that Poles have so become invested in the wound that the wound has come to stand for identity itself.

The Katyń case is also symptomatic of the persistent difficulty in Russians coming to terms with the repressed suffering and transgressions of the Soviet era,[28] the reasons for which lie to a large extent in the sheer scope and nature of the Soviet terror, which included brutal state-led efforts at modernisation (for example, "dekulakization"; the Ukrainian famine, and so forth), the arrest and deportation of targeted nationalities in the 1930s and 1940s, crimes directly related to the Second World War and its aftermath, and many others.[29] Apart from the long-awaited admission of guilt regarding the Katyń crime, the truth about the mass murder of the regime's own subjects has also been slow to emerge. Since the late 1980s, numerous mass-grave sites created by Stalin's NKVD containing the remains of tens of thousands of victims have been uncovered across the Soviet Union.[30] But while for some the bodies represented a tangible sign of the final break with the past regime, over the last two decades there has been neither a proper explanation nor a proper commemoration of their deaths.[31]

The difficulties in recalling traumatic experiences from the Soviet era further remind us of the comparative silence with which Western Europe regards this memory: while all sorts of cultural and historical remembrance evoke the crimes of Nazism and Fascism, comparable markers of the crimes of Stalinism are much fewer. By comparison, historians in the countries of the former Soviet Bloc have only just begun to revise their understanding of Soviet domination, and to reappraise the consequences of communism (Jarausch and Lindenberger, 2007: 6). Yet the status of that "wound" – along with legal and socio-psychological implications – remains contested and ambivalent to this day. At the pan-European ceremonies held in Gdańsk on 1 September 2009, on occasion of the seventieth anniversary of the outbreak of the Second World War, the Poles and the Baltic states pressed Russia to atone for Stalin's collusion with Nazi Germany, while Putin rejected a comparison of Stalinist repression with Nazi German genocide and the demands for Russian accountability. As Thompson notes, "When the collective memories of neighbouring countries differ so dramatically, it is virtually impossible to achieve closure" (Thompson, 2005: 8).

As I point out in the book's Introduction, the vocabulary of grievance that infuses the recent "work" of mourning through the difficult Soviet legacy in the Baltic region (but also elsewhere in Europe), has deflected attention away from pain and other less tangible traces of the past occasioned by the enormous losses from the Second World War. Wajda, whose father was among the Polish officers killed by the NKVD in Kharkov in 1940, knows this hurt. As he confesses, "I remember well the disquiet, hope, and desperation of my mother, who, until her death in 1950, waited for a sign from father, a prisoner of war in Starobelsk" (2008: 97). Much of his film is devoted to picturing the fates of women in similar circumstances to those of his mother. He shows the mother and the wife of a cavalry captain awaiting his return even after the war has ended, until they come into possession of his diary that reveals to them the last hours of his life; the sister of a Polish pilot murdered at Katyń, who like Sophocles' Antigone, chooses to mourn the death of her brother openly even though it goes against the sovereign law, leading to her disappearance into the darkness of the secret police underground prison; and the wife of a Polish general also murdered in Katyń, who suffers pain, loneliness, and resentment. In a short sequence, Wajda also depicts the deportations of the families of the Polish POWs to the Soviet Union, while leaving us to imagine their fates.

A recently published assembly of impassioned, conflicting testimonies of the deported children of the Katyń victims (Kaczorowska, 2006) now tells us about the separation, adversity and survival endured in Soviet and German camps, permanent exile, and of losses that cannot be undone. The stories in these pages, along with the dramas of the families depicted in *Katyń*, confront us with all that is incommensurable and unquantifiable when it comes to their pain. Like the stories of women and children depicted in Wajda's film, their testimonies repeatedly remind us that there may never be enough expressions of individual or national justice, reparation, guilt, pain, or anger to make up for the wounds cleaved into the Polish psyche, remembered as inconsolability itself. Revealing all that cannot be healed, they undermine the hope that grievance can adequately do the work of mourning. Like Wajda's characters, they demonstrate that there is no simple "moving on" from or "getting over" that history. Yet, as Sara Ahmed reminds us, the "solitariness of pain is intimately tied up with its implication in relationship with others" (2004: 29). In other words, pain requires acknowledgement; if it is witnessed it can be granted "the status of an event, a happening in the world" (29). She signals a tension between the impossibility of sharing pain and the necessity for an ethics of pain that is witnessed by another. This paradox points to the importance of seeking and examining ways to attend and represent the pain of others so it might be witnessed, if not vanquished, despite the difficulty of such a project.

Pain, ethics, and politics are also central to the final thoughts that I wish to offer here. I want to attend to a lacuna *in Katyń's* content, which is difficult yet important to articulate. This lacuna concerns the representation of loss in Wajda's film, which, I would like to propose, oscillates between mourning, where there is a recognition of what has been lost, and melancholia, which stands for the relation with the disavowed past. Earlier I pointed to the affirmative, healing quality of Wajda's film (as did many critics elsewhere, as well as the director himself). The Katyń victims may have died as isolated individuals, the argument goes, but their witnessing by the film's audiences in contemporary Poland could be seen as a ritual of incorporation into the social body from which the dead had been subtracted by violence. The healing of the wound inflicted in Katyń is represented as the healing of the nation; the covering over the wound allows the nation to become whole again. According to Anne Applebaum, with *Katyń* Wajda "wanted to create something that would get Poles to talk to one another, to reflect upon common experiences, to define common values, to admire similar virtues, to forge a civil society out of an anonymous crowd" (2008: 4). In Applebaum's view, "*Katyń* is deliberately intended to inspire patriotism, in the most positive sense of the word" (2008: 4). As such, the film appeals strongly to "Poles' need for national identification at the beginning of the twenty-first century" (Falkowska, 2007: 262). However, and this is my point, in Wajda's film some losses come to embody the collective loss more than others. Some losses are taken in as "ours," and others excluded. Polish-Jewish losses suffered at Katyń do not appear as losses at all.

As I point out in the book's Introduction, in their reading of Freud's "Mourning and Melancholia," Nicolas Abraham and Maria Torok have criticised the misleading synonymy between introjection and incorporation that he posited. They insist on the necessity of recognising incorporation, rather than introjection, as defining all possible pathological forms of mourning. They have also introduced the concept of a "psychic crypt," a space effected by a disavowal of loss in which the other is kept inside the self unconsciously, as though buried alive. For Abraham and Torok:

> Incorporation results from those losses that for some reason cannot be acknowledged as such. The words that cannot be uttered, the scenes that cannot be recalled, the tears that cannot be shed – everything will be swallowed along with the trauma that led to that loss. Swallowed and preserved. Inexpressible mourning erects a tomb inside the subject. (1994: 128)

Thus, incorporation of the object, which brings about the melancholic condition, emerges out of a failure of symbolisation. Bringing this model of intrapsychic structure and dynamics in relation to Wajda's film, it could be said that while *Katyń* can certainly be seen as an expression of (nationalist) mourning, it also reveals the presence of latent melancholia, an inability to mourn adequately. This inability manifests itself in the forgetting of the detail of difference regarding the losses that the film invokes.

For, as Anna Cienciala reminds us, "about 10 percent of all Polish Army officer prisoners were Jewish" (2008: 28).[32] In Simon Schochet's estimate, 462 Polish Jews lost their lives at Katyń (1989), but it is believed that this number was much higher. In a preface to the memoirs of Solomon W. Slowes, a Polish-Jewish officer who survived the camps, Władysław Bartoszewski notes that about 1,000 Jewish officers perished in Katyń, including Major Baruch Steinberg, the chief Rabbi of the Polish Armed Forces (1992: xiv). These facts, though they sometimes make their way into the historiography of Katyń, are hardly registered in popular collective awareness; they remain, for the most part, in a sphere of denial. In Wajda's *Katyń* too, the Polish-Jewish losses are absorbed into the traditional nationalistic scripts of Polish martyrdom. This elision in the film's content, which is otherwise infused with Christian iconography, thus works to reinforce the dominant notion of Polish identity, free from the unsettling and "diluting" influence of the other.[33] While in Kantor's *Let the Artists Die* bereaved memory manifests itself merely as "a trace eluding all attempts at appropriation," Wajda's film shows that "even the contestation of political prohibitions that establish the boundaries between grievable and ungrievable lives can still repeat the repudiation of unspeakable losses within the public performance of mourning" (Plonowska Ziarek, 2006: 153, 151).

My attention to the simultaneity of recognition and disavowal at work in Wajda's film is not meant to eclipse its significance or Wajda's important contribution to the discussion of the "Jewish question" in Poland. In several of his films such as *Korczak, Holy Week,* and *Pan Tadeusz* (1999) Wajda has dealt overtly with Judaism and the Polish-Jewish relationship. But, if one of Wajda's goals with *Katyń* was to bequeath a painful memory to the young generation, especially "those moviegoers for whom it matters that we are a society, and not just an accidental crowd" (2008: 3), as he put it recently, then this omission should give us pause. His silence about the Polish-Jewish losses suffered at Katyń is all the more puzzling in light of the ongoing re-evaluation of Polish national identity and the place of Jews in it (see, e.g. Polonsky and Michlic, 2004; Glowacka and Zylinska, 2007), which was invigorated recently by Jan Gross's book about the murder of the Jewish residents of the small town of Jedwabne by their non-Jewish neighbours in July 1941. We may even say that the symbolic exhumation of the Polish losses in Wajda's film (cleansed of all Jewish traces), and the unprecedented media attention it received at home, *screen* (in a Freudian sense) the symbolic dimension of the recent exhumation of Jedwabne's victims' remains during the inquiry by the Polish Institute of National Memory. But if one of the film's main tasks was to commemorate a national trauma, to reconstruct the vitality and identity of the nation in the wake of the event, then, in present-day Poland, this task also includes a radical rethinking and reformulation of the very notions of boundaries and borderlines regulating exchange between the inside and the outside, between self and other, indigenous and foreign. As Ewa Plonowska Ziarek has argued, it is only by exercising a certain capacity of moral hospitality to its other and working through the painful past "that contemporary Poland stands a chance of inventing new, more ethical modes of collectivity and solidarity, no longer predicated on the narcissistic investment in its own suffering but more concerned with the responsibility for the suffering of others" (2007: 322). Working through the past here does not mean a taking leave of the past or a facile integration of the lost other, nor is it reducible to individual grieving. Rather, it entails "a re-visioning of Polish identity that incorporates the historical reality of Poland as a set of multicultural communities, each distinct in historical and social development but all linked by common experiences of citizenship, occupation, violence, and loss" (Holc, 2005: 325).

Entire histories and identities were buried at Katyń. After their long sojourn in the earth, they resurfaced once more on Kantor's stage and Wajda's screen, forcing their audiences to become excavators of these lives and pasts. In Kantor's performance these historical remnants are exposed in disarray, placing upon the spectators the task of locating the displaced artefacts and organising a mnemonic field of the dead. Wajda's film has also renewed our affective engagement with this past by mixing reality and fiction, while serving as a reminder that we are all responsible for what we make visibly available and want to share. In the face of the trauma of Katyń, these artists neither give us justice nor assert the redemptive value of bearing witness. Instead, they make us acknowledge that which can never leave us. Moreover, they remind us that the ethics of digging up bodies, both literal and metaphorical, should be based upon more than an instrumental relation to the traumas of the past.[34]

Marked by loss: mourning and melancholia in Kantor's *I Shall Never Return*

As I have shown in my analysis of *Wielopole, Wielopole* and *Let the Artists Die*, memory as mourning and melancholy is central to Tadeusz Kantor's "Theatre of Death." Indeed, one can argue that each of the performances from this cycle, from *The Dead Class* to *Today Is My Birthday* (*Dziś są moje urodziny*, 1990), moves through the mortuary zones of grief and mourning. Positioned within the Polish discourse of national remembrance in which they intervene, these performances draw their effectiveness from the irreparable wounds of trauma, to which they appeal. In this sense, they aim precisely to summon up the presentness of memory, to insist on the unfinished business: guilt and reparation remain the dominant themes. Embracing not only the past, but also the future, they open spaces for cultural convalescence to be achieved through the performance of mourning.

Here I will discuss *I Shall Never Return*, the penultimate production of Kantor's "Theatre of Death," which commemorates the death of his father who perished in Auschwitz.[35] Engaging recent conceptualisations of mourning and melancholia articulated by Nicolas Abraham and Maria Torok, Jacques Derrida, and Judith Butler, I argue that for most of his lifetime Kantor was unable to mourn the loss of his father, not only because the loss was painful and traumatic, but also because of the ambivalence felt towards him. I suggest that Kantor incorporated and encrypted this loss inside himself until late in his life, beginning the process of mourning only after a discovery he made about his father in 1984. While I argue that it is precisely this process of coming to terms with the loss of his father that Kantor stages in *I Shall Never Return*, I also show that this performance should not be understood as expressive of a singular subjective account of loss, but as reaching outward towards the collective sites of memory, history, and trauma.

But before I move on with my analysis of *I Shall Never Return*, I would like to mention a few details from Kantor's biography that crucially inform this performance. Tadeusz Kantor was the second child of Helena Kantor, née Berger (1880–1962) and Marian Kantor-Mirski (1884–1942). Kantor's father never returned home to his family after he went with the Second Division of the Polish Legion to fight in the First World War. Upon leaving the army on 15 December 1921, he first settled in Sląsk (Silesia), and then in Zagłębie Dąbrowskiego, before finally returning to Tarnów, his home town, in 1938. On 8 September 1940 he was arrested and put in a prison in Tarnów, from which he was deported to the Auschwitz concentration camp on 20 February 1942. He was executed there on 1 April 1942.[36] In *I Shall Never Return* Kantor quotes the telegram that was sent to his mother by German authorities in which she was notified that her husband died of a "heart attack."

As Marie-Thérèse Vido-Rzewuska has suggested, "The fact that his father never returned is one of the major ambiguities of Kantor's work" (1995: 233).[37] She has also argued that Kantor's attitude to his father changed after he attended a conference dedicated to the memory of Marian Kantor-Mirski. Organised by the Zagłębie Museum in Będzin in June of 1984, the conference celebrated Kantor-Mirski's accomplishments as a soldier (he was decorated with the "Cross of Merit" and the "French Order of Victory"), and as an ethnologist who wrote a number of papers about the history of Silesia – the accomplishments that played a part in his arrest and confinement in Auschwitz. Participating in this event allowed Kantor to see his father in a new light. As Vido-Rzewuska describes, Kantor emerged from the conference "quite shattered, saying, 'Why did I only get evil reports of him?'" (1995: 235). The blurred image of Kantor's father – the result of first his absence, and then his untimely death – introduces a degree of uncertainty and indirectness to the considerations of his influence on the author, which nevertheless testify to the strength of this influence. Some kind of disguise, metamorphosis, or recontextualisation accompanies the continuing influence of the dead. In this essay I propose that this influence is most intelligible in *I Shall Never Return*, where Kantor stages the return of his dead father as the return of the mythical figure of Odysseus.

Significantly, this was not the first time that the figure of Odysseus appeared in Kantor's theatre. On 21, June 1944, in Cracow, Kantor and his Underground Theatre troupe illegally staged *The Return of Odysseus* (*Powrót Odysa*, 1904–07), a play written by Stanisław Wyspiański (1869–1907), the creator of the "Polish Theatre of Death."[38] Wyspiański's play, written in 1904 and published shortly before his death in 1907, belongs to the last stage of his work in which the theme of death is predominant. In this text, the playwright closely followed Dante's bold reappropriation of Homer in the Ulysses canto (canto 26) of *Purgatorio*. While in *The Divine Comedy* Odysseus is sent to hell in punishment for destroying Troy, Wyspiański's protagonist suffers from traumatic memories related to the siege of Troy and his long voyage home. That Kantor's decision to stage this play in Cracow in 1944 was influenced by its topicality at the time is suggested by the fact that Odysseus in this performance was presented as a German soldier returning from Stalingrad.[39]

The sense of estrangement between the son and the father thematised in Wyspiański's play may also have had strong bearings on the young Kantor. In a comment written on the margins of his stage script (*partytura*) of *The Return of Odysseus* from 1944 Kantor underlined this feeling: "Father is back after years of war. They have little in common now, father and son, and little to say to each other. All their attempts to come close to each other remain futile and ludicrous" (Kantor n.d.d: 5).[40] Furthermore, after Odysseus kills a herdsman in Act I of Wyspiański's play, Telemachus kills another servant with an identical gesture and is overwhelmed by a feeling of joy and euphoria. In this way, Wyspiański illustrates not only a violent legacy bequeathed from one generation to another, but also a strong urge on the part of the son to identify with his ego ideal (father). Considering the ambivalent feelings that Kantor had for his father, I believe that this motif may have provided the subterranean motivation for his decision to stage the play both in 1944 and in 1988.[41]

However, it is only with his performance of *I Shall Never Return* that Kantor makes an ingenious use of Wyspiański's play as a figural vehicle for his act of bearing witness to Auschwitz and the death of his father. The artist may have drawn his inspiration here from the first act of Wyspiański's drama where the author puts into doubt the ontological status of his protagonist, when in his address to the Herdsman Odysseus says: "You know, old man, maybe I'm a ghost and frighten people" (1966: 12). The precedent was already established by Dante whose Ulysses and his men are swallowed up in open sea beyond the Pillars of Hercules, in sight of Mount Paradise, and at the pleasure of the Christian God. Analogous to Ulysses and his companion Diomedes, who return only as a speaking flame encountered by Dante and Virgil in purgatory in order to tell their story of passing the limit and a consequent submersion, Kantor's father returns to Ithaca (Cracow) only as a spectre on his son's stage.[42] Thus, in the aftermath of Auschwitz, Kantor rewrites Wyspiański so as to substitute for Odysseus's return to Ithaca a very different story, in which return is resignified once again.

The trope of return is crucial for Kantor's theatre practice. Commenting on his wartime staging of Wyspiański, in a 1980 prose piece entitled "The Infamous Transition from the World of the Dead into the World of the Living (Fiction and Reality)," Kantor wrote:

> It is not merely the war and Troy that Odysseus returned from. More importantly, he returned from "out of the grave," from the

realm of the dead, from the "other world" into the sphere of life, into the realm of the living, he appeared among us. *The Return of Odysseus* established a precedent and a prototype for all later characters of my theatre. (1993: 145)[43]

On another occasion Kantor offered a similar definition of his theatre:

I hold that theatre is a ford across the river. It is a place through which the dead figures from that shore, from that world, cross over into our world and now into our lives. . . . And what happens next? The answer might be given by the Dybbuk . . . the spirits of the dead who enter into the bodies of others and speak through them. (Pleśniarowicz, 1994a: 145)

The idea of the dybbuk, "the soul of a dead person who has not come to complete rest" (Rokem, 2000: 54), which inhabits the body of a living person, speaking through the mouth of the host, is a potent metaphor for Kantor's theatre. His productions could be thought of essentially as a raising of the dead. As we shall also see later, the old Jewish scenarios of dybbuk possession and exorcism bear some striking similarities to the psychoanalytic process of incorporative melancholia, which I will employ here in order to illuminate the work of mourning performed in Kantor's *I Shall Never Return*.

Kantor sees each work as both text and pretext for further texts and performances. I would propose that what Jeanette Malkin claims for Heiner Müller's intertextual approach to writing could be equally said of Kantor's: both approaches are "impregnated by a view of memory as coexistent with the present" (1999: 79), a view that their collage texts and performances further encourage. According to Denis Bablet, with his 1988 production of *The Return of Odysseus* Kantor wanted to create a retrospective of his theatrical career, from the war times to the present moment. While he initially considered restaging *Balladyna* by Juliusz Słowacki, the first performance he staged in his underground theatre in 1942, he finally opted for Wyspiański's piece. In Bablet's estimate, the text "held an evident advantage over *Balladyna* (hardly known abroad). It came from the very heart of European mythology" (1989: 153).

Kantor's *I Shall Never Return* is a palimpsest composed not only of Kantor's texts, performance sequences, and characters from his earlier productions, but also of parts and particles from such diverse cultural artefacts as myth, autobiography, dreams, literary paraphrase, quotation, and self-citation. The story of the return of Odysseus is presented in the form of recycled images and sequences from Kantor's earlier performances: *Wielopole, Wielopole, Dainty Shapes and Hairy Apes*, and *The Dead Class*, "building up a structure of interlocking memories as audiences experience each new element of the work as haunted by the experience of previous works" (Carlson, 2001: 104).[44] Towards the middle of the performance, after a wedding ceremony between a Dead Bride and a Young-Kantor-Mannequin a knocking at the door is heard. A Cleaning Woman rushes and opens the door. In the doorframe stands the Ghost of Odysseus. In one of his guides for the performance Kantor writes:

> He comes from the depths of time./ Wartime, 1944./ But it's only his R E M A I N S./ As if they had been pulled out of the grave./ A Military Uniform,/ Stretched out, like on a cross./ . . . And, from somewhere above we hear a voice saying: " . . . I am Odysseus,/ Lord of Ithaca./" The Cleaning Woman cries:/ "On the night of January 24 / 1944/ Odysseus returned to Kraków,/ his Ithaca." (n.d.c: 319–20)

A repeated knocking is heard. There is a new guest in the doorframe – the spectre of Kantor's father. It is a mannequin bound to a pillory with a rope, like Odysseus to the mast of his ship. A machine gun is fastened to the pillory, and points at the back of the father's head. We hear the song "Ani maamin," and then the voice from a loudspeaker, "I died on 24 January / 1944 / That same date" (Kantor, n.d.c: 319–20). The voice that we hear, however, does not belong to the spectre of Kantor's father, but to his son Tadeusz. The phrase, "That same date," refers to the explanatory lines of the Cleaning Woman from the previous sequence when she announced the date of Odysseus's return to Cracow. While Kantor's first staging of Wyspiański's *The Return of Odysseus* took place in occupied Cracow on 21 June 1944, in *I Shall Never Return* the artist has Odysseus return to the same war-torn city for the first time on 24 January 1944, the same day that he remembers receiving the news of his father's death in Auschwitz (Lawson, 1995: 433).

To mourn effectively is to dispense with the dead; to mourn unsuccessfully is to remain permeable to the dead. As David Savran suggests:

> virtually every ghost in the contemporary theatre signals a crisis in the constitution of the subject, for whom the ghost represents an other who has been lost and yet is imagined to inhere both inside and outside the self. For these bereaved subjects, the ghost functions as a symptom of a melancholic process whereby the subject attempts to incorporate that which he or she has lost. (2000: 121)

To refuse or to be unable either to mourn or to stop mourning is to encourage the admission of a foreign body into oneself that will play havoc with all manner of fortifications and defence, in an exemplary disruption of understanding. Such may be the painful consequences of the death of a father, and of the preservation of the dead father.

Kantor's *I Shall Never Return* marks such unresolved, deeply personal loss. However, as Freud observed, finding in archaeological excavation a metaphor for the psychoanalytic recovery of the past, that which is shoved "underground" into the unconscious and sealed up may simply be better preserved. "There is, in fact, no better analogy for repression, by which something in the mind is at once made inaccessible and preserved," wrote Freud, "than burial of the sort to which Pompeii fell victim and from which it could emerge once more through the work of spades" (1953–72: 40). As we shall see, in *I Shall Never Return* that which is buried down also comes up to the surface, reiterating that what is sealed up or forced under does not disappear, but festers until the moment when it can erupt into consciousness once again. Following Vido-Rzewuska, I suggest that for Kantor this moment came in 1984, when he attended the exhibition which honoured the memory of his father, after which he was able to begin the process of grieving and "decorporation" of the cryptic object.

Let us remember here that, for Freud, melancholia is characterised by the inability of the subject to separate itself from the object and thus recognise what has been lost, while a successful work of mourning constitutes an articulated reaction to loss. Julia Kristeva, too, saw the "cure" for melancholy in interpretation and representation in addition to cathartic exercises, such as art, religion, and literature, which discharge drive and affect associated with the repressed (1989: 24). In line with this thinking, one could argue that Kantor's act of calling up the theatrical ghost of his father, allowing him to tell his story in *I Shall Never Return*, could be seen as signifying the process of transforming melancholia into mourning, unconscious into conscious.

Writing after Freud, Nicolas Abraham and Maria Torok make a distinction between "introjection," a mechanism of so-called normal mourning where the object of loss is acknowledged as lost, and "incorporation," which characterises mourning where the object of loss cannot be dispensed with. The latter mechanism belongs more properly, therefore, to melancholy – the state of disavowed or suspended grief in which the object is magically sustained "in the body" in some way.[45] For Maria Torok "incorporation" intervenes when introjection, for any reason, fails. According to Derrida, "cryptic incorporation always marks an effect of impossible or refused mourning" (1986: xxi). Mourning that is impossible, refused, or unaccomplished represents the failure or unwillingness to settle debts with the past, to abandon a loved one – the father, say – to the past, to a dead memory. But to stay in touch in this way, to perpetuate an identification by incorporating a loved object, involves never being able to come to terms with a death of the loved one. In Abraham and Torok's words, "incorporation is the refusal to acknowledge the full import of the loss, a loss that, if recognised as such, would effectively transform us" (1994: 127).

But how can the dead live inside someone? Where would they find "lodging"? Abraham and Torok use the concept of the crypt to designate a unique intrapsychic topography that inexpressible mourning erects inside the subject as a secret tomb that houses the dead "other" as "living." They see the crypt as a formation constituted through the fantasy of incorporation, which simulates introjection. In "Mourning *or* Melancholia," Abraham and Torok describe the crypt's structure as follows:

> Reconstituted from the memory of words, scenes, and affects, the objectal correlative of the loss is buried alive in the crypt as a full-fledged person, complete with its own topography. The crypt also includes the actual or supposed traumas that made

introjection impracticable. A whole world of unconscious fantasy is created, one that leads its own separate and concealed existence. Sometimes in the dead of night, when libidinal fulfilments have their way, the ghost of the crypt comes back to haunt the cemetery guard. (1994: 130)

Thus, mourning that operates – or fails to operate – by incorporation can never be reconciled to the lost object that it is able to preserve. Incorporative mourning keeps the loved object at bay by including it within the ego. In other words, the loved object can be included within the ego only if it is at the same time withheld, held in. According to Derrida:

Incorporation is a kind of theft to reappropriate the pleasure object. But that reappropriation is simultaneously rejected: which leads to a paradox of a foreign body preserved as foreign but by the same token excluded from a self that henceforth deals not with the other, but only with itself. The more the self keeps the foreign element as a foreigner inside itself, the more it excludes it. The self *mimes* introjection. But this mimicry with its redoubtable logic depends on clandestinity. Incorporation negotiates clandestinely with a prohibition it neither accepts nor transgresses. (1986: xvii)

Such incorporation ensures that what is perpetually disavowed will always return, even if what perpetually returns continues to be disavowed. Cryptogenic incorporation is, among other things, the means by which a loved one is neither "digested" in the mind, nor vomited out. Derrida describes incorporation as "an act of vomiting to the inside;" cryptic incorporation involves a process – neither purely a fantasy, nor the consequence of a "real" event – of "eating the object (through the mouth or otherwise) . . . in order to vomit it, in a way, into the inside, into the pocket of a cyst" (1986: xxxviii). A door is silently sealed off like a condemned passageway inside the self.

Discussing the phenomenon of melancholic incorporation, Abraham and Torok further assert that the "shadow of the object . . . comes back to haunt by being *reincarnated in the person of the subject.*" The moment of uncanniness is brought about through the shadow-effect of the other that, in Abraham and Torok's terms, "*carries the ego* [or some other façade] *as its mask*" (1994: 141). Where the phantom (i.e. an incorporated object) indicates a rift in the ego, it returns to haunt its host through a mechanism that, according to these authors, "consists of exchanging one's own identity for a fantasmatic identification with the 'life' – beyond the grave – of an object of love . . . " (1994: 142). Although it takes many forms in endocryptic identification, "the 'I' is understood as the lost object's fantasised ego" (1994: 148) that haunts the subject through a kind of ventriloquism. As Judith Butler further explains, "The experience of loss compels the subject to incorporate that other into the very structure of the ego, taking on attributes of the other and 'sustaining' the other through magical acts of imitation" (1990: 57). I propose that it is precisely this act of melancholic sustenance that is dramatised in *I Shall Never Return*.

Several scenes in the performance, in which Kantor identifies with his father, suggest such an act. During a wedding ceremony, for example, a Priest recites the marriage service to a couple addressing a Young Tadeusz Kantor Mannequin as Marian Kantor, and a Dead Bride as Helena Berger, Kantor's mother. Even without this explicit address, the intertextual reference to Kantor's parents' wedding ceremony from *Wielopole, Wielopole* in this scene establishes a certain parallelism, and suggests Kantor's identification with his father. Moreover, as already mentioned, after the appearance of Marian Kantor's mannequin in the midst of the performance, it is Tadeusz Kantor's voice that comes from the loudspeaker, and says: "I died on 24 January 1944." This too, I believe, implies that the oscillation between the "self" (Kantor) and the "other" (his father) is precarious. Finally, in the description of one of the last scenes provided in one of his performance guides Kantor makes his identification with the father figure/Odysseus quite explicit when he writes: "Odysseus (mannequin) departs for ever. I remain. I – Odysseus" (n.d.c: 331).[46]

Because the melancholic (unlike the mourner) refuses to relinquish the love-object, "internalisation becomes a strategy of magically resuscitating the lost object, not only because the loss is painful, but because the ambivalence felt toward the object requires that the object be retained until the differences are settled" (1990: 61–2). Discovering a positive image of his father during the conference in Będzin enabled Kantor to start the process of mourning, namely "introjection" and "decorporation" of the cryptic object with the respect to his father. The false "I" was reconverted into the third person, as Kantor understood that it was possible to evoke the prodigal love of his father – the love of forgiveness and acceptance – without subjecting him to shame, or losing him morally. The entombed experience was acknowledged, and the crypt unlocked, its contents laid out in the open and recognised as the unalienable property of the subject. However, no totalising answer seems possible to the question whether this change means "letting an object go," whether mourning can be successful or not.

That mourning is and remains cryptic is suggested near the end of the performance, in the scene of an encounter between Kantor and the stage figure of his father (Odysseus), following the play-within-a-play representing the return of Odysseus (Figure 3.5). Here Kantor takes his stage-script from the 1944 production of Wyspiański's *The Return of Odysseus*, and sits down at the centre table at which Odysseus sits as well. He adjusts Odysseus's scarf, and lightly touches his hand. "But Odysseus, sitting stiffly / in his Wartime Uniform / gives one the impression / of a MANNEQUIN," writes Kantor (n.d.c: 330). What does this silent encounter tell us? Does this (im)possible return of the father ensure that what is outstanding between generations continues to be unresolved? It seems that the ambivalence between

Figure 3.5   Scene from rehearsals for Kantor's *I Shall Never Return*; photograph by Jacquie Bablet; courtesy of J. Bablet

son and father is renewed rather than dissipated. But if this suggests, in whatever way, a facility of transgenerational communion, this communion is shrouded in an overdetermined unintelligibility. The return of the father, the extraordinarily enduring influence of the dead, is achieved at the price of expository fluency, of the ability to act or communicate intelligibly. Kantor can renew contact with the dead, but this contact, it seems, tends not to the efficiency of understanding between generations, but to irresolution, to an uncertain communication that does not exhaust itself in a definitive reconciliation of the parties involved. The return of the dead, it could be said, coincides with certain interruptions of communication, which nevertheless indicate an uncanny communicative power.

As Kantor begins to read the lines from the third act of Wyspiański's *Return of Odysseus*,[47] he and Odysseus are joined by the Cleaning Woman, who sits by the table and starts translating the Polish text into Italian from the line "The shores of my fatherland:"

> I found a Hell in my own Fatherland,
> Entering a graveyard. . . .
> I slaughtered everything, pushed all away;
> And all deceptive happiness fled from me.
> Nothing, nothing behind me, or in front . . .
> . . .
> these shores of my fatherland, Ithaca . . .
> I raced along these paths in my boyhood,
> Chasing the birds – hey! Gulls fly over the seas:
> The birds of my youth . . .
> There! There! There is Ithaca!
> . . . There – is my fatherland . . .
> there is the song of my life consummate!
> No one – alive – finds out his childhood home . . .
> My fatherland – I've carried it in my heart,
> And now I carry it in my desire,
> Today I only long for it, a shade . . .
> A shade myself, I long after a shade . . .
> I hear a crowd . . .
> A boat full of people!
> They look at me – they call to me!
> . . .

I cannot make them out. Who may they be?
They call out – they complain – or, they rejoice?
The waves divide me from their voices, waves,
Dividing us – The boat of the dead![48]

(quoted in Kantor, n.d.c: 330–1)

The story being read by Kantor reflects the stage picture we see: to the sounds of *Salve Regina*, the stage figures follow Charon's boat in a stylistic representation of the crossing of the Styx. They all exit. After Kantor has finished his reading, Odysseus gets off the table, and starts leaving the stage. Then, suddenly, he turns and glances at Kantor. For the first time in the performance they look at each other. The two men enter each other's eyes, and thus a sense of communion, of repair or healing, of recognition might be felt. Then, as Kantor writes in his notes for the performance "Odysseus (mannequin) departs for ever. / I remain. I – Odysseus" (quoted in Kantor, n.d.c: 331).

Early on in this chapter I pointed out that the phenomenon of incorporative melancholia, which I engaged in order to illuminate the act of mourning enacted in Kantor's performance, could be seen as analogous to the process of dybbuk possession expressed in Jewish folklore. In the final part of this chapter, I would like to pursue this argument further in order to tease out a broader relevance of this claim for my analysis here. Dybbuk possession involved spirits of the dead as possessing agents, and as in other cultural variants of possession-as-disease, the exorcism of the dybbuk was construed as a patterned sequence of steps, through which the spirit's identity and posthumous vicissitudes were disclosed, and the conditions for its departure negotiated.

The mystical doctrine of transmigration of souls (*gilgul*), which provided the ideational basis in which the dybbuk phenomenon germinated, was formulated as early as the twelfth century (Scholem, 1971; Chajes, 2003). While most of the early cases of dybbuk possession were recorded in Italian and Middle Eastern Sephardic communities in the sixteenth and seventeenth centuries, "during the eighteenth and nineteenth centuries Eastern European Hasidic communities, mainly in Russia and Poland, supplied most of the reports" (Bilu, 1987: 165). According to Yoram Bilu, "the general disintegration of the Jewish traditional centers in Europe and the Middle East in our time has eliminated them altogether. As a result, no contemporary cases of dybbuk possession have been available since the 1930s" (1987: 163). S. Anski, the pseudonym for Shlomo Zanvil Rappoport, who from 1912 through 1914 conducted ethnographic expeditions to study Jewish communities in Volhynia and Podolia, revitalised these beliefs with his enormously successful play, *The Dybbuk*, performed in Yiddish by the Vilna troupe in 1920.[49]

In the play, a young woman, Leah, is possessed by the soul of her late beloved, on the day of her wedding to another man. The dybbuk speaks from within Leah, refusing to leave her body until painful exorcism is performed and certain secrets from the past revealed. From a psychoanalytic point of view, one could argue that the reason behind Leah's insanity is unfulfilled mourning, and that possession here could be seen as "a cultural device through which an intrapsychic conflict is assigned an 'interpersonal' dimension" (Bilu, 1987: 165). In this respect, the similarities in regards to the psyche's play between internal and external objects, between processes of identification and separation, at work in *The Dybbuk* and *I Shall Never Return*, are, I believe, overt. In both, the living cannot forget the dead and the dead refuse to be forgotten by the living.

In *I Shall Never Return* as well as his other "Theatre of Death" performances, Kantor reactivates historical scenarios of dybbuk possession (what Schechner calls "strips of behavior" [1985: 35]); he makes use of these historical antecedents for his theatrical practice in order to dramatise the scarce boundary between the living and the dead, the interpenetration of the dead with the world of the living. While Pierre Nora has famously argued that in the modern society textual memory (*lieux de mémoire*) has essentially replaced embodied memory (*milieux de mémoire*), Kantor's theatre shows the ways in which embodied memory operates in conjunction with the archive, here Anski's text, to create and sustain cultural memory.[50]

This becomes explicit in the last section of *I Shall Never Return*, which overtly transforms the subjectivity of grief into a broader historical and collective context, or, where, in Pleśniarowicz's words, "The end of the biography is identified with the end of the epoch" (1994a: 146). In this scene, titled "The Great Emballage of the End of the XXth century," a group of "Those Serious Gentlemen," the masters of power, spread black shrouds of oblivion over the figures and objects on the stage, thereby constructing a mountainous graveyard for a lifetime of Kantor's memories. The tune of the "Rakoczi March" from Berlioz's oratorio accompanies this act of annihilation. From this mass-grave Emballage, the priest's cross sticks out for a while only to disappear a moment later into the sea of black shrouds. Then, singing the old Hasidic chant "Ani maamin", replete with suffering, the Cleaning Woman/Songstress of the Promised Land slowly exhumes the corpses buried under this immense mourning veil – the memories will not be completely obliterated.[51] As she leads them away from the stage, the doors close after them for the last time.

As the finale of the performance strongly suggests, Kantor's Kaddish for his father – his most personal work, and his most heartfelt – is also his requiem for the twentieth century. Pleśniarowicz calls it Kantor's "most legible invocation of the Holocaust so far" (1994a: 142). As I attempted to demonstrate here, with this performance Kantor provides an example of a work of mourning in which the ghosts and phantoms of culture are to be entertained rather than exorcised. Like the rest of the performances from his "Theatre of Death," this performance of Kantor's is not the work of mourning in the Freudian sense. It does not enforce the gradual detachment of libido or desire from the object. Instead it reframes the question of mourning in ethical terms, thus functioning as a resonant text, a complicated web of temporality in which memory is not only taken in, introjected, or accrued, but reworked, projected, and given back to a collective subject, thus allowing the past to find a "place" within the identity of the remembering community.

4
Postmemory, Testimony, Affect

The grey zone of witnessing in Pinter's *Ashes to Ashes*

Pinter's *Ashes to Ashes* (1996) combines features of his early memory plays and his overtly political dramas, such as *One for the Road* (1984), *Mountain Language* (1988), and *Party Time* (1991), as well as his sketches *Precisely* (1983) and *The New World Order* (1991), which he started writing after the mid-1980s. As in *Landscape* (1967), which marks the beginning of Pinter's long and fruitful obsession with the subject of memory, the setting is a ground floor room in a country house, with a garden outside, where a woman – Rebecca, and a man, Devlin – talk about the past. It is the woman, again, who reminisces, while the man relentlessly and obsessively provokes the flood of memories with his questions. Yet, while in Pinter's early memory plays the past is always frozen into monologic "mindscapes" through the language, stage images, and the behaviour of his characters, *Ashes to Ashes* expands this self-circulation, transforming the subjectivity of grief into a broader historical, and collective, context.

All the memories reported in the play are elusive, amputated, fragmented. First, in an account in which the difference between compulsion and voluntary compliance gets oddly blurred, Rebecca recalls how her former lover – who may or may not have existed – would make her kiss his fist, and then she would ask him to put his hand round her throat. Rebecca initially describes this man as a "guide" or a "courier" for a travel agency, only soon thereafter to recall that he ran a factory that "wasn't the usual kind of factory," a reference, it would seem, to labour camps (1996, 19: 23).[1] He is also identified with a man "who would go to the local railway station and walk down the platform and tear all the babies from the arms of their screaming mothers" (27). While Devlin makes attempts to clarify her stories as well as to talk her back into the everyday life from which she seems so radically estranged, she goes on to describe images of people led to their deaths in the sea off the coast of Dorset and refugees walking along an icy street. Towards the end of the play, Rebecca identifies with a woman whose baby was torn from her arms at a railway station by a man who was once her lover, while Devlin adopts the role of Rebecca's former lover, ordering her to kiss his fist and to put his hands around her throat. In this final sequence, Rebecca's words are repeated by an echo, reminding us of similar tales of loss and atrocities not limited only to the past. The play concludes with a *"Long Silence"* (85). *Ashes to Ashes* neither specifies the atrocities that Rebecca relates, thus prescribing a fixed object of memory, nor does it predetermine the viewer's reaction to that memory. Whereas in Pinter's earlier memory plays such as *Landscape* and *Silence* (1968), followed by *Old Times* (1971), *No Man's Land* (1975), and *Other Places* (1982), the spectator is never addressed, implied, or acknowledged, this memorial text shares with his "overtly political" dramas a demanding relation to their audiences, insisting upon the spectator's coproductive work. Although attesting to the past and the continuing presence of the past, it also invites the audience into the recognition that the torture, pain, and loss it relates are part of a larger context of violence happening in the world in the present.

Hanna Scolnicov speaks for many Pinter critics when she states: "The gap between Rebecca's vivid recollection of the Nazi atrocities and the everyday calm of her English surroundings poses the central hermeneutic problem of the play, for how can she remember what she never saw, what happened before she was ever born" (2001: 19). Scolnicov reads *Ashes to Ashes* as Pinter's Holocaust play, claiming that "Rebecca identifies so closely with the experiences of the Shoah, that they become part of her internal landscape, images incised in her memory, from which she cannot extricate herself" (2001: 20). A few critics, for instance Marc Silverstein (1999) and Susan Hollis Merritt (2000), leave open other interpretative possibilities, acknowledging the fact that the atrocities which Rebecca describes in her "recollections" remain unspecified in the play. Even they, however, analyse the play primarily with reference to the Holocaust. By and large, Pinter critics read Rebecca's identification with a woman whose baby is taken by the end of the play affirmatively, and commend her ethical stance of taking the role of a witness to a historical atrocity. However, they often disavow the erotic components of the play and Rebecca's fascination with authoritarian violence, which trouble the ethics of her position as a sympathetic witness. Furthermore, while several critics, including Marc Silverstein (1999) and Katherine Burkman (1999), make attempts to situate the play in the context of current discourses on witnessing, trauma, and intergenerational transmission of memory, they generally endorse Shoshana Felman's and Cathy Caruth's theories without further qualification. For instance, Scolnicov claims, without seriously elaborating her argument or acknowledging an evolving theoretical discussion on witness testimony that "despite their hallucinatory nature, and although she could not have possibly experienced the atrocities herself, Rebecca's harrowing memories are none the less authentic" (2001: 19). While I find these critics' readings of the play insightful and engaging in many respects, I also find that some of their claims need to be further qualified in order to illuminate and address with more precision some of the key issues which I think the play raises: in particular, the workings of memory and transmission, the resonant after effect of trauma, as well as sex and gender as potent and troubling idioms of remembrance for the generation who came after those who witnessed a historical trauma.

Marianne Hirsch's concept of "postmemory" will furnish an initial point of reference for thinking about history, subjectivity, and ethics as problematised in Pinter's *Ashes to Ashes*. I will argue that the play testifies that our attempts to constitute an ethical relation to the past and historical injustices such as the Holocaust continue to be vexed by contradictory forms of a desire to take the other's place. As the recent work of Ruth Leys, Dominic LaCapra, and Amy Hungerford, among others, has shown, such dislocations are common, if not constitutive, features of engaging the Holocaust through the lens of trauma. Their important work in this field focuses on the problems that arise when testimonies and theories enact an identification with the trauma of the Holocaust itself. They rightly criticise those approaches that transform the Holocaust into a site of perpetual retraumatisation, thus giving rise to a discourse of the negative sublime. Dominic LaCapra (1994; 2004), for instance, also cautions against the valorisation of "acting out" over "working through" trauma, and the temptation of identifying with the experience of the victim (surrogate victimage). I will return to LaCapra's work, as well as to the work of other critics in the field of trauma studies, throughout this essay, since much of my analysis of *Ashes to Ashes* is a dialogue with these critics' assessment of such "identificatory," or transferential, approaches to the Holocaust.

However, as I argue in the second part of my analysis, alongside Rebecca's stance of melancholic identification and surrogate victimage runs her fascination with authoritarian violence, which has elements of a sadomasochistic fantasy. I propose that by disintegrating the official line that divides good and evil, Pinter blurs the aesthetics of domination, Nazism, victimisation, and submission. Taking as points of reference Susannah Radstone's insights on fantasy at work in testimonial witnessing (2001; 2007a; 2007b), Laura Frost's work on the cultural fascination with fascism and its relation to sadomasochism (2002), and Karyn Ball's investigation of the rules of critical conduct that shape the scholarly investigation of the Holocaust (2008), I argue that Pinter's play testifies to the role of fantasy in the way that we narrate and make sense of past traumatic events and invites us to consider the ethical stakes involved in "adoptive witnessing." Ultimately, I contend, *Ashes to Ashes* attests to the ongoing challenge of rethinking the ways in which we can strive to make past experiences that are not our own proximate, rather than intimate, and thereby avoid repeating the violent dislocations that constitute such experiences.

After his public reading of *Ashes to Ashes* in New York on 21 October 1996, Pinter gave his own perspective on the play:

> I think that one of the things that was happening to me when I was writing the play is the realisation that what we term "atrocities" and "catastrophes" throughout the world – by the way, not, by any means, limited to what happened in the Holocaust – there's a holocaust more or less every day of the week. Certainly, the Holocaust images do stay with me. They are contained within people's experience. . . . I think for those of us who live in this world, we – our identification – if our antennae are at all active and alive – with the facts – the atrocious facts – of the world are a constant fact in our lives. Now my

point, therefore, is that this woman . . . the woman that I felt to be haunted – and if you like, possessed – by this world around her, which, I remind you, she had never herself experienced – I mean, she had never herself gone through *any* of these things *at all*, and, I hope that that's made absolutely clear in the play. So that we're talking about, I think, we're talking about a *haunted* person, and a man who really essentially wants to bring her back to just the ordered state of affairs . . . (qtd. in Merritt, 2000: 74–5)

A few months later in Barcelona, Spain, in an interview with Mireia Aragay, the author also explained his personal experience of the Second World War, which informs the play:

Ashes to Ashes is about two characters, a man and a woman, Devlin and Rebecca. From my point of view, the woman is simply haunted by the world that she's been born into, by all the atrocities that have happened. In fact they seem to have become part of her own experience, although in my view she hasn't actually experienced them herself. That's the whole point of the play. I have myself been haunted by these images for many years, and I'm sure not alone in that. I was brought up in the Second World War. I was about fifteen when the War ended; I could listen and hear and add two and two, so these images of horror and man's inhumanity to man were very strong in my mind as a young man. They've been with me all my life, really. That's the point of *Ashes to Ashes*. I think Rebecca inhabits that. (qtd. in Aragay, 1997: 10)

It seems that what Pinter relates in these two passages is a certain capacity of moral hospitality – a capacity that Rebecca exercises in an unusual measure when she experiences the pain of another woman as wholly or partly indistinguishable from a "remembered" pain of her own. In what follows, I want to further investigate the ethical implications of Rebecca's confusing the historical consciousness of events involving extreme violence with painful personal memories – confusing them to the point of being inhabited (i.e. haunted) by the events as though she actually lived through them.

One way to better understand both the necessity and the potential pitfalls of identification with the victims of past (and present) atrocities, and the process of how this identification is affected regardless of whether one has a direct connection to such events, is through the notion of postmemory. The term postmemory was initially coined by Marianne Hirsch to describe a familial memory of children of Holocaust survivors, the so called "second-generation." Through their parents' stories and silences, they were the recipients of a second-hand, delayed, and indirect form of memory that "is distinguished from memory by generational distance and from history by deep personal connection" (Hirsch, 1997: 22). Postmemory, therefore, is seen as the relationship of the second generation to "the stories of the previous generation shaped by traumatic events" (1997: 22). As she further explains: "Postmemory is a powerful form of memory precisely because its connection to its object or source is mediated not through recollection but through projection, investment, and creation. This is not to say that survivor memory itself is unmediated, but that it is more directly connected to the past" (1999: 8). Although Hirsch's formulation was inspired by familial experiences of the Holocaust, she also suggests, as does Andrea Liss (1988; 1991), that postmemory need not be defined by this "familial inheritance and transmission of cultural trauma" (Hirsch, 2001: 9).[2] This is because, even though "familial inheritance offers the clearest model for it, postmemory need not be *strictly* an identity position" (2001: 10, emphasis in the original). After all, as Leslie Morris argues, "as the memory of the Holocaust circulates beyond the actual bounds of lived, remembered experience . . . it seeps into the imaginary of other cultures (and other geographical spaces) as postmemory. . . . " (2002: 291). Thus, "outsiders" too have access to this "intersubjective transgenerational space of remembrance" (Hirsch, 2001: 10).

The notion of postmemory, therefore, can be used to understand a familial as well as a non-familial relationship to the Holocaust and other historical atrocities. This does not mean that the two forms of postmemory are the same, however. Hirsch, for instance, suggests that the postmemory of "outsiders" may be understood as an act, as a *"retrospective witnessing by adoption"* (2001: 10; emphasis in the original). This process is made "more broadly available" through "particular forms of identification, adoption, and projection" (2001: 9–10). This form of identification provides a means of access for those who were not there: "It is a question of adopting the traumatic experiences – and thus also the memories – of others as experiences one might oneself have had, and of inscribing them into one's own life story" (2001: 10). The difference, then, between familial and non-familial (extra-familial or cultural) postmemory is one of degree: both involve processes of identification with a history not experienced first-hand, and in both cases one may find instances of over-appropriation and over-identification.

I am drawn to this second, non-familial, reading of postmemory because it breaks the link between experience and identity, and thus interrupts the discourse of authenticity that I believe to be also at work in Pinter's *Ashes to Ashes*. The revivifications of the past, which in the register of postmemory happen through the process of imaginative investment and creation, share much in common with what Alison Landsberg has referred to as "prosthetic memory." This form of memory is neither the scar of the past trauma nor the result of a long relation to the past based on family heritage or ethnic birthright. It "emerges at the interface between a person and a historical narrative about the past" (Landsberg, 2004: 2). Physically and emotionally engaging media such as cinema and experiential museums can enable consumers who have never lived through the events represented to "inhabit" other people's memories and *"experience* an event or a past without having actually lived through it" (Landsberg, 2004: 48; emphasis in the original). Landsberg, for instance, offers the example of the Holocaust Museum in Washington, DC, where each visitor receives a facsimile identity card and biography, which is meant to help him or her to develop an individual and affective relationship to his or her historical counterpart while proceeding through the exhibit. According to Landsberg, in this process "the person does not simply apprehend a historical narrative but takes on a more personal, deeply felt memory of a past event through which he or she did not live" (2004: 2). Ultimately, she argues, this new form of social memory has the ability to ring changes on our emotions, identity, and affiliation and progressively shape our politics. And while in her view the "experiential site" of the museum tries to approximate the sensory and emotional experiences of the original sufferer, this is only meant to guide the museum-goer to connect the historical as well as the personal past to the present. Even though "one comes to owe" the memories resulting from this encounter with the past, "one never confuses them with one's own lived experiences" (Landsberg, 2007: 629). But this is, I contend, exactly what happens in *Ashes to Ashes*, where Rebecca confuses, voluntarily or not, her personal experiences with those that she has never lived through.

In the course of the play, as Rebecca describes (past) cruelties, so they become alive in her imagination. In one of her last recollections, she returns to her vision of "the frozen city," with an old man and a boy stalking icy, star-lit streets while "dragging suitcases," and herself looking out of the window at them, "wondering where they were going" (71). Then she describes "a woman following them, carrying a baby in her arms" (71). As the light in the room darkens, Rebecca switches from a perspective of a witness to a perspective of a participant in the scene – she "recognises" the woman as herself:

REBECCA: She listened to the baby's heartbeat. The baby's heart was beating.
. . .
The baby was breathing.
Pause.
I held her to me. She was breathing. Her heart was beating.

(73)

At this point, Rebecca's monologue is interrupted by Devlin, who approaches her and enacts the gestures of the lover Rebecca described in the first scene of the play, thus appearing to identify himself with the man. Devlin's fist-clenching, throat-gripping gestures leave Rebecca immobile and speechless until Devlin loosens his grip. Then, maintaining her identification with the woman that she described before Devlin's invasion, she resumes her testimony:

REBECCA: They were taking the babies away
ECHO: the babies away
Pause.
REBECCA: I took my baby and wrapped it in my shawl
ECHO: my shawl
REBECCA: And I made it into a bundle
ECHO: bundle
REBECCA: And I held it under my left arm
ECHO: my left arm
Pause

REBECCA: And I went through with my baby
ECHO: my baby
Pause.
REBECCA: But the baby cried out
ECHO: cried out
REBECCA: And the man called me back
ECHO: called me back
REBECCA: And he said what do you have there
ECHO: have there
REBECCA: He stretched out his hand for the bundle
ECHO: for the bundle
REBECCA: And I gave him the bundle
ECHO: the bundle
REBECCA: And that's the last time I held the bundle
ECHO: the bundle
Silence.

(79–81)

Both Geoffrey Hartman (2000) and Susan Hollis Merritt (2000) have discovered (it seems independently of each other) that Rebecca's story about handing over the bundle at the train station bears striking similarities with the Holocaust testimony of Bessie K., "who was born in Vilna, Poland, in 1924 and lived in Kovno ghetto before being sent to Estonian and Stutthof concentration camps" (Merritt, 2000: 81). The following are the words of Bessie K. from the documentary *Witness: Voices from the Holocaust*:

BESSIE K.: I saw them [the Germans] taking away the men separate, the children separate, and the women separate. So I had the baby and I took the coats that I had – the bundle – and I wrapped [it] around the baby, and I put it on my left side, because I saw that the Germans were saying: "left to right" and I went through with the baby, but the baby was short of breath, started to choke, and it started to cry. So the German called me back. He said, "What do you have there?" in German. Now . . . I didn't know what to do, because everything happened so fast and everything happened so suddenly. I wasn't prepared for it. [Pause.] To look back

> – the experience was – I think I was numb, or something
> happened to me – I don't know. But I wasn't –
> I wasn't there. And – um – he stretched out his arms,
> I should hand him over the bundle, and I hand him over
> the bundle. And this was the last time I had the bundle.
> (qtd. in Merritt, 2000: 81)

At the end of her speech, Rebecca is also in denial of ever having
had a baby:

REBECCA: And we got on the train
ECHO: the train
REBECCA: And we arrived at this place
ECHO: this place
REBECCA: And I met a woman I knew
ECHO: I knew
REBECCA: And she said what happened to your baby
ECHO: your baby
REBECCA: Where is your baby
ECHO: your baby
REBECCA: And I said what baby
ECHO: what baby
REBECCA: I don't have a baby
ECHO: a baby
REBECCA: I don't know of any baby
ECHO: of any baby
          Pause
REBECCA: I don't know of any baby
          Long silence.

(81–5)

In response to Rebecca's final words Hartman writes:

> I read them first in a *New Yorker* review of Pinter's play after it was
> staged in America two years later. We glimpse here how diffusion
> occurs: how Holocaust memory influences affectively a wider
> public. For it is improbable that Pinter could have seen the Yale
> testimony in question. It is far more likely that he saw those words
> in a book by Lawrence Langer, who was the first to study the Yale

archive in *Holocaust Testimonies: The Ruins of Memory*. That book does not quote these particular words, but a later book by Langer, *Admitting the Holocaust* (1995), does. (2000: 15)

Hartman's guess is that "key phrases" from Bessie K.'s testimony "have migrated from a videotaped testimony to a scholarly book to a popular play to an influential magazine's review of the play" (2000: 16). Pointing out how this particular testimony may have travelled from one medium to another, Hartman also shows the workings of postmemory in the present. However, the image of women as mothers trying to protect their children marked for exterminations is so iconic of the Holocaust experience – even though it has multiple resonances – that no validation is necessary here. James Young reminds us, for instance, that "Women and children had to be killed to eliminate 'the germ cell of a new Jewish revival,' as described in the Wannsee Protocol, or to 'deprive Jewry of its biological reserves,' in the words of Otto Six of the Reichssicherheitshauptamt ('Reich Main Security Office')" (2009: 1779). And as Janet Jacobs writes, "As a trope of memory, the suffering of mothers, their death and the death of their children, act as a powerful reminder of a type of human evil that the Holocaust has come to represent in the collective imagination" (2008: 214).[3]

To return to Pinter's play: according to Merritt, "The final section of Rebecca's speech reveals the 'numb' denial that Holocaust survivors like Bessie K. and other women whose experience Rebecca has apparently introjected might have felt after 'handing over' the 'bundle'" (2000: 81). In Silverstein's view, through the scene in which Rebecca identifies with the mother "Pinter gives powerful dramatic expression to this 'involvement beyond ourselves' as Rebecca engages in the empathetic projection through which she speaks *for* the other by speaking *as* the other" (1999: 82; emphasis in the original). While agreeing with these critics' insights as well as recognising postmemory's significance for enlarging the circle of witnesses, I would like to argue with Hirsch that some of this identification, "the imaginative capability of perceiving . . . what is happening to others in one's own body," can also become potentially problematic if it remains unexamined (1999: 17). Hirsch warns that these "lines of relation and identification" need to be theorised further in order to resist appropriation and incorporation. It is the kind of identification that leads to adoption, appropriation, and the erasure of difference between self and other in our confrontation with the Holocaust that concerns me, as it allows the viewer or reader to become "a surrogate victim," blurring "context, specificity, responsibility, history" (Hirsch, 1999: 17). Landsberg also carefully delineates between sympathy and empathy. In her view:

> Unlike sympathy, empathy does not depend on a "natural" affinity, on some kind of essential underlying connection between the two subjects. Empathy recognises the alterity of identification and the necessity of negotiating distances and is therefore essential to an ethical relation to the other. A practice of empathy is an essential part of taking on prosthetic memories, of finding ways to inhabit other people's memories as other people's memories and thereby respecting and recognising difference. (2004: 24)

Both Hirsch and Landsberg draw in turn on Kaja Silverman's discussion of empathy, in which she makes a distinction between idiopathic and heteropathic identification.

In *The Threshold of the Visible World* (1996), Silverman discusses two main forms of empathic identification: idiopathic identification and heteropathic identification, derived from the German philosopher Max Scheler. Idiopathic identification assimilates or appropriates the experience of the other, which is to say, the distinctiveness of the other's experience is only interpreted with reference to one's own experience. The conflation of subject positions that is at work here involves the confusion of compassion with unchecked identification, vicarious experience, even surrogate victimage. We are familiar with this suspension of alterity "through that formula with which we extend sympathy to someone less fortunate than ourselves without in any way jeopardising our *moi*: 'I can imagine myself in his (or her) place'" (Silverman, 1996: 25). In other words, operating along a trajectory of incorporation, this kind of identification fundamentally confuses object with subject.

Silverman believes that if imaginary processes of identification are sufficiently tempered by symbolic functions, identification can be modulated so that one could identify with the other's perspective without usurping or distorting it. "Heteropathic identification" is a movement out from the self to identify with the other's position that would preserve a perception of the other as a separate subject. Here emotional response comes with respect for the other and the realisation that the experience of the other is not one's own. It is an ethical, nonappropriative and not self-serving relation to the other that recognises the other as a separate, individual, and equal subject.

Empathy also figures prominently in Dominic LaCapra's recent work (and in historical theory in general), as part of his attempts to defend a historiographical practice and more general ethic in approaching the Holocaust. In *History and its Limits* (2009), as in his previous four books – *Representing the Holocaust* (1994), *History and Memory After Auschwitz* (1998b), *Writing History, Writing Trauma* (2001), and *History in Transit* (2004), LaCapra examines the problem of the Holocaust, trauma, and their representation in and for history, illuminating the ways historians and other scholars enact transferential relations with their object of study that express their investment in or disavowal of a particular subject position. LaCapra introduces empathy to think about the Holocaust narrator's relationship with traumatised sources (though his writing about it makes clear that it is not to be restricted to such Holocaust and trauma-related sources), and develops what he terms "empathic unsettlement." The concept entails "being responsive to the traumatic experiences of others" (2001: 41), while insisting that an empathy that "resists full identification with, and appropriation of, the experience of the other would depend both on one's potential for traumatization . . . and on one's recognition that another's loss is not identical to one's own loss" (2001: 79).

Working according to the logic of health and illness, he draws on Freud's distinction between mourning and melancholia – the former a restorative "working through" of traumatic loss, the later "acting out" that remains fixated upon a traumatic event – arguing that it can be applied to the subjectivity of both the survivor and the secondary witness, though differently for each. LaCapra is sympathetic to the idea that pathological acting out may be inevitable for survivors or intimates of victims and survivors; he further suggests that in the context of secondary witnessing "identification with the victim may take place on an unconscious level such that one may be haunted or even possessed by another in whose halting or broken voice one may find oneself speaking" (2009: 66). He acknowledges that such an occurrence "would be misconstrued if seen as merely pathological or as a simple choice" (2009: 66). However, LaCapra sharply critiques a critic (but also an artist) who fails to stand apart from identificatory processes and "rhetorically validates or advocates vicarious identification and takes up the gap-ridden voice of the victim or survivor, attempting to speak for and in that voice rather than with respect to, and respect for, it" (2009: 66). When the critic does fail, when the relationality that provides the basis of a capacity for putting oneself in the place of another collapses, limit events such as the Holocaust acquire a negative sublimity. As he argues in his critique of Claude Lanzmann's directorial and interviewing strategies in his seminal film *Shoah* (I will invoke this critique later in my discussion of traumatic affect and transference at work in Artur Żmijewski's video-testimony), in such instances these events become sanctioned as incomparable and unrepresentable, unavailable for the act of collective history-making. It is important to observe here that LaCapra does not define empathy as beyond intersubjective identification altogether; rather, he suggests that "a viable ethic of response" (2009: 67) depends on the extent to which the identificatory tendency detracts from relationality itself. However, some scholars have criticised his tendency "to foreground the ethical and conscious valences of working through while expropriating Freud's theses on the drives and fantasy" (Ball, 2008: 15); I will address this issue shortly.

It may be helpful at this point, however, to refer to a recent, and by now widely discussed case of Binjamin Wilkomirski's book *Fragments: Memories of a Wartime Childhood* (1996). As one of the most infamous expressions of a peculiar identification with Jewish victims of the Holocaust, this "child survivor" memoir can help to illuminate, at least in part, what is at stake in Rebecca's imaginative identification with the women she describes in her "recollections." Wilkomirski's book proclaims itself a survivor's account depicting the author's fragmented and recovered memories of his early childhood in the concentration camps. Initially hailing *Fragments* as one of the greatest Holocaust accounts, critics awarded the book a variety of literary prizes, including the National Jewish Book Award for autobiography and memoirs, and the *Prix Mémoire de la Shoah*. Three years later, however, journalist Daniel Ganzfried exposed Wilkomirski as a fraud. After having unsuccessfully attempted to document and verify the particular details of the story, Ganzfried claimed that Wilkomirski was, in fact, Bruno Grosjean, an illegitimate child raised in foster care before being adopted and renamed Bruno Dössekker. While Wilkomirski had always admitted to being Dössekker, he had also maintained that, upon adoption, Grosjean's identity had been retroactively forced upon him, thereby effectively erasing his own past, and his Holocaust experiences. As he describes in the Afterword to his text "for decades I was silent but my memory could not be wiped clean. . . . It is so easy to make a child mistrust his own reflection, to take away his voice" (2001: 495). Only many years later, when attempting to come to terms with his anxieties, fears, and nightmares, Wilkomirski supposedly recovered and reclaimed his true identity so forcefully denied to him: "I wanted my own certainty back, and I wanted my voice back, so I began to write" (2011: 495). In so doing, Wilkomirski collapses his writing with the process of remembering his true past, thereby forcing his readers to admit the truth status of his story even as many of the facts and details question this truth.

The Wilkomirski affair testifies to the overwhelming collective meaning placed upon the Holocaust. Whether purposefully or unconsciously, Bruno Dössekker chose this historical event to symbolise the very personal pain of his childhood. Using not only the imagery, but also the collective suffering of the Holocaust as symbolic of his own psychic pain, he fashioned himself as a Holocaust survivor, this seemingly being the only way to sufficiently render his emotional pain. Unlike Sylvia Plath, however, who also uses the Holocaust imagery to express her psychic pain, but clearly differentiates between herself and her narrative voice, Wilkomirski *becomes* his own fiction.[4] As Susan Suleiman aptly summarises the case: "The problem with *Fragments*, as a text, is precisely that it does not recognise – or at any rate, does not admit – its own fictionality" (1999: 552). In her view: "Using the criterion of truth claim, therefore, we must call *Fragments* not a novel but a false – or better, a deluded – memoir" (2000: 552).[5] For Suleiman, Wilkomirski's *Fragments* poses the following questions: "Where does literature end (or begin) and psychopathology begin (or end)? Where should the line be drawn? – between personal memory and imagined or 'borrowed' memory? To whom does the memory of the Holocaust belong?" (2000: 554).

Amy Hungerford has argued that recent theorisations of trauma by Felman and Caruth posit it as an experience without a subject, a floating force whose existence and transmission occurs through language alone. With LaCapra, she shows how the textualisation of experience in deconstruction and trauma theory has allowed critics to identify with victims of the Holocaust. Hungerford focuses on the process of this transformation of experience (and people) into memorial language, or text. She argues that imitation – or memorisation – of past texts can take the place of experience, and furnish the basis for personal identity, thus allowing readers as disparate as Shoshana Felman and Binjamin Wilkomirski to identify with the Holocaust as victims. In regard to Wilkomirski she writes:

> He absorbed the accounts of camp life, the stories of extreme violence, the testimonies and histories and photographs, and they finally became him, finally made him Binjamin Wilkomirski. I want to suggest that, despite the difference we understand between what we memorise – like the multiplication tables – and what we call our memories . . . , our recollections of "the things that made" us – in the case of Bruno Dössekker, *memorising and memory have become the same thing.* Without setting out to memorise the map of Auschwitz, he nevertheless did. In doing so, he became a child survivor. (2001: 88; emphasis added)

While the space here does not allow me to elaborate on the finest points of Hungerford's argument, it is worth noticing that in her larger argument she identifies an important strand of twentieth-century literature and literary theory (notably Caruth and Felman) that combining "deconstruction and psychoanalysis makes trauma both generic and transmissible" (2001: 88). Hungerford does not deny that "to receive traumatic experience one must feel an identification with the victims of the Holocaust," nor does she question the value of "a commitment to the importance of sentiment and desire in the production of that identification, over and above lived experience of trauma represented" (2001: 74). However, and this is her central point:

> [I]t is worth acknowledging the specific nature of the sentiment and the experience at issue here, for it is true that seeing the survivor's testimony must be understood as a lived experience that can have intense emotional effects on the viewer. My point, then, is not that watching – or reading, or hearing – survivor testimonies

is not in its own way traumatic, but that it is so *in its own way*. It seems important – in the interest of actual factual accuracy, but also in the interest of understanding exactly what trauma theory accomplishes in the realm of culture – to distinguish this experience of trauma, if one wishes to call it that, from the trauma that the survivor herself has experienced and then represents in her testimony. (2001: 74; original emphasis)

Primo Levi's voice also reminds us throughout the pages of *The Drowned and the Saved* that "one is never in another's place" (1989: 60). In the chapter entitled "Shame," Levi stresses the irreducible singular nature of the prisoners' affective experience of psychic death and hopelessness in Auschwitz: "The mental mechanisms of the *Häftlinge* were different from ours; curiously, and in parallel, different also were their physiology and pathology" (1989: 85). So much of what he witnessed in the camp was incredible, and not comparable to anything he previously experienced or imagined, that he suggests in one passage that "knowledge that has been built up and tested 'outside' in the world that, for the sake of simplicity, we call civilian" is irrelevant to the conditions of the struggle for survival in Auschwitz (1989: 85). Levi instructs us that the suggestion that primary witnesses and those that have never directly experienced the camps have a comparable experience of the traumatic past constitutes an untenable conflation of literal and metaphorical victimisation.

While acknowledging the problematic ways in which affective relations to victims are mobilised and constituted in contemporary culture, however, Carolyn Dean warns that "the historical and psychological experience of some Jews is erased or diminished in the high-stakes effort to distinguish between history and memory, true and false claims to having been victimized" (2010: 54). In her excellent study *Aversion and Erasure: The Fate of the Victim after the Holocaust*, Dean argues that the iconic status of the Holocaust in the West (she focuses on the United states and France) and the tendency amongst some to treat the Holocaust survivor accounts as sacred texts "have created a consensus about the ostensibly narcissistic appropriation of Jewish suffering, its consequences and impact" (2010: 32). In her view a certain variant of trauma theory that often comes with a discourse of the sublime, represented by critics such as Felman and Agamben, which I addressed above, also contributed to this trend. This discourse about the so-called surfeit of Jewish memory, which emerged most forcefully in the 1990s, is in her view "now articulated primarily as an argument about how Jewish memory exemplifies a pathological cultural attachment to having been or being a victim" (2010: 32). She assesses this phenomenon "in terms of the discrepancy between fantasmic concepts of 'too much' and the right amount of identification with victims" and in light of the "the pervasive assumption that the experience and memory of Jewish genocide have dramatically undermined the rational contestation of grievances in democratic societies" (2010: 32; 181). One of the problematic aspects of this discourse, argues Dean, is that in order to delineate clearly between history and memory many contemporary critics tend to "advocate a mode of testimony commensurate with the mastery of symptoms" (2010: 143). For instance, Primo Levi's deliberately chosen minimalist style that gives an appearance of an objective witness is problematically favoured over testimonial styles that may manifest overwhelming and excessive traumatic symptoms. Thus, in this rhetorical context, in the worst cases, the traumatised Jewish victim's testimony, which cannot be reconciled to this normative pattern, may be conceived as not a real one. Dean notes that the pervasive reference to "surfeit memory" also figures strongly in voluminous literature on the "second generation," marked by critics' anxious attempts to distinguish between the real victims of historical atrocities and those "who choose to play victim, embrace injury, or wish they had been victims" (2010: 7).

The literature of the "second-generation" writers – the children of the Holocaust survivors – is preoccupied with the ways in which the Holocaust shaped not only the lives of those who survived the atrocities of the Holocaust, but also the lives of the children who grew up in the shadow of this catastrophe. As I pointed out earlier in my discussion of Marianne Hirsch's formulation of the concept of postmemory, such proximity to this historical injury, however vicariously and abstractedly viewed, has marked indelibly the lives of the children of Holocaust survivors. In *After Such Knowledge* (2004), Eva Hoffman offers a powerful meditation on the meaning of this difficult legacy for children of survivors, who like her, lived with their parents' "splintered signs of acute suffering, of grief and loss" (2004: 34), and its accompanying "[d]epression, anxiety, psychic numbing, panic attacks. And further, or below these, burning rage and corrosive guilt, an inadmissible shame and a mourning so encompassing that it could surely have no 'resolution' within a single frame" (2004: 53). As she adds, to these experiences must be added the additional lifelong struggle to avoid pitfalls of vicarious witnessing and to keep a critical distance from survivors. It is worth noticing here, however, that the catastrophe has also marked deeply the lives of many who have not grown up with the intimate familial knowledge of the Holocaust. Susan Sontag, for instance, describes her life as divided into two parts, "before I saw those photographs (I was twelve) and after, though it was several years before I understood fully what they were about" (1989: 19–20). She describes how, when she first encountered the photographs of the Holocaust "something broke. Some limit has been reached, and not only that of horror; I felt irrevocably grieved, wounded, part of my feelings started to tighten; something was dead; something was still crying" (1989: 20).

Concerned primarily with the transmission of Holocaust memory, Gary Weissman's *Fantasies of Witnessing: Postwar Efforts to Experience the Holocaust* problematises this memory discourse making a powerful argument that a "desire to make the survivor's experiential understanding one's own" drives those who study and memorialise the Holocaust (2004: 112). In his view:

> It is the unspoken desire of many people who have no direct experience of the Holocaust but are deeply interested in studying, remembering, and memorializing it. It is a desire to know what it was like to be there, in Nazi Europe; in hiding; at the sites of mass shootings; in the cattle cars; in the concentration camps; in the death camps; in the gas chambers and crematoria. (2004: 4)

This desire, he says, is indulged through identification with Holocaust victims, the proliferation and consumption of media representations and memorials of the Holocaust, and the figure of the survivor. The attempts on the part of the second-generation to come to grips with the memory of Jewish genocide and their apparent need to identify with the survivors, argues Weissman, may in the end be self-serving, self-satisfying, even dishonest, hindering "historical and moral comprehension of the Holocaust" (2004: 210).

As Dean has argued, Weissman and other critics of "victim culture" who problematically attend to posttraumatic symptoms in second generation fiction, art, memoir, and testimony conceive this intergenerational inheritance "as part of the presumably excessive affect attached to victims that voids historical understanding" (2010: 38–9). That is to say, they "treat traumatic symptoms and their potential transmission over time as if they were instrumental or self-indulgent responses unbefitting the dignity of those who have really suffered" (2010: 29). In the process, the second generation's struggle to find an appropriate way to relate to the experiences of those who have survived massive historical trauma and their own sense of belatedness "is recast not as a tormenting psychological struggle but as narcissistic self-indulgence" (2010: 39). As she rightfully argues, the problem posed by that suffering and critics' own investments in delineating clear lines between "better and worse ways of remembering, between respectful, bounded memory, and self-indulgent appropriation of memory" requires further critical scrutiny (2010: 46).

To slowly make our way back to Pinter's *Ashes to Ashes*, the play's fragmented discourse functions as a mimesis of amputated, free-floating memories bereft of a specific historical context. The play does not specify where the sinister-sounding factory was, nor the identity of the people obediently walking into the sea and the screaming mothers whose babies were torn from their arms at a railway platform, which compels a "symbolic" interpretation, a narrative amplification, on the part of its readers and audiences. Rebecca's identity is never specified (nor is that of the woman with whom she ultimately identifies); it comes into being only in the reader's and spectator's imaginative attempts to make sense of the play or performance. Even though many critics (for instance, Hartman, 2000; Merritt, 2000; Scolnicov, 2001) read Rebecca's bits of memory as metonyms of the *univers concentrationnaire*, the universe of the camps set up by the Nazis, the work does not necessarily serve to articulate a postmemorial experience of the Holocaust – it sets up a dialogue, requiring us also to acknowledge the other experience.

Indeed, Rebecca's testimony regarding her baby-girl forcefully taken from her resonates with many similar historical events, and I will mention here just a few pertinent examples. As in the case of residential schools in Canada (closed in the early 1970s), and in Australia as well, Indigenous children were forcefully taken from their families and communities to mission school and to adoption by white families. This genocidal policy, clearly visited many traumas upon children, families and communities in both countries. In her book *Haunted Nations*, where she discusses this legacy in respect to both nations, Sneja Gunew even proposes that "These abductions of so-called 'light skinned' children, in order to force them to assimilate, are not so far removed from the traumatic history of slavery" (2004: 130). The controversial Human Rights and Equal Opportunity Commission report *Bringing Them Home*, tabled in the Australian parliament in 1997, which addresses the policies, effects, and legacy of the separation of Indigenous children in Australia, also interprets this forced removal in traumatic terms. An excerpt from this report relates well the effects of separation and assimilation that are still lived today by members of the Stolen generation, and their families and communities: "Separation and institutionalisation can amount to traumas. Almost invariably they were traumatically carried out with force, lies, regimentation and an absence of comfort and affection. All too often they also involved brutality and abuses. Trauma compounded trauma" (qtd. in Kennedy and Wilson, 2003: 119).[6]

By referencing these two examples of historical injustice and collective and individual suffering, I wish to propose that the play may be viewed as concerned with a range of experiences that are not anchored in a singular or specific identity, or atrocity. Just as Rebecca draws on collective memory and offers hospitality of an identity to the probably imagined woman – though not unproblematically, as we have seen – reading *Ashes to Ashes* or viewing it in performance, we draw on our knowledge and memory, but in order to recognise now the horrors that we have forgotten, denied, or ignored. In this way the play intervenes in the politics of memory and repression, engaging the memoried consciousness of its audience – with whose memory, and repression, this play is in a constant dialogue.

While evocative of many past atrocities as well as those unfolding on the global stage, the play is much less explicit than Pinter's more overtly political dramas created in the eighties and early nineties. Its dramaturgy is also far removed from the genre of verbatim theatre which came to prominence in the West in the last couple of decades. In search for truth and political efficacy, this kind of theatre often presents testimonies of individuals and collectives who have undergone traumatic experiences and suffered various human rights violations, and sometimes even brings these subjects on stage as is the case, for example, with some performances created in collaboration with refugees and asylum seekers in the UK and Australia (see, for instance, Gilbert and Lo, 2007; Forsyth and Megson, 2009). However, to Lisa Fitzpatrick, the Pinter play's efficacy lies precisely in its indeterminacy, which allows performative evocation of various past and contemporary atrocities each time the play is staged in a different context. She makes her point by discussing the play's staging at the Tarragon Theatre in Toronto in 2007. Vahid Rahbani's postdramatic interpretation of the play at this venue referenced directly the death of the Iranian-Canadian photojournalist Zahra Kazemi, who died in custody in Iran in July of 2003 after she was arrested for taking pictures outside a prison in the aftermath of a student protest in Tehran. But, Fitzpatrick also goes to argue, the imagery employed in the performance also invoked the injustices of Guantánamo, Abu Ghraib, and the War on Terror, inviting its audience to recognise that the "fictional events performed on the stage have 'real world' resonances" (2011: 65).

Both Fitzpatrick and I see the potential of Pinter's play to provide a form of witnessing to human rights violations in the past and present. As I pointed out earlier, Fitzpatrick argues that the Toronto staging of *Ashes to Ashes* hailed the viewers to witness suffering on a global stage, soliciting their concern and demanding "an individual conscientious response" (2011: 63). Drawing on Baz Kershaw's claim that performance efficacy is very much dependent on authenticating conventions or signs that "allow the audience to identify a 'a real world' in the performance" (2011: 65), Fitzpatrick argues that some directorial choices in this Toronto staging of Pinter's play, for example the moment when Rebecca takes a photo of the audience, referencing Kazemi's plight in Iran, and the appearance of two soldiers who spoke in Russian and German, indexing the Soviet and Nazi regimes (Figure 4.1), enabled the audiences to establish correspondences between the stage action and the places, events, and political actions that occur "at distance" from them or took place in the past. At the end of the performance the audiences was confronted with a projection of the photograph taken from the stage before the start of the show, "in the moment before witnessing and therefore before the knowledge" (Fitzpatrick, 2011: 66). The picture was meant to hit the audience with the shock of recognition that the events represented on stage and their own world are coextensive rather than separate and to inspire them "to engage with suffering and to act" (2011: 66).

Figure 4.1 Scene from Harold Pinter's *Ashes to Ashes*, dir. Vahid Rahbani, SummerWorks, Toronto, 2007, photo by Pooyan Tabatabaei; courtesy of Lemaz Productions and Pooyan Tabatabaei

Fitzpatrick's claim is consonant with Hans-Thies Lehmann's attempts to articulate a new politics appropriate to a postdramatic theatre that he offers in the epilogue of his influential book *Postdramatic Theatre* (German edition 1999; English edition 2006). Arguing that "the mode of perception in the theatre cannot be separated from the existence of theatre in a world of media that massively shapes all perception," he draws connections between the search for ethical vision in theatre and visual cultures and practices proliferating in various arenas today that foster passive rather than engaged, even empathetic, looking. According to Lehmann, "Theatre can respond to this only with a *politics of perception*, which could at the same time be called *an aesthetic of responsibility or (response-ability)* . . . It can move the mutual implication of actors and spectators in the theatrical production of images into the centre and thus make visible the broken thread between personal experience and perception. Such an experience would be not only aesthetic but therein at the same time ethico-political" (2006: 185–5; emphasis in the original). In his view it would be absurd to see theatre as an effective alternative to the mass media spectacularisation of political conflicts; instead, he is asking us to recognise the dialogic interactions between ethical engagement and spectacle embedded in visual acts of witnessing.

I would like to follow up on these compelling arguments with further reflections on the complex ways in which visual witnessing is implicated in histories of imperialism, militarization, and unequal access to human rights and political visibility. In particular, I wish to comment on the correspondences between the fragmentary discourse of *Ashes to Ashes* – whose images of a frozen street with escaping refugees, a slave labour factory, and babies being torn from mothers' arms at a railway platform, though evocative, do not explicitly point out to specific socio-political contexts – and the selective nature of media images of various political conflicts, both of which in their different ways promise to witness human rights violations. As scholars such as Judith Butler (2004; 2009), Susan Sontag (2004), Wendy Kozol (2004; 2008) and Ann Kaplan (2005) have argued, given the powerful role of popular culture in shaping our understanding of conflicts that occur in the world, it is crucial to interrogate the credibility of documentary genres as truth-gathering mechanisms. For instance, Kozol argues that representational strategies employed by photo reportage and other visual news practices often visualise trauma replicating a predominately Western gaze that tends to exoticise or elide the racial and ethnic identities of those involved in humanitarian crises. Focusing on the coverage of the NATO bombings in the former Federal Republic of Yugoslavia at the height of the Kosovo crisis in 1999, which according to the NATO officials aimed to prevent the persecution and ethnic cleansing of the ethnic Albanians by Serbian forces in the region, she demonstrates how three major US newsmagazines: *Time, Newsweek,* and *U.S. News* framed this conflict through racial and gender categories, ignoring complex historical factors that shaped the crisis. Featuring prominently photographs of Albanian refugee women holding small children and babies, the magazines relied on these vulnerable bodies to function as metonyms for the crisis and to provide the visual alibi for this US-led military intervention.

While she acknowledges that episodic images of violence and victimisations can be powerful tools in eliciting emotional responses and financial support for international relief efforts, which were also underway during the war, Kozol shows how the selective nature of the photographs that were published diverted "attention from the historical causes of this war, including the integral role of American and European economic and political interests in the persistent instabilities in this region" (2004: 5). The camera focus on Albanian refugees fleeing in mountainous landscapes or in refugee camps exposed in all their vulnerability, ignored any agency the Albanians may have had, eliding their subjectivity in the process. These media images perpetuated a Western gaze at the Balkans that since the Enlightenment portrayed the region and its people as the geopolitical abject on the fringes of civilisation (see, for instance, Wolff, 1994; Boatcă, 2007). What Ann Kaplan convincingly argued in regard to the March 2003 US coverage of the war in Iraq, equally applies to the coverage of the NATO military intervention against the former Yugoslavia: through its practice of providing isolated images of violence, aggression, and individual pain, media coverage aroused only "'empty' empathy, closely allied to sentimentality" (2005: 94).

In a "Letter from Paris" published in the aftermath of the bombings, Tzvetan Todorov writes that each of the parties involved in the Kosovo conflict: the Western powers, the Serbs, and the Kosovo Albanians "attempted to find arguments justifying its policies in the memory of and assimilation with hero, victim or evildoer figures, and parallels were always easy to find" (2000: 11). Many of the photos published in the Western media raised the historical spectre of the Holocaust (Kozol, for instance, refers to a photo of a train overflowing with refugees, published in several magazines, which made the visual allusion to the deportations of the Jews by the Nazis), while the Western politicians employed the slogan "Auschwitz never again" invoking this historical trauma for the sake of power politics in the present (Probst, 2003). Neglecting the norms of international law – from the Geneva Convention of 1947 and the UN Charter to the Statute of NATO itself to the total neglect of national parliaments of the countries involved in the action, NATO justified its military involvement in Kosovo as a moral obligation to intervene on behalf of innocent civilians. As Milan Brdar puts it ironically, this "had to be a moral justification in the strongest terms in order to justify such obvious crimes as bombing hospitals, schools, TV stations, etc." (2003: 163). Brdar's shows how the triumphal rhetoric of the NATO leaders covered up the fact that the main victims of the NATO's punitive expedition in Serbia were Serbian civilians; foregrounding innocent victimisation of ethnic Albanians it also ignored the violence perpetrated by the Kosovo Liberation Army (KLA) and their paramilitary supporters against the Serbian population (Petras, 1999).

Speaking out against the NATO bombardment of Serbia, Pinter described this "humanitarian action" as a neo-colonial tool of world domination. Refusing the idea that crimes committed against one population can serve as an excuse for the "collateral damages" inflicted against the other, he put his objection against the NATO bombing this way: "The problem with a missile that tears the head of a little girl, and the mother holding the little girl's head, is that their image is not taken into account by those launching the missiles" (qtd. in Todorov, 2000: 10–11). Here, as in the two US-led invasions of Iraq, fighting from a distance, "NATO accepted the sacrifice of civilian 'enemies' and thereby introduced a hierarchy in the worth of human life" (Todorov, 2000: 11). What Judith Butler wrote about the US Government's mobilisation of grief in the context of the current war in Iraq equally applies here: "Some lives are grievable, and others are not; the differential allocation of grievability that decides what kind of subject is and must be grieved, and which kind of subject must not, operates to produce and maintain certain exclusionary conceptions of who is normatively human: what counts as a livable life and a grievable death?" (2004: xvi–xv). This question cannot be adequately addressed within the confines of this chapter, but haunts debates about empathy and failure and difficulties involved in forging ethical solidarities.

It is also beyond the remit of this chapter to undo the ideological web of the evolving international human rights regime, political geography, and historical trauma(s) that was spun during the Kosovo conflict. As Sheila Benhabib writes, "when, why, and under what conditions military intervention to stop massive human rights violations is justifiable remains a question in political ethics" (2008: 103); however, as I tried to point out here, this question can be closely tied to a rhetorical manipulation of the discourse of memory. True, in the last couple of decades, we have been constantly reminded that it is our duty to remember. At the heart of much contemporary memory work across disciplines as well as in other public discourses lies a belief in the relationship between remembering and transformation. Researchers interpreting the memorial traces of individual or collective sufferings and abuse do so not only to honour history's victims, dead and alive, but in the hope that memory can vanquish repetition. For instance, Daniel Levy and Nathan Sznaider have argued that memories of the Holocaust can "facilitate the formation of transnational memory cultures, which in turn, have the potential to become the cultural foundation for global human rights politics" (2006: 4). While I would like to take part in their optimism that Holocaust memory may "provide the foundations for a new cosmopolitan memory" that would aid collective efforts to stop genocide from being committed yet again (2006: 4), I would also like to recall here Claude Lefort's comment, made in response to the NATO bombing of Serbia, that "without the duty to think, the duty to remember will be meaningless" (qtd. in Probst, 2003: 58). The refusal to think of the totalitarian temptation as something which is emerging (only) from the outside of democratic societies and not from the inside is one of the dangers of our time.

When Aragay asked Pinter if *Ashes to Ashes* is "a play about Nazism," he replied:

> No, I don't think so at all. It *is* about the images of Nazi Germany. I don't think that anyone can ever get that out of their mind. . . . But it's not simply the Nazis that I'm talking about in *Ashes to*

Ashes, because it would be a dereliction on my part to simply concentrate on the Nazis and leave it at that. . . . I'm talking about us and our conception of our past and our history, and what it does to us in the present. (qtd. in Aragay, 1997: 10–11; emphasis in the original)

If Pinter is somewhat ambivalent on the issue (the play is about, but "not simply" about, the circulation of Nazi atrocities in postmemorial imagination), the fact that most of the critical interpretations of the play foreground the Holocaust as its primary historical reference in itself testifies to the iconic nature of the Holocaust in the contemporary imagination (postmemory), and – perhaps equally so – to the academia's own ideological legitimation in historical narratives and theories of history. I have followed this path, perhaps inadvertently so, but with the understanding that this was a necessary interpretative choice in order to address the larger discourse on witnessing, which has been developed primarily in the context of the Holocaust studies, and which for the most part informs the existing critical account of the play. This choice is also pertinent for the second part of my analysis of *Ashes to Ashes*, where I focus on "erotic" postmemories in the play.

To engage with Pinter's "eroticised hauntology," to use Elizabeth Freeman's term (2008: 57), we need to start with the play's opening scene. It shows Devlin "*standing with a drink*" and Rebecca "*sitting,*" and a "*Silence.*" After the silence, as if already in *media res* of remembering, Rebecca relates to Devlin the details of a relationship she once had with another man:

REBECCA: Well . . . for example . . . he would stand over me and clench his fist. And then he'd put his other hand on my neck and grip it and bring my head towards him. His fist . . . grazed my mouth. And he'd say, "Kiss my fist."
DEVLIN: And did you?
REBECCA: Oh yes. I kissed his fist. The knuckles. And then he'd open his hand and give me the palm of his hand . . . to kiss . . . which I kissed.
Pause.
And then I would speak.
DEVLIN: What did you say? You said what? What did you say?
Pause.

REBECCA: I said, "Put your hand round my throat." I murmured it
through his hand, as I was kissing it, but he heard my
voice, he heard it through his hand, he felt my voice in
his hand, he heard it there.
Silence.

(103–5)

Is Rebecca telling Devlin about a former or current lover here?
Perhaps she is telling him about a dream or a fantasy that she might
have had, "perhaps even a moment from a film or book" (Milne,
2001: 207). Throughout the play, Rebecca re-enacts the act of obsessive recall, of melancholy remembrance, centred on the lover and
some unspecified atrocities, frustrating Devlin's attempts to verify
her stories or to divert their conversation to the concerns of their
everyday lives. Towards the end of the play, the exchange between
Rebecca and her lover, which Rebecca recounts in the play's opening
sequence, is re-enacted, but with an important difference:

Devlin goes to her. He stands over her and looks down at her.
He clenches his fist and holds it in front of her face.
He puts his left hand behind her neck and grips it. He brings her head
towards his fist. His fist touches her mouth.

DEVLIN: Kiss my fist.
She does not move.
He opens his hand and places the palm of his hand on her
mouth.
She does not move.
DEVLIN: Speak. Say it. Say "Put your hand round my throat."
She does not speak.
Ask me to put my hand round your throat.
She does not speak or move.

(73–5)

Devlin does not seem to be able to take the place of the man desired
or imagined by Rebecca.

Some early reviews of *Ashes to Ashes* expressed concern that Pinter
may have gone too far by establishing a close analogy between
the political, public violence at home and abroad and personal, in

this case sadomasochistic, violence. Reviewing the original staging of the play by the Royal Court Theatre at the Ambassador theatre in London, Paul Taylor of *The Independent* wrote warily of "the connection the play makes between sadomasochistic mutual violence in a private relationship and the brutalities inflicted in a totalitarian state – the one type of fascism a reflection of the other. If such equivalence exists, this play does not persuade me of it" (1996: 4). He also wondered how "those mooted comparabilities might strike someone actually living in a totalitarian regime, or, indeed, a Holocaust survivor" (1996: 4). This concern was echoed by John Peter who raised a question whether Pinter was "using images of the Nazi Holocaust and a woman's need for a bit of rough sex to illustrate one another" (1996: 1188). Michael Billington, too, argued in a similar vein that "Pinter is not writing specifically about Nazis, but about the umbilical connection between the kind of sexual fascism so graphically described in the opening scene and its political counterpart; about a world of brute masculine power and naked submission" (1996: 374).

More extended scholarly critiques of the play, when not glossing over the images or invocations of sexualised violence in Pinter's play, typically rehearse this anxiety, reading the play's opening and closing scenes as a metaphor for the thinness of the line between large-scale wartime violence elsewhere and the so-called normal in a world filled with catastrophic suffering. And while many critics read the play in relation to the Holocaust (for example, Burkman, 1999; Scolnicov 2001; Sakellaridou, 2003), they too display an unease in regard to the images of sexual and sexualised violence portrayed in the play. But this evasiveness is also something these critical accounts share with an otherwise increasingly voluble discourse on the Holocaust. As Sonja Hedgepeth and Rochelle Saidel, the editors of the first English-language volume to address the sexual violation of Jewish women during the Holocaust note, despite "an impressive proliferation of Holocaust memorials and museums since the late 1970s, sexual abuse has hardly been acknowledged as a theme, much less a central topic, worthy of investigation" (2010: 2). Going beyond previous studies of women's experience during the Holocaust, and moving away from perspectives that relied on falsely neutral treatments of gender and sexual differences, the essays featured in their *Sexual Violence Against Jewish Women During the Holocaust* address explicitly the sexual abuse of women, shedding new light on the apparatus of genocide and the suffering they endured. If we posit that Pinter taps into this history of the sexual violation of women during the Holocaust, confronting his readers and viewers with the challenge of bearing witness not just to the "unspeakable" exhibited in the play, but, to paraphrase Young, to the splitting off of the sexual abuse of women during the Holocaust from Holocaust history and memory (2009: 1779), then how the are we to read the images of the gender-specific as well as sexualised violence portrayed in the play? How do we account for them with a measure of moral sensitivity and care and without adding to the injustice experienced by the victims of these crimes? How are we to understand ourselves in relation to these images evocative of Nazi torture and violence? How are we to bear witness to them? Keeping in mind that the atrocities depicted in *Ashes to Ashes* do not necessarily have their historical referent in the experience of the Holocaust, but may also resonate with other past and present atrocities, these scenes also prompt a question: what does it mean when an author simultaneously eroticises authoritarian violence and repudiates it politically?

Conjuring up the history of rape and sexual abuse of Jewish and non-Jewish women in the Holocaust – which is to say "the history of the absence of women's voices and their experiences as women" within Holocaust representation (Young, 2009: 1779), the play invites both audience interpretation and a certain amount of audience discomfort, if not outright evasion and denial. However, the play's purpose is not simply to return to that which has been left out in or ignored within representation. *Ashes to Ashes* does not just invoke what is missing from much contemporary scholarship on the Holocaust. After all, as Young reminds us, "in many popular representations, the Holocaust has been eroticized, whether we like it or not" (2009: 1781). "In popular movies like Stephen Spielberg's *Schindler's List* or Liliana Cavani's *The Night Porter*, as well as in novels like *The White Hotel*, for example," writes Young, "Eros and Thanatos are twinned as constituent elements of Holocaust victimization, projected reflexively onto victims by a culture obsessed with both, a culture that has long fatally connected the two – a culture that has grown dependent on their union for commercial and entertainment success" (2009: 1781). Rather, engaging Radstone's and Ball's writings on the role of fantasy and the unconscious in the contexts of giving testimony and Frost's work on the cultural fascinations with fascism, as well as several critical responses to *Ashes to Ashes*, in the discussion that follows I will argue that the play's opening scene and its repetition-with-a difference at the end are suggestive of the complex identifications at work in postmemorial testimonial scenarios. As Teresa De Lauretis explains, mass-produced images from movies, television, the internet, and so forth "provide material and scripts, or forms of content and expression, to the subjective activity of fantasising" (1998: 866). These modes of visual symbolisation also share "a permeable border with unconscious wishes including aggressive and/or sadomasochistic urges that may be further specified through Nazi iconography" (Ball, 2008: 209). Taking a cue from De Lauretis and Ball, I am arguing that Rebecca's comments in the opening scene point to the possibility that her identification with an unnamed woman, who is a victim of authoritarian violence, is imbued with a fascination with authoritarian violence, with elements of sadomasochistic fantasy. Rebecca's refusal to see the man who "used to go to the local railway station and walk down the platform and tear all the babies from the arms of their screaming mothers" (27) as anything but her adoring "lover," I contend, is indicative of the ways in which the feared/loaded images of Nazi violence might serve as a site of transgressive identifications with Nazi perpetrators and their victims. Thus I argue that an attention to fantasy may illuminate Rebecca's sympathetic yet fantastic reconstruction of the atrocities she narrates and the relation between fantasy and cultural memory of historical trauma at work in this play.

In her recent writings, Radstone complicates the assumed workings of empathic identification, which in her view inform much of contemporary trauma theory, by shifting it away from often implicit calls to identify with victimhood. While acknowledging the ethical impulse behind trauma theory – its attempts to give shape and meaning to past acts of violence and suffering – she proposes that trauma theory's analyses of testimonies, texts, and other artefacts are limited by their almost exclusive focus on, and empathetic identification with, traumatised groups and individuals, including, most particularly, Holocaust survivors. Radstone challenges the tendency in recent work on trauma and testimony to reproduce an absolute distinction between good and evil by foregrounding potential identifications with sufferers as well with perpetrators (2007b: 191–8). She argues that trauma theory's "focus on texts of catastrophe and suffering is bound to be inflected, also, by less easily acknowledge-able fascinations and fantasies concerning victimhood grounded in aggressivity, or a drive to voyeurism and control" (2007a: 23). She consequently argues for a value of a psychoanalytic perspective that emphasises the role of fantasy and the unconscious in the ways in which we narrate and make sense of traumatic experiences and takes prospect of these sadomasochistic identifications into consideration. Following Gillian Rose's critique of a certain "Holocaust piety" that she thinks characterises those representations of the Holocaust marked by morally proper identifications with victimhood that leave no room for ethical empathic engagement with ambiguity, unsettle-ment, and a whole range of subject positions beyond the witness/vic-tim relationship, she urges us to recognise "the hidden *violence* that subtends identification solely with victimhood, since it is only from the position of absolute power that the predatory capacity of others can cease to be a point of identification" (2001: 66; emphasis in the original).

While maintaining that the distinction between perpetrators and victims must be upheld, Radstone criticises the testimonial perspec-tives of Caruth, Felman, Laub, and Hirsch for their exclusive focus on the identificatory relationship between witness and victim (she takes as her case study Marianne Hirsch's writings on the ethical aesthetics of postmemorial photography). Instead, she invites us to read the cultural remnants of the traumatic affect "in the 'grey zone,' that is, in a zone in which neither 'pure' victimhood, not 'pure' perpetration hold sway" (2001: 75). Radstone borrows the term "grey zone" from Primo Levi (1989), who uses it to refer to situations in which survival imperatives overcome human solidarity and complicity with dehu-manisation can become inescapable even among victims, thereby challenging the binary opposition(s) of "friend" and "enemy," "good" and "evil."

Radstone's argument resonates with Frost's *Sex Drives* in which she examines the modernist aesthetic and its "fascination" with the tropes of fascism. Frost looks at a number of artists (Plath, Genet, Duras, Lawrence, and others) who confronted National Socialism in their work before, during, and after the Second World War, and formulates an argument linking sadomasochistic fantasies inspired by Nazi imagery to cultural anxieties concerning nation building, democracy, gender inequity, homosexuality, and racism (among others). Frost's central claim is that political identities are constructed, in part, around sexual identities, and that that "[f]ascism offers libidinal gratification and solicits pleasures that are otherwise denied by liberalism and Marxism" (2002: 157–8). In her view, liberal democracies have privileged sexual respectability as essential to their own political self-conceptions: "a selected form of sexuality – heterosexuality founded on equality, respect, and non-violence – was validated as a reflection of democratic national ideals," while alternative sexual modes (homosexuality, sadomasochism) were linked to fascist perversion and "institutions of oppression and domination" (2002: 6–7). Therefore, concludes Frost, the erotic allure that the Nazi imagery still retains in contemporary culture may be a by-product of a tradition that casts normative sexuality as a reflection of democratic political ideals, while associating sexual deviance with fascism and upholding the taboo against morally forbidden identifications with Nazi violence.[7]

Like Frost's study, Karyn Ball's *Disciplining the Holocaust* touches on many uncomfortable questions for scholars in this area. Ball employs "the concept of the disciplinary imaginary to describe the nexus of scientific, aesthetic, moral, and rhetorical ideals that scholars in different fields invoke as they defend an 'appropriate' (rigorous and ethical) approach to the Holocaust" (2008: 8). The disciplinary imaginary refers here to the mimetic dimensions of scholarship "that conscripts its producers and readers into reinvesting in particular models and protocols as the parameters of knowledge, authority, and social conduct" (2008: 4). The goals of Ball's study share much in common with those of Radstone and Frost. However, while Frost examines the implications of cultural fascination with fascism and the sadomasochistic fantasies inspired by Nazi imagery, and Radstone invites us to acknowledge the complex interplay of affect, desire, and interest at work in testimonial settings, Ball is concerned with a disciplinary code existing in relation to the production and reception of texts about the Holocaust.

Taking as her point of departure a conference on the Holocaust where women Holocaust survivors testified about gendered forms of violence and humiliation, in the final chapter of her book she examines how traumatic history operates as both an object of knowledge and of desire. Prompted by her response to these testimonies, she writes: "My imagination gags on these images, which seem at once to crystallize and seduce my horror; it is nevertheless driven to return to them again and again. This compulsion betrays a shamefully perverse side to my attempts to assimilate the traumatic significance of the Holocaust through its imagery of death and destruction" (2008: 214). An interrogation of her own potential for voyeuristic and fetishistic pleasure that she discerned in her own responses to the testimonies prompts her discussion of voyeurism in relation to the Holocaust and the ethical dimensions of witnessing such testimony. Thus, through her own confessional performance, Ball invites scholars "to assume responsibility for the unconscious aspects of our fascination with the Holocaust" (2008: 218). This commitment "may seem controversial when we are talking about the postmemorial reception of survivor testimony," writes Ball, but, as she goes on to argue, "it is essential to any reflection on the ethics of this encounter" (2008: 209). Drawing on these critical insights by Ball, Radstone, and Frost as well as engaging several critical responses to Pinter's play that have examined the erotic allure of sexualised violence exhibited in *Ashes to Ashes*, in the next pages I address the issue of "postmemorial" fantasies involved in "adoptive witnessing" at work in the play.

While acknowledging that "the fictional temporality of the play definitely excludes every possibility of a personal involvement of the characters with the Holocaust as a historical event," Elizabeth Sakellaridou reads the play "metaphorically, as a case of PTSD (post-traumatic stress disorder)" (2003: 92). She singles out "repetition and denial" as two common strategies that individuals resort to when coping with this ailment, and observes that "the repetition of the traumatic event usually takes the form of a ritualistic game, which is repeated again and again with healing effects." She argues that Pinter's play follows this psychoanalytic pattern of role-playing, noticing also that it shares this characteristic with his earlier short piece *The Lover*. The author then concludes that by yielding to Rebecca's demand to join the ritual by impersonating the Nazi lover Devlin "discloses, inadvertently, the sadistic pleasures hidden behind the authoritarian infliction of pain and death" (2003: 92), while Rebecca loses herself completely in a masochistic identification with the Jewish victims of the Holocaust.

I find Sakellaridou's interpretation of the play contentious in several respects. First, like few other critics (for instance, Scolnicov, 2003), she identifies Rebecca as Jewish, although there is not enough textual evidence in the play to support this claim even if her name is suggestively Jewish. Next, Sakellaridou identifies the sadomasochistic dynamics in Rebecca's fantasy, as well as in her relationship with Devlin at the end of the play, but, like other Pinter critics, she views sadomasochism as an equivalent to the historical forces that oppress and, ultimately, to the Nazi violence. Sadomasochistic scenarios, as Linda Williams's work has shown, present a difficult problem in the assessment of violence in sexual representation. For, as Williams writes, "here the violence is depicted not as actual coercion but as a highly ritualised game in which the participants consent to play pre-determined roles of dominance and submission" (1989: 18). Following Leo Bersani, Frost acknowledges as well that "the dynamics of sado-masochistic fantasy – domination and submission – are structurally similar to that of fascism," but she also qualifies this view by observing that "to speak of 'submission' to fascism is a grotesque distortion of those who were victimised by it" (2002: 33). She further argues that, "in sadomasochistic fantasy, the characters are engaged with one another's desires and move, however circuitously, toward pleasure. In scenes of fascist violence, consent, recognition, and exchange among the characters are missing, as is erotic pleasure" (2002: 33). She reminds us that "when we note merely the fascist images in sexual scenarios" we lose the track of these important differences (2002: 33). Thus, Frost argues that a distinction must be made between erotic sadomasochism and violence that may, or may not be, sexualised. Following Frost, I contend that *Ashes to Ashes* needs to be read with an eye for erotic investment and incitement, for shifts in agency, and for the differences between historically faithful representations of fascism, and a clearly distorted fantasy of fascism.

Equating a sadomasochistic game with fascist or other manifestations of authoritarian violence leads Sakellaridou to conclude that, in the course of the play's action, "Rebecca moves into the subject position of the victimised, then into that of the redeemed" while "Devlin takes on the subject position of the tormentor/lover and consequently that of the unredeemed" (2003: 94). In her view, even though both characters transgress certain boundaries by reanimating historically specific social roles of a fascist brute and his Jewish victim, "the binary opposition of ethical values persist" (2003: 94). She claims that by the end of the play Rebecca is redeemed through her empathy with the victims of the past injustices, whereas Devlin "is reduced to silence, marginalized for his remorseless endorsement of the forbidden pleasures of oppression and torture" (2003: 94). Thus, in her opinion Pinter's moral position is clear: he "endangers his characters by pushing them into the liminal zone of experience, but spares his spectators the agonies of ethical indeterminacy" (2003: 94).

It seems that in the course of her analysis Sakellaridou implicitly endorses the all too common interpretation of sadomasochistic intercourse as a transgressive behaviour incommensurate with liberal democracy, and that, like some other Pinter critics, she searches for interpretative possibilities that would exculpate Rebecca for this transgression. In my view, it is not Pinter's play, but rather Sakellaridou's interpretation of it, that is shaped by a Manichean vision, making the latter unable to address the complex web of identifications that is arguably constitutive of testimonial witnessing in the play. Sakellaridou's reading of the play, as we shall see, shares much in common with the one offered by Marc Silverstein.

In his study of *Ashes to Ashes*, Silverstein too puts the sign of equation between sadomasochistic behaviour and political violence by interpreting the play's opening dialogue as "marked by the same kind of authoritarian violence Pinter explores in his recent plays" (1999: 76–7). The play's opening scene, in which Rebecca "recollects" finding sexual enjoyment through a submissive role in (what looks like) a sadomasochistic encounter, raises some troubling questions for Silverstein: "How could Rebecca accept her lover's designation of what we clearly perceive as acts of violence, as expressions of 'compassion' and adoration? How can she find gratification in submitting to the kind of sexual brutality that the guards in *One for the Road* inflict on Gilla?" (1999: 45; 77).

In his next interpretative move, Silverstein explains Rebecca's fantasy as an elaborate game on her part aimed at revealing "Devlin's fascination with sexual power" (1999: 80) and making apparent the close link between political authoritarianism and (sadomasochistic) eroticism. In his view, Devlin is drawn to this kind of role playing and exercising power over her but refuses to acknowledge that using the trappings of violent and even genocidal moments from the past or those unfolding on the global stage in sexual games and/or practices may be tantamount to repeating them. Rebecca, however, performs the statement "the personal is political" insisting on connecting the two in an attempt to force Devlin "to confront the nightmare of history to which his dreams of power inexorably lead" (1999: 80).

I am not entirely convinced that Rebecca is quite so consciously attempting to make Devlin aware of this connection, nor that she is as detached from her fantasy as Silverstein would want us to believe. As we have seen, by the end of the play she completely identifies with the woman whose baby is taken from her. Furthermore, the assumed equation between authoritarian violence and the sadomasochistic play/fantasy situates Silverstein's interpretation on the same axes with other interpretations of the play, which in their quest for ethical aesthetics in Pinter's play fail to address more politically sensitive and morally troubling issues involved in witnessing testimony. In other words, they fail to acknowledge what Radstone calls "testimonial witnessing's darker side" (2001: 61).

Despite my disagreement with some of the key tenets of Silverstein's argument, I am drawn to it because it invites us to problematise the operation of sadomasochistic violence in Pinter's play in temporal terms. Engaging Bersani's and Frost's ideas, earlier in my discussion I have emphasised the structural character of an S/M dialectic, which ostensibly focuses on the ritualised exchange of power between two or more people. However, as Elizabeth Freeman points out, sadomasochistic role playing could also become "a means of addressing history in an idiom of pleasure" (2008: 35; see, also Freeman, 2010). Following Simone de Beauvoir, she traces the rise and elaboration of this stigmatised form of sexual practice to the figure of the Marquis de Sade and the time of the French Revolution, when he and other members of the deposed aristocracy revived their lost imperial power symbolically, in the bedroom. By reanimating historically specific social roles related to particular historic injustices, Sadean sex enacts a kind of "time travelling" enabling its participants to engage viscerally with the past. "S/M roles," writes Freeman, "move their players back and forth between some kind of horrific then in the past and some kind of redemptive now in the present, allegedly in the service of pleasure and a freer future" (2008: 45). She illuminates her points by discussing Isaac Julian's film *The Attendant* (1993), where S/M role playing takes place between black and white men sexually allegorising scenes of transatlantic slavery. While aware of the political implications of mimicking slave relations, Julien posits that "a black British man might willingly incorporate the iconography of the transatlantic slave trade into his sexual fantasies and activities" (2008: 42), thus controversially asserting the capacity of the dead slaves' descendants to recalibrate pain into pleasure. In Freeman's view Julien's revivifications of the past injustices do not confuse pleasure with historical amnesia; rather, his achievement is precisely in holding sensuality and historical accountability in productive tension.

Going back to *Ashes to Ashes*, while in the world of Pinter's play S/M appears to work as a mode of connecting otherwise separate historical moments, his characters do not seem to consider S/M as a catalyst for any genuinely historicist inquiry. Granted, towards the end of the play Rebecca's narrative gains erotic force enticing Devlin to enact the Sadean tableau vivant invoked by Rebecca early on; however, he still refuses to acknowledge any continuity between historically specific injustices and the body's erotic economy. He certainly does not emerge at the end of the play recognising the experiences Rebecca recounts. On the other hand, Rebecca relentlessly insists on the encounter with history, bleeding the borders between public and private, collective and individual subjectivities. Though to Silverstein Rebecca appears as someone who self-consciously manipulates time, feeling a painful, and/or a pleasurable link to the past she invokes, in the end she fuses a collective past with the present tense by identifying completely with the woman whose experiences she relates, surmounting the very difference between self and other. While in the world of the play mixing of a traumatic past and eroticism does not seem to yield new possibilities for being and knowing for its characters, this may play out differently for its audiences, who are invited to confront, on an affective register irreducible to a traditional historical inquiry, what has been at once acknowledged and disavowed. That is, invoking personal pasts and collective suffering in an idiom of pleasure, the play could be seen, to quote Freeman, as a way of invoking history through "nonsequential forms of time . . . unconscious, haunting, reveries, and the afterlife . . . that may be invisible to the historicist eye" (2010: xi). Moreover, as Fitzpatrick asserts in her article on the play's staging in Toronto in 2007, for its audiences *Ashes to Ashes* may also open up new registers for critically exploring convergence between sadomasochistic eroticism, whatever its moral valences, and the seemingly weightier matters of time and history. Her argument implies, for instance, that the play may prompt reflections on the specific operations of power at work in the scene of production at Abu Ghraib that gave rise to the photographs of torture, in which torturers disavowed their own S/M and homosexual excitement even as they engaged in S/M and homosexual acts to shame and humiliate Muslims. Furthermore, the play may also trigger thinking about the way in which the dissemination and reception of these photos in new contexts brought about unveiling the mechanism of disavowal that produced them in the first place.

Finally, I would like to address briefly Hanna Scolnicov's study of Pinter's portrayal of sexual violence in *Ashes to Ashes*. While offering a sensitive analysis of the inscription of traumatic memory in the play, she too – just like Sakellaridou and Silverstein – displays anxiety over the play's violence. Referring to Billington's suggestion that Pinter might have based the play on Gitta Sereny's "Postscript" in her book on Albert Speer, which tells of his love affair with a young English woman (Scolnicov claims she was in fact German), she speculates that "Rebecca's fascination, on the verge of hypnosis, with her lover's sexual violence may be Pinter's way of coming to grips with the preposterousness of the unnamed young woman's attraction to one of the central figures of the Third Reich" (2001: 16). She further argues that "Rebecca's compassion for, and even identification with, the victims is incommensurate with the anonymous young woman's infatuation with the former Nazi chief" (2001: 16). In the final analysis, for Scolnicov, the concerns raised by Sereny's narrative and Pinter's play are too dissimilar.

Scolnicov's argument begs a question: Are "infatuation" and "identification" invoked in her analysis necessarily mutually exclusive? By dismissing the "attraction" of the young women to a former Nazi as mere "preposterousness" and suggesting an alternative direction for interpreting the play, Scolnicov completely disregards the problems posed by the opening scene involving the lover, that is, the question of Rebecca's sadomasochistic fantasy involving an authoritarian figure responsible for various atrocities. There is a certain presumptuousness at work in her argument, a presumptuousness that, quoting Radstone on Primo Levi (1989), "can shade into self-righteousness" (2001: 65).

Contra Sakellaridou, Silverstein, and Scolnicov, I argue that, by disintegrating the official line that divides good and evil, Pinter indeed blurs the lines between self and other, victim and victimiser, and memory and fantasy. This transgression of set identities does not describe a sexual dynamics in the context of war and the "Final Solution," but postwar eroticised obsessions with the memory of Nazism and the sites of pain and extermination. What makes the games of erotic enslavement and domination presented in the opening scene of *Ashes to Ashes* so unpalatable for many critics is that this mutually consensual theatre of cruelty opens up onto questions of morality that are deeply embedded within historical, sexual, and gender discourses. Re-enacting imaginatively the limit-experience of excessive violation and enslavement that would enable her to efface boundaries between pleasure and terror, and life and death, Pinter's Rebecca challenges stable subjective identifications that would accord her the status of a "pure" victim that is morally irreproachable. Further on in the play, she imaginatively memorialises the horror of some unspecified atrocities (that transpire in the past, present, and future), but also bypasses their implications and transposes their impact to the realm of fantasy, to "a grey zone where scenarios of domination and sadistic bloodlust alternate with images of masochistic abjection before the sublime tortures of authoritarian masters" (Ball, 2008: 214). In portraying this the play reveals that beneath and "alongside the progressive goal of forestalling future violence by exposing its myriad forms and affects," for instance, through the acts of adoptive witnessing, may lie "an erotic fascination with power and violence" (Ball, 2008: 216).

Pinter and the critics I have invoked here leave us with some provocative ideas and gripping questions about the relation between political authoritarianism and the erotic. For instance, why is transgressive, authoritarian politics so often eroticised in fantasy? In Frost's view, this is because "the politically forbidden and repudiated is just as likely, if not more so, to be the substance of erotic fantasy as the permitted" (2002: 10). However, it seems that it is not just the "politically forbidden" that has the erotic lure, but specifically power and aggression. Furthermore, if we claim that sexual fantasy, even when it finds its inspiration in the master and slave scenario that Nazism offers, "is not necessarily coherent, politically useful, or instrumental" (Frost, 2002: 9) and that it cannot be held to the same standards as political ideology, we are still left to account for how the erotic dimension of fantasy and unacknowledged obsessions structure our engagement with political reality and with what kind of consequences.

In her book *Women As Weapons of War* (2007), Kelly Oliver tellingly explores precisely this interplay between gender, sex, and violence, mediated by the media, in the context of the ongoing American occupation of Iraq. For instance, she relates the 2005 Hollywood blockbuster *Mr. & Mrs. Smith* – featuring Brad Pitt and Angelina Jolie as a married couple whose brutality towards each other rekindles their desires and saves them from their empty lives – to the torture photographs from Abu Ghraib, offering insights into larger contemporary, political, and social practices. Oliver suggest that the line between the acts of sexual violence performed at Abu Ghraib – ranging from acts closely associated with homosexuality such as anal and oral sex, via sadomasochistic practices of bondage, leashing, and hooding, to rape – and the fictional images of sadomasochistic violence (be it blockbusters of S/M porn popular with soldiers) is not as fixed and clearly demarcated as we would like to believe. Here Oliver asks a simple yet salient question, "weren't the young soldiers at Abu Ghraib not only following orders to 'soften up' the prisoners but also acting out their own fantasies?" (2007: 84).

Days after the photographs had been circulated among the foreign press, George Bush dismissed the abuse in Abu Ghraib by saying, "This treatment does not reflect the nature of American people" (qtd. in Raijiva, 2005: 12). As Jasbir Puar aptly comments, "Bush denies that the psychic and fantasy life of Americans is depraved, sick, or polluted and rather affirms that it is naturally free from such perversions – that Americans could never enjoy inflicting such abuse as occurred at Abu Ghraib and would never even have the mindset or capacity to think of such acts" (2004: 523). Although many accounts of the actions of the US military in Saddam's former torture chambers see them as exceptional, Oliver stresses that the torture depicted in these pictures is part of a larger context of violence and points to a loss of meaning in our world. Following on recent insights by Julia Kristeva, Oliver interprets these violations as symptomatic of the predicament of the modern subject who is losing the ability to find satisfactory narratives for its interior states. "Without the ability to articulate our violent fantasies," argues Oliver, "we end up acting on them – confusing fantasy with reality" (2007: 91). Rather than denying our capacity for violence, she suggests that we need to cultivate our "ability to imagine, interpret, and represent desires and fears" (2007: 91). To Oliver, the human capacity to interpret violent impulses prevents acting on those impulses. This process of perpetual questioning and interpretation is also central to her witnessing model of ethics in the service of justice, nonviolence, and freedom, which I will engage in my discussion of Żmijewski's artwork in the second half of this chapter.

Examining Pinter's work through the lens of postmodernist culture, Mireia Aragay also raises the issue of the personal vs. the political in Pinter's work, arguing that what crucially informs Pinter's openly political plays written since the mid-1980s, especially *Ashes to Ashes*, is "a concern with articulating a social, shared sense of subjectivity, arguably the necessary condition for the emergence of a truly transformative kind of agency that will bypass the individualism underlying both the liberal humanist and the postmodernist subjects" (2001: 252). In Aragay's view, Rebecca "ultimately comes to embody the claim that it is only by extending ourselves beyond ourselves, only by truly taking on the implications of a shared, social sense of subjectivity, that any kind of effective resistance may be envisaged" (2001: 255). This critic also convincingly argues that, as in postmodernism, in Pinter's recent work there is an inextricable link between the "private" and the "public," which may also be related to his increasing political activities over the last two decades. On the other hand, in his article "Pinter's Sexual Politics," Drew Milne takes a different stance on *Ashes to Ashes* arguing that: "The imaginative juxtaposition of holocaust 'memories' with female desire for misogynist authoritarianism . . . leaves political responsibility disturbingly ambiguous" (2001: 209). In his view, Pinter does not provide terms by which different perspectives could be judged, which "confirms the structural gulf between politics and sexual politics in Pinter's works as a whole" (2001: 209).

However, I contend that, if following the play, we group Rebecca's erotic fascination with authoritarian male power and violence together with her ethical impulse to take a witnessing stance in regard to the atrocities she relates, we can reintroduce the concept of fantasy as that which links both of these responses. Moreover, we can take their co-presence as a counter-narrative or caution against any straightforward interpretation of the play as a whole. In this context, there seems no point in trying to establish a one-way relation between the personal and the wider political history the play evokes, as Aragay and other critics discussed in this essay seem to argue. The play offers the implication of the one in the other – implication, rather than determination, precisely because one cannot establish a single, one-track relation between the two. In this regard, what is most striking about *Ashes to Ashes* is its mobility of fantasy, the extent to which it takes up psychic positions which, it is often argued, if not clearly distinguished, lead to the collapse of morality itself. Pinter, on the other hand, moves from one position to the other, implicating them in each other, forcing the spectator to enter into something which she or he is often willing to consider only on condition of seeing it as something in which, psychically no less than historically, she or he plays absolutely no part.

To spell this out a little more clearly: I suggest that morality does not collapse if the relations between fantasy and history are two-track or even more complex and multi-valenced. It may be possible to choose to act out fantastical scenarios of S/M while condemning actual historical acts of torture, abuse, and extermination. It may even be compulsive and unconscious to some extent in the first case and conscious and conscience-laden in the second. Pinter's *Ashes to Ashes* asks us to acknowledge that complexity. Marooned from her own present, burdened with a traumatic legacy, grieving the loss of what was never hers to relinquish, driven by the pressure of postmemorial desires and fantasies, Pinter's Rebecca testifies to the stubborn lingering of pastness, the way it splits the present and our selfhood, while also articulating an ethics of responsibility towards the other across time. Perhaps what is left open in *Ashes to Ashes* and, indeed, in my critique of it, is the appropriate value or judgement to place on the psychic investment in S/M. The gendered nature of the play would seem to make it even more difficult than in a homosocial economy where arguably gender is not already in play as a power relation between the consenting adults. Throughout my analysis, however, I have resisted a moral discourse against S/M as such (that is, as an extremely marginalised sexual practice). Rather than disavowing our fascination with violence and holding onto a purified vision of humanity (that would construe humanity as fundamentally non-violent), I suggest that it may be infinitely more productive to acknowledge and channel that violence productively. But, of course, *Ashes to Ashes* presents only one of many possible scenarios for reanimating the past, even if only in imagination and by proxy. As the theatrical re-enactment of a scene of humiliation from Auschwitz in Żmijewski's *80064*, which I analyse next, indicates, other power differentials could inflect our postmemorial "playful" engagements with the past. Here, a Holocaust survivor, in an encounter with an artist, exchanges a material and symbolic sign of his victim status or identity as a commodity or currency producing additional moral and ethical dilemmas.[8]

Holocaust testimony, ethics, and affect in Artur Zmijewski's *80064*

Earlier in this chapter, when discussing ethical stakes involved in postmemorial witnessing at work in Pinter's *Ashes to Ashes*, I pointed to a noticeable turn to testimonial discourse in much recent cultural theory, especially in the context of finding ways to bear witness to human suffering, tragedy and trauma. In their study *Testimony: Crisis of Witnessing in Literature, Psychoanalysis and History* published in 1992, which played a significant role in launching the field of trauma studies in the Anglo-American academy, Shoshana Felman and Dori Laub claim that that the twentieth century was "an era of testimony," although how testimony became a significant cultural form remained unexplained in their work. In her essay "On Testimony" (1994) and the book *The Era of the Witness* (2006, originally published in French in 1998), the historian Annette Wieviorka does precisely this, tracing the evolution of testimony about the Holocaust from its beginning during the war years, through its next phase in the trial of Adolf Eichmann, to what she calls the "the current era of testimony." To Wieviorka, the Eichmann trial made a profound change in the function of testimony:

> Testimony has changed direction. Print has been replaced by the tape recorder and the video camera. At the same time, the function of testimony has also changed. In the years following the war, the primary aim of testimony was knowledge – knowledge of the modalities of genocide and the deportation. Testimony had the status of an archival document. Today . . . the purpose of testimony is no longer to obtain knowledge. Time has passed and the historian does not trust a memory in which the past has begun to

blur and which has been enriched by various images since the survivor's return to freedom. The mission that has devolved to testimony is no longer to bear witness to inadequately known events, but to keep them before our eyes. Testimony is to be a means of transmission to future generations. (Wieviorka, 1994: 24)[9]

As it took survivors' stories from within the family sphere to the public, the trial also transformed the role of the witness in contemporary culture. The survivors acquired legitimacy as bearers of truth as well as "the social identity of survivors because society now recognized them as such" (Wieviorka, 2006: 88). With the trial, the witness emerged from the shadows of the Holocaust to become an "embodiment of memory (*un homme-mémoire*), attesting to the past and to the continuing presence of the past" (Wieviorka, 2006: 88).

Discussing Pinter's play I focused not on actual survivors and their testimonies but on the problem of adoptive witnessing and melancholic fixations that may accompany it, in order to illuminate the sense of second-hand culpability that sometimes inflects the cultural imagination of the postmemorial generation and the challenges this poses for our thinking about history, subjectivity, and ethics after the Holocaust. The circulation of innocence and guilt at work in *Ashes to Ashes* (but, as I have shown, also in current theorisations of the Holocaust), risks erasing the historical specificity of the concentration camp experience and conflating the irreducibly distinct subject positions of victim, executioner, witness, and secondary witness. Continuing on this trajectory, I would like to examine Artur Żmijewski's video work *80064* from 2004, which, I contend, conflates distinct subject positions and histories with disturbing ethical consequences. For this work, Żmijewski persuaded an Auschwitz survivor, Józef Tarnawa, featured in the film, to have the prisoner number tattooed on his forearm restored (Figure 4.2). The film was made for the exhibition "The Auschwitz Trial: History and Reception" (*Auschwitz Prozess – Geschichte und Rezeption*, 2004) organised by the Fritz Bauer Institute to mark the 40th anniversary of a trial of Nazi war criminals in Frankfurt-am-Main, but was eventually rejected. It was realised for the first time as part of Żmijewski's individual exhibition at the *Centre d'Art Contemporain de Bretigny* in France. Since then it has been shown in many countries. While this work and the rest of Żmijewski's oeuvre to date have received considerable

Figure 4.2 Still from Artur Żmijewski's *80064*, courtesy of the artist, Foksal Gallery Foundation Warsaw and Galerie Peter Kilchmann, Zurich

approbation from critics and curators in Poland and internationally, the equivocations that surround the issue of the consensual re-tat-tooing of Tarnawa, the amorphous "public good" that mandated the humiliation, and the term "consent" employed by Żmijewski and some of his critics to designate the displacement and euphemisation of violence in the discourse on *80064* warrant further scrutiny.

Focusing on the ethics of the encounter between the artist and the survivor, in this chapter I seek to reckon with the doubling of pain or wounding as well as the nature and value of pains-taking in this memory-based work. Situating my analysis in the context of recent debates on reenactment in contemporary art and culture, and continuing my engagement with the discourses of witnessing and trauma theory, I will examine the questions, criticisms, and concerns around the ethics and politics of this work as well as the model of subjectivity it posits in relation to theories of trauma and its rep-resentation. I further show that this work by Żmijewski testifies to the ways in which the Holocaust continues to affect the generations who emerge in its wake, but also to the fraught and sensitive issues that emerge from the postmemorial generations' engagements with this past.

Between 1990 and 1995 Żmijewski studied at the Sculpture Department of the Academy of Fine Arts in Warsaw, but later on became increasingly interested in photography and film. Today he is one of the most challenging, provocative, and established Polish artists of the younger generation working in Poland today. A survey of his work opened at the prestigious MIT List Visual Arts Center in Boston in May 2004, and he represented Poland at the 51st Art Biennale in Venice in 2005. He is currently the curator for the 2012 Berlin Biennale and an art editor of *Krytyka Polityczna* (*Political Critique*), a respected Polish magazine that brings the fields of philosophy, politics, and art together.[10] He is also a regular collaborator of the Foksal Gallery Foundation based in Warsaw, one of the most significant independent galleries in Poland today.

Many of Żmijewski's works from the last decade or so are devised as experimental situations in which the participants are subjected to a specific scenario. As Claire Bishop notes, "it is never clear to what degree his participants are acting with their own agency, or being manipulated to fulfil the requirements of his predetermined narrative" (2010: 266), hence his works often raise strong ethical criticism. Filmed and edited by Żmijewski, who occasionally takes part in them, these situations often deal with individual and collective suffering, social taboos, disability, and human vulnerability. For instance, in *Singing Lesson* (*Lekcja śpiewu*, 2001), he employed a conductor to teach students from a school for the deaf to sing the "Kyrie" from Jan Maklakiewicz's *Polish Mass* (1944) in the Augsburg-Evangelican church in Warsaw. For *Repetition* (*Powtórzenie*), produced for the Venice Biennale in 2005, he employed seventeen Polish men paying them forty dollars a day to re-enact the infamous Stanford Prison Experiment in Warsaw's historical district of Praga. Two years later, at the Documenta 12 in Kassel, he presented *Them* (*Oni*, 2007), involving representatives from four different ideological groups in Warsaw; the work was structured around a series of painting workshops in which each group produced an artwork depicting their values and then, encouraged by Żmijewski, responded to each other's paintings by altering them in whatever way they wanted. Finally, an important strand in this artistic inquiry includes works dealing directly with the issues of individual and collective memories related to the Second World War.[11] In *Our Songbook* (*Nasz śpiewnik*, 2003), shot in Israel, he asks elderly Polish Jews living in nursing homes in Tel Aviv to sing in Polish songs from their pre-war childhood. For *The Game of Tag* (*Berek*, 1999), which Michael Moynihan (2012) has found the most controversial work of the 2012 Berlin Biennale, Żmijewski asked a group of adults of various ages to enter a former Nazi death camp gas chamber naked and play a game of tag.[12]

Repetition is also present in *80064*. Filmed in what looks like a tattoo parlour, the film starts with then 92-year-old survivor answering Żmijewski's questions about his life in the camp. He is still hesitant about undergoing the act of re-tattooing, unsure whether a "restored" number will still be authentic. Żmijewski insists, reminding him that they made a previous agreement about this, and the elderly man finally gives in. In an interview given to a Polish magazine, Żmijewski explains the rationale for this risky experiment. The quote is lengthy but telling:

> After 60 years, the prisoners of Auschwitz remember only fragments, pieces, misremembered and deformed, far from being truthful to the events. . . . I know, that their narratives are flawed, due to their age as well as due to their fear of annihilation, which erased many events . . . . [T]he narratives of the survivors are "constructed," and the witnesses themselves are not capable of reconstructing some events – their memory is hidden from them. Something else is also hidden – emotions. Emotions from the time of extermination (*Zagłady*), emotions of witnesses are locked in them – their coming out is maybe a more significant witnessing than words, stronger than text – it is a true proof of the brutality of past events, and for us, the audience, also a spectacle of history, a history which lives in a person and can flow out of him as a scream, fear, a cry, a sigh, returning fright/terror and regret. This history is different than one described in words. This history is one which can truly wound, and the least safe is the witness. But his kind of witnessing is irrefutable, aggressive, penetrating emotions of the audience in the same way as pain penetrates the body. It was my purpose to awake these kinds of emotions and that is why I asked a former Auschwitz prisoner for his agreement for the

re-tattooing of the number. This was a vehicle of time, a tool for the trip to that world. (2005c: n.p.)[13]

Żmijewski does not dismiss testimony in general. Rather he argues that survivors' efforts to pass on their stories are in and of themselves inadequate to transmit their traumatic experiences. His views are consonant with the views held by literary theorists such as Felman and Caruth who have shown how traumatic memory and its delayed aftereffects throughout one's life compromises history conceived as a straightforward narrative account of the unfolding of events, which I have addressed at length in this book's Introduction. This anxiety about transmission of Holocaust experiences also reso-nates Interestingly with Ernst van Alphen's dissatisfaction with the Holocaust education he received growing up in the Netherlands. An overdose of information about the Holocaust that he was exposed to resulted in boredom and created an obstacle for a more affective engagement with this past. Van Alphen evokes this experience in an essay titled "Playing the Holocaust," where he examines works by a younger generation of artists – "second or third generation descen-dants from survivors or bystanders who represent the Holocaust or Nazi Germany" (2005: 181), who share with him a negative assess-ment of the Holocaust education they acquired in their respective countries. Analysing their imaginative attempts at working through the Holocaust memory and history he commends their creative strat-egies devised to solicit affective engagement with their audiences. He praises David Levinthal's (USA) *Mein Kampf* (1994–96), with photographed scenes from Auschwitz, previously staged by means of little dolls or figurines; Ram Katzir's (Israel/the Netherlands) series of installations with colouring books based on Nazi photographs (the audiences were invited to colour the images), and Zbigniew Libera's *Lego, Concentration Camp* set (Poland, 1994) for removing any obsta-cles standing in the way "of a 'felt knowledge' of the emotions these events entailed . . . " (2005: 203).

Van Alphen sees these works as "purposeful attempts to shed the mastery that Holocaust narratives provide," which "entice the viewer to enter into a relationship that is affective and emotional rather than cognitive" (2005: 201). What he seems to be suggesting here is that affect is somehow independent of signification and meaning, a belief he shares with new Deleuze-inspired affect theorists such as

Brian Massumi (2002), William Connolly (2002), and Nigel Thrift (2004).[14] As Ruth Leys has written, unlike Freud and "appraisal theorists," these affect theorists "posit a constitutive disjunction between our emotions on the one hand and our knowledge of what causes and maintains them on the other, because according to them affect and cognition are two separate systems" (2011: 437). While there is no space here to engage these discourses on affect and their theoretical, political and other implications, I should like to point out that one of the reasons Leys finds these theorists' views troubling is that they imply such a radical separation of emotion or affect from cognition and meaning "as to make disagreement about meaning, or ideological dispute, irrelevant to cultural analysis" (2011: 472). Leys does not elaborate on this argument, but I find it keenly relevant for my discussion here. For instance, neither van Alphen nor Żmijewski ask how affective relations to the history and memory of the Holocaust and its victims are mobilised, constituted, and institutionalised in different national settings and how this may affect their audiences' engagement with these artworks. They also do not address recent discussions and debates on the politics of memory in Europe and how certain cultural attitudes towards survivors may erase their experiences in ways great and small. Van Alphen makes valid points that traditional learning that leads to the mastery of the subject studied fails in the face of the Holocaust, and that the legacy of this historical trauma cannot be taught along traditional pedagogical lines, where the memory of the event is drummed into pupils' minds. Yet, while favouring "a performative mastery of the emotions triggered by the happenings" over "an epistemic mastery of what happened" (2005: 203), it never occurs to him to subject the existing textbooks (and gaps and silences they may be perpetuating) to critical analysis or question the kind of knowledge that is being transmitted on to future generations, as if it were somehow wholly unproblematic and the same all over Europe, in Israel, and the USA. The fascinations and preoccupations with the Holocaust and the aesthetic strategies that he employs in his work are what Żmijewski shares with these and other artists from Europe and beyond, as I will show shortly when discussing his work in relation to recent fascinations with re-enactment in arts and a wider public sphere.

But to return to Żmijewski's video: the admittedly selective incidents that comprise Tarnawa's narrative: the arrival to the camp in 1942, the tattooing – the first permanent insult to his bodily integrity – and his struggle to survive, obscure the full materiality of violence that he experienced in Auschwitz, perhaps in order to avoid the pain and humiliation necessarily part of its retelling. That is to say, the language of fact – criticised by van Alphen – and the emotional withholding that characterise the narrative are determined by complex factors: the degradations he experienced, the strictures of decency, the pain of recollection, and the impossibility of representing the magnitude of violence experienced in the hands of Nazis and their collaborators. The conventions of the video film genre and the intentions of the filmmaker – an issue I will expand on further below – also account for the selective character of the story presented here. These elisions both display and displace the searing wounds of his violated body. As Cathy Caruth has noted, "the transformation of the trauma into a narrative memory that allows the story to be verbalised and communicated, to be integrated into one's own, and others', knowledge of the past, may lose both the precision and the force that characterizes traumatic recall" (1995: 153). In the story of Pierre Janet's patient Irène, for instance, explains Caruth, "her cure is characterised by the fact that she can tell a 'slightly different story' to different people" (1995: 153). In other words, the capacity to remember is also the capacity to shape the narrative or even to forget.

As Charlotte Delbo, a French political prisoner who survived Auschwitz, also shows in her prose and poems, factual accounts of the past (such as those that inform Tarnawa's testimony) can also serve as a protective shield to ward off the memory of trauma and pain associated with Auschwitz. Delbo distinguishes between two distinct modes of personal memory, the "ordinary" intellectual memory connected to the thinking process, and the "deep memory" that "preserves sensations, physical imprints" (1990: 3). Common memory enables her to speak about her experiences of the camps, and translate the past for others. Hence "when I talk to you about Auschwitz, it is not from deep memory my words issue. They come from external memory, if I may put it that way, from intellectual memory, the memory connected with thinking process" (1990: 3) When, however, "deep memory" ruptures the present and her reconstructed universe, "I feel it throughout my whole body which becomes a mass of suffering; and I feel death fasten on me, I feel that I am dying" (1990: 3). Deep memory defies historicisation and resists turning into controlled narrative, threatening to collapse the distinction between present and past and re-engulf the survivor. It comes to represent the immediacy and lasting presence of the camp (when Auschwitz is supposedly over): "Auschwitz is there, unalterable, precise, but enveloped in the skin of memory, an impenetrable skin that isolates it from my present self. . . . I live within a two-fold being" (1990: 2–3). As many critics have noted, the structure of Delbo's text too mimes the effects of massive trauma on the emplotment of the past, contesting the hegemony of more conventional Holocaust testimonies that construct tragic yet linear, coherent, and possibly redemptive narratives of inspiration, courage, and triumph.

While Delbo uses this epidermal metaphor to convey daily challenges of surviving traumatic experience, Żmijewski, in pursuit of a certain re-enacting distinct from retelling, literally cuts through the survivor's skin in order to access his history and to allow his memories to bleed out. With the act of re-tattooing – some would say, the replicated dehumanisation – Żmijewski wishes to trigger the emotional memory of the survivor that, in his view, would reveal the "truth" of Auschwitz. To be sure, the re-enactment employed in this artwork to reach back to historical events (be it at an emotional cost to the survivor) is not peculiar to Żmijewski and other art re-enactment practices but exists rather more broadly in a whole range of popular activities not exclusive to art. Hence a brief detour to engage the cultural practice of re-enactment in circulation today may throw some light on Żmijewski's staging of testimony in *80064*.

While the term "re-enactment" has circulated in various discourses in the past, its popularity has increased enormously in the last two decades. As Rebecca Schneider writes in *Performing Remains*, the term covers a wide range of forms and practices: from "re-playing or re-doing a precedent event, artwork, or act" to historical re-enactments in living history museums, historical reality television shows, and preservation societies. "In many ways," writes Schneider, "reenactment has become the popular and practice-based wing of what has been called the twentieth-century academic 'memory industry'" (2011: 2). There is a wide range of types of re-enactment in the art and performance worlds today, which exhibit a variety of aesthetic and political goals and engage their audiences in many different ways. For instance, some restage artworks and historically significant events with as much exactness as possible – Schneider offers here the examples of the Wooster Group's recreation of Grotowski's *Akropolis* and Rod Dickinson's repetition of Dr Stanley Milgram's infamous 1961 social psychology experiment "Obedience to Authority" (inspired in part by the 1961 trial of Adolf Eichmann), which tested how far participants would go to obey an authoritative scientist and inflict pain on other persons. Others, such as Jeremy Deller's *The Battle of Orgreave*, which reconstructs a 1981 confrontation between striking British coal miners and the police, take artistic liberties and depart from the established account about this event.

According to Amelia Jones, common to vastly different examples of re-enactments in the visual and performing arts "is an interest in how time, memory, and history work – and how or whether we can retrieve past events . . . by redoing them in some fashion" (2011: 24–5). While some critics argue that artistic re-enactments exhibit greater critical reflexivity than more widely consumed forms of popular history such as the re-creation of historic battles, I think that Jones's comments also hold for a wide array of living history events, mock battles, and heritage scenes, which seem to promise their participants access to history through direct involvement and empathy in a way that various forms of historical representation cannot. "This short-circuiting of the present with the past," argues Inke Arns, "makes it possible to experience the past in the present – actually, an impossible view of history" (2007: 59). In Arns's celebratory view of the phenomenon, re-enactment offers great possibilities for imaginative and empathetic encounters with the subjects from the past eras. "By eliminating the safe distance between abstract knowledge and personal experience, between then and now, between the others and oneself, re-enactments make personal experience of abstract history possible" (2007: 59).

Other critics are more cautious about re-enactment's epistemological and political claims and promises (for example, Cook 2004; Agnew 2007; Schwarz 2007). To Vanessa Agnew, contemporary re-enactment is indicative of the recent "affective turn" in the study of history and marks a departure from more traditional forms of historiographical inquiry. "As a form of affective history – i.e. historical representation that both takes affect as its object and attempts to elicit affect – reenactment is less concerned with events, processes, or structures than with the individual's physical and psychological experience" (Agnew, 2007: 301). While not questioning its cultural and sociological significance, she asks to what extent affect can be considered evidentiary. In her view "reenactment's collapsing of temporalities and its privileging of experience over event or structure – raise questions about its capacity to further historical understanding and reconcile the past to the present" (2007: 301). Finally, Agnew asks questions about the kind of the cultural and political work re-enactment as a form of affective history performs and the nature of the new knowledge it advances. While re-enactments place modern individuals in dialogue with a historical imaginary, too often they "promote a form of understanding that neither explains historical processes nor interrogates historical injustices" (2007: 302). Instead, as she illustrates through her discussion of contemporary German reality television shows such as *The Black Forest House, 1902* (*Das Schwarzwald Haus, 1902*; 2002) and *Adventure 1900: Life in the Manor House* (*Abenteuer 1900: Leben im Gutshaus*; 2004), where a group of people faced the challenges posed by living in a reconstructed historical setting without the modern-day conveniences, history here is the conceit "for coming to terms with the present" (2007: 302).

Writing about re-enactments of colonial encounter in Australia, Anja Schwarz also sees re-enactments well-equipped for the "reconciliatory task of summoning ghosts and being claimed by the spectres of the past" (2007: 439–40). Focusing on the role of Indigenous actors in these historical re-enactments, she shows how they simultaneously exhibit recognition and containment of hurtful pasts associated with the Australian landscape. Ultimately Schwartz argues that re-enactments have been crucial in the creation and contestation of public memory (see, for instance, Taylor, 2006), but she also warns that all too often they offer redemptive narratives that present a sanitised version of the past.

Trying to account for the continued popular appeal of Civil War re-enactments in the USA, Schneider notes: "The *feel* – the affective engagement – is key" (2011: 50). In her view, the re-enactors that she interviewed and observed "wanted to touch something they deemed authentic, real, and actual in experience – something about fighting and falling on the field that would be other than what they could glean from textual accounts, photographic images, or watching film actors re-enacting on screen" (2011: 54). In other words, these people "wanted to *experience it for themselves* and add to their historical acumen by way of their own physical engagement" (2011: 54; original emphasis).

However, this "communing with" the spectre is not without its own moral dilemmas and difficulties, especially in the societies still haunted by their unsettled pasts. "No one has ever worked through an injury without repeating it," Judith Butler reminds us. "There is no possibility of not repeating. The only question that remains is: How will that repetition occur, at what site . . . and with what pain and promise?" (1997b: 102). Claude Lanzmann's attempt to generate a form of access to an (unmediated) truth about the Holocaust through *Shoah* (1985 [2003]) – his monumental, nine and a half hour long film made up of testimonies of Jewish survivors, bystanders, and perpetrators of the Holocaust, much of which employs re-enactment as its crucial epistemic and aesthetic strategy – is a case in point and of much relevance to our discussion of the re-enactment that Żmijewski employs in his film.

Video testimony has been privileged by many scholars for its capacity to communicate survivors' experiences of the Holocaust in the way that, for instance, written memoirs could not. It is seen as "the genre most able to communicate the sense memory of the survivor," while some of its proponents such as Lawrence Langer "even believe that through the embodied presence of the survivor and the bodily re-enactment of the camp experience, this genre can give us a form of access to an 'unmediated truth' about the Holocaust or to 'the thing itself'" (qtd. in Hirsch and Spitzer, 2009: 158). However, as Thomas Trezise usefully reminds us, Lanzmann's *Shoah* – subtitled *An Oral History* – is different from the kind of videotaped testimony found in archives around the world – in Warsaw, at Yad Vashem, at Yale University, in Washington, DC, and other places. It is different in its "drive to elicit from interviewees a re-enactment," which seems to be designed to "to afford immediate access to the experience of atrocity, to enable those who 'were not there' to participate in, and hence in some measure to appropriate, the traumatization of those who were" (2008: 35). In *Shoah*, Lanzmann brings some of his interviewees back to the sites of atrocity, such as former extermination camps in Poland and their environs, or even constructed sets, leading them insistently towards the reliving of their traumatic experiences in the present (instead of simply describing them) so as to be able to remember and testify about the past. For instance he asks Henrik Gawkowski to drive a locomotive in Treblinka; he takes Simon Srebnik back to Chelmno where Srebnik sings again the ballad he sang to save his life; and he places Abraham Bomba, a former *Sonderkommando*, in a barber shop in Israel, where he asks him to imitate cutting the hair of Jewish women inside Treblinka's gas chambers. In this last instance, Lanzmann relentlessly questions the survivor, insisting that he resumes his testimony – "You have to do it" (Lanzmann, 1985: 117) – even when Bomba breaks down emotionally and asks to be permitted to stop his account. Many critics have discussed ethical issues that the scene with Bomba raises. To Tony Kushner, the director's questioning of Bomba "can have no ethical justification" on either historical or artistic grounds (2006: 290). For instance, he supports this claim by invoking Wieviorka's essay "On Testimony," which I mentioned earlier, where she claims that the testimonies of the survivors featured in the film bring little that was not already familiar from other sources, such as trials and written testimonies. While Lanzmann seems to be using testimony to gather evidence, LaCapra suggests that the staging of the scene with Bomba may serve another purpose altogether. In his view, the object of Lanzmann's quest (and Żmijewski has professed as much about his own pursuit in *80064*) is "the incarnation, actual reliving, or compulsive acting out of the past – particularly its traumatic suffering – in the present" (1997: 235). He finds Lanzmann's working method ethically dubious: "My feeling is that it is acceptable if a survivor in the course of an interview he or she has willingly entered into finds him- or herself transported out of the present and into his or her initial experience of traumatic events" (1998a: 834). "However," LaCapra continues, "I find it ethically dubious if the survivor is led in the direction of retraumatisation by an intrusive interviewer. The fact that the experience is made 'available to the viewer' does not justify the interviewer's procedure. In fact it increases its dubiousness" (834).

As I mentioned earlier, scholars such as Wievorka have highlighted the performative quality of testimony – its capacity to transmit affect and body memory. To Geoffrey Hartman, too, testimony is not just a source of historical information but also "a humanizing and transactive process" (1996: 155). Drawing on Aharon Appelfeld's *Beyond Despair* (1994), he states that testimony "works on the past to rescue the 'individual, with his own past and proper name' from the place of terror where that face and name were taken away" (1996: 155). This is to say, if the victim has been dehumanised by the camp experience, then during the testimony the survivor gains access to his self and reclaims the position of witness to the history that he has lived through. Dori Laub, a psychiatrist and cofounder of the Fortunoff Video Archive for Holocaust Testimonies at Yale University, made a significant contribution to testimonial discourse by highlighting this relational nature of testimony (see, Laub, 1992; 1995; 2009). He articulates this aspect of testimony as follows: "The survivors did not only need to survive so that they could tell their story; they also needed to tell their story in order to survive" (1992: 78). Laub also places an important emphasis on the listener, who in his view plays an indispensable part in the initiation and elaboration of testimonial narrative. "To a certain extent," writes Laub, "the interviewer-listener takes on responsibility for bearing witness that previously the narrator felt he bore alone, and therefore could not carry out" (1992: 85). To him it is precisely this "encounter and the coming together between the survivor and the listener, which makes possible something like a repossession of the act of witnessing. This joint responsibility is the source of the re-emerging truth" (1992: 85). Wieviorka also foregrounds this interhuman situation of testimony when she writes that: "The one who testifies signs a 'compassionate pact' with the one who receives the testimony . . . " (2006: 143). However, as LaCapra points out, Lanzmann himself asserted that "there are no real encounters or dialogic relations between people in the film even when they are in the same place" (1997: 265). In *80064*, too, the artist who is positioned as the receiver of Tarnawa's testimony may not be engaged in receiving it at all; rather, he seems to be "doing nothing more . . . than establishing a certain site, a position, a structural place where the relation to a possible reception is articulated" (Butler, 2005: 67). A collaboration involving a meeting between two different people and a mutuality of engagement is missing here. It could be argued that for Żmijewski, just as for Lanzmann, the process of interviewing the survivors and listening to their stories does not serve the purpose of restoring their humanity and identity. Instead they both aim to break (sometimes coercively and violently) through the protective layers of their consciousness in order to capture the feeling of what having been in the Nazi extermination camps was like, and make their "deep memory" of the traumatic past literally accessible to those who were not there.

About half way into the video, when Żmijewski tells Tarnawa that he would like to re-tattoo his Auschwitz number and Tarnawa resists expressing his concern that the tattoo would lose its authenticity, the artist reminds him that he has already agreed to this procedure. The video leaves the nature of this agreement ambiguous, leaving its viewers in the dark as to why Tarnawa agreed to this humiliating procedure. In an interview given to Miklós Erhardt in Budapest, Żmijewski reveals that Tarnawa agreed because he was financially compensated for doing so. "Of course, he said 'yes', because I paid him," states Żmijewski. "It was a deal: we met before and he signed a contract stating that I pay him 500 Euro for renewing the tattoo" (Żmijewski, 2008: n.p.). This less commonly circulated piece of background information about the making of *80064* raises of course the issue of the commodification of the individual and collective suffering of the past as well as of the exploitation of a Holocaust survivor whose life story has been turned into a commodity for circulation on the global art market.

Scholars in many disciplines have critically engaged the problems of the ongoing historical refashioning of cultural attitudes to victims as well as commodification of traumatic suffering. For instance, commenting on the place of trauma in the contemporary politics of reparation, testimony, and proof the authors of *The Empire of Trauma*, Didier Fassin and Richard Rechtman note: "Survivors of disasters, oppression, and persecution adopt the only persona that allows them to be heard – that of victim. In doing so, they tell us less of what they are than of the moral economies of our era in which they find their place" (2009: 279). Erica Caple James has argued in a similar vein how humanitarian and development interventions in Haiti, aimed at facilitating its postconflict transition following the period of military rule in the early 1990s inadvertently, contributed to "the commodification of suffering in the political economy of trauma" (2010: 106). Patricia Yaeger (2002) too has written convincingly of the academy's consumption of trauma in light of its search for a politics of empathy and moral dilemmas that attend it. Finally, anthropologist Arthur Kleinman finds "the globalization of suffering" worrisome "because experience is being used as a commodity, and through this cultural representation of suffering, experience is being remade, thinned out, and distorted" (qtd. in Illouz, 2003; 219). In other words, "the experience of suffering is transformed into something that is qualitatively different – entertainment and an aestheticization of suffering – and is incorporated in the predatory commercial engine of capitalism" (Illouz, 2003: 219). As Eva Illouz demonstrates convincingly, talk shows such as *The Oprah Winfrey Show*, in which ordinary actors expose their life stories, are a case in point.

While vastly different from Żmijewski's work, Oprah Winfrey's famous talk show might offer an interesting point of comparison here and allow for further reflection on Żmijewski's piece. Both entrepreneurs (after all, Żmijewski receives artistic commissions, fees, and royalties from an artworld network of biennial, museum, and gallery systems) are motivated by certain social agendas and both offer social platforms to the victims and bearers of trauma as well as other socially marginalised constituencies, for instance deaf-mute children in Żmijewski's *The Singing Lesson 1* (*Lekcja śpiewu 1*, 2001) and *The Singing Lesson 2* (*Lekcja śpiewu 2*, 2003) and paralytic patients in *Out for a Walk* (*Na spacer*, 2001). As Żmijewski states in his essay/manifesto "The Applied Social Arts" (2010) and the interview with Erhardt, his goal is to reintegrate art into society, claim back a practical, concrete position for it in the social-political discourse, and create opportunities for his collaborators "to tell people their stories, their message, to include their story in the repository of all stories" (2008: n.p.). Furthermore, adds Żmijewski, "they know their story will be heard out, so it will have the potentially political power to effect change, create knowledge, or aid the paradigm-transformation process" (2008: n.p.). Similarly, as Illouz observes, "*The Oprah Winfrey Show* is such a powerful cultural form because it provides a forum in which to expose and discuss disrupted lives and various forms of suffering, from terminal disease to a variety of neuroses and childhood traumas to such life-disrupting events as divorce and bereavement" (2003: 101).

On Oprah's show the guests' biographies are not paid for with money. This is because, Illouz argues, Winfrey "frames her enterprise in moral rather than economic and instrumental terms" (2003: 53). And while some take the fact that her guests are not paid to explain Oprah's financial success, she suggests that it also maintains the boundary between commodity exchange and storytelling ensuring that some life stories are not perceived as more valued than others. Furthermore, Oprah's show has become endowed with a capacity to induce moral action on the part of its viewers, which gives it ethical

weight and increases its legitimacy. Żmijewski's *80064* displays nearly
the opposite sort of humanising impulses to those at work on *Oprah*.
His pieces such as *80064*, *Repetition*, and *The Game of Tag* transform
"collaboration" into a hiring relationship and make little or no mention of the histories of participants. As he states in the interview with
Erhardt, he treats the participants as employees who sell him their
labour, so he pays them because he respects them as well as "their
time and courage" (2008: n.p.). But, when asked by Erhardt whether
the fact that he pays his participants is a kind of alibi for him, which
calms his conscience, Żmijewski answered in the negative, adding:
"I like to be able to say openly that I made something bad, immoral
or unethical" (2008: n.p.).

In addition to the issues Żmijewski's *80064* raises in regard to the
employment of testimonial witnessing in a public sphere, the work
could be also examined in the context of a larger discourse on the
uses of human subjects in "delegated performance," which I would
like to address briefly here before examining further the epistemic
claims Żmijewski makes about his work and ethical claims that come
with them. This genre of performance has gained in popularity since
the early 1990s, and it involves use of everyday people and non-
professionals (often an economic or ethnic "other") as performers,
which has often raised ethical issues and questions of exploitation.
According to Claire Bishop, who has theorised this genre from a
perspective of the visual arts, "Manipulation and coercion do not
invalidate a work if it exists in critical dialogue with a larger social
and political context." She believes that "Looking at the works of
Collins and Żmijewski, for instance, through a reductively humanist
framework of reification ensures that the greater import of their work
is misunderstood" (2009: 122). In her view, "The criteria for judging
[this kind of work] should not be the exploitation of the performers,
but rather its resistant stance towards the society in which it finds
itself and the modes of subjectivity produced therein" (122). "At
their best," writes Bishop, "delegated performances produce disruptive events that testify to a shared reality between viewers and performers, and that throw into question agreed ways of thinking about
subjectivity, ethics, and economics" (123). Bishop does not elaborate
on these points, nor does she discuss Żmijewski's *80064* more than
to describe it, which does not leave much room for critical engagement with her abstractions. While endorsing Żmijewski's works, for

instance, she does not consider the kind of impact Józef Tarnawa's submission to Żmijewski's procedure may have had on Tarnawa from either a psychological, ethical, or economic point of view.

As an act of physical violence, the act of re-tattooing 80064 on Tarnawa's forearm obliterates the indexical bond between the time of extremity and endless deprivation and the present time, and hence the evidentiary status of the old tattoo that confirms Tarnawa as the Holocaust survivor. And while Nicholas Chare reminds us that the tattoo "never entirely vanishes" (it often remains under the skin's surface even after the use of laser tattoo removal [2011: 99; 168l]), the tattooist's needle that suffuses Tarnawa's skin with new pigment removes forever the visibility of the old scar that marked Tarnawa as a Holocaust witness and survivor. The ink from Auschwitz that penetrated Tarnawa's skin several decades ago leaving on his body the mark of the Nazi master, now receives a new inscription. The old, fading numerals that told the story of the body that has survived Auschwitz are replaced with more visible ones. The act as such could be also seen as inflicting symbolic if not psychological violence. But perhaps we can go one step further to argue that Żmijewski's experiment poses the same ethical problems as those provoked by the practice of torture. As Diana Taylor writes, "Even if the [torture] practices were highly efficacious in providing vital information, their means render them inadmissible, undoing the very notion of good that that might come out of that knowledge" (2007: 721). The act of re-tattooing, contrived to send Tarnawa back into a traumatic past so that he may act it out in front of Żmijewski's camera – and so that he and his audiences could see what Auschwitz really was – threatens to collapse whatever precarious emotional distance the survivor has established between the purgatorial time of the camp and his living after-Auschwitz. The artist is interested only in reaching the "memory of the senses," the embodied memory of the survivor, without showing concern whether this may cause further psychic damage to the survivor. That much is clear. I will revisit the issues of torture scenarios as they pertain to Żmijewski's work later in the chapter; for now, let us look at some other arguments put forward by Żmijewski and some of his critics as to significance of this artwork, which, they deem, legitimise this brutal procedure.

"When I undertook this film-experiment with memory," stated Żmijewski, "I expected that under the effect of the tattooing the 'gates of memory' would open, that there would be an eruption of remembrance of that time, a stream of images or words describing the painful past (Żmijewski, 2005a: 24). While this did not happen, something else worth reflecting did happen, notes Żmijewski. He then singles out the part of the interview in which he asked Tarnawa whether during his internment in the camp he had any feeling of revolt, to which Tarnawa responded: "No, no revolt whatsoever. One had to put up with the situation as it was. . . . One had to endure, that's all" (Żmijewski, 2011: 120). In Żmijewski's view, "In the memory of this former prisoner, the condition for survival, necessitated by the extremely oppressive and restrictive environment, was extreme conformity" (2005a: 24). And, according to the artist, "in the film such an act of conformism, consent and subordination is repeated. The protagonist agrees to have his camp number re-tattooed. He protests a little at first, argues, but eventually gives in and is once again victimised" (2005a: 24). Joanna Mytkowska, who curated the Polish Pavilion at the 2005 Venice Biennale, where Żmijewski's works, including *80064*, represented Poland that year, underscores the social significance of this experiment (without any reflection on its ethics): "By obliging him [Tarnawa] to consent to it, he [Żmijewski] affirmed that surviving the camp succeeded usually at the cost of consent to inhuman rules, acceptance of one's fate, and conformity. There is no public discourse capable of considering survivors in this way, of re-negotiating this kind of memory" (2005: 16). Furthermore, adds Mytkowska, "the established discourse of solidarity with victims and against evil does not allow such memory to emerge" (2005: 16).

However, the thesis or truth that Żmijewski seems to be advancing here was of course put forward long ago by many Holocaust testimonies, fictional accounts of the event as well as scholarship on the Holocaust. It is enough to remember Primo Levi's narrative entitled "The Grey Zone" (1989 [1986]) and its controversial thesis that the survivors often survived, or survived longer, through their blurring of the subject positions of victims and executioners. Levi, in this defining essay, talks primarily about particular groups or individuals such as the *Sonderkommandos* or *Kapos* of Auschwitz-Birkenau, those who collaborated with Nazis through motives of "terror, ideological seduction, servile imitation of the victor, myopic desire for any power whatsoever, even though ridiculously circumscribed in space and time, cowardice, and, finally, lucid calculation aimed at eluding the imposed orders and order" (Levi, 1989: 43). Other authors such as Zygmunt Bauman, in his chapter on "soliciting the co-operation of the victims" in his book *Modernity and the Holocaust* (1989), and Barbara Engelking in her chapter "Daily Life in the Ghetto" in her book *Holocaust and Memory* (2001; Polish edition 1994), have also shown that the thesis can be applied more generally to those victims trapped in the Jewish ghettos in Poland under the Nazi occupation.

Furthermore, Mytkowska's and Żmijewski's discursive alchemy shrouds direct forms of violence under the veil of the public good, disappearing the violation of Tarnawa's body through the assertion of his complicity and wilful submission, then and now. (The complicity of the survivor displaces the act of violence.) I contend that the unspoken and the non-thematised background of what is represented that haunts the artwork, makes the issues of consent, will, and agency more complicated and ungainly than they seem to propose. Saidiya Hartman's insights from her book *The Scenes of Seduction* – an exploration of racial subjugation during slavery and its aftermath – may be instructive here. "If the commonplace understanding of the 'will' implies the power to control and determine our actions and identifies the expressive capacity of the self-possessed and intending subject," writes Hartman, "certainly this is far afield of the condition or terms of action available to the enslaved" (1997: 81). In other words, "the notion of the will connotes more than simply the capacity to act or do; rather, it distinguishes the autonomous agent from the enslaved, the encumbered, and the constrained" (1997: 81). To Hartman, "The opportunity for nonconsent is required to establish consent, for consent is meaningless if refusal is not an option" (1997: 111). Therefore, "the very effort to demonstrate consent reveals its impossibility if consent is understood as a voluntary agreement free from constraint or compulsion or as unimpinged by relations of power and dominance" (1997: 111). This applies to slavery as well as to the inmates in Auschwitz whose bodies were broken by the inhuman regime of work, the regularity of punishment, and the persistence of torture.

For Tarnawa to consent to have his Auschwitz number re-tattooed many decades after the original procedure, no matter how coercive the actual soliciting of this consent may have been, is certainly different from being forced to submit to the humiliating procedure within the horror of extermination. Furthermore, the nexus of conditions and system of power relations, hierarchies, and values that have produced the tattooed and disciplined body of Tarnawa, the body as object, instrument, and commodity, could not be reproduced. That is to say, the two acts of tattooing that Tarnawa underwent (one in the extermination camp, the other in civilian life more than half a century later) belong to two vastly different orders of violence altogether. By making an analogy between these two incommensurate gestures, Żmijewski and Mytkowska merge incommensurate contexts and temporalities erasing the distinction between victim, executioner, witness, and secondary witness. The logic at work in Mytkowska's argument that Tarnawa's agreement to have his Auschwitz tattoo refreshed confirms that those who survived Auschwitz did so usually at the cost of submitting to and participating in the traumatic conditions of camp life – she does not mention that Tarnawa was paid for the job – disregards the irreducible particularity of the infernal conditions of the grey zone as mapped by Levi. This goes against his explicit injunction against conflating the extermination camp and civilian life. In *The Drowned and the Saved*, Levi writes: "The mental mechanisms of the Häftlinge were different from ours; curiously, and in parallel, different also were their physiology and pathology" (1989: 85). Highlighting the irreducible difference of the camp inmates' experiences, he proposes to his readers that "knowledge that has been built up and tested 'outside' in the world that, for the sake of simplicity, we call civilian" (1989: 85) is irrelevant for heretofore the uncharted and volatile ethical space of the grey zone. Moreover, while for some, those who participated in the murder and cremation of their own should be judged for having chosen to save themselves by injuring others, Levi states his belief that "no one is authorised to judge [the *Sonderkommando*], not those who lived through the experience of the Lager and even less those who did not" (1989: 59).[15]

Moreover, examining "the on-going historical refashioning of cultural attitudes to victims," Carolyn Dean shows that some historians' assessment of (particularly Jewish) alleged passivity during the Holocaust is symptomatic "of a more profound cultural problem with and scepticism of constrained agency, constrained intention, and constrained will, even or perhaps especially in the context of the terrorized disempowerment that confronts so many victims" (2010: 62; 159). Like Levi, she argues that judgements concerning degrees of agency victims may have had in the camps "avoid asking difficult questions about the parameters of action in a radically rede-fined moral economy . . . " (2010: 156).[16] Żmijewski's video does not allow for such kind of elaboration: we never find out what kind of agency Tarnawa had in the camp and how it might have been exer-cised, nor do we learn how he survived against the odds. When he remembers the violence inflicted on his fellow inmates by Gerhard Palitzsch, an SS officer notorious for his activities in Auschwitz, or when he recounts briefly his dreams about the camp, these are the only instances in this short video when Tarnawa has a chance to talk about abjection to which he and other prisoners were reduced as well as its physiological and psychological effects. As Didier Fassin and Richard Rechtman note in *The Empire of Trauma*, where they examine the history of trauma and explore the transition of the victim from a marginalised to a respected role, surviving a cataclysmic event "does not necessarily imply that one's experience is circumscribed by this event, or even that one desires that it be reduced to this event" (2009: 281). Regrettably, in his encounter with Tarnawa, Żmijewski ignores the survivor's life before entering Auschwitz, and his struggle to live and recover in its aftermath; focused only on reopening his old wounds and documenting the process, he demonstrates no inter-est in showing the full complexity of survivor identity. This reduc-tionism does not allow any space for Tarnawa to communicate about his social, affective, and physiological life after the camps. The film is not only silent on these realities; it actually obscures them.

As I have already mentioned, Żmijewski as well as some of his crit-ics (for example, Mytkowska, 2005; Verwoert, 2008; Stott, 2012) often attribute epistemic validity to his performance experiments such as *80064*, *Repetition*, and *Them* comparing them to scientific ones. I will broach this subject further below, but first I would like to expand on this epistemic aspect of his work by engaging Diana Taylor's concept of scenario, and then draw some parallels between his performance scenarios and some famous scientific scenarios he references. In an essay on torture, Taylor distinguishes among three paradigms – the (exemplary) case study, the limit case, and the scenario (2007: 715). "Limit cases are irreproducible and ungeneralizable – the exception that serves only as illustration rather than the rule" writes Taylor (2007: 715). The limit cases such as the Holocaust, Hiroshima, and 9/11 represent "the incommensurable, singular, universally relevant, paradigmatic, and at times quasi-sacred . . . " (715). Our knowledge of limit events comes from testimonies by those who survived or witnessed these events rather than the scientific data. Scenarios, on the other hand, are hypothetical. Rather than furnishing evidence, establishing cause and effect, or offering reproducible findings in the ways case studies do, "they reveal deep social imaginaries, fears, and desires" (715). Covering a wide range of activities, from play staging to healing scenarios, "they demand staging and embodiment – whether real or virtual" (728). In her book *The Archive and the Repertoire*, Taylor also defines the scenario as "a paradigm that is formulaic, portable, repeatable, and often banal because it leaves out complexity, reduces conflict to its stock elements, and encourages fantasies of participation" (2003: 54). Questioning their epistemic value, she argues that scenarios "often boil conflict and resolution down to known positions and assumptions" (728). They prove persuasive not because of their scientific rigour but "but because the outcomes, so often re-enacted, seem inevitable and prescripted" (729).

Stanley Milgram's series of obedience experiments and Philip Zimbardo's Stanford Prison Experiment – probably the two best-known psychological studies today, each of which staged a scenario, in a theatrical sense – may throw some more light on Żmijewski's assumptions, methods, and ambitions exhibited in *80064*. While Milgram's experiment involved actors, Zimbardo's test-subjects remained themselves throughout the experiment; they knew from the beginning that they were to be involved in role play. First carried out at Yale University in 1961, Milgram's experiment "questioned how much injury one person would inflict on another when obeying authority" (Taylor 2007: 719). Taking as its departure point the atrocities of the Nazi regime, which he understood in line with Hannah Arendt's conceptualisation of "the banality of evil" – the thesis that people who carry out unspeakable crimes may not be fanatical at all, but rather ordinary individuals who simply accept the premises of their state and participate in any ongoing enterprise with the energy of good bureaucrats – he endeavoured to advance knowledge of the psychology of obedience, with the hope that, with research and knowledge, people could be inoculated from the tendency to blindly obey authority (see, for instance, De Vos 2010 and 2011).

A decade later, in August 1971, the Stanford University psychologist Philip Zimbardo and his team of investigators began the famous Stanford Prison Experiment. The study involved twenty-four young men who were offered fifteen dollars per day for two weeks to participate in their study of the psychology of imprisonment (Zimbardo, 2007). Shortly into the experiment, the situation began to go bad: the prisoners began to exhibit symptoms of depression, while the guards engaged in acts of humiliation and violence. On the fifth day of the expected two weeks, Zimbardo stopped the experiment. He concluded that "it is not authority, as in Milgram's experiment, but role assignment which explains obedience and consequent reprehensible and shocking behaviour" (De Vos, 2010: 166). In his critique of Zimbardo, Jan De Vos argues that his whole experimental setup was flawed. Referring to an orientation meeting for the group who played the guards, he shows that they were also asked to "play the role of social scientists conducting an experiment" and that the brutal and humiliating behaviour they engaged in came precisely from their identification with the role of experimental psychologists (De Vos, 2010: 166). He asserts that "mistaking a totally psychologized situation for the real thing," Zimbardo was convinced that he "has laid bare the truth of the human species in his experiment" and revealed "the abyss of humanity as it really is" (De Vos, 2011: 297–8).[17]

In claiming that his experiment with Tarnawa brought to light some kind of truth about the mechanism of submission to the Nazi authority at work in Auschwitz and other camps, Żmijewski seems equally misguided. Drawing on Giorgio Agamben's theorisations of lives lived on the margins of social, political, juridical, and biological representation, De Vos further proposes that the de-humanisation and de-subjectivation of the prisoners that took place during the Stanford Prison Experiment constituted "the prisoners as the humiliated and debased *homo sacer* of the psychological discourse" (2010: 164). Likewise, critics have drawn parallels between human subjects that populate Żmijewski's projects – often stripped down to the point of physical and mental humiliation – and Agamben's *homo sacer* (see, Möntmann, 2006; Downey, 2009). Some, like Jan Verwoert, even go as far as to argue that Żmijewski's collaborators "are stripped bare and unconditionally subject to a social experiment performed on their bodies . . . demonstrating how little it takes to isolate people in the position of bare life" (2008: n.p.). For instance, he argues that the guards involved in Żmijewski's *Repetition* "become progressively more sadistic as they realise that the bare life of the prisoners is completely at their disposal" (2008: n.p.). Similarly, Tim Stott argues that in Żmijewski's *Game of Tag* "players are quite explicitly reduced to the condition of bare life before a sovereign power, who abandons them to their play. Żmijewski no doubt knowingly demonstrates how easy it is for an artist to do this, as one whose sovereignty is exemplary" (2012: 3–4). For these two critics then, Żmijewski's works function as evidence, as if they were the object of analysis in a scientific experiment. They do not question the films' aesthetic choices and their biases and mediations, treating them as almost transparent representations of the conflicts enacted in Żmijewski's morally provocative scenarios.

Agamben has developed his theory of *homo sacer* primarily in his book of the same name (Italian edition 1995; English edition 1998) and *State of Exception* (Italian edition 2003; English edition 2005); for him this obscure figure of Roman law, reduced to "bare life" by the ruling order and deprived of basic rights such as representation before law, is paradigmatic of modern subjectivity lived precariously under the rule of sovereignty and its power over the life and death of its subjects. He sees this form of subjectivity ("bare life") as an impossible negotiation of biographical life (*bios*) and biological life (*zoe*). He criticises modern politics for exploiting the gap between these two forms of life in order to produce sovereign power, which is invested with an exclusive authority to kill or let live, and "bare life," a politicised form of disposable life deprived of national civil rights and international human rights. While Auschwitz is one of the key places where "bare life" came into an unmediated relationship with sovereign power, he notes that nowadays such a correlation of sovereign power and bare life can be located in places such as Guantánamo. Labelled enemy combatants, subject only to raw power while having no legal existence the detainees of Guantánamo are *homini sacri* reduced to "pure life without any mediation" (Agamben, 1998: 171). To De Vos, this is precisely "why psychology serves Guantánamo and other extraterritorial black sites so well. The psy-sciences are the tools that remove the mediation; they deliver the technologies to reduce someone to bare life" (2011: 309).

While it is difficult not to posit a profound, if ironic, connection between the brutal coercing of testimony in these two very different settings (Guantánamo and Abu Ghraib on one hand and the tattoo parlour presented in *80064* on the other), perhaps there is a line to be drawn between the instrumentalisation of knowledge obtained by psychoanalysis and its unethical implementation in the US detention camps and its uncritical application in iconoclastic artistic experiments such as Żmijewski's piece. But while I have critiqued Żmijewski's assumptions about replicating a Holocaust experience, more could be said about the model of trauma and psyche that informs his concept for *80064*. As I mentioned earlier, Żmijewski professed that his violent handling of Tarnawa was motivated by his search for an "unmediated truth" about the Holocaust. To him, *88864* is "about radical modes of memory, about the fact that trauma infects the body, engraves itself in the mind and refuses to be symbolized, and thus eventually tamed, neutralized" (Żmijewski, 2008: n.p.). The procedure of re-tattooing was a "vehicle of time" that was supposed to transpose Tarnawa into the time of the camps, induce an outpour of emotions associated with that time, and enable the artist to "get to the heart of trauma" (Żmijewski, 2008: n.p.).[18]

Żmijewski seems to subscribe here to the "hydraulic" model of the emotions as liquids within each person ready to be let out, presented for instance in Freud's early work, "Project for a Scientific Psychology" (1895) and that prevails today in popular conceptions of emotions. The understanding of trauma he uses to explain why he decided to expose Tarnawa to the painful procedure of re-tattooing of his Auschwitz number resonates alongside Freud's description of trauma. In his *Beyond the Pleasure Principle* (first published in 1920), which originated in the experience of First World War shell shock, Freud describes trauma as a breach of the organism's protective shield as follows: "We describe as 'traumatic' any excitations from outside which are powerful enough to break through the protective shield. It seems to me that the concept of trauma necessarily implies a connection of this kind with a breach in an otherwise efficacious barrier against stimuli" (1953–74a: 29). According to Freud, the emotional damage stays hidden and manifests itself only belatedly. As Shoshana Felman writes, expanding on Freud, "The trigger of the symptoms is often an event that unconsciously reminds the subject of the original traumatic scene, and is thus lived as a repetition of the trauma" (2002: 171). By piercing Tarnawa's body, Żmijewski wishes to breach the defensive crust or shield of the survivor's consciousness and provoke an enactment of trauma. But as we know, Tarnawa fails to experience the floods of memory that Żmijewski is after.

While this model of trauma has been hugely influential, many critics have also argued that adopting it as universal runs the risk of erasing essential differences between traumatic experiences, cultures, histories, and geographies in which they are embedded, as well as individual variations of the human condition (see, Leys, 2000; Didier and Rechtman, 2009; Thomson, 2009; Craps, 2013). In other words, individual experiences, basic to Freud's talking cure, could be lost in a diagnosis that finds the same symptoms everywhere. Żmijewski, however, adopts this particular model of trauma and deploys it in his experiment with Tarnawa as if it was universal, and without any immersion into the subjective world of the survivor. In this respect, Żmijewski's act could be seen as an instance of what Freud termed as "wild analysis." In his paper "'Wild' psychoanalysis" ([1910] 2002), he discusses a distortion of psychoanalytic technique, considering "wild" any psychoanalytic treatment conducted with preconceived ideas about what is likely to be discovered. And while "wildness" in itself "could be a source of creativity and of therapeutic power," and the image of the wild analyst could serve as a metaphor for "the deeply involved, personally motivated analyst, whose work is intense and emotionally risky" (Berman 2007; 214; 212), my use of the term here is closer to Freud's discussion of wild analysts and their blind spots, and his critique of the deductive use of theory to conceptualise experience.

To take this line of critique of *80064* a bit further, let us engage Radstone's recent critique of trauma theory. Arguing that this theory "is becoming almost a new theoretical orthodoxy," Susannah Radstone invites us to reflect on its implications for the Humanities as well as on it uncritical applications in various contexts beyond academia, because, as she argues, "trauma theory seeps into to the broader cultural domains, where there's a danger of its unreflexive applications" (2007a: 22). While trauma theory is explicitly concerned with the empathetic witnessing of the suffering of others and its ethical impetus is beyond dispute, Radstone wants us to reflect further on the ethics of trauma criticism and its "tendency of trauma analysis to foreground the analyst's sensitivity and emphatic capacities" (2007a: 22–3). In her view, "that critical 'empathy' is not without its darker aspects," and "the empathetic recovery of the voices of traumatised testifier and texts may be at the expense of those for whom trauma criticism claims to speak" (2007a: 23). Furthermore,

Radstone urges to consider that an engagement with painful histories or artefacts memorialising them "may be inflected, also, by less easily acknowledgeable fascinations and fantasies concerning victimhood grounded in aggressivity," or it may screen potential identification with aggression (2007a: 23). While in my analysis of Pinter's *Ashes to Ashes*, I showed how Rebecca's projection into the past is shaped, to some degree, by a masochistic identification with victimhood, aggressivity (unconscious or not) informing Żmijewski's encounter with Tarnawa is easy to discern. I will return to Żmijewski in a moment, but let us revisit the scene of address from Lanzmann's film, which I discussed early on in the paper. The ethical valence of Lanzmann's encounter with Bomba bears a certain resemblance to the one that inflects the encounter between Żmijewski and Tarnawa, and dwelling further on them in proximity of each other may bring us closer to an understanding of ethical stakes in these two works and illuminate the artists' complicity with violence that they exhibit.

Commenting on coercive techniques employed by Lanzmann to convince the barber Abraham Bomba to recount a particular experience from a gas chamber in Treblinka and to describe his feelings about it at the time of its occurrence, LaCapra asserts that "it would be wrong to see this scene in terms of Lanzmann's somewhat sadistic insistence on going on" (though he never quite explains why [1997: 255]). Rather, he maintains that Lanzmann's insistence on having Bomba and other survivors relive traumatising events derives not only from his self-professed desire to bring them into the light of day but also from his disguised and unconscious desire to "identify empathetically [with them] and relive their reliving" (1997: 260). "Fully empathetic identification with people and places enabled Lanzmann to feel that he was reliving – indeed suffering through – a past that he never in fact lived. He would even be phantasmatically able to die others' death with them" (1997: 264). He then quotes Lanzmann who comments on his work on *Shoah* in a similar vein: "A meaning for me that is simultaneously the most profound and the most incomprehensible in the film is in a certain way . . . to resuscitate these people, to kill them a second time, with me; by accompanying them" (qtd. in LaCapra, 1997: 24). LaCapra even goes on to tentatively propose, drawing on Nicolas Abraham and Maria Torok's concept of incorporative melancholia, that Lanzmann's unchecked transferential subject position enacted in *Shoah* may be "based on an encrypted or hidden wound caused by the fact that he was not in reality a victim of the Shoah sharing the fate of his objects of study" (1997: 250). So, while LaCapra here addresses the role of the unconscious in the process of working through the past, even his interpretation seems founded upon a certain Manicheanism (Radstone 2001; 2007a; 2007b), as it wards off a possibility that Lanzmann's aggressivity displayed in the scene with Bomba manifests his potential (unconscious) identification with aggression (that is, he postulates only Lanzmann's not fully conscious overidentifications with the victim).[19]

When, in a conversation with Żmijewski, Agata Araszkiewicz points out a similarity between Lanzmann's coercive technique employed in his interview with Bomba and his own handling of Tarnawa, he comments that "Lanzmann fights for memory in a ruthless way" (2005b: n.p.). As for himself, he states: "And when I speak about remembering, I mean remembering pain and oppression. I mean cruelty remembered in a cruel way" (2005b: n.p.). As I mentioned earlier, Żmijewski is not overtly anxious to posit his engagement with the Holocaust material in general and Tarnawa in particular as an index of his ethical commitment with and empathetic witnessing of Tarnawa's testimony, but when moments earlier Araszkiewicz asks "But don't you position yourself as an executioner . . . ?" (referencing the act of re-tattooing of Tarnawa), Żmijewski responds that that is an over-exaggeration (2005b: n.p.). The artist evacuates all "badness" from the act of repeated humiliation of Tarnawa by insisting that he only exposed Tarnawa's conformism that was instrumental for his survival in the camp. When Araszkiewicz comments on a certain dose of humour exhibited by Tarnawa at the end of the video, where he compares his "refreshed" number to a renovated piece of furniture, Żmijewski asserts that these words are a variation of an explanation he offered to the survivor before filming him, thus insisting that the desubjectification Tarnawa underwent in Auschwitz had lasting consequences for his sense of agency in the present. However, later, commenting on Marek Edelman's reflection on his fight against the Nazis (Edelman was the last surviving leader of the armed Jewish revolt against the Nazis in the Warsaw ghetto in 1943), he notes: "He [Edelman] was able to position himself not only in the place of the victim, but also the enemy, the occupier, the killer" (2005b: n.p.). If we entertain here Radstone's idea that "scenarios that include the

exercise of power and authority arguably prompt a particular identification *with* the wielder of that power, as well as with the object
of upon whom it is exercised" (2001: 65; original emphasis), then
it could be argued that in *80064* Żmijewski too displays less easily
acknowledgeable fascinations with aggressivity, an affect that the
author disavows but that his work symptomatically represents.

In *Giving An Account of Oneself*, her recent exploration of the
intersections of identity and responsibility, Judith Butler proposes
a rethinking of responsibility in relation to the limits of self-understanding that make us human. She argues: "If the subject is opaque
to itself, not fully translucent and knowable to itself, it is not thereby
licensed to do what it wants or to ignore its obligations to others. The
contrary is surely true" (2005: 19–20). Kelly Oliver also approaches
the very issue that concerns Butler, and in her important study
Witnessing: Beyond Recognition (2001) she develops a model of subjectivity in relation to the intersubjective structures of witnessing and
psychoanalytic working through. She writes:

> Subjectivity is founded on the ability to respond to, and address,
> others – what I am calling witnessing. Insofar as subjectivity is
> made possible by the ability to respond, response-ability is its
> founding possibility. The responsibility inherent in subjectivity
> has the double sense of the condition of possibility of response,
> response-ability, on the one hand, and the ethical obligation to
> respond and to enable response-ability from others born out of
> that founding possibility, on the other. (2001: 15)

Thus, she argues, the processes of witnessing and working through
trauma, though never complete, depend on the supportive responsibility of the other. These processes also require witnessing (on the
part of the hearer of testimony) to the unconscious of the survivor, to what cannot be recognised by the witness himself. In *The
Colonization of Psychic Space* (2004) and *Women As Weapons of War*,
Oliver radicalises this ethical responsibility by maintaining that
we are also responsible for our unconscious desires and fears. She
writes:

> If we are not transparent to ourselves, our bodies and behaviours
> demand incessant interpretation. If a part of ourselves always

remains inaccessible and to a greater or lesser extent resists any one interpretation, then we will be compelled to continually call into question our own motives and desires. (Oliver, 2007: 106)

Especially in the context of witnessing difficult or even traumatic histories, argues Oliver, ethics requires an ongoing, vigilant self-interrogation of our own conscious and unconscious aggressive impulses and fascinations with violence and war as well as "owning up to the ways in which we profit both materially and psychologically from the suffering of others" (2007: 164–5). In her desire to expunge our fascination with violence and to restore the boundary between fantasy and reality (so we do not play out our violent fantasies on others), Oliver may be overemphasising free will and suppressing the agency of the unconscious and the kind of role it plays in working through the past. But, while her desire to see overcoming violence as fundamentally constitutive of humanity may be utopian, her injunction to learn to see differently, to see the world as fundamentally about connection and dependency and to engage on a continual self-interrogation is critical.

Both Butler and Oliver offer theories of subject formation that acknowledge the limits of self-knowledge and can serve as conceptions of ethics and responsibility. As Butler writes: "It would be perhaps, an ethics, based on our shared, invariable, and partial blindness about ourselves" (2005: 41). And in the reading I have offered here, *80064* has certainly emerged as a site where the relationship between mimesis and ethics in the performing of testimony enters a hiatus, raising also difficult questions as to the fragility, integrity, and unity of the self, both of the survivor and the witness. In his statements about *80064*, Żmijewski has repeatedly emphasised the deadly effect of Auschwitz time on Tarnawa. In an interview with Agata Araszkiewicz, for instance, the artist argues that the burden of his Auschwitz knowledge "changed the character of his [Tarnawa's] existence," and that the "person who he was before the camp . . . sank into the interior of subjectivity – imploded" (Żmijewski, 2005b: n.p.).

His view of the survivor is consonant with the following statement by Agamben, made in his *Remnants of Auschwitz: The Witness and the Archive*: "The survivor is therefore familiar with the common necessity of degradation; he knows that humanity and responsibility are something that the deportee had to abandon when entering the camp" (1999: 59–60). This argument, largely grounded in a partial reading of Primo Levi, focuses primarily on the "limit-figure of 'bare life,' the *Musselmann*, who in passively submitting to his fate without resistance stands as an image or icon of horror" (Leys, 2007: 171), but in the book he seemingly denies agency to every Auschwitz inmate. Similarly, Żmijewski perceives the Tarnawa from the time of the camps as an empty shell of a man, degraded and diminished, dislocated from any meaningful relationality, and intent only on self-preservation.

In the process of replicating an experience of cruelty and utter degradation from the camp, in order to elicit an affective and visceral form of remembering from the survivor, Żmijewski fails to try for entanglement, proximity, or a personal bonding with the survivor-witness of collective disaster, necessary for the transmission of memory. If anything, he downright denies empathy any kind of ethico-political or epistemological currency. Throughout my analysis of *80064*, however, I have tried to emphasise not the issue of desubjectification but of human relatedness and responsibility, which did not cease to exist even amidst the extreme destitution and degradation of human life to bare life subject to mass extermination. As Lisa Guenther argues, engaging the writings on the Holocaust by Primo Levi, Robert Antelme, and Maurice Blanchot, "even when exposed to an unimaginable extremity of need and affliction . . . , the subject retains a relation to alterity which provides a starting point, however minimal, for resistance" (2011: 18) To Guenther, "This relationality remains even when every relation to every particular other has been severed, and it remains even when the subject who would be in relation to others – the I, the ego – has been utterly destroyed" (2011: 18). As she simply concludes, "Humanity makes sense only as an irreducible relation to alterity which cannot be destroyed, not even through murder or mass extermination" (20011: 18).

Where Żmijewski perhaps succeeds is in causing a secondary traumatisation of those who watch his video, especially the young. The viewers often feel disturbed, if not irretrievably wounded, by the procedure they have witnessed in *80064*. They often have an unwarranted gut feeling that a human life has been violated here. If attentiveness to the irreducible difference between a Holocaust survivor and those not directly affected by the catastrophe is a prerequisite for an ethical engagement with this difficult past, a question that remains is perhaps less "whether we should expect some kind of decorum even in the depiction of extremity" (Hartman, 2006: 255), but whether it was worthwhile to subject an aging Holocaust survivor to a humiliating procedure, to reinscribe a story of his past victimisation, so that we – the audiences – could deepen our knowledge of the "unimaginable" extremity of the events related.

5
Conclusion: European Memories and the Margins of Europe: *Sarajevo Theatre Tragedy* and Three Prayers for One Wish

The end of the forty-year Cold War that split the postwar European continent provided an impetus for rethinking the past all over Europe, as well as for the study of "European memory." A commitment on the part of European countries to "work through the past" as individual nations, and the often contentious negotiations about what to remember and what to forget, ran parallel with the search for a transnational memory of the conflicts, contentions, complexity, and ambiguity of Europe's past. In *Performing European Memories* I joined these debates to explore the intersections between contemporary European theatre and performance, the interdisciplinary field of memory studies, and current preoccupations with the politics of memory in Europe. Asking whether a genuinely shared European memory is possible while simultaneously addressing the dangers of a single homogenised European memory, I examined the contradictions, specificities, continuities, and discontinuities in the European shared and unshared pasts as represented in the works of Harold Pinter, Tadeusz Kantor, Andrzej Wajda, Heiner Müller, and Artur Żmijewski. Showing the different ways in which these artists engage with the traumatic experiences of the Holocaust, the Stalinist Gulags, colonialism, and imperialism, I argued that their works challenge their audiences' historical imagination and renew their affective engagement with Europe's past. Embracing not only the past, but also the future, they open spaces in which cultural convalescence can be achieved through the performance of mourning.

"Few phenomena in contemporary Polish culture have evoked such a wealth of commentary in so many languages," writes Pleśniarowicz

248

in regard to Kantor's theatrical oeuvre, but, at the same time, "few have been analysed in a way so dependent on the direct action of the artist's personality and commentaries on his work" (1994a: 165–6). Kantor sought a kind of continuity and philosophical structure in his work, and held his theoretical writings to be the very foundation of his theatrical art – the bedrock of how his work would be remembered and considered by future generations of theatre artists and historians. In this study, I read Kantor's theoretical writings as an extension of his theatre, as poetic confessions that are symbiotically interwoven with his performances. At the same time, in order to establish the stakes of the mnemonic for Kantor, I attempted to pull Kantor's seemingly eccentric obsession with memory back into the context of Polish history and culture before and after the Holocaust, where it rightfully belongs. Furthermore, locating Kantor's texts and performances within a wider contemporary fixation upon the mnemonic, I tried to denaturalise Kantor's own seemingly sovereign self-understanding.

The full depth and complexity of Kantor's accomplishments appear only in light of comprehensive knowledge of the Polish context in which he struggled and evolved. Although the rigour of the theatrical form and spirit of Kantor's works has had a gripping hold on international audiences (his work has been performed in more than twenty countries), the particulars of Kantor's particular national, ethnic, and personal milieus often remain inaccessible to them. Engaging the Second World War historiography and Kantor's writings, I showed how *Let the Artist Die* reminds us of the tragic life stories of many thousands of Poles who perished at the hands of the NKVD or in Gulag camps, and how *Wielopole Wielopole* raised the complex issue of Polish-Jewish relations before, during, and after the Holocaust, a subject still surrounded by high emotions and confounding taboos on both sides. As the nexus between the subjective and the objective – memory and history – Andrzej Wajda's film *Katyń* that I have analysed here in relation to Kantor's *Let the Artist Die*, provides an excellent counterpoint and accompaniment to Kantor, while making his work less hermetic. Kantor's presence on stage places him simultaneously in the role of a silent witness and a re-creator of the events portrayed. His witnessing is active, not reactive; it is agency, not passive victimisation. His witnessing narratives, in other words, are not ends in themselves, but potential means of healing and growth; they are collective, enabling recovery narratives. They avoid a negative fixation on the past by incorporating both a present interventionist orientation and a future progressivist one. Thus, his performances provide a means to chart the past and, along with it, the future in a positive manner, by undoing the traumas of "misrecognition" that can inflict grievous wounds. Furthermore, his memory-theatre demands from his audience the ethically responsible witnessing of these traumas, the stories of which must be told and retold in order to be fully understood, and then acted upon positively and productively.

Like Kantor's works, Müller's theatre also protests against indifference and oblivion. Theatre, Müller suggests, must remain faithful to historical legacy; it must not betray the victims of the violent past, the millions of those who perished as victims of the transatlantic slave trade, and the millions of the murdered, burnt, and gassed who were neither buried, nor mourned. In my analysis of Müller's *The Task*, I showed the ways in which this play questions the relationship between the modernity of European expansionism, racial subordination, and genocide, and modernity as emancipation and democratisation. As I argue along with Fischer (2004), memory alone could not counter the disavowal of revolutionary antislavery thematised in the play. Understanding the gaps and silence at the heart of the play's ideological landscape, which, as we have seen, also became an ingredient in hegemonic conceptions of modernity, would not be possible without engaging with existing scholarship about the French Revolution and the Caribbean during the Age of Revolution. As I further argued, Müller's play demonstrates that writing historically in terms of reclaiming the repressed, the blocked out, and the marginalised means openly addressing the forces that caused the repressing, the blocking, and the marginalising in the first place. True, there are obvious dangers to wallowing in victimhood that should not be ignored, but another way to look at Müller's injunction to memory is to see such witnessing (even by belated witnesses) as agency – for theatre, of course, as well for theatre history.

In my analysis of Müller's *A Description of A Picture*, I suggested that the subtle elaborations of the subject of loss in this play are best detected when contrasted with the standard Freudian approach to mourning. Questions about mourning and loss that Müller's play raises are at odds with the central tenet of Freud's study "Mourning and Melancholia," namely that grief can be resolved. Like Kantor's "The Theatre of Death," this play speaks of the failure immanent to the work of mourning, which keeps the work of mourning in process, always unfinished. And if *A Description of a Picture* points to the difficulty of coming to terms with intractable grief, and the ethical stakes involved in this process, Müller's *Mommsen's Block*, which I read along Benjamin's formulation of "Left melancholy," renders palpable the ambiguity of such melancholic fixations.

Memory is one of the defining themes of Pinter's plays. As my study shows, it also motivates a lot of his political thinking. Moving away from the notion of memory as a personal and individual experience, in *Ashes to Ashes* Pinter shows how the maintenance, communication, and breakdown of memory operates across temporal, cultural, political, and interpersonal boundaries. In this play, memory – and trauma itself – does not issue from within. Remembering something is not simply a question of "expressing" inner, subjective feelings, or of retrieving a linear past, but rather of tracing one's trajectory through a cultural space, a contemporary landscape of memory. Drawing attention to the ways in which in this play's empathetic identification follows certain trajectories, I argue that unreflexive empathetic responses to traumatic events may have significant costs in as much as they reinscribe cultural hierarchies, and that we should understand trauma and empathy in terms of our positioning in a global network. In this way, I suggest, the culturally invisible traumas of marginal groups such as refugees might be acknowledged. In a similar vein, I suggest that Żmijewski's *80064* invites us to be mindful of the dangers involved in witnessing "the pain of others." Situating my analysis in the context of recent debates on oral history performance and testimony, historical re-enactment and delegated performance, I examined the ethics and politics of this work, as well as the model of subjectivity it posits in relation to prevailing theories of trauma currently in circulation in the humanities. Ultimately, I argue that, like Pinter's *Ashes to Ashes*, Zmijewski's *80064* attests to the ongoing challenge of finding ways in which we can make past experiences of others proximate, rather than intimate, and thereby avoid repeating the violent dislocations that constitute such experiences.

To discuss "a specificity of a European memory," Luisa Passerini argues, "one would have to take into consideration at least two directions of research: the impact of accelerated processes of mediatisation, and generally of change in the field of communication, on the contemporary phenomenon of proliferation/cancellation of memory; and the relationship between memory and guilt – for colonialism, for persecutions and massacres" (2003: 251). In this study, I engaged with both of these issues, mapping their particular contextualisation in the work of the artists under my investigation. Most certainly, this kind of undertaking could not be exhaustive. The landscape I mapped out here consists of heterogeneous facts, practices, and ideas that remain mostly separated by disciplinary boundaries to this day. A number of other studies that explore the intersection between memory and theatre, which I have mentioned in this book's Introduction, have by necessity covered some similar points, since, as Passerini puts it, "the dialectics between memory and silence in this continent cannot avoid colonialism, totalitarianism, and wars, and their sites within and outside of Europe" (2003: 252).

In a collection of essays entitled *A European Memory? Contested Histories and Politics of Remembrance*, edited by Małgorzata Pakier and Bo Stråth, Jan-Werner Müller has argued that the attempt to develop a "common European memory" could lead to a "process of mutual opening and civilized confrontation of collective memories under the guidance of something like a Rawlsian 'public reason'" (2010: 26). Engaging theatrical representations of the Holocaust, Second World War atrocities, Stalinist gulags, imperialism, and colonialism, as well as the historical imagination of these chapters in Europe's past and the proliferation of collective memories in Europe, this book reveals that the process propagated by Müller, while commendable, is fraught with difficulties and challenges. For most western Europeans (and Germans in particular), the Holocaust plays a central role in the public discourse of national remembrance. This is not necessarily the case in Europe's central, southern, or eastern regions. The beginning of the twenty-first century in Spain, for instance, has been dominated by a complex, painful, and contested process of coming to terms with the Spanish Civil War of the 1930s and almost forty years of the Franco Dictatorship (1939–75), which gradually led to a greater interest in the memory of the Holocaust (already present to some extent in the previous decade through media, literature, and historical research). Furthermore, as Jo Labanyi notes, "a general supposition that modern Spain had nothing to do with the Jews, having expelled them in the late fifteenth century, and hostile relations towards Israel, fully recognized by Spain only in 1986" also helps explain the friction, resistances, and meanings associated with the discourses on the Holocaust in contemporary Spain (2009: 27). On the other hand, the memory of the Yalta Conference held in 1945, which largely decided the post-Second World War geopolitical division of Europe, has an enormous resonance in Eastern Europe and the Baltic states. Moreover, as Todorova notes, the comparatively long East European experience of communism "went through different stages and displayed amazing geographical varieties" (2010a: 11). Unlike fascism, she adds, the "diverse communist episode has actually had no *Stunde Null* and has been fading out in a more or less energetic, but essentially gradual way" (2010a: 12). As my analysis of selected works by Müller, Kantor, and Wajda shows, remembering communism involves a range of diverse and often contested issues: from the records of violence of communism and its totalitarian and authoritarian practices, via contested memories of the Holocaust and the Second World War in general, to the positive communist legacies of the real existing communism (for instance, in the spheres of education, healthcare, and culture), which are now threatened with obsolescence and forgetting. Finally, in this book I reflect on the difficulty of addressing the history of European colonialism, and show that the colonialist legacy of the European past has not yet been adequately incorporated into the discussions about a common European past. Engaging some of the most powerful and challenging theatrical and screen representations of this new memory discourse, *Performing European Memories* seeks to show the many ways in which theatre and performance evoke, contest, and provide for complex examinations and redresses of European collective pasts.

The itinerary that I took on my journey through the universe of memory has led us from the Caribbean during the time of the global slave trade to twentieth-century Berlin, Cracow, and Wielopole, and on to the extermination camps in Auschwitz and to the Katyń forest. In its course I have touched on the firestorms in Hamburg and Dresden during the allied bombing raids of the Second World War, and human rights abuses perpetrated by the US military personnel in the Abu Ghraib prison. I have alluded to Australia's and Canada's colonial pasts, and the difficult legacies of the Stolen Generation and residential schools survivors respectively. My route, therefore, has gone back and forth between Europe and other parts of the world, although its focus has remained on the twentieth century and the European continent. An analytical tension between common and diverse elements in Europe's past has produced a complex, and certainly non-celebratory view of European history, which transcends both the histories of individual nation-states, and that of Europe as the sum of its various national histories.

In closing, I would like to turn briefly to my native Bosnia. As a scholar of East European history, Norman Naimark, writes, some critics have suggested that we need "to learn how to forget painful historical events rather than to remember," and that this is especially true of the Balkans, where "there is a surfeit of historical memory rather than a dearth of it" (2009: 15). However, to Naimark, "the issue of collective memory is not really one of choice; the question is, really, how will the participants remember and how will we remember" (2009: 15). To start answering these questions, I will share my reflections on a theatre performance entitled *Sarajevo Theatre Tragedy* (*Sarajevska pozorišna tragedija*), which I saw in Sarajevo in the spring of 2011, as well as one personal story about Sarajevo. With these I hope to tie together this book's inquiries into remembering, understanding, and absorbing European pasts with the struggle of coming to terms with the difficult legacy of the Bosnian civil war, 1992–95, as it continues in contemporary Bosnia and Herzegovina.

The social, political, and economic situation in which all people of Bosnia and Herzegovina found themselves at the beginning of the 1990s, at the onset of the dissolution of the former Yugoslavia, is too complex to narrate here. This is also true of the complex causes behind the Bosnian war, which was prefaced by a declaration of Bosnia and Herzegovina's sovereignty in October of 1991, and a referendum for independence from Yugoslavia in early 1992, which was boycotted by the great majority of Bosnia's Serbian population. The war that followed brought about a division of the country into largely ethnically homogenised territories, through the process now known as ethnic cleansing. It also saw the destruction of cultural materials such as mosques, churches, bridges, and libraries that bore witness to Bosnia's rich multicultural and multi-confessional past, and the obliteration of human lives on a scale not seen in Europe since the Second World War. The Dayton Agreement, signed at the peace conference in Dayton, Ohio, in November 1995, ended the war, preserving the Bosnian state. The country was divided into two large ethno-territorial units: the Federation of Bosnia and Herzegovina (with largely Bosniak and Croat population) and the Republic of Srpska (Bosnian Serb Republic with predominantly Serbian population). Meanwhile, the International Criminal Tribunal for the Former Yugoslavia (ICTY), a United Nations court of law established in 1993 to deal with war crimes that took place during the conflicts in the Balkans in the 1990s, continues with its work until this day.

Sarajevo Theatre Tragedy had its premiere at the National Theatre in Sarajevo on 23 April 2010 as part of that year's International Theatre Festival Sarajevo (MESS). The performance was based on a play with an eponymous title and several other shorter texts by Peđa Kojović, and it was directed by Gorčin Stojanović, both of whom originally hailed from Sarajevo. After a long sojourn in the US, where he worked as a journalist for Reuters, Kojović returned to his native city, while Stojanović has been living in Belgrade for more than two decades, and is currently the artistic director of the Yugoslav Drama Theatre there. *Sarajevo Theatre Tragedy* was performed as part of the MESS's programme entitled the Memory Module. Initiated by the festival's executive producer Nihad Kreševljaković in 1996 in order to examine the artistic productions that emerged from Sarajevo during the war, the module is now a regular component of the festival, featuring performances, documentaries, art exhibitions, and symposia on the themes of memory and history in the Balkans and beyond.

The collaboration between Kojović and Stojanović, however, could also be seen as part of the ongoing attempts by cultural workers from Bosnia and Herzegovina, Serbia, and other former Yugoslav republics to develop new creative ways of thinking and working together after a long hiatus since the 1990s. For instance, in 2007, NGOs from Belgrade and Sarajevo, led by the Youth Initiative for Human Rights of Serbia, started an annual festival called the Days of Sarajevo in Belgrade in order to renew and strengthen cultural links between these two cities. Each year the festival offers its audiences performances, photo exhibits, concerts, staged readings, and films. In 2012, the festival attracted nearly 10,000 people between 22–6 May. Artists from Serbia have also been going to Bosnia to present their work in its cities and towns, and to collaborate with Bosnian artists.

The cultural activity in Sarajevo continued in some form even during the war, as Davor Diklić's book *Theatre in Sarajevo during the 1992–1995 War, Testimonies (Pozorište ratnom Sarajevu, svjedočanstva, 1992–1995)* amply documents. In her excellent book *Performance, Space, Utopia: Cities of War, Cities of Exile* (2012), my colleague at the University of Warwick, Silvija Jestrović, also examines theatre and performance in the city within the broader context of the war in Sarajevo, as well as against the backdrop of postwar developments in the city. The last two decades also saw a number of theatre productions, films, performances, and other arts coming from other parts of Bosnia and Herzegovina and the former Yugoslavia in which the experience of the Bosnian war, the disintegration of the socialist homeland, and life after the war is explored. I cannot even begin to survey this field of cultural production: suffice it to mention a few recent outstanding plays and performances such as such as devised pieces *Born in YU (Rođeni u YU,* 2010) and *Hypermnesia (Hipermnezija,* 2011), directed by Dino Mustafić and Selma Spahić respectively, which through the personal testimonies of actors who play in them talk about the life that was shared in a country that no longer exists, and the impact of its dissolution on the identities of its citizens. Also worth mentioning is Mirza Fehimović's *Ćeif,* a play about returnees to Sarajevo after the war – those who had moved to safety and run away. The drama explores the Bosnian trauma by focusing on the ethical dilemmas and guilt of the returnees, their fear of not being understood, and the possibility of forgiveness and healing. I focus here on *Sarajevo Theatre Tragedy* because it opens a wider conceptual discussion about the ways the war in Bosnia is remembered today, and the country's current political dilemmas, impasses, and prospects for the future.

The performance engages not only with the nostalgia for a country that ceased to exist, but also the traumatic experiences of the civil wars in the former Yugoslavia from the early 1990s which ended with country's collapse. Fragmentary in form, it features a rock concert, a play-within-a-play about reconciliation between warring parties in the Bosnian civil war (1992–95), and several short films by Ivica Matić (1948–76), one of Bosnia's most important filmmakers. In its first half, the characters, a group of men and women in their twenties and thirties, reminisce about their youth spent in Sarajevo before the war. Often talking directly to the audience, they describe

funny incidents from their past, often with a good dose of the pro-
verbial Sarajevan dark humour, arousing bursts of laughter from the
audience. More often than not, their stories betray a certain kind of
melancholy feeling, though perhaps nostalgia is the word that would
better capture the sentiment evoked. Their narratives suggest that
something was lost with the disintegration of the former Yugoslavia,
but they do not say what was lost exactly: Our youth? Our country?
The promise of the twentieth century? Humanity? A future?

The theme of loss of one's country is particularly foregrounded in
a series of monologues by of one the stage figures, a woman dressed
in black, who delivers the lines directly to the audience. The monologues consists of long passages that director Stojanović chose from
the book *My Country* by Emil Cioran, a Romanian writer and philosopher who spent most of his adult life in France. I quote here parts of
Cioran's texts used in the performance:

> I had written at the time a book on my country: it may very well be
> that no one has ever attacked his country so violently. It was ravings
> of a wild madman. But in my negations there was such a fire that,
> from a distance, I can only imagine it as a sort of love in reverse,
> a negative idolatry. This book was like a hymn of a killer, a theory of
> screams of a patriot without a homeland. (qtd. in Kojević, 2010: 11)

And the author goes on:

> And to a certain extent, I was grateful to my country for provid-
> ing me with such a marvellous occasion for torment. I loved it
> because it did not answer my expectations. Those were the good
> times: I believed in the prestige of unhappy passions. I loved chal-
> lenge, and the biggest seemed to be that of having been born in
> my country. (qtd. in Kojević, 2010: 11–12)[1]

In this work, which Cioran probably wrote in the early 1960s (see
Zarifopol-Johnston, 2009), but which was published posthumously,
the author reveals his ambivalent feelings for his homeland while
also dramatising the sense of estrangement and distance from his
younger self. As Ilinca Zarifopol-Johnston writes, here "the older,
French Cioran still vividly remembers the wound of pride from
which his writing sprang" (2009: 96).

However, the melancholy sentiment that this text engenders in the performance of *Sarajevo Theatre Tragedy* also derives from very specific Bosnian present-day circumstances, where the negative consequences of the war are still deeply felt. The country still lacks political stability and a sense of common purpose as it stands divided along ethnic and religious lines. The economy is recovering very slowly, unemployment figures are high, and public frustration and resentment over corruption is mounting. Many of the political values that oriented the period of actually existing socialism, such as progress, equality, and a strong, sovereign nation state have been already lost, and people are still coming to terms with new geopolitical and economic realities. The recent financial meltdown in Europe is exacerbating already harsh economic conditions. Neoliberal strategies for economic transformation have had a negative impact on ordinary people's lives in terms of jobs, benefits, retirements, access to education, health, and housing. This economic devastation and deracination is compounded by the wounds of war, which are healing slowly.

Telling here, for instance, is Selma Leydesdorff's exploration of the memories of women from Srebrenica, a town in eastern Bosnia where about 7500 Bosnian Muslims were killed by Bosnian Serb armed forces in 1995 (Ankersmit, 2006: 330). As her project shows, there are several layers of meaning to the way in which suffering is remembered. According to Leydesdorff, a professor of oral history and culture at the University of Amsterdam, "the main problem is not how memories are constructed versus 'reality,'" that is, the historical accuracy with which an "event" is recollected; anthropological research shows that events always bear complex relation to identity, memory, and history (2009: 24). Rather, for Leydesdorff, "The main problem is what *cannot* be remembered and put into words" (2009: 24–5). The women whose testimonies she has heard were not forthcoming in relating their experiences of violence and loss. She concludes that, as is often the case when we work with trauma, "the survivors either did not wish to remember or, more frequently, certain episodes were too difficult to recall in the light of their present lives. I am referring not to the trauma, but to their past of peaceful co-existence with those who eventually betrayed them. This past can hardly be understood now" (2009: 25).

Leydesdorff also emphasises here the relationship between the individual and the collective reconstruction and re-narration of the past: "These good memories of co-existence with 'the other' have become problematic. It is easier not to talk about them, to deny past feelings and replace them with stronger emotions of hatred and disappointment" (2009: 30). In attempting to negotiate the relation between the history of peaceful co-habitation before 1992, the war and the catastrophe of 1992–95, and their present, the memories recalled by Leydesdorff's interviewees often elide the material concerned with their pre-war pasts. The traumatic event, as trauma theory tells us, wounds the psyche. And it is because of this wound, concludes Leydesdorff, that these Bosnian women "can hardly imagine positive feelings when they talk about the past" (2009: 30).

In light of this kind of sentiments, several clips from Matić's short films (titled *Theme 1* and *Yellow-Green*) which were screened during the performance assume novel meanings. Matić is perhaps best known to international audiences for his first and only feature film, *Landscape with a Woman* (*Žena s krajolikom*, 1989), although he died in 1976, and the film was completed after his death. Made during the 1960s as part of his film studies, *Theme 1* captures ordinary Sarajevans on a sunny spring day in one of the city's main parks, with friends, lovers, and pensioners passing by (Figure 5.1), while *Yellow-Green* presents countryside scenes from various former Yugoslav republics.

The second half of the performance reflects some of the ways in which both Bosnian Muslims and Bosnian Serbs are creating narratives about their intertwined pasts, how these narratives diverge and converge, and the formation of contested memories about the Bosnian civil war (but also about the Second World War and the years of peaceful cohabitation in between). It features a play within a play in which a character named Muhamed recounts how the Commission for European Integration advertised a public competition in a Bosnian daily newspaper for the best theatre play that would speak "about turning from the past towards the future, about peace and progress" (Kojović, 2010: 14). In other words, as he translates the EU-speak, the play was supposed to envision "the better and happier future our country will be facing as soon as we stop behaving as primitive Balkan jerks and join the European Union" (Kojović, 2010: 13). Having won the competition, Muhamed now narrates the plot of the play with the rest of the cast, and then they enact an incident that took place during a rehearsal, in which Sasha (a Serbian actor) and Amir (a Bosnian Muslim actor) clash and exchange a set

Figure 5.1 Still from *Sarajevo Theatre Tragedy*, dir. Gorčin Stojanović, the National Theatre in Sarajevo, 2010; courtesy MESS Sarajevo

of insults. Holding a gun to Sasha's face, Amir then questions Sasha about the Bosnian war asking why, as he puts it, Bosnian Serbs started the armed conflict.

While Sasha insists that "everybody was waging with everybody else and [that] this was a civil war by definition," Amir responds, "No Shit. You man, you committed genocide – GENOCIDE . . ." (Kojović, 2010: 28). After the exchange reaches an impasse, Sasha states resignedly:

> I say I am sorry, and you do nothing. I do not know what else to do. I would understand if you said, "After what you have done, we do not want to live with you and you can go and fuck yourself." But you really do not want to say that. You say you want to live with us, but it seems that this is how you want to live with us, to keep us on the aim and to hit us on our head with this war every

now and then. . . . You don't even want to hear my side of the story. (Kojović, 2010: 28–9)

The scene illustrates well the ongoing Bosnian predicament of what Judith Butler calls "'up againstness' – the result of populations living in conditions of unwilled adjacency, the result of forced emigration or the redrawing of the boundaries of a nation-state" (2011b: 1). While Butler discusses her notion of cohabitation primarily within the context of the Israeli-Palestinian conflict, her ideas, as I will elaborate later, are deeply relevant for Bosnian society today. Seventeen years after the war, as the country's history is being re-written, a new memorial culture is being created in which the narratives of the "fact of war," such as the defence of Sarajevo, the role of the political leadership, military strategies, and the reaction of the international community, form part of the founding myths of a new nation. The ethical and political challenges of living together in democracy are many. The debate between Sasha and Amir on the main stage of the National Theatre in Sarajevo is thus deeply evocative of ethno-religious and political divides in Bosnia that have and "will continue to exacerbate the state of a divided memory, in which each group's legitimate victimization blinds and desensitises them to that of their countryman, who they themselves may have had a hand in victimizing" (Miller, 2006: 323).

The Bosnian government's lawsuit against Serbia-Montenegro, decided in the International Court of Justice (ICJ) in The Hague in February 2007, illustrates the current political stalemate well. The court concluded that Bosnian Serb armed forces perpetrated genocide in Bosnia and Herzegovina in Srebrenica in July 1995. However, the Court also concluded that Serbia was neither responsible for the genocide nor complicit in it, "but was responsible for failing to prevent it and for failing to punish its perpetrators" (Dimitrijević and Milanović, 2008: 65). In the aftermath of the war, the Bosnian genocide case deliberated in The Hague constituted an affectively charged reality, a "device through which both parties attempted to validate their broader, collective narratives as to the character of the Bosnian conflict, especially as to who were its heroes and who were its villains" (Dimitrijević and Milanović, 2008: 66). In this respect, according to these two authors, both the Government of the Republic of Bosnia and Herzegovina (BiH), which instituted the proceedings

before the ICJ, and the Federal Republic of Yugoslavia were less interested in "presenting their best legal case" than in "telling their *story*
of the Bosnian war" (2008: 66; original emphasis). As these authors
conclude, the trial was "a true juridical drama", a veritable "play
within a play, in which the actors in the courtroom were taking their
cues from the larger, political play outside it" (2008: 66).

Following this resolution, the Bosniak and Croat members of the
BiH presidency have stated publicly on several occasions that the
Court's judgement "has as its basic implication the 'annulment of all
results of genocide,' by which they of course mean the abolishment
of the Republika Srpska" (Dimitrijević and Milanović, 2008: 92). The
same body sent a joint letter to the UN Secretary General calling for
the abolition of Bosnian political entities – the Federation of Bosnia
and Herzegovina and Republika Srpska – in favour of a more unitary
state of Bosnia and Herzegovina. On the other hand, the political
elites of Republika Srpska saw the BiH lawsuit before the ICJ as a
threat. They maintain that reasons for establishing this entity derive
from the condition of extreme precarity in which Bosnian Serbs
found themselves after a declaration of Bosnia and Herzegovina's
sovereignty in October of 1991, and its secession from Yugoslavia
in 1992. The historical memory of the Bosnian Serbs, especially that
of their suffering and genocide during the Second World War, also
played a role, they argue (Dimitrijević and Milanović, 2008: 73).
And not much has changed since 2007. General elections of October
2010, which did not bring any significant political changes, have
been followed by a post-election stalemate. At the end of *Sarajevo
Theatre Tragedy*, a female character called Irma relates the tragic
ending of the scene between Sasha and Amir witnessed earlier in
the performance. After their long discussion, they shake hands, and
then Amir hands over his gun to Sasha to show him that it is not
a real gun after all. And this is when two members of the Bosnian
special military units burst onto the scene and kill Sasha. I found
the ending disappointing, abrupt, and arbitrary: if this was an ending to the play within the play we witnessed, where is the ending
to the performance, I wondered? Some critics called *Sarajevo Theatre
Tragedy* a postdramatic piece of theatre, perhaps because of its collage
structure, but this is perhaps where the similarities end. I appreciated
the experience of trying to reconstruct our collective tragedy, the
opportunity to visit again the familiar auditorium of the National

Theatre after nearly two decades, and the proximity of an audience that shares my sense of humour, but I could not relate to the fatalistic outcome of the piece. The Bosnian reality still seems infinitely more complex than the ending of this performance seems to suggest.

The epilogue to the Bosnian political crisis is yet to be written. For Naimark, the key problem standing in the way of plural cohabitation in Bosnia is that of identity. Having witnessed an international conference dedicated to the tenth anniversary of the genocide in Srebrenica, which took place in Sarajevo in 2005, he draws sombre conclusions. He argues that, like the other two main ethnic groups in Bosnia and Herzegovina, Bosniaks strive to develop "their own national institutions and culture, based primarily on their identity as victims," while simultaneously advocating the dissolution of ethnically-based institutional arrangements inherited from Dayton in exchange for "a united, democratic, and multi-national Bosnia-Herzegovina" (2009: 16). For this historian, the main obstacle for the country and its future is that the Bosniaks perpetuate the narrative of victimhood at the hands of the Serbs, while at the same time they seek "to incorporate a substantial Serbian population into the new Bosnia-Herzegovina," adding that "[t]here are similar, but less vital questions about the Croats" (2009: 16). He concludes: "If the genocide is at the core of national consciousness, then it is hard to imagine [that] a multi-national state can succeed in the future. But there are no workable alternatives" (2009: 18).

It is hard to disagree with Naimark, especially now that Europe is also going through a period of diminished expectations. As the European financial crisis has unleashed the destruction of public goods, from education to provisions for human welfare, older dreams of tolerance and social inclusion are losing ground. Faced with the Greek financial crisis, Europe, or rather the EU did not show any real solidarity towards this member state, signalling that the political, social, and cultural future of Europe is in a precarious condition (Balibar, 2010a; 2010b; 2012). Furthermore, European leaders such as David Cameron, Angela Merkel, and Nicolas Sarkozy have pronounced the ideal of a multicultural society as utterly failed. To this already grey picture we can add the thinning of key democratic values combined with novel forms of economic and political power. There is, indeed, little cause for hope.

To better address the problem of cohabitation in Bosnia in light of all these aforementioned difficulties, I want to return briefly to

Butler. The reader may recall that I introduced her idea of cohabitation when discussing Polish-Jewish relations in Poland. Butler has written on the subject in an article published in an edited collection *The Power of Religion in a Public Sphere*, where she – along with Habermas, Charles Taylor, and Cornell West – reflects on the political status of modern religion. She has also addressed this theme in her latest book entitled *Parting Ways: Jewishness and the Critique of Reason* and a number of public lectures, where she engages the thought of Emmanuel Levinas, Hannah Arendt, and Edward Said in her attempts to articulate a version of co-habitation that could be a resource for thinking about current global challenges and obligations. Butler insists upon a certain "intertwinement" between the lives of others and her own life, which she finds irreducible to the markers of national or other kinds of belonging. "It seems to me that even in situations of antagonistic and unchosen modes of cohabitation," writes Butler, "certain ethical obligations emerge. Since we do not choose with whom to cohabit the earth, we have to honour those obligations to preserve the lives of those we may not love, we may never love, we do not know, and did not choose" (2011b: 24). As vulnerable, injurable, and limited beings, we must recognise our own shortcomings as a way of recognising them in others. Butler recognises, however, that the application of this notion of precarity within the context of the Israeli-Palestinian conflict comes with the struggle "for social and political forms that are committed to fostering a sustainable interdependency on egalitarian terms" (2011b: 21). Here Butler revisits and affirms Arendt's and Said's critique of the state of Israel, and their respective proposals for a one-state solution, that is, a bi-national state in which both Jews and Arabs would maintain their cultural autonomy.

To Craig Calhoun, the significance of Butler's notion of political cohabitation "comes from underwriting recognition of the importance or at least inevitability of continued life in the same place, even when values, identities, and practices cannot be readily reconciled" (2011: 130–1). And this is also where I find her ethical and political ideal of living together applicable to the Bosnian case. The two political entities in the land are in the throes of creating single national narratives of past events, institutions, culture, and politics, often making massive simplifications that not only distort the country's past, but threaten to impoverish its future. In these circumstances, promoting an ethical position in which the obligations of cohabitation do not derive from cultural sameness, but from the unchosen character of social plurality seem paramount. Only time will tell whether the necessity of co-habiting the land will prevail as a guiding principle behind the actions and policies of Bosnian peoples and their leaders, and lead them to greater cultural heterogeneity.

I would like to end on an optimistic note, by relating a story about my visit to Sarajevo in August 2010, when I learned about one of the city's surviving multicultural practices. It was a sunny summer day, and I was waiting for my friend Nina in front of the BBI Centre, where one of the city's former landmarks, the old shopping centre *Sarajka*, used to stand. Nina now lives in Canada, and we do not have a chance to see each other very often. That summer our respective visits to Sarajevo luckily coincided, so we arranged to meet for a cup of coffee in Baščaršija, Sarajevo's old town, hoping to catch up after several years of not seeing each other. Popular with Sarajevans, the old shopping centre was demolished during the war; the new structure now features boutiques with expensive global brands that most Sarajevans are not able to afford, and the headquarters of Al Jazeera Balkans news television station owned by Qatar Media Corporation. On my way to meet Nina, between the shopping centre and a big city park (*Veliki park*), the same one in which Matić's recorded footage for his *Theme 1*, I noticed a Nick Danziger's street exhibition called *Missing Lives*. Produced in collaboration with the International Commission on Missing Persons (ICMP) and the BiH Missing Persons Institute (MPI), the exhibition featured large photographs of men and women whose family members had gone missing during the civil wars in the former Yugoslavia (1991–95), which were accompanied by their testimonies recalling the circumstances in which their loved ones had disappeared. Other photos captured acts of forensic exhumations and human identification across the Western Balkans (former Yugoslavia), where, according to the exhibition narrative, more than fifteen thousand people are still considered missing.

Nina arrived and, after our customary hugs and kisses, suggested that we go visit several religious shrines in the old town. There is an old custom, she explained, according to which people visit three successive sites: the (Islamic) Seven Brothers *Turbe* (a tomb, a mausoleum), the Catholic (Franciscan) Church of St Ante and the Old Orthodox Church in Baščaršija. At each site they leave donations, pray, and make a wish. The sites are visited by people of different ethnic and religious affiliations, who come to pray and wish for their health and happiness, or that of their closest friends and relatives. Nina had heard about this custom from her mother some years ago and had performed the ritual already, and she wanted to share the experience with me. The prospect made me smile, and we headed towards the old town. Along the way we exchanged some bills for the coins that we would need for donations. The route took us across the Gavrilo Princip bridge and we reached the tombs of the Seven Brothers, located at Bistrik on the left side of the Miljacka river, a few minutes later. The tombs are placed in a covered structure with a door and seven windows, just below the entrance to the Mosque of Hadži Sulejman Čokadžija. Legend has it that the men buried there were not really related by blood, but rather that six of them were unjustly executed sometime during the Ottoman period. People insert coins of the same value at each window, starting from the door on the left and moving to the right, as they pray and make their wishes. We were there during a week day, and there were only a few people at the site. A middle-aged woman and a young man made their donations as they performed their Muslim prayers. I was not sure how to proceed: I remembered in that moment going to a mosque as a child with my Muslim schoolfriends, and the feeling of embarrassment – of intruding upon them – that came over me as they started praying in Arabic. Then I noticed a woman crossing herself after donating some coins and moving from one window to another, and Nina already standing at one of the windows. I silently joined her.

Next on our journey was the Church of St Ante, built in the new Romanesque style in the early twentieth century, and located just across the street from the Seven Brothers. Here we enjoyed some beautiful organ music and gorgeous stained-glass windows for a while, before making our donations and heading to the Old Orthodox Church on Baščaršija. Along the way we stopped by the beautiful Gazi Husrev-beg Mosque at the heart of Baščaršija, and took some pictures. Upon entering the Old Church – the Church of Sts Michael and Gabriel the Archangels – we went upstairs to visit a wooden canopied table with a little casket on top of it, a picture of the Madonna, and offerings of flowers all around. People believe that the casket contains the remains of a child found during the restoration of the church in the eighteenth century. Over time, the dead child has become sacred among Sarajevans of all faiths. Women who have trouble becoming pregnant, whether Muslim, Christian, or Jewish, come here to perform a ritual (which involves passing three times on one's knees under the table holding the casket), believing that it will help them to conceive and bring into the world a healthy new-born. Nina and I lit some candles for the dead and for the living, and then admired a large iconostasis with old frescos that covers the entire right wall. Later, we had a drink of water in the courtyard just as a big group of tourists arrived at the site. There I suggested to Nina that we add an old Sephardic synagogue, now converted into a Jewish museum, to our itinerary, since it was only a short walk from where we were. Unfortunately, the museum was closed, so we headed to one of many street cafes on Baščaršija for a cup of coffee instead; there was still so much catching up to do.

For some this ritual bears witness to the legacy of Bosnia's multi-confessional community, for others it is an invented tradition. It can be also seen to reflect well the dominant foreign representation of Sarajevo as a city that has heroically preserved its cosmopolitan diversity in spite of all adversity and nationalist box-thinking – a belief that also inflects the narratives of many Sarajevans. Culture workers promote this unique expression of interethnic intimacy as an example of the city's intangible heritage by adding it to the range of city tours on offer. Whichever view one takes, this evocation of an eclectic multicultural practice can be seen as indicative of an existing process of social mediation and transformation in the city that, less than two decades ago, emerged from the ravages of a civil war. Experienced within layered contexts of embodiment – collective, intersubjective, individual – this performative practice shows the interdependence between its inhabitants' daily practices, cultural legacies, collective memories, and political processes. As such, it could be seen as a sign of Sarajevans' mutual assertion of difference and their commitment to a pluralistic, tolerant, and integrated society. Performed by both religious people and atheists, it also signals the significance of both religion and the secular in both the Bosnian, and a wider public sphere.[2]

At the same time, I realise that this narrative about a multicultural and unitary Bosnia, which can fold into many Bosniak nationalist narratives, is less easily absorbed by others: for instance, "many Serbs and Croats in Bosnia see their separate communities as not part of a putative Bosnian nation" (Hayden, 2007: 117). The narrative also occludes the fact that most of the city's Serb population now lives in its suburbs, known today as East Sarajevo (*Istočno Sarajevo*).[3] Furthermore, this narrative about Sarajevan conviviality does not cast any light on the various other minorities and marginalised groups who inhabit the city such as Roma, refugees from eastern Bosnia, small entrepreneurs from China, illegal immigrants, asylum seekers, or women trafficked from former Soviet republics and other countries; their presence remains overshadowed by relations between the three dominant ethnic groups. And while it is difficult to tell at this juncture what kind of a future Bosnians really wish for themselves, it is to be hoped that, despite all difficulties and challenges, fragile processes of social mobilisation and democratisation currently underway will result in social and political forms committed to fostering a sustainable interdependency of Bosnians on egalitarian terms and social inclusion based on solidarity, justice, and ethics.

Notes

1 Introduction: Theorising Europe and Recollection

1. I am indebted to an anonymous reader for providing a succinct account of this book's aims in an anonymous reader's report for Palgrave Macmillan; some of these observations have inflected this paragraph.
2. Independently of a query concerning the relation of memory and history in recent scholarship focusing on the twentieth century, a number of studies have attempted to place the idea of memory in historical perspective during premodern periods. Frances A. Yates's *The Art of Memory* (1966) traces transformations in *ars memoria* – the rhetorical art of memorising through spatial images – from Roman times through the Renaissance, where the art of memory persisted in the humanist tradition despite its decline due to the spread of the printing press. Janet Coleman's *Ancient and Medieval Memories: Studies in the Reconstruction of the Past* (1992) offers a comprehensive history of theories of memory from antiquity through later medieval times. In *The Book of Memory: A Study of Memory in Medieval Culture* (1990) and *The Craft of Thought: Meditation, Rhetoric, and the Making of Images, 400–1200* (1998), Mary Carruthers demonstrates the persistence of memory training even with the spread of texts, which resulted in the highly mixed oral-literate nature of medieval cultures. Lina Bolzoni's study, *The Gallery of Memory: Literary and Iconographic Models in the Age of the Printing Press* (2001) deals with the practices related to memory in sixteenth-century culture. A number of other recent works in the field of intellectual history have attempted to grapple with the intriguing problem of the historicity of the phenomenon of memory in the West. This idea of historicity of memory has been inspired in part by Pierre Nora's essay "Between Memory and History" (1989) which introduced the multivolume series he directed, *Realms of Memory: Rethinking the French Past* (1996–98). In this vein, Patrick H. Hutton's *History as an Art of Memory* (1993), Mat K. Matsuda's *The Memory of the Modern* (1996), and Richard Terdiman's *Present Past: Modernity and Memory Crisis* (1993) all centre on the historical transformations to which, according to the different perspectives of their works, "memory has been subject." Like Nora, they link this historicity of the social and cultural role of memory to the radical transformations that Western civilisation has undergone in the modern period.
3. See especially Caruth (1995; 1996); Felman and Laub (1992); and Van der Kolk, McFarlane, and Weiseth (1996). Leys (2000) provides a critical assessment of this consensus position, offering a history of the concept of trauma in the fields of psychology, neuroscience, and literary criticism.

Also, in recent years critics have called attention to the limitations of trauma theory claiming that notions of class, race, gender, and sex have not received due attention within its boundaries. Many of them have argued for the importance of rethinking trauma theory from a postcolonial perspective and the need to address the traumas visited upon members of non-Western cultures. For this critical trend in twenty-first century trauma studies see, for instance: Huyssen (2003); Bennett and Kennedy (2003); Hodgkin and Radstone (2003); Kaplan and Wang (2004); Kaplan (2005); Bennett (2005); Ball (2007); Radstone (2007a; 2007b; 2011); Fassin and Rechtman (2009); Rothberg (2009); and Craps (2013). See also the special issues of the journals *Life Writing* 5.1 (2008), edited by Kate Douglas, Gillian Whitlock, and Bettina Stumm and *Continuum* 24.1 (2010) edited by Antonio Traverso and Mick Broderick that explore a wide range of uses and applications of trauma theory beyond the scope of the conventional theory of trauma.

4. Obviously, our access to the witnesses' testimonies is limited by a number of languages we speak. Translation has helped to overcome this problem to some extent, but the linguistic and cultural complexity of many original texts has been lost, or seriously reduced in the process of transfer. For instance, there is an issue of languages in which these memoirs were written. For many Eastern European Jews Yiddish was the first language, and many authors wrote in Yiddish without even suspecting that after the war Yiddish would cease to be a living language spoken in Europe. If a memoir written in Yiddish were to reach the wider reading public, it would have to be translated into a modern European language. As a result, translations often displaced originals, and we can only try to guess whether there is another original behind a Polish or German memoir. There are also texts written in the author's first language, and then translated but the translation is often marked as the original and the real original cannot be easily traced.

5. As Craps notes, scholars such as Wendy Brown (1995) and Lauren Berlant (2007) have expressed strong doubts about the political value and efficacy of focusing on traumatic suffering, offering powerful critiques of the depoliticising tendencies of hegemonic trauma discourses seen to privilege psychological recovery "over the transformation of a wounding political, social, and economic system" (2013: 28). However, I would argue along with Craps that, though "trauma research does not in and of itself lead to political transformation," it can act as an impetus for individuals and communities to work through their histories and memories of suffering and conflict from more active positions of political agency (2013: 126). In recent years, for instance, we have seen trauma discourses combined with other cultural strategies of working through a traumatic past that emphasise the establishment of truth and delivery of social and institutional justice, or apology, forgiveness, reconciliation, and compensation.

6. In a very different setting and evoking very different histories, Sandra Richards' research on African-American cultural travel to slave sites in the Black Atlantic also grapples with the layered and fractured memories of

trauma and displacement. As Richards asserts, though in their encounters with the sites that memorialise the transatlantic slave trade, such as Ghana's slave castles "diasporic visitors enact conflicting identities – emotionally distraught surrogates for enslaved ancestors, smiling tourists, quarrelsome members of a reunited African family, or disruptive critics complicit with American hegemony," Ghana and other West African nations still exert a special pull on African-American tourists as sites that mark their ancestral beginning (2005: 63).

7. Kristeva calls this loss a maternal "Thing" rather than an object because unlike an object this lost maternal is not yet specified, or separate from the subject (1987, 262 n.7).

8. In recent years several psychoanalytic authors working within the European tradition of contemporary critical thought have addressed anew the problem of the constitution of the human subject (Kristeva, 1989; 1995; Butler, 1990; 1997a; Oliver, 2001; Laplanche, 1989; Elliot, 2004). Essential to all such recastings of subjectivity is a shift away from an Oedipal-centred to a pre-Oedipal perspective, from a Lacanian-inspired theory of the linguistification of the subject to a post-Lacanian theory of pre-verbal, imaginary signification. Often taking their cue from Freud's classic essay, "Mourning and Melancholia" (1917), these theories have typically concerned themselves with the boundaries of the ego and with the processes of identification that constitute the ego's economy. Moreover, these far-reaching investigations have raised afresh the question of human creation, the question of representation and fantasy, and the question of the imaginary constitution of the socio-symbolic world. For more traditional intellectual histories that focus on the figure of melancholia, see: Babb (1951); Jackson (1986); Klibansky, Panofsky, and Saxl (1964); and Wittkower (1963). For an assessment of the similarities and differences between the melancholic states of past eras and today's depression, see Radden (2003). On the gendered distinction between melancholia and depression see Radden (1987), and Schiesari (1992).

2   History, Memory, and Trauma in Heiner Müller's Theatre

1. Hannah Arendt's insight into the connections between oversees imperialism and Nazism has recently given rise to a more detailed literature tracking possible links between colonial genocide and the Holocaust. While postcolonial authors such as Aimé Césaire, Frantz Fanon and W. E. B Du Bois drew parallels between extermination of indigenous populations in Africa and the war of annihilation against the Jews of Europe, they did not give this problem as much attention as Arendt did in her book *The Origins of Totalitarianism* (1951a). (*The Burden of Our Time* [London: 1951] is the title of the first British edition of *The Origins of Totalitarianism*.) Some claim that Arendt argued that colonial violence paved the way for National Socialism; acts of colonial genocide in German Southwest Africa

during the early 1900s are often cited as the best proof of Arendt's thesis (Hull, 2005; Zimmerer and Zeler, 2008; Melber, 2011). Other scholars have criticised this thesis as unduly teleological (for example, Grosse, 2005; Kundrus, 2011; Moses, 2011). See Langbehn and Salama (2001) for different viewpoints about "continuity" and "discontinuity" between colonialism and the genocide of Nazi Germany. See Stone (2011) for the adoption and adaptation of Arendt's ideas in the context of genocide studies.

2. Haiti and the Haitian Revolution have been present as topoi in German literature from the early nineteenth century. The first German literary work to deal with Haiti, written in the aftermath of the Haitian revolution, is Heinrich Kleist's *The Betrothal in Santo Domingo* (*Die Verlobung in St. Domingo*, 1811). After Kleist, the most significant literary engagements with the Haitian revolution in German language come from Anna Seghers (1900–83) and Müller. As a Jew and a Marxist, Seghers fled Germany in 1933, and spent most of her exile years in Latin America, including brief stays in Santo Domingo and Martinique. After her return to Soviet-occupied Germany in 1947, she soon became one of leading literary voices in the GDR. For a book length study of Haiti in German literature, see Uerlings (1997). On the idea of negritude in East German Literature, including Muller's work, see Pizer (2011).

3. *The Task* was first performed at the Volksbühne in Berlin in 1980. It was directed by Müller in collaboration with his second wife, Ginka Tscholakowa. See Barnett (1998) for an account of this and several other German stagings of the play. In her commentary on the play, for instance, Arlene Akiko Teraoka notes that Müller's use of Brecht's *The Measures Taken*, "which deals with the export of the *socialist*, Russian Revolution, marks 'Paris' as a metaphor also for 'Moscow'" (1985: 167; her emphasis). As it is well known, ever since the failure of the Spartacus Uprising in January 1919, German communism was forced to enter a relationship of complete dependence on the Soviet Union. In the wake of the Second World War the German communists came to power, but as governors for an occupying power rather than on the foundation of a revolution. Thus the reading that Teraoka reminds us of was certainly topical at the time Müller wrote the play.

4. Madureira also points out to "an analogous process of subalternisation in the theoretical formulations of East German intellectuals concerning the revolutionary processes in African countries, which expectedly relegated them to an inferior or lower status in relation to the East European countries" (2011: 288).

5. For comprehensive discussions of Brecht's influence on Müller, see for instance Fehervary (1976) and Teraoka (1985).

6. One of the seminal texts on the Haitian Revolution still remains C. L. R. James's *The Black Jacobins* (1938). For an excellent survey of the "Greater Caribbean" between 1789–1815, see a volume edited by David Gaspar and David Geggus (1997), especially the opening essay by Geggus that provides an overview of the period. For a critical review of various tendencies within the historiography of the Haitian Revolution,

see Trouillot (1995). For a comprehensive account of the revolutionary age in the Americas, see Langley (1996). Furthermore, Haiti's bicentennial was marked by publication of works by scholars such as Laurent Dubois (2004a; 2004b), Sibylle Fischer (2004), Nick Nesbitt (2004; 2008), and David Patrick Geggus (2002) to whose excellent insights into the French Atlantic world during the revolutionary epoch my analysis here is particularly indebted.

7. The term *gens de couleur* refers to free people of colour; those of varying African descent freed by masters or born of two free parents.

8. Apart from being ignored by Arendt, the revolution that led to Haiti's independence from France in 1804 is barely acknowledged even in Eric Hobsbawm's seminal *Age of Revolution* (1962). If you search through recent canonical histories of the French Revolution by people like François Furet (1992) and Simon Schama (1989) you will find little or no trace of the issue of slavery and the "colonial question." Mona Ozouf's and François Furet's *Critical Dictionary of the French Revolution* (1989) does not mention the Haitian Revolution and has no entry for either colonialism or slavery.

9. Stevens's letters speak directly of the mission described in *The Task*. They are preserved at the Department of State in Washington and were published in *The American Historical Review* 16.1 (Oct., 1910): 64–101. While there were many slave uprisings in Jamaica, the British crown abolished slavery on the island only in 1834. Jamaica gained independence in 1962.

10. For a cogent reading of Müller's *The Task* in relation to Genet's *The Blacks*, see Kalb (2001: 127–37). On historical plays dealing with the French Revolution, some of which have been completely forgotten, see: Carlson (1966); Buckley (2006); and Maslan (2005). For a comprehensive analysis of first known piece of political theatre in Saint Domingue entitled *General Liberty, or The Planters in Paris* (*La Liberté Générale, ou Les Colons à Paris*), dealing with the intrigues of colonists and slave holders in Paris and the passage of law abolishing slavery on 4 February 1794, see Fischer (2004: 214–26).

11. On gender and the French Revolution, the literature is vast. See, for instance, Hunt (1992) and Desan (1992).

12. In his *Black Atlantic* (1993), one of the most sustained and influential critical assessments of the issue of modernity and slavery, Paul Gilroy also offers an account of the diasporic African cultures as a vital reservoir for utopian ideas as well as a source for a critical revision of modernity.

13. In her article "Hegel and Haiti," which initially appeared in *Critical Inquiry* (2000) and then in her book *Hegel, Haiti, and Universal History* (2009), Buck-Morss offers a compelling exploration of the impact of the Haitian Revolution on philosophical developments in Europe. Presenting compelling evidence, she insists that Hegel was deeply aware of and responding to events in Haiti, that the Haitian Revolution played a central role in his articulation of the master–slave dialectic, and that he initiated a tradition of ignoring the Revolution in Western scholarship. Furthermore, she goes on to argue that Hegel scholarship has ignored this obvious connection for two

centuries. As Fischer writes, "The issue goes to the heart of the question of how silence operates, and whether, why, and when Haiti and revolutionary antislavery vanished from the Western records" (2004: 28).

14. As Buck-Morss further relates, Jean-Jacques Dessalines, a leader of the Haitian Revolution and the first ruler of an independent Haiti, "in gratitude, and in acknowledgement of what Poles suffered at home . . . allowed them to stay in Haiti after independence (whereas all other whites were barred by Article 12 of the 1805 constitution from owning property)" (2009: 75).

15. On the resonances of the French Revolution in German philosophical circles at the time see Max (2003), and Comay (2011).

16. Here I quote the original versions of these poems:

> Da ist die Brücke
> Und ich seh dich gehen
> Über die Planken aus Holz
> Drei fehlen in der Mitte.
> Ich reiche dir die Hand
> Und du siehst sie nicht.
> Du siehst das Wasser Unter dir
> Und den Wind, der Stark ist.
> Da zittert meine Hand
> In der Mitte zwischen Wasser
> Und Wind.
> Und da ist die Brücke.
>
> Inge Müller (1954)

[Inge Müller: *Daß ich nicht ersticke am Leisesein*. Aufbau Verlag GmbH & Co. KG, Berlin 2002.]

> Ins Wasser blickend sah ich
> Deine Augen, die mich suchten. Da
> Fand ich mich. Und ich fürchtete den Wind
> Nicht mehr. Er trägt uns
> Die sich an den Händen halten.
>
> Heiner Müller (1954)

[Heiner Müller, *"Ins Wasser blickend sah ich."* From: *Heiner Müller, Werke, Volume 1: Die Gedichte.* © Suhrkamp Verlag Frankfurt am Main 1998. All rights reserved by and controlled through Suhrkamp Verlag Berlin.]

Here and throughout this chapter – when there are no existing translations of the texts in German which I quote – I have provided my own translation.

17. Formally speaking, we may say that this text belongs to the kind of writing for theatre that Hans-Thies Lehman terms as "postdramatic theatre."

In his book *Postdramatic Theatre* (2002; English version, 2006), Lehman uses this concept to refer to tendencies and experiments defining theatre outside the (dialogic) paradigm of dramatic texts. As the major exponents of postdramatic theatre he lists Robert Wilson, Tadeusz Kantor, and Müller, to name only a few.

18. In his autobiography, Müller provides an explanation for the genesis of the text:
   "A drawing, slightly coloured, of a female stage design student in Sofia. She had made a drawing of a dream. She had not read Freud, so that this was one to one, without any inhibitions about symbols. I started to describe the picture. Associations to the picture followed, which essentially started from the incorrectness of the drawing, the flaws leaving room for imagination. To describe a picture also means to paint it over with writing. The description translates it into a different medium . . . One layer extinguishes the preceding one and the points of view change. Finally the onlooker himself is called into question and thus also the person describing the picture" (qtd. in Vaβen, 1995: 169).

19. For autobiographical information on Inge Müller see, for instance, Herta Müller (2000) and Geipel (2002).

20. As the published draft of *Obituary* indicates, Müller first wrote this text in the first person singular, then changed it into the third person singular, and finally decided for the original choice (Müller, 1999: 35–9). The draft is not dated. It is published in an exhibition catalogue by the Heiner Müller Archive at the Academy of Arts, Berlin. For a cogent reading of *Obituary*, see Kreikebaum (2003).

21. It seems that Müller responds to this criticism on some level when he writes in the second version of *Obituary*: "to write a story of a woman, impossible" (Müller, 1999: 41).

22. Sebald's novels evoke fragmentary memories of wartime Europe, and in several of them he writes about the sufferings of German Jews.

23. It is interesting to notice that Inge Müller invokes Hiroshima in one of her poems, "Who gives you a right to play dumb" ("Wer gibt dir ein Recht den Stummen zu spielen"):

> The Earth does not bear you?
> The sun does not warm you? –
> Have you seen the dead in the stone
> The shadows of the suns; the living dead:
> Hiroshima.

[Die Erde trägt dich nicht? / Die Sonne wärmt dich nicht? – / Hast du die Toten im Stein gesehen / Die Schatten; die Toten die leben: / Hiroshima.] (Inge Müller, 1997: 118–19.)

24. See, for instance, Markusen and Kopf (1995), Barkan (2000), and Naimark (2001).

25. In her article entitled "Hamburg Memories," for instance, Angelika Bammer argues that while in the immediate postwar years "the suffering

and losses that Germans had inflicted on others during the Nazi and war years was publicly acknowledged and remembered, it was the memory of German suffering and loss that clearly predominated" (2001: 362). Bammer then demonstrates how Hamburg's memorial landscape was redefined in the 1980s. As the emphasis shifted to a focus on German agency, and the consequences of German actions, a number of memorials were erected that tell the story of Holocaust destruction. To Bammer this indicates "less a change in what is remembered than a shift in emphasis and stance. In neither period is either of the two catastrophic events that mark this history – the war and the Nazi genocide – forgotten or ignored" (359).

26. At the same time, together with Christa Wolf, Müller became a key figure in the German public confrontation with socialist culture. With the publication of Wolf's novel *What's Left* (*Was bleibt*) in the summer of 1990, there followed a heated debate among German cultural critics surrounding these intellectuals' role and alleged failure in the face of the German Democratic republic's political collapse of 1989. The debate sharpened after the discovery of these authors' involvement with the East German secret police. This "literature controversy," in Katrin Sieg's words, "operated as a performative text that organised inter-German relations in a constellation that accorded former East Germany a morally and culturally inferior position" (1995: 151). Andreas Huyssen observes that the *Was bleibt* controversy served to "freeze" critical reception around Christa Wolf's work. It was as if her entire career culminated and imploded in those diaries. See Huyssen (1995: 60–6).

27. Müller spells the Count's name as York. In Demandt's text he is referred as Count Yorck (1992: 2).

28. As a matter of fact the event occurred on *Marchstrasee* (March Street) (Demandt, 1992: 22).

29. In his recent *Illusion of the End*, Jean Baudrillard notes that rejection of the past "consists in reviewing everything, rewriting everything, restoring everything, face-lifting everything, to produce, as it seems, in burst of paranoia a perfect set of accounts at the end of the century, a universally positive balance sheet" (1994: 12).

30. In *The Foundling* (*Der Findling*, 1987) as well, Müller sees the urban landscape of West Berlin as a palimpsest of memories: "Half-city of the old and the new windows / Corpses in closets money in the bank / Corpses with David's star in brown / In armygray / . . . / Smoke through the chimney dust from carpet bombings / Plötzensee monument on butcher hooks / the plaque that disappeared at Landwehr canal" (Müller, 1989: 143–4).

31. Immediately upon the unification of the Federal Republic of Germany and the German Democratic Republic in 1990, Müller pronounced: "The separation of the communists from power concerns the emigration into a dream. In this process an idea again becomes a force. . . . Reality can cease to exist, can be erased by a new reality. But dreams cannot be erased, they exist in another time. . . . Communism exists in the dream-time and this is not dependent on triumph or defeat" (qtd. in Herzinger, 1995: 113).

32. Contra Huyssen, Bochow argues that Müller "did not share the utopian hope and the enthusiasm of many intellectuals in Eastern Germany in the weeks of October and November of 1989 who, by pursuing an utopian project of reconciling socialism with democracy, remained within the very concepts of European history" (2005: 5).

3 Contested Pasts and the Ethics of Remembrance in Tadeusz Kantor's "Theatre of Death"

1. For excellent discussions of Kantor's avant-garde experiments prior "The Theatre of Death" (1975–1990), see Kobialka (1993; 2009), and Suchan (2000).
2. In this respect Kantor is associated with artists such as Czesław Miłosz, Tadeusz Borowski, Miron Białoszewski, Henryk Grynberg, Hanna Krall, Tadeusz Różewicz, Stanisław Lem, and Jan Błoński, who also tried to assimilate the experiences of the Holocaust.
3. While acknowledging the "work" memory has done and continues to do in the production of subjectivity, I agree with Susannah Radstone and Katherine Hodgkin, who have suggested that the "regimes of memory," which they define as "the kinds of knowledge and power . . . carried, in specific times and places, by particular discourses of memory," cannot be equated with regimes of subjectivity with which they are associated. Instead, they propose that "study of regimes of memory might complicate as well as deepen our understanding of related regimes – for instance, of subjectivity, of history, or of the mind" (2003: 2–3).
4. I explore Polish-Jewish relations at more length in this chapter after my analysis of Kantor's *Wielopole, Wielopole*.
5. Here and throughout this part of the chapter, unless otherwise indicated, I am quoting from Mariusz Tchorek and G. M. Hyde's English translation of Kantor's "theatrical score" (in Polish, *partytura*) for *Wielopole, Wielopole*. I consulted various recordings of *Wielopole, Wielopole* in the Cricoteka, the Centre for the Documentation of the Art of Tadeusz Kantor, in Cracow; however, my performance analysis here is mostly based on the following two records: Andrzej Sapija's recording of the performance filmed in Wielopole Skrzyńskie, Kantor's home town in 1984, and the TV recording of the performance made by Stanisław Zajączkowski at Sokol Hall in Cracow in 1983. From 2006–08, the Cricoteka released ten DVDs of film, filmed performances, and documentaries featuring Kantor's work.
6. This act of "naming" as well as Kantor's stage presence throughout his performances of "The Theatre of Death" bears much resemblance to the figure of the Buddhist priest in Noh theatre. Etsuko Terasaki writes: "In order for a reincarnation or a ghost to make its presence known, a link to the human world is necessary – a need that is filled by the Buddhist priest. . . . If the priest's presence signifies the living world, the natural world, and the continuum of empirical time, the figure of reincarnation represents the dead at the very threshold of the living, restlessly

wandering and seeking a link with the living. Without the mediation of the priest, the dead cannot communicate its intentions. . . . By the gesture of apostrophe, the priest's task is to 'give a face to a ghost,' that is, to enable it to speak out the grievances it harbours, so as to lead it to a personal confession of its transgression" (2002: 19–20).

7. In *The Poetics of Space* Bachelard sees in the house "a tool for analysis of the human soul" (1994: xxxiii), and he asserts that "the things we have forgotten are 'housed'" (p. xxxiii), that "the unconscious abides" (p. 9).

8. "Even memory has a history," writes Richard Terdiman in his *Modernity and the Memory Crisis* (1993: 3).

9. As Mary Carruthers also points out, "Zeno the Stoic (4th–3rd century BC) defines memory as *'thesaurismos phantasion'* or 'storehouse of mental images.' *Thesaurus* is used metaphorically both in Romans (2:5) and the Gospel of Matthew (6:19–20) in the sense of storing up intangible things for salvation. . . . The *Rhetorica ad Herennium* calls memory the treasure house of found-things, 'thesauru[s] inventorum' (iii, 16), referring particularly to a memory trained by the artificial scheme, which the author proceeds to recommend. Quintilian, also recommending a cultivated memory, calls it *'thesaurus eloquentiae'* (xi, 2, 2)" (Carruthers, 1990: 34–5).

10. According to Cicero, Simonides "inferred that persons desiring to train this faculty select localities and form mental images of the facts they wish to remember and store those images in the localities, with the result that the arrangement of the localities will preserve the order of the facts, and the images of the facts will designate the facts themselves, and we shall employ the localities and images respectively as a wax writing tablet and the letters written on it" (*De oratore*, II: 354).

11. Many critics have compared Kantor's role on stage to that of a priest conducting a sermon. In a conversation with Jean-Pierre Thibaudat, Kantor tells the following anecdote from his childhood in Wielopole: "On Sunday, at Christmas and Easter, I watched superb ceremonies in church. I was four or five years old, I had no idea of the theatre whatso-ever, but I used to re-enact the mass in the presbytery's hall. I was playing the priest, in a white shirt, with my sister helping me. I always invited the priest, grandmother and mother; I treated the show very seriously and they were my audience. Each time I ended it with a sermon" (qtd. in Thibaudat, 2003: 183).

12. This secret protocol agreed between Hitler's Germany and Stalin's Soviet Union on 23 August 1939 effectively divided Poland (and the rest of Central Europe) between their two spheres of influence.

13. It was only in April 1989 that the Polish side of the Polish-Soviet histori-cal Commission, established in late spring 1987, examined and rejected the Soviet Burdenko report, and a year later (on 13 April 1990) that the Soviet President Mikhail Gorbachev officially laid the blame for the Katyń massacre on the NKVD. Two and a half years later, on 14 October 1992, Russian President Boris Yeltsin handed over to Polish President Lech Wałęsa key archival documents concerning Katyń, including the document containing the Politburo resolution (from 5 March 1940) that

ordered the liquidation of the Polish prisoners of war and the deportation of a hundred thousand Polish nationals.

14. However, as George Sanford notes, in this decade, Katyń appeared repeatedly in Solidarity press, and the issue of commemoration of the Polish prisoners of war was raised in Solidarity's negotiations with the Government (2005: 212).

15. Of course, photography's deeply rooted kinship with death has been noted by many authors. Among the very interesting sources on the subject are Roland Barthes' classic *Camera Lucida* (1981), Eduardo Cadava's *Words of Light* (1997), and more recently Susan Sontag's *Regarding the Pain of Others* (2003), and Judith Butler's *Precarious Life* (2004) and *Frames of War* (2009).

16. As Douwe Draaisma notes, after the discovery of photography the medium became a frequent metaphor for memory: "After 1839 the human memory became a photographic plate, prepared for the recording and reproduction of visual experience" (2001: 78).

17. Here and throughout this essay, unless otherwise indicated, I am quoting from Charles S. Kraszewski's unpublished and undated translation of Kantor's performance text for *Let the Artists Die*, which I consulted in the Cricoteka archives in Cracow: Tadeusz Kantor, *Let the Artist Croak*, trans. Charles S. Kraszewski (Cracow: Cricoteka, n.d.), 231. Hereafter referenced as (Kantor n.d.b).

18. I will expand on this stage figure below.

19. Michel Beaujour also comments on the importance of the notion of flashing images before death or fainting in the construction of self-portraits (1991: 140–1); see also Draaisma (2001: 135).

20. You-Know-Who sings the popular soldier's song "Blossom for me, O My Rosemary" ("O, mój rozmarynie rozwijaj się"), from the First World War.

21. During the Polish-Soviet War (1919–20), Piłsudski led the Poles to victory in the Battle of Vistula (August 1920). As Cienciala writes, "It is worth noting that many of the Polish officers taken prisoner by the Red Army in September 1939 had fought against it in 1920" (2008: 10). She also notes that "After the Soviet invasion of Poland in September 1939, the Polish commander, General Władysław Langner, a Piłsudski Legionnaire in World War I and veteran of the Polish-Soviet War, decided to surrender [his troops] to the Soviets rather than the Germans. . . . In the surrender agreement, even though Timoshenko's representatives agreed that the Polish military should go free, they were arrested and imprisoned in Starobelsk, near Kharkov, Ukraine. Once there, the officers protested that their captivity violated the surrender terms" (2008: 20).

22. Several other filmmakers who are known for their cinematic experiments in imaging trauma are more oriented towards formal innovation in their approach. These include Alain Resnais, Isztván Szabó, and Aleksandr Sokurov.

23. The character of the General's wife was inspired by the description of General Smorawiński's wife found in the book *Return to Katyń* (*Powrót do Katyńia*, 1990) by Stanisław M. Jankowski and Edward Miszczak, who,

like Róza in the film, refused to make a public statement after the massacre had been revealed in Lublin (Wajda, 2008: 86).

24. In addition to the footage from Katyń, this film also featured a section showing mass graves of the victims of the Soviet terror, mostly from 1937 and 1938, uncovered by the Germans in the Ukrainian city of Vinnytsia in May 1943 (this imagery is not presented in Wajda's film). The images of the exhumations at Katyń, however, were never shown to the German general public during the war. Aiming to regulate affect and shield their audiences from the "excessive expressivity" (Barthes, 1981: 41) of this footage, they subjected it to explicit censorship, afraid that it might fuel public fears in Germany about their own soldiers fighting the Soviets or held captive by them and turn public opinion against the war. This decision was in line with the German general policy at the time that "no pictures should be shown which are apt to produce fear, horror or revulsion [of or at, the war]" (Raack, 1986: 190).

25. "Thus," writes Paperno, "the Criminal Investigation Report identified the officials blamed for the executions not only by name and rank, but, in most cases, also by using an additional qualification, '*Jude*'" (2001: 96).

26. Wajda, quoted in Brian Hanrahan's "Film Reopens Poland's Katyń Wound," BBC News, 5 October 2007, http://news.bbc.co.uk/1/hi/world/europe/7028365.stm [accessed 29 July 2009].

27. Wajda, quoted in Hanrahan (as above).

28. The post-Gorbachev history of Polish-Russian relations around Katyń bears this out. During his visit to Warsaw in August 1993, President Yeltsin placed flowers at the Katyń memorial and asked for forgiveness, in what was widely interpreted as a personal gesture (see, Cienciala et al., 2008: 260). Two years later, in his letter to President Wałęsa, he objected to unofficial Polish demands for a Russian apology and compensation for victims' families. In 2002, President Putin also rejected a notion of an apology. In March 2005, the Russian Prosecutor's Office announced that the Katyń investigation, which had been running since 1990, was closed. The Russian Procuracy investigations concluded that there was no evidence of genocide: the victims were condemned under the Soviet criminal code as it stood in 1940, which at the time did not include categories such as a crime of genocide, a war crime, and a crime against humanity (see, Cienciala et al., 2008: 262). Therefore, the crime fell under the statute of limitations, a juridical concept which "has been compared to the 'natural' forgetting of an offence through the passage of time, despite the fact that this concept does not apply to crimes against humanity" (Suleiman, 2006: 225). The Katyń families, as well as the majority of Polish opinion, however, view the Katyń massacre as genocide and demand an official Russian apology and compensation (see, Cienciala et al., 2008: 262). While the reasons for Stalin's decision to murder the prisoners remains unresolved to this day, most Polish and Russian historians now agree that Stalin ordered the execution of the prisoners "because they constituted an elite, the potential leaders of a future, independent Poland" (141–2). Some scholars add that social class was also a factor, arguing that the Katyń massacre can

be seen as the epitome of "class cleansing" (see, e.g. Davies, 1982: 452; Zaslavsky, 2008: 5).

29. Dekulakisation involved imprisonment, deportation, and even execution of supposedly rich peasants (*kulaks*) and their families as part of the state's attempt to destroy organised class resistance in the countryside, mainly in the early 1930s (see, for instance, Werth, 2008).

30. On the popular memory and memorialisation of Soviet crimes, see, e.g. Adler (2005); Etkind (2004; 2009), and Smith (1996). On the history of the Soviet gulag see, for instance, Applebaum (2003). For "dead-body politics" in Eastern Europe in the 1990s, see Verdery (1999).

31. The campaign for recovery of memory (the opening of the multiple archives, the onslaught of memoirs, oral history collections, as well as artworks grappling with the painful past) from the early 1990s gave way to a state-sponsored nostalgia for the Soviet past, while the victory in the Great Patriotic War (1941–45) that resulted in the triumph of the Stalinist state continues to provide a unifying bond for historical identity in Russia. This selective approach to national history, with an emphasis on national unity and national pride, is perceived to be better suited to Russia's national interest than the anti-communist message associated with the legacy of unconfronted memories of the Stalinist terror. It also leaves little space for critical questioning. While many survivors and victims' organisations still require a complete disclosure of what happened, most Russians are generally reluctant to bear witness to this past and more concerned about their own safety in light of current terrorist threats than past wrongs. See, Boym (2001) and Adler (2005).

32. The gender of the Katyń victims is also a little-discussed subject, and one that remains to be fully investigated; the one documented female victim of whom I am aware is Janina Dowbor-Muśnicka Lewandowska, a well-known Polish pilot. She was executed at Katyń on 21 April 1940. Her sister, Agnieszka Dowbor-Muśnicka, was executed by the Nazis at Palmiry near Warsaw two months later. There is a brief mention of Lewandowska's biography in Łukasz Kamiński, 'Warstwy kierownicze należy zlikwidować' (The Management Structures must be Liquidated), *Tygodnik Powszechny*, 39 (22 September 2009) http://tygodnik.onet.pl/35,0,33540,8222warstwy_kierownicze_nalezy_zlikwidowac8221,artykul.html [accessed 20 December 2009]. I thank Halina Filipowicz for this information.

33. This is not to deny that many of the Jewish-Polish POWs who perished in Katyń *felt* Polish; in other words, many of them belonged to the culturally and politically assimilated Jewish elite who treated their Jewish faith as a private matter and considered themselves Polish citizens. However, as Antony Polonsky points out, in the pre-Second World War period, "on the Polish lands the great majority of Jews defined themselves and were regarded by most of the population as a separate national group". See Polonsky, "Introduction," *Polin*, 13 (2000): 8.

34. As I mentioned earlier, much political, aesthetic, cultural, and scholarly work has been done in Poland in the last few decades to integrate Poland's

Jews into the nation's consciousness. This includes new developments in Polish-Jewish scholarship, a series of Polish public debates on wartime Polish-Jewish relations, as well as the efforts to recover Poland's Jewish heritage and culture through events such as the annual Jewish Cultural Week in Cracow. See, for instance, Zimmerman (2003) and Polonsky and Michlic (2004).

35. *I Shall Never Return* premiered on 23 April 1988 at Piccolo Teatro Studio in Milan. My analysis here is based on my viewings of a video recording of the performance played at Piccolo Teatro Studio the following night (24 April), as well as a version filmed by Polish Television for their Teatr Telewizji series (March/April 1990, director Andrzej Sapija), both housed at the Cricoteka. I also refer to the Polish and English versions of the programmes for the performance, and Charles Kraszewski's unpublished translation of the programme in Polish supplemented by his translation of the verbal parts of the text taken from two video recordings of the performance: from the theatre Albeniz in Madrid (February/March 1989) and the Polish Television version, as well as his description of the scenic action (from the Madrid stage production). Finally, in the Cricoteka, I consulted numerous video recordings of the rehearsals of this performance conducted in 1987 in Cracow and in 1988 in Milan.

36. The date of his father's death noted above comes from a recent monograph on Marian Kantor-Mirski, written by Zdzisław Kantor. The author bases this information on the entry in Archiwum Państwowego Muzeum Oświęcim-Brzezinka, Księga Stanów Dziennych w K.L. Auschwitz B-AU-I-3/1/2, nr inw. 31534, T. 2, s. 209 (26–7). Urszula Rzewiczok provides the same date in *Drodzy Nieobecni Tadeusza Kantora* (2002: 9).

37. In a piece of poetic prose entitled "Father" Kantor writes: "His imprint / My eyes could not look high enough, / so there are only his / b o o t s , /which are knee high. / My sensitive ear would catch / incomprehensible / curses of the father and / his strange walking pattern:/ one two, one two. . . . / Nobody else walked like this. / Then I learned words to describe it:/ To march, marching." (Kantor, 1993: 183). Vido-Rzewuska refers to this fragment as the only memory Kantor as a child had of his father (233). Based on an interview with Kantor, Guy Scarpetta records a much later encounter between Kantor and his father: "Suddenly, one day in the 1930s in Cracow, a certain very elegant man, with a platinum plate visible in his skull (a war wound? a trepanation?) addresses him: 'You are my son' . . . He offers young Tadeusz Kantor a coffee and, in front of his fascinated son, begins to play all instruments in the band, surrounded by young women" (Scarpetta, 2003: 192).

38. On Kantor and the Polish "theatre of death" see, for instance, Pleśniarowicz (1993) and Morawiec (1979).

39. In his "Odysseus Must Really Return," Pleśniarowicz makes an attempt at reconstructing this production, and finds that it evolved through three conceptions. According to him, "Perhaps, due to these numerous versions and transfers (for safety reasons), it is impossible to establish the

exact dates." He further observes that "Kantor himself referred to the date of June 21 (Rostworowski: 1968; Chrobak: 1994), but it is not possible today to state whether the date was precise and which version of *The Return of Odysseus* is concerned" (Pleśniarówicz, 1994b: 57–9).

40. This text, entitled "Powrót Odysa. Partytura sztuki Stanislawa Wyspiańskiego 'Powrót Odysa'" can be found in an edited collection of Kantor's writings (2000).

41. I am aware that in light of Wyspiański's and his critics' interpretation of the figure of Odysseus as "a destitute man morally equal to the degenerate suitors" (Sugiera, 1999: 86), "a compulsive killer" (Terlecki, 1983: 123), "a criminal" (Clarke, 1966: xiv), and "a war criminal" (Kantor, n.d.d, 1), the analogy that I establish between Kantor's father and Odysseus might appear troublesome. Furthermore, as already noted, Odysseus in Kantor's performance from 1944 was presented as a German soldier returning from Stalingrad. My intention is not to conflate the positions of victim and perpetrator, or to blur the distinction between inflicting and receiving a wound. However, I believe that Kantor's choice of conflating the date of his father's death with the date of the return of Odysseus to Cracow in this performance allows for this kind of interpretation.

42. In this regard Kantor's performance could be compared to Primo Levi's text *If This Is a Man* (*Se questo è un uomo*), in which Levi makes use of Dante's Ulysses canto, that is, Dante's revision of Homer, in an act of bearing witness to Auschwitz.

43. In 1905, Wyspiański wrote an essay on *Hamlet*, which might have influenced his shaping of this and subsequent scenes in Act I. The ghost returning from the world of the dead is also a common figure of the Polish Romantic drama, to which both Wyspiański and Kantor are indebted.

44. Carlson employs such terms as "recycling" and "ghosting" to describe this kind of intertextual approach to theatre, and mentions Kantor as one of its major exponents (2001: 104–5; 107).

45. In this essay I am referring primarily to a compilation of their essays in *The Shell and the Kernel* (1994). They write on related issues in their *The Wolf Man's Magic Word: A Cryptonimy* (1986).

46. In the *partytura* for *I Shall Never Return* Kantor uses the Latin version of the name: Ulysses (in Polish, Ulisses). But, when he talks about the 1944 production of Wyspiański, he uses the Greek version of the name. I have amended the translation by Kraszewski in this respect and used name Odysseus throughout. Kobialka proceeds in the same way in his chapter on *I Shall Never Return*, which, I believe, helps to avoid confusion.

47. In the performance, Kantor read the lines from the copy of the play he used when staging it in 1944. Wyspiański's text shows Odysseus at an empty shore reliving his chaotic memories that bear an indelible mark of trauma: the burning of Troy, the nymph Calypso, a Harpy, repetitive callings of singing Sirens, and a boat of the dead.

48. I quote here from Kraszewski's translation of Kantor's *partytura*, not from Clarke's translation of Wyspianski's play.

49. Kantor saw the famous Evgeny Vakhtangov production of *The Dybbuk* performed by the legendary Yiddish Habima troupe at the Bagatela Theatre in Cracow in 1938, which made a deep impression on him (Pleśniarowicz, 2004: 19).

50. Freddie Rokem, in his book *Performing History*, refers to Anski's *The Dybbuk* as a "central intertext of the Israeli [theatre] productions" and explains why the play continues to have a strong grip on Israeli audiences: "After the war, however, with six million Jewish souls who had not been properly buried, and who had thus not reached complete rest, the Israeli cultural discourses gradually developed an unconscious obsession with becoming possessed by these Dybbuks" (2000: 55). In Kantor's performance, as well as in a more recent production of *The Dybbuk* by Krzysztof Warlikowski and a 1996 short story by Hannah Krall about the Holocaust dybbuk, the legend of a spirit who possesses a living person could be also seen as a figure for Poland's relationship to its missing Jews. These works suggest that the past lives in the present and that to exorcise it may be misguided – may, in fact, not be possible.

51. In his Cracow rehearsals Kantor used the song "Lily Marlen" for this sequence. However, as he revealed in an interview with Denis Bablet, while rehearsing the performance in Milan he "met a Jewish singer . . . who sang [him] a song once sung by the Jews entering gas chambers, the religious song 'We Trust the Messiah Will Come' " (Bablet, 1989: 158); ultimately he decided to include it in the performance.

4   Postmemory, Testimony, Affect

1. All subsequent quotes from the play are from this edition of the play.

2. Hirsch and Andrea Liss seem to have developed this concept simultaneously, and independently of each other. For Liss's first and later use of the term, see Liss (1988) and Liss (1991). For Hirsch, see Hirsch (1997; 1999; 2001). Liss does not define postmemories as familial at all, but uses the term to define all postwar Holocaust memory projects, regardless of whether the creator is the child of survivors (Liss, 1988: 86). I draw here primarily on Hirsch's definition of the term.

3. On recent gendered approaches to the Holocaust see Ofer and Weitzman (1998), Baer and Goldenberg (2003). See also Gurewitsch (1998), an edited collection of oral histories of women who survived the Holocaust, with a separate section on "mothers."

4. For a reading of Plath's metaphorical usage of the Holocaust as an "imaginative misappropriation of atrocity," see Rosenfeld (1980: 175–82). For an excellent defence of Sylvia Plath's use of the Holocaust as archetypal imagery, see Young (1988: 117–32).

5. The most thorough version of the Wilkomirski/Dössekker story to date is Mächler's (2001). Elena Lappin (1999) and Philip Gourevitch (1999) also offer compelling versions of the case. Ross Chambers offers an affirmative reading of Wilkomirski's *Fragments* by employing the metaphor of "phantom pain" and the fantasy of incorporation (2002).

6. Rosalyn Ing's doctoral thesis *Dealing With Shame and Unresolved Trauma: Residential School and Its Impact on the 2nd and 3rd Generation Adults* (2001) provides a painful account of the Canadian residential schools.

7. Frost's argument in *Sex Drives* also extends the arguments about the link between sadomasochism and fascism put forward by Michel Foucault (1996) and Susan Sontag (1974). Sontag, for instance, writes that never before was "the relation of master and slaves so consciously aestheticised" as in the "master scenario" that Nazism offers, in which the "colour is black, the material is leather, the seduction is beauty, the justification is honesty, the aim is ecstasy, the fantasy is death" (1974: 105).

8. I am grateful to Janelle Reinelt and Brian Singleton for their comments on the final section of my analysis of *Ashes to Ashes*; several of their observations have inflected this paragraph.

9. Wieviorka's argument that the main role of the Holocaust testimony today is to transmit affectively in order to elicit emotions and empathy from its listeners needs to be further qualified. As the new scholarship on the Holocaust in Eastern Europe shows, oral testimonies still offer crucial evidence in reconstructing the Second World War crimes. Jan Gross's study on the atrocity at Jedwabne would have not been possible without the testimony of witnesses and participants.

10. In 2010, he published a collection of interviews with various Polish artists entitled *Trembling Bodies: Conversations with Artists* (in English and German; first published in Polish in 2006). The anthology features artists related to the "critical art" movement in Poland: Paweł Althamer, Katarzyna Górna, Andrzej Karaś, Grzegorz Kowalski, Katarzyna Kozyra, Zbigniew Libera, Jacek Markiewicz, Joanna Rajkowska and Monika Zielińska, whose works share strong preoccupations with the issue of corporality and its entanglement in power structures.

11. Żmijewski shares this preoccupation with other representatives of the young generation of Polish artists working in different media, whose works explore traces, remnants, and memories of the Holocaust. These include, to name just a few: Zbigniew Libera, well-known internationally for often provocative and scandalous pieces such as *Lego, Concentration Camp* (*Lego, Obóz koncentracyjny*, 1994) and his *Positives* series (*Pozytywy*, 2002–03); Miroslav Balka with captivating videos (for example, *Winterreise*, 2003) and installations such as *Soap Corridor* (1993) and *How It Is* (2010), which offer powerful invocations of history, human suffering, and the plight of the body; and Joanna Rajkowska, whose provocative yet poignant installations such as *Oxygenator* (*Dotleniacz*, 2006) and *Patriotic Literature* (*Literatura patriotyczna*, 2006) and the video entitled *Maja Gordon Goes to Chorzow* (*Maja Gordon jedzie do Chorzowa*, 2007) address the complex issue of Polish-Jewish relations. The Holocaust also emerged as a key theme in the younger generation of Polish theatre makers. For instance, Krzysztof Warlikowski's important production of the *Dybbuk* (*Dybuk*, 2003), based on Solomon Anski's drama titled *The Dybbuk* and a short story by Hanna Krall of the same title, examines

repressed elements of Polish history – the past that returns yet resists assimilation or integration. In a similar vein, Tadeusz Słobodzianek's play *Our Class* (*Nasza klasa*, 2010), which pays homage to Tadeusz Kantor, addresses the Jedwabne pogrom. The play had its world premiere at the National theatre in London in 2009, won the 2010 Nike Literary award – Poland's most prestigious literary prize, and was ranked by European Theatre Convention among the best contemporary European plays written during 2009 and 2010. For interesting overviews on diverse strategies of Holocaust representation in visual arts in Poland, see Bojarska (2008). On the key tendencies in Polish drama since 1990, see an excellent review by Trojanowska (2005). For a cogent reading of the reception of Słobodzianek's play *Our Class* in the UK and Poland, see Murjas (2011).

12. In 2011 the work was withdrawn from Berlin's prestigious Martin-Gropius Bau exhibition hall after members of the Jewish community complained about the work.

13. I thank Olga Ponichtera for her help with translating this passage and other parts of Żmijewski's interview with Agatą Araszkiewicz, which I quote later in this chapter. Hereafter, this interview article is marked as: Żmijewski, 2005b.

14. For excellent edited collections on the affective turn in critical theory see Clough (2007), and Liljeström and Paasonen (2010).

15. The extension of the "grey zone" to civilian life at work in Żmijewski's and Mytkowska's reflections on *80064* is analogous to some recent theorisations of the Holocaust (Agamben, 1999) and trauma (Felman and Laub, 1992; Caruth, 1995), criticised for conflating of distinct subject positions and histories. As Debarati Sanyal (2002) and Ruth Leys (2007) show, in his analysis of life under extremity as epitomised by Auschwitz, Agamben offers less nuanced and more totalising elaboration of the grey zone than that put forward by Levi. Telling here, for instance, are different ways in which Levi and Agamben employ the German word *Befehlnotstand*, which, as Leys explains, Levi used to denote "the state of compulsion following an order" when trying to capture the experiences of the *Sonderkommandos* in the camps. Agamben used this concept indiscriminately to both the SS and the *Sonderkommando*, whereas "Levi distinguishes between the compulsion to obey orders experienced by the *Sonderkommando* and the 'impudent' appeal by the Nazis to the same concept as a way of excusing their conformist behaviour, since the Nazis could always find a way out, but the *Sonderkommando* could not" (Leys, 2007: 171).

16. For instance, Amos Goldberg shows that the emerging Israeli historiography made strong efforts to dismantle allegations that Jews did not resist their murderers and "to prove the opposite: that the Jews had undertaken, as far as circumstances had allowed, civil, cultural, communal, and religious resistance in almost all spheres of life, and had, wherever possible, also resorted to armed resistance" (2009: 225). Berel Lang (2005)

has also recently confronted questions over alleged Jewish passivity during the war, proving them to be logical fallacies.

17. De Vos defines psychologisation as "the overflow of the knowledge of psychology into society altering the way in which 'man' is present with himself, others and the world" (2010: 158).

18. For instance, as mentioned earlier, *The Game of Tag* by Żmijewski shows the situation in which men and women of various ages play the game of tag in a former gas chamber. The artist articulates his concept for this video as follows: "This resembles a clinical situation in psychotherapy. You return to the traumas that brought about your complex. You recreate them, almost like in the theatre" (2005c: 152). While bringing sexuality and murder into direct association here, Żmijewski does not try to account for voyeuristic aspects of his work or the violence perpetrated by this installation on the memory of the Holocaust. And while some may see the loss of moral affect (and compass) at work in this installation, the author recognises in it certain therapeutic qualities. However, to my best knowledge, he has never revealed anything about the subjects he hired to implement this scenario, their familial or cultural relations to the Holocaust, or their motivations to take part in it. While the endeavour does not engender a greater historical understanding of the Holocaust, the psychological postulates and practice put in place by Żmijewski here would be perhaps best seen as a version of "wild" psychoanalysis (Freud, 2002 [1910]), that is, "psychoanalysis undertaken without due rigor and outside the consulting room" (Radstone, 2007b: 190). See also Gene Ray's article (2003) on the exhibition entitled "Mirroring Evil: Nazi Imagery/Recent Art" held at the Jewish Museum in New York in 2002 that presented works that were strongly criticised by many for their iconoclastic tackling of representational taboos associated with the Holocaust.

19. In the chapter 4 of her *Disciplining the Holocaust* (2008), Ball offers a cogent critique of what she sees as LaCapra's over-emphasis on the processes of working through, which in her view underplays the power of our often-unconscious investments in traumatic pasts.

5   Conclusion: European Memories and the Margins of Europe: *Sarajevo Theatre Tragedy* and Three Prayers for One Wish

1. I quote here from an unpublished English translation of *Sarajevo Theatre Tragedy*, which I have accessed through the MESS office in Sarajevo. I have modified the translation significantly, drawing on Ilinca Zarifopol-Johnston's translation of the same passages found in her book *Searching for Cioran* (2009: 96–7).

2. A number of critical theory studies that explore the role of religion in the public sphere and ways of reconceiving the significance of religion and the

secular in the context of contemporary national and international politics have appeared in recent years. Theatre and performance scholars are only beginning to engage with these important questions. In November 2011, Jisha Menon from Stanford University and I co-organised a panel at the American Association for Theatre Research (ASTR) conference in Seattle, titled "Rethinking the Secular: Performance, Religion, and the Public Sphere," which explored the itineraries of "the secular" within the modern world through the lens of performance. We are currently working on an edited collection that will explore these themes further.

3. East Sarajevo is also the capital of Republika Srpska, although its government is seated in the city of Banja Luka.

Bibliography

Abraham, Nicolas, and Maria Torok. 1986. *The Wolf Man's Magic Word: A Cryptonymy.* Trans. Nicolas T. Rand. Minneapolis: University of Minnesota Press.

———. *The Shell and the Kernel.* 1994. Ed. and trans. Nicolas T. Rand. Chicago and London: University of Chicago Press.

Adler, Nanci. 2005. "The Future of the Soviet Past Remains Unpredictable: The Resurrection of Stalinist Symbols amidst the Exhumation of Mass Graves." *Europe-Asia Studies* 57.8 (December): 1093–119.

Agamben, Giorgio. 1998. *Homo Sacer: Sovereign Power and Bare Life.* Trans. Daniel Heller-Roazen. Stanford: Stanford University Press.

———. 1999. *Remnants of Auschwitz: The Witness and the Archive.* Trans. Daniel Heller-Roazen. New York: Zone Books.

———. *State of Exception.* 2005. Trans. Kevin Attell. Chicago: Chicago University Press.

Agnew, Vanessa. 2004. "Introduction: What is Reenactment?" *Criticism* 46.3: 327–39.

———. 2007. "Historical Reenactment and Its Work in the Present." *Rethinking History* 11.3: 299–312.

Ahmed, Sarah. 2004. *The Cultural Politics of Emotion.* Edinburgh: Edinburgh University Press.

Albrecht, Monika. 2011. "(Post-) Colonial Amnesia? German Debates on Colonialism and Decolonization in the Post-War Era." *German Colonialism and National Identity.* Eds. Michael Perraudin and Jürgen Zimmerer. New York: Routledge. 187–96.

Aleksiun, Natalia. 2003. "Jewish Responses to Antisemitism in Poland, 1944–1947." *Contested Memories: Poles and Jews during the Holocaust and Its Aftermath.* Ed. Joshua D. Zimmerman. New Brunswick: NJ; and London: Rutgers University Press. 247–61.

———. 2004. "Polish Historiography of the Holocaust: Between Silence and Public Debate." *German History* 22.3: 406–32.

Ankersmit, Frank R. 2006. "'Presence' and Myth." *History and Theory* 45.3: 328–36.

Applebaum, Anne. 2003. *Gulag: A History of the Soviet Camps.* London: Allen Lane.

———. 2008. "A Movie that Matters." *The New York Review of Books* 55.2 (14 February): 1–6.

Aragay, Mireia. 1997. "Writing, Politics, and *Ashes to Ashes*: An Interview with Harold Pinter." *The Pinter Review: Annual Essays 1995 and 1996.* Eds. Francis Gillen and Steven H. Gale. Tampa: University of Tampa Press. 4–15.

Aragay, Mireia. 2001. "Pinter, Politics and Postmodernism (2)." *The Cambridge Companion to Harold Pinter*. Ed. Peter Raby. Cambridge: Cambridge University Press. 247–59.

Arendt, Hannah. 1951. *The Burden of Our Time*. London: Secker & Warburg.

——. 1951a. *The Origins of Totalitarianism*. New York: Harcourt, Brace and Company.

——. 1990 [1963]. *On Revolution*. Harmondsworth: Penguin.

Arns, Inke. 2007. "History Will Repeat Itself." *History Will Repeat Itself: Strategies of Re-Enactment in Contemporary (Media) Art and Performance*. Frankfurt: Revolver. 36–63.

Augustine, Saint, Bishop of Hippo. 2002. *Saint Augustine's Memory*. Trans. and ed. Garry Wills. New York: Viking.

Babb, Lawrence. 1951. *The Elizabethan Malady: A Study of Melancholia in English Literature from 1580–1642*. East Lansing: Michigan State College Press.

Bablet, Denis. 1989. "The Second Return of Ulysses." *Cricot 2 Theatre – Information Guide 1987–1988*. Ed. Anna Halczak. Cracow: Cricoteka. 151–60.

Bachelard, Gaston. 1994. *The Poetics of Space*. Boston: Beacon Press.

Baer, Elizabeth R., and Myrna Goldenberg, eds. 2003. *Experience and Expression: Women, the Nazis, and the Holocaust*. Detroit: Wayne State University Press.

Balbus, Isaac D. 2005. *Mourning and Modernity: Essays in the Psychoanalysis of Contemporary Society*. New York: Other Press.

Ball, Karyn. 2008. *Disciplining the Holocaust*. Albany: State University of New York Press.

Balibar, Étienne. 2010a. "Europe: Final Crisis? Some Theses." *Theory and Event* 13.2: n.p.

——. 2010b. "The Greek Crisis." *Journal of Modern Greek Studies* 28.2: 306–9.

——. 2012. "Lenin and Ghandi: A Missed Encounter?" *Radical Philosophy* 172 (March/April): 9–17.

Balme, Christopher. 2004. "Editorial." *Theatre Research International* 29.1: 1–3.

Bammer, Angelika. 2001. "Hamburg Memories." *The German Quarterly* 74.4: 355–67.

Baraban, Elena. 2007. "*The Fate of a Man* by Sergei Bondarchuk and the Soviet Cinema of Trauma." *Slavic and East European Journal* 51.3: 514–35.

Barkan, Elazar. 2000. *The Guilt of Nations: Restitution and Negotiating Historical Injustices*. New York: W. W. Norton.

Barnett, David. 1998. *Literature versus Theatre: Textual Problems and Theatrical Realization in the Later Plays of Heiner Müller*. Bern; New York: Peter Lang.

Bartana, Yael. 2007. *Mary Koszmary (Nightmares)*. HD video, 10'27". 26 July 2012. http://www.artmuseum.pl/filmoteka/?l=1&id=200

Barthes, Roland. 1981. *Camera Lucida: Reflections on Photography*. Trans. Richard Howard. New York: Hill and Wang.

Bartoszewski, Władysław. 1969. *Righteous Among Nations: How Poles Helped the Jews, 1939–1945*. London: Earlscourt Publications.

——. 1987. *Polish-Jewish Relations: A Current Debate among Polish Catholics*. Institute of Jewish Affairs Research Report no.7, October.

———. 1992. "Foreword." *The Road To Katyn A Soldier's Story.* By Salomon W. Slowes. Trans. Naftali Greenwood. Oxford: Blackwell Publishers. vii–xxxii.

Bartov, Omer. 2008. "Contemporary Issues in Historical Perspective: Eastern Europe as the Site of Genocide." *Journal of Modern History* 80.3: 557–93.

Baudrillard, Jean. 1994. *The Illusion of the End.* Trans. Chris Turner. Stanford, Calif.: Stanford University Press.

Bauman, Zygmunt. 1988. "On Immoral Reason and Illogical Morality." *POLIN* III: 294–30.

———. 1989. *Modernity and the Holocaust.* Ithaca, NY: Cornell University Press.

———. 1992. *Mortality, Immortality.* London: Polity Press.

Beaujour, Michel. 1991. *The Poetics of the Literary Self-Portrait.* Trans. Yara Milos. New York and London: New York University Press.

Beck, Ulrich. 2003. "Understanding the Real Europe." *Dissent* 50.3: 32–8.

Becker, Daniel. 2006. "Coming to Terms with *Vergangenheitsbewältigung*: Walser's Sonntagsrede, the Kosovo War, and the Transformation of German Historical Consciousness." *Victims and Perpetrators, 1933–1945: (Re)presenting the Past in Post-Unification Culture.* Eds. Laurel Cohen-Pfister, Dagmar Wienroeder-Skinner. Berlin: Walter de Gruyter, 337–61.

Beckles, Hilary McD. 1997. "Capitalism, Slavery and Caribbean Modernity." *Callaloo* 20.4: 777–89.

Beevor, Anthony. 2002. *The Fall of Berlin 1945.* New York and London: Penguin Books.

Beilharz, Peter. 2003. "Budapest Central: Agnes Heller's Theory of Modernity." *Thesis Eleven* 75 (November): 108–13.

Benhabib, Sheila. 2008. "The Legitimacy of Human Rights." *Daedalus* 137.3: 94–104.

Benjamin, Walter. 1968. "Thesis on the Philosophy of History." *Illuminations: Essays and Reflections.* Ed. Hannah Arendt. Trans. Harry Zohn. New York: Schocken Books. 253–64.

———. 1977. *The Origin of German Tragic Drama.* Trans. John Osborne, London: Verso.

———. 1979 [1939]. *One-Way Street, and Other Writings.* Trans. Edmund Jephcott and Kingsley Shorter. London: NLB.

———. 1994. "Left-Wing Melancholy." *The Weimar Republic Sourcebook.* Eds. Andreas Keas, Martin Jay, and Edward Dimendberg. Berkeley: University of California Press. 304–6.

Bennett, Jill. 2005. *Empathic Vision: Affect, Trauma, and Contemporary Art.* Stanford, Calif.: Stanford University Press.

Bennett, Jill, and Rosanne Kennedy, eds. 2003. *World Memory: Personal Trajectories in Global Time.* New York: Palgrave Macmillan.

Berg, Eiki, and Piret Ehin. 2009. *Identity and Foreign Policy: Baltic-Russian Relations and European Integration.* Farnham, UK; Burlington, Vt.: Ashgate.

Berlant, Lauren. 2007. "The Subject of True Feeling: Pain, Privacy, and Politics." *Traumatizing Theory: The Cultural Politics of Affect in and beyond Psychoanalysis.* Ed. Karyn Ball. New York: Other Press. 305–47.

Berman, Emanuel. 2007. "Call of the Wild." *The American Journal of Psychoanalysis* 67: 211–20.

Biddick, Kathleen. 2007. *The Shock of Medievalism.* Durham: Duke University Press.

Billington, Michael. 1996. *The Life and Work of Harold Pinter.* London: Faber and Faber.

Bilu, Yoram. 1987. "Dybbuk Possession and Mechanisms of Internalization and Externalization." *Projection, Identification, and Projective Identification.* Ed. Joseph Sandler. Madison, Conn.: International Universities Press, 163–78.

Bishop, Claire. 2009. "Outsourcing Authenticity? Delegated Performance in Contemporary Art." *Double Agent.* Eds. Claire Bishop and Mark Sladen. London: Institute of Contemporary Arts, 112–27.

———. 2010. "Delegated Performance: Outsourcing Authenticity." *Twenty-First Century: Art in the First Decade.* Ed. Miranda Wallace. Brisbane: Queensland Art Gallery. 264–73.

Blaive, Muriel, Christian Gerbel, and Thomas Lindenberger, eds. 2011. *Clashes in European Memory: The Case of Communist Repression and the Holocaust.* Innsbruck; Vienna; Bozen: Studienverlag

Blonski, Jan. 1990. "The Poor Poles Look at the Ghetto." *'My brother's keeper?': Recent Polish Debates on the Holocaust.* London; New York: Routledge in association with the Institute for Polish-Jewish Studies, 34–52.

Boatcă, Manuela. 2007. "The Eastern Margins of Empire: Coloniality in 19th Century Romania." *Cultural Studies* 21.2: 368–84.

Bochow, Jörg. 2005. "Müller's Hamlet/Hamletmachine 1989/1990: The Collapse of Utopia." Unpublished essay. 1–8.

Bojarska, Katarzyna. 2008. "The Presence of the Holocaust in the Work of Polish Artists." 10 June 2012. http://www.culture.pl/web/english/resources-visual-arts-full-page/-/eo_event_asset_publisher/eAN5/content/the-holocaust-in-the-works-of-polish-artists

Bolzoni, Lina. 2001. *The Gallery of Memory: Literary and Iconographic Models in the Age of the Printing Press.* Toronto, Buffalo, and London: University of Toronto Press.

Boym, Svetlana. 2001. *The Future of Nostalgia.* New York: Basic Books.

Brammer, Angelika. 2001."Hamburg Memories." *German Quarterly* 74.4: 355–67.

Brdar, Milan. 2003. "Humanitarian Intervention and the (De)Nazification Thesis as Functional Simulacrum." *Lessons of Kosovo: The Dangers of Humanitarian Intervention.* Ed. Aleksandar Jokic. Peterborough, Ont.: Broadview Press. 153–72.

Brown, Vincent Aaron. 2003. *Slavery and the Spirits of the Dead: Mortuary Politics in Jamaica, 1740–1834.* Diss. Duke University. Ann Arbor: UMI.

Brown, Wendy. 1995. *States of Injury: Power and Freedom in Late Modernity.* Princeton: Princeton University Press.

———. 1999. "Resisting Left Melancholy." *Boundary 2* 26.3: 19–27.

———. 2005. *Edgework: Critical Essays on Knowledge and Politics.* Princeton: Princeton University Press.

Buck-Morss, Susan. 1989. *The Dialectics of Seeing: Walter Benjamin and the Arcades Project.* Cambridge: MIT.

——. 2000. *Dreamworld and Catastrophe: The Passing of the Mass Utopia in East and West*. Cambridge: MIT.

——. 2009. *Hegel, Haiti, and Universal History*. Pittsburgh, Pa.: University of Pittsburgh Press.

Buckley, Matthew S. 2006. *Tragedy Walks the Streets: The French Revolution in the Making of Modern Drama*. Baltimore: Johns Hopkins University Press.

Buffery, Helena. 2007. "The 'Placing of Memory' in Contemporary Catalan Theatre." *Contemporary Theatre Review* 17.3: 385–97.

Burkman, Katherine. 1999. "Harold Pinter's *Ashes to Ashes*: Rebecca and Devlin as Albert Speer." *The Pinter Review: Collected Essays 1997 and 1998*. Eds. Francis Gillen and Steven H. Gale. Tampa: University of Tampa Press. 86–96.

——. 2001. "Displacement in Time and Space: Harold Pinter's *Other Places*." *Pinter at 70: A Casebook*. Ed. Lois Gordon. London and New York: Routledge. 109–18.

Butler, Judith. 1990. *Gender Trouble: Feminism and the Subversion of Identity*. London: Routledge.

——. 1997a. *The Psychic Life of Power: Theories of Subjection*. Stanford: Stanford University Press.

——. 1997b. *Excitable Speech: Politics of the Performative*. New York: Routledge.

——. 2004. *Precarious Life: The Powers of Mourning and Violence*. London; New York: Verso.

——. 2005. *Giving an Account of Oneself*. New York: Fordham University Press.

——. 2007. "Torture and the Ethics of Photography." *Environment and Planning D: Society and Space* 25.6: 951–66.

——. 2009. *Frames of War: When is Life Grievable?* London; New York: Verso.

——. 2011a. "Is Judaism Zionism?" *The Power of Religion in the Public Sphere*. Eds. Eduardo Mendieta and Jonathan Vanantwerpen. New York: Columbia University Press. 70–91.

——. (May) 2011b. "Precarious Life and the Obligations of Cohabitation." Nobel Museum, Stockholm: 18 July 2012. http://www.nobelmuseum.se/sites/nobelmuseet.se/files/page_file/Judith_Butler_NWW2011.pdf: 1–25.

——. 2012. *Parting Ways: Jewishness and the Critique of Zionism*. New York: Columbia University Press.

Cadava, Eduardo. 1997. *Words of Light: Thesis on the Photography of History*. Princeton: Princeton University Press.

Calhoun, Craig. 2009. "Cosmopolitan Europe and European Studies." *The Sage Handbook of European Studies*. Ed. Chris Rumford. Los Angeles; London: SAGE. 637–54.

——. 2011. "Afterword: Religion's Many Powers." *The Power of Religion in the Public Sphere*. Eds. Eduardo Mendieta and Jonathan Vanantwerpen. New York: Columbia University Press. 118–34.

Calle, Sophie. 1996. *Die Entfernung*. Berlin: G+B Arts International.

Caple James, Erica. 2010. *Democratic Insecurities: Violence, Trauma, and Intervention in Haiti*. Berkeley: University of California Press.

Carlson, Marvin. 1966. *The Theatre of French Revolution*. Ithaca, NY: Cornell University Press.

———. 2001. *The Haunted Stage: The Theatre as Memory Machine*. Ann Arbor: University of Michigan Press.

Carruthers, Mary. 1990. *The Book of Memory: A Study of Memory in Medieval Culture*. Cambridge: Cambridge University Press.

———. 1998. *The Craft of Thought: Meditation, Rhetoric, and the Making of Images, 400–1200*. Cambridge: Cambridge University Press.

Caruth, Cathy. 1995. "Introduction." *Trauma: Explorations in Memory*. Ed. Cathy Caruth. Baltimore: Johns Hopkins University Press. 3–12; 151–7.

———. 1996. *Unclaimed Experience: Trauma, Narrative and History*. Baltimore: Johns Hopkins University Press.

Césaire, Aimé. 1960. *Toussanint Louverture: la Révolution française et le problème colonial*. Paris: Présence africaine.

Chajes, Jeffrey Howard. 2003. *Between Worlds: Dybbuks, Exorcists, and Early Modern Judaism*. Philadelphia: University of Pennsylvania Press.

Chambers, Ross. 2002. "Orphaned Memories, Foster-Writing, Phantom Pain: *The Fragments* Affair." *Extremities: Trauma, Testimony, and Community*. Eds. Nancy K. Miller and Jason Daniel Tougaw. Urbana: University of Illinois Press. 92–111.

———. 2004. *Untimely Interventions: Aids Writing, Testimonial, and the Rhetoric of Haunting*. Ann Arbor: University of Michigan Press.

Chare, Nicholas. 2011. *Auschwitz and Afterimages: Abjection, Witnessing and Representation*. London: I. B. Tauris.

Cheah, Pheng. 2008. "Crises of Money." *Positions* 16.1: 189–219.

Cheng, Anne Anlin. 2001. *The Melancholy of Race*. New York: Oxford University Press.

Cicero. 1976. *De oratore* and *De partitione oratoria*. Ed. and trans. H. Rackham. 2 vols. [Loeb Classical Library. 1942]; Cambridge: Harvard University Press.

Cienciala, Anna M., Natalia S. Lebedeva, and Wojciech Materski, eds. 2008. *Katyn: A Crime Without Punishment*. Trans. Anna M. Cienciala and Maia A. Kipp. New Haven and London: Yale University Press.

Clapp, Elizabeth J., and Julie Roy Jeffrey, eds. 2011. *Women, Dissent and Anti-Slavery in Britain and America, 1790–1865*. Oxford: Oxford University Press.

Clarke, Howard. 1966. "Introduction." *The Return of Odysseus*. By Stanisław Wyspiański. Bloomington: Indiana University Press.

Clough, Patricia Ticineto, ed., with Jean Halley. 2007. *The Affective Turn: Theorizing the Social*. Durham, NC: Duke University Press.

Cohen-Pfister, Laurel, and Dagmar Wienroeder-Skinner, eds. 2006. *Victims and Perpetrators, 1933–1945: (Re)presenting the Past in Post-Unification Culture*. Berlin: Walter de Gruyter.

Cole, Catherine, M. 2010. *Performing South Africa's Truth Commission: Stages of Transition*. Bloomington: Indiana University Press.

Coleman, Janet. 1992. *Ancient and Medieval Memories: Studies in the Reconstruction of the Past*. Cambridge: Cambridge University Press.

Comay, Rebecca. 2004. "Dead Right: Hegel and the Terror." *The South Atlantic Quarterly* 103.2–3: 375–95.

——. 2011. *Mourning Sickness: Hegel and the French Revolution.* Stanford, Calif.: Stanford University Press.

Connolly, William E. 2002. *Neuropolitics: Thinking, Culture, Speed.* Minneapolis, Minn.: University of Indiana Press.

Conrad, Sebastian. 2012. *German Colonialism: A Short History.* Trans. Sorcha O'Hagan. Cambridge: Cambridge University Press.

Cook, Alexander. 2004. "The Use and Abuse of Historical Reenactment: Thoughts on Recent Trends in Public History." *Criticism* 46.3: 487–96.

Craps, Stef. 2010. "Wor(l)ds of Grief: Traumatic Memory and Literary Witnessing in CrossCultural Perspective." *Textual Practice* 24.1: 51–68.

——. 2013. *Postcolonial Witnessing: Trauma out of Bounds.* Basingstoke; New York: Palgrave Macmillan.

Davies, Norman. 1982. *God's Playground: A History of Poland.* New York: Columbia University Press.

Dean, Carolyn J. 2010. *Aversion and Erasure.* Ithaca: NY: Cornell University Press.

De Lauretis, Teresa. 1998. "The Stubborn Drive." *Critical Inquiry* 24: 851–77.

Delbo, Charlotte. 1990. *Days and Memory.* Trans. Rosette Lamont. Marlboro, Vt.: Marlboro Press.

Demandt, Alexander. 1992. "Einleitung." *Romische Kaisergeschichte: Nach den Vorlesungs-Mitschriften von Sebastian und Paul Hansel 1882/86.* Eds. Barbara and Alexander Demandt. Munich: C. H. Beck. 1–35.

——. 1996. "Introduction." *A History of Rome Under the Emperors.* Trans. Clare Krojzl. London and New York: Routledge. 15–50.

Derrida, Jacques. 1986. "Foreword: Fors: The Anglish Words of Nicolas Abraham and MariaTorok." *The Wolf Man's Magic Word: A Cryptonymy. Theory and History of Literature.* Vol. 37. Trans. Barbara Johnson. Minneapolis: University of Minnesota Press. xi–xlviii.

——. 1995. *The Gift of Death.* Chicago: University of Chicago Press.

——. 1996. "By Force of Mourning." Trans. Pascale-Anne Brault and Michael Naas. *Critical Inquiry* 22.2: 171–92.

Desan, Suzanne. 1992. "'Constitutional Amazons': Jacobin Women's Clubs in the French Revolution." *Recreating Authority in Revolutionary France.* Eds. Bryant T. Ragan, Jr., and Elizabeth A. Williams. New Brunswick, NJ: Rutgers University Press.

De Vos, Jan. 2010. "From Milgram to Zimbardo: The Double Birth of Postwar Psychology/Psychologization." *History of the Human Sciences* 23.5: 156–75.

——. 2011. "Depsychologizing Torture." *Critical Inquiry* 37.2: 286–314.

Diklić, Davor. 2004. *Teatar u Ratnom Sarajevu, 1992–1995: Svjedočanstva.* Sarajevo: Kamerni Teatar 55.

Dimitrijević, Vojin, and Marko Milanović. 2008. "The Strange Story of the Bosnian Genocide Case." *Leiden Journal of International Law* 21.1: 65–94.

Domdey, Horst. 1995. "Writer's Block, or 'John on Patmos in the Haze of a Drug High:' Heiner Müller's Lyrical Text *Mommsen's Block.*" *Heiner Müller: Contexts and History: A Collection of Essays from the Sydney German Studies Symposium 1994 "Heiner Müller, Theatre-History-Performance."* Ed. Gerhard Fischer. Tübingen: Stauffenburg Verlag. 233–42.

Douglas, Lawrence. 1995. "Film as Witness: Screening Nazi Concentration Camps before the Nuremburg Tribunal." *The Yale Law Journal* 105.2: 449–81.

Douzinas, Kostas, and Slavoj Žižek. 2010. "Introduction: The Idea of Communism." *The Idea of Communism.* Eds. Kostas Douzinas and Slavoj Žižek. London; New York: Verso. vii–x.

Downey, Anthony. 2009. "Zones of Indistinction: Giorgio Agamben's 'Bare Life' and the Politics of Aesthetics." *Third Text* 23.2: 109–25.

Draaisma, Douwe. 2001. *Metaphors of Memory: A History of Ideas about the Mind.* Cambridge: Cambridge University Press.

Dubois, Laurent. 2004a. *Avengers of the New World: The Story of the Haitian Revolution.* Cambridge, Mass.: Belknap Press of Harvard University Press.

——. 2004b. *A Colony of Citizens: Revolution and Slave Emancipation in the French Caribbean, 1787–1804.* Chapel Hill and London: University of North Carolina Press.

Duprey-Colon, Jennifer. 2010. "Memory and Urban Landscapes in Contemporary Catalan Theatre: Benet i Jornet's *Olors* and Jordi Coca's *Antigone.*" *New Spain; New Literatures.* Eds. Luis Martín-Estudillo and Nicholas Spadaccini. Nashville, Tenn.: Vanderbilt University Press. 61–80.

Eke, Norbert Otto. 1989. *Heiner Müller: Apokalypse und Utopie.* Padeborn: Ferdinand Schöningh.

Elliott, Anthony. 2004. *Subject to Ourselves: Social Theory, Psychoanalysis and Postmodernity.* Boulder, Colo.: Paradigm.

Enders, Jody. 1999. *The Medieval Theatre of Cruelty: Rhetoric, Memory, Violence.* Ithaca and London: Cornell University Press.

Eng, David L., and David Kazanjian. 2003. "Introduction: Mourning Remains." *Loss: The Politics of Mourning.* Eds. David L. Eng and David Kazanjian. Berkeley, Calif.; London: University of California Press. 1–24.

Engelking, Barbara. 2001. *Holocaust and Memory. The Experience of the Holocaust and Its Consequences: An Investigation Based on Personal Narratives.* Trans. Emma Harris. Ed. Gunnar S. Paulsson. London; New York: Leicester University Press.

Erikson, Kai. 1995. "Notes on Trauma and Community." *Trauma: Explorations in Memory.* Ed. Cathy Caruth. Baltimore: John Hopkins University Press. 183–99.

Etkind, Alexander. 2004. "Hard and Soft in Cultural Memory: Political Mourning in Russia and Germany." *Grey Room* 16 (Summer): 36–59.

——. 2009. "Post-Soviet Hauntology: Cultural Memory of the Soviet Terror." *Constellations* 16.1: 182–200.

Euripides. 1999. *Alcestis.* Trans. Ted Hughes. London: Faber and Faber.

Falkowska, Janina. 2007. *Andrzej Wajda: History, Politics, and Nostalgia in Polish Cinema.* New York and Oxford: Berghahn Books.

Fassin, Didier, and Richard Rechtman. 2009. *The Empire of Trauma: An Inquiry into the Condition of Victimhood.* Trans. Rachel Gomme. Princeton: Princeton University Press.

Fehervary, Helen. 1976. "Enlightenment or Entanglement: History and Aesthetics in Bertolt Brecht and Heiner Müller." *New German Critique* 8.

Felman, Shoshana. 2002. *The Juridical Unconscious: Trials and Traumas in the Twentieth Century*. Cambridge, Mass.: Harvard University Press.

Felman, Shoshana, and Dori Laub. 1992. *Testimony: Crises of Witnessing in Literature, Psychoanalysis and History*. New York: Routledge.

Fick, Carolyn E. 1990. *The Making of Haïti: The Saint Domingue Revolution from Below*. Knoxville: University of Tennessee Press.

——. 1997. "The French Revolution in Saint Domingue: A Triumph or Failure?" *Turbulent Time: The French Revolution and the Great Caribbean*. Eds. David Barry Gaspar and David Patrick Geggus. Bloomington: Indiana University Press. 51–77.

Fiebach, Joachim. 1990. *Inseln der Unordnung: Fünf Versuche zu Heiner Müllers Theatertexten*. Berlin: Henschelverlag.

——. 2003. "Self-Reflexivity in Heiner Müller." *Mirror or Mask: Self-Representation in the Modern Age*. Eds. David Blostein and Pia Kleber. Berlin: VISTAS Verlag. 169–77.

Fischer, Sibylle. 2004. *Modernity Disavowed: Haiti and the Culture of Slavery in the Age of Revolution*. Durham and London: Duke University Press.

Fitzpatrick, Lisa. 2011. "The Performance of Violence and the Ethics of Spectatorship." *Performance Research* 16.1: 59–67.

Forsyth, Alison, and Chris Megson. 2009. *Get Real: Documentary Theatre Past and Present*. Basingstoke and New York: Palgrave Macmillan.

Foucault, Michel. 1996. "Film and Popular Memory." *Foucault Live: Collected Interviews, 1961–1984*. Ed. Sylvère Lotringer. Brooklyn: Semiotext(e).

Freeman, Elizabeth. 2008. "Turn the Beat Around: Sadomasochism, Temporality, History." *Differences* 19.1: 32–70.

——. 2010. *Time Binds: Queer Temporalities, Queer Histories*. Durham; London: Duke University Press.

Freud, Sigmund. 1953–72. "Delusions and Dreams in Jensen's Gradiva." *The Standard Edition of the Complete Psychological Works of Sigmund Freud*. Trans. and ed. James Strachey. London: Hogarth Press. 7–95

——. 1953–74a. *Beyond the Pleasure Principle. The Standard Edition of the Complete Psychological Works of Sigmund Freud*. Vol. 18. Trans. and ed. James Strachey. London: Hogarth Press.

——. 1953–74b. "Inhibitions, Symptoms, and Anxiety." *The Standard Edition of the Complete Psychological Works of Sigmund Freud*. Vol. 20. Trans. and ed. James Strachey. London, Hogarth Press.

——. 1955. "The Ego and the Id." *The Standard Edition of the Complete Psychological Works of Sigmund Freud*. Vol. 19. Trans. and ed. James Strachey. London: Hogarth Press. 1–59.

——. 1957 [1917]. "Mourning and Melancholia." *The Standard Edition of the Complete Psychological Works of Sigmund Freud*. Vol. 14. Trans. and ed. James Strachey. London: Hogarth Press. 243–58.

——. 1961. *Beyond the Pleasure Principle*. Trans. James Strachey. New York: W.W. Norton.

Freud, Sigmund. 1966. "The Splitting of the Ego as a Mechanism of Defence." *The Standard Edition of the Complete Psychological Works of Sigmund Freud*. Trans. and ed. James Strachey. Vol. 23. London: Hogarth Press. 271–8.

———. 1966. "Project for a Scientific Psychology." *The Standard Edition of the Complete Psychological Works of Sigmund Freud.* Vol. 1. Trans. and ed. James Strachey. London: Hogarth Press. 283–397.

———. 1966. *An Outline of Psychoanalysis. The Standard Edition of the Complete Psychological Works of Sigmund Freud,* Vol. 23. Trans. and ed. James Strachey. London: Hogarth Press.

———. 2002. *Wild Analysis.* Trans. Alan Bance. London; New York: Penguin Books.

Friedland, Paul. 2002. *Political Actors: Representative Bodies and Theatricality in the Age of the French Revolution.* Ithaca: Cornell University Press.

Friedrich, Jörg. 2002. *Der Brand: Deutschland im Bombenkreig 1940–1945.* Munich: Propyläen.

Frost, Laura. 2002. *Sex Drives: Fantasies of Fascism in Literary Modernism.* Ithaca: Cornell University Press.

Fuchs, Elinor. 1996. *The Death of Character: Perspectives on Theatre after Modernism.* Bloomington: Indiana University Press.

Furet, François. 1992. *Revolutionary France, 1770–1880.* Trans. Antonia Nevill. Oxford: Blackwell Publishers; Cambridge, Mass.: Three Cambridge Centre.

———. 1999. *The Passing of an Illusion: The Idea of Communism in the Twentieth Century.* Trans. Deborah Furet. Chicago: University of Chicago Press.

Gardiner, Michael E. 2000. *Critiques of Everyday Life: An Introduction.* New York; London: Routledge.

Gaspar, David Barry, and David Geggus. 1997. *A Turbulent Time: The French Revolution and the Great Caribbean.* Bloomington: Indiana University Press.

Geggus, David P. 1985. "Haiti and the Abolitionists: Opinion, Propaganda, and International Politics in Britain and France, 1804–1838." *Abolition and Its Aftermath: The Historical Context, 1790–1916.* Ed. David Richardson. London: Frank Cass. 113–40.

———. 1987. "The Enigma of Jamaica in the 1790s: New Light on the Causes of Slave Rebellions." *William and Mary Quarterly* 44.2: 274–99.

———. 2002. *Haitian Revolutionary Studies.* Bloomington: Indiana University Press.

Geipel, Ines. 2002. *Dann fiel auf einmal der Himmel um. Inge Müller. Die Biographie.* Berlin: Henschel Verlag.

Genovese, Eugene. 1979. *From Rebellion to Revolution: Afro-American Slave Revolt in the Making of the Modern World.* Baton Rouge: Louisiana State University Press.

Gilbert, Helen, and Jacqueline Lo. 2007. *Performance and Cosmopolitics: Cross-Cultural Transactions in Australasia.* Basingstoke and New York: Palgrave Macmillan.

Gilroy, Paul. 1993. *The Black Atlantic: Modernity and Double Consciousness.* Cambridge, Mass.: Harvard University Press.

Glissant, Édouard. 1989. *Caribbean Discourse: Selected Essays.* Trans. J. Michael Dash. Charlottesville, Va.: University of Virginia Press.

Glowacka, Dorota, and Joanna Zylinska. 2007. *Imaginary Neighbours: Mediating Polish-Jewish Relations after the Holocaust.* Lincoln: University of Nebraska Press.

Goldberg, Amos. 2006. "Trauma, Narrative, and Two Forms of Death." *Literature and Medicine* 25.1: 122–41.

——. 2009. "The Victim's Voice and Melodramatic Aesthetics in History." *History and Theory* 48.3: 220–37.

Gordon, Avery F. 1997. *Ghostly Matters: Haunting and Sociological Imagination.* Minneapolis and London: University of Minnesota Press.

Gourevitch, Michael. 1999. "The Memory Thief." *The New Yorker* 14 June: 48–68.

Graham, Helena, and Alejandro Quiroga. 2012. "After the Fear Was Over: What Came after Dictatorships in Spain, Greece, and Portugal." *The Oxford Handbook of Postwar European History.* Ed. Dan Stone. Oxford: Oxford University Press. 502–25.

Graham-Jones, Jean. 2000. *Exorcising History: Argentine Theatre under Dictatorship.* Lewisburg, Pa.: Bucknell University Press; London: Associated University Presses.

Grass, Günther. 2002. *Crabwalk.* Orlando: Harcourt.

Greer, Donald. 1935. *The Incidence of the Terror during the French Revolution: A Statistical Interpretation.* Cambridge, Mass.: Harvard University Press.

Griffiths, Aled. 2000. "The Last Days of Heine Müller." *Dying Words: The Last Moments of Writers and Philosophers.* Ed. Martin Crowley. Amsterdam; Atlanta, Ga.: Rodopi. 39–55.

Gross, Jan Tomasz. 2001. *Neighbors: The Destruction of the Jewish Community in Jedwabne, Poland.* Princeton, NJ: Oxford: Princeton University Press.

Grosse, Pascal. 2005. "What Does German Colonialism Have to Do with National Socialism? A Conceptual Framework." *Germany's Colonial Pasts.* Eds. Eric Ames, Marcia Klotz, and Lora Wildenthal. Lincoln: University of Nebraska Press. 115–34.

Gunew, Sneja. 2004. *Haunted Nations: The Colonial Dimensions of Multiculturalism.* London and New York: Routledge.

Guenther, Lisa. 2011. "Resisting Agamben: The Biopolitics of Shame and Humiliation." *Philosophy and Social Criticism* 1–21.

Gurewitsch, Brana, ed. 1998. *Mothers, Sisters, Resisters: Oral Histories of Women Who Survived the Holocaust.* Tuscaloosa; London: University of Alabama Press.

Habermas, Jürgen. 2001. *The Postnational Constellation: Political Essays.* Cambridge, Mass.: MIT.

Habermas, Jürgen, and Jacques Derrida. 2005. "February 15, or, What Binds Europeans Together: A Plea for a Common Foreign Policy, Beginning in the Core of Europe." *Old Europe, New Europe, Core Europe: Transatlantic Relations after the Iraq War.* Eds. Daniel Levy, Max Pensky, and John Torpey. London; New York: Verso. 3–13.

Hallward, Peter. 2007. *Damming the Flood: Haiti and the Politics of Containment.* London: Verso.

Hanrahan, Brian. 2007. "Film Reopens Poland's Katyn Wound." BBC News (5 October). http://news.bbc.co.uk/1/hi/world/europe/7028365.stm [accessed 29 July 2009].

Hansen, Peo. 2002. "European Integration, European Identity and the Colonial Connection." *European Journal of Social Theory* 5.4: 483–98.

——. 2004. "In the Name of Europe." *Race and Class* 45.3: 49–62.

Hartman, Geoffrey H. 1996. *The Longest Shadow: In the Aftermath of the Holocaust.* Bloomington, Ind.: Indiana University Press.

——. 2000. "Memory.com: Tele-suffering and Testimony in the Dot Com Era." *Raritan* XIX: 1–20.

Hartman, Saidiya V. 1997. *Scenes of Subjection: Terror, Slavery, and Self-Making in Nineteenth-Century America.* New York: Oxford University Press.

Hayden, Robert M. 2007. "Moral Visions and Impaired Insight: The Imagining of Other Peoples' Communities in Bosnia." *Current Anthropology* 48.1: 105–31.

Hedgepeth, Sonja M., and Rochelle G. Saidel. 2010. "Introduction." *Sexual Violence against Jewish Women during the Holocaust.* Eds. Sonja M. Hedgepeth and Rochelle G. Saidel. Waltham, Mass.: Brandeis University Press. 1–10.

Heller, Agnes. 1993. *A Philosophy of History in Fragments.* Oxford and Cambridge, MA.: Blackwell.

——. 1999. *A Theory of Modernity.* Oxford: Blackwell.

Hertz, Robert. 1960. *Death and the Right Hand.* Trans. Rodney and Claudia Needham. Aberdeen: Cohen and West.

Herzinger, Richard. 1995. "*Deutschland ortlos*: Heiner Müller's Image of Germany in the Context of German Cultural Criticism." *Heiner Müller: Contexts and History: A Collection of Essays from the Sydney German Studies Symposium 1994 Heiner Müller/Theatre-History-Performance.* Ed. Gerhard Fischer. Tübingen: Stauffenburg. 103–16.

Hirsch, Joshua. 2004. *Afterimage: Film, Trauma, and the Holocaust.* Philadelphia: Temple University Press.

Hirsch, Marianne. 1997. *Family Frames: Photography, Narrative, and Postmemory.* Cambridge: Harvard University Press.

——. 1999. "Projected Memory: Holocaust Photographs in Personal and Public Fantasy." *Acts of Memory: Cultural Recall in the Present.* Eds. Mieke Bal, Jonathan Crewe, and Leo Spitzer. Hanover and London: University Press of New England. 2–23.

——. 2001. "Surviving Images: Holocaust Photographs and the Work of Postmemory." *The Yale Journal of Criticism* 14.1: 5–37.

——. 2012. *The Generation of Postmemory: Writing and Visual Culture After the Holocaust.* New York: Columbia University Press.

——. and Leo Spitzer. 2009. "The Witness in the Archive: Holocaust Studies/Memory." *Memory Studies* 2.2: 151–70.

——. 2010. *Ghosts of Home: The Afterlife of Czernowitz in Jewish Memory.* Berkeley: University of California Press.

Hobsbawm, Eric J. 1962. *The Age of Revolution.* New York: Mentor.

——. 1994. *The Age of Extremes: A History of the World, 1914–1991.* New York: Pantheon.

Hobsbawm, Eric, and T. Ranger. 1983. *The Invention of Tradition.* Cambridge: Cambridge University Press.

Hodgkin, Katherine, and Susannah Radstone, eds. 2003. *Contested Pasts: The Politics of Memory.* London; New York: Routledge.

Hoffman, Eva. 1998. *Shtetl: The Life and Death of a Small Town and the World of Polish Jews*. London: Secker and Warburg.
——. 2004. *After Such Knowledge: Memory, History and the Legacy of the Holocaust*. New York: Public Affairs.
Holc, Janine P. 2002. "Working through Jan Gross's 'Neighbors.'" *Slavic Review* 61.3: 453–9.
——. 2005. "Memory Contested: Jewish and Catholic Views of Auschwitz in Present-Day Poland." *Antisemitism and Its Opponents in Modern Poland*. Ed. Robert Blobaum. Ithaca and London: Cornell University Press. 301–25.
Homans, Peter. 2000. *Symbolic Loss: The Ambiguity of Mourning and Memory at Century's End*. Charlottesville; London: University of Virginia.
Honegger, Gitta. 1986. "Forms of Torture: Found Meanings between Bausch and Kantor." *Theater* 17.2: 56–60.
Huet, Marie Hèlene. 1997. *Mourning Glory: The Will of the French Revolution*. Philadelphia: University of Pennsylvania Press.
Hull, Isabel V. 2005. *Absolute Destruction: Military Culture and the Practices of War in Imperial Germany*. Ithaca: Cornell University Press.
Hungerford, Amy. 2001. "Memorising Memory." *Yale Journal of Criticism* 14.1: 67–92.
Hunt, Alfred N. 1988. *Haiti's Influence on Antebellum America: Slumbering Volcano in the Caribbean*. Baton Rouge: Louisiana State University Press.
Hunt, Lynn. 1992. *The Family Romance of the French Revolution*. Berkeley, Calif.: University of California Press.
Hüppauf, Bernd. 1993. "Experiences of Modern Warfare and the Crisis of Representation." *New German Critique* 59: 41–76.
Hutchison, Yvette. 2013 (forthcoming). *South African Performance and the Archives of Memory*. Manchester; New York: Manchester University Press.
Hutton, Patrick H. 1993. *History as an Art of Memory*. Hanover and London: University Press of New England.
Huyssen, Andreas. 1995. *Twilight Memories: Marking Time in a Culture of Amnesia*. New York and London: Routledge.
——. 2003. "Rewritings and New Beginnings: W. G. Sebald and the Literature on the Air War." *Present Past: Urban Palimpsests and the Politics of Memory*. Stanford, Calif.: Stanford University Press, 138–57.
Illouz, Eva. 2003. *Oprah Winfrey and the Glamour of Misery: An Essay on Popular Culture*. New York: Columbia University Press.
Ing, N. Rosalyn. 2001. *Dealing with Shame and Unresolved Trauma: Residential School and Its Impact on the 2nd and 3rd Generation Adults*. Diss. University of British Columbia.
Jacobs, Janet. 2008. "Gender and Collective Memory: Women and Representation at Auschwitz." *Memory Studies* 1.2: 211–25.
Jackson, Stanley, W. 1986. *Melancholia and Depression: From Hippocratic Times to Modern Times*. New Haven: Yale University Press.
Jakovljević, Branislav. 2008. "From Mastermind to Body Artist: Political Performances of Slobodan Milošević." *TDR: The Drama Review* 52.1: 51–74.
James, C. L. R. 1963 [1938]. *The Black Jacobins: Toussaint L'Overture and the San Domingo Revolution*. New York: Vintage Books.

James, Erica Caple. 2010. *Democratic Insecurities: Violence, Trauma, and Intervention in Haiti*. Berkeley: University of California Press.

Jarausch, Konrad, H., and Thomas Lindenberger. 2007. "Introduction: Contours of a Critical History of Contemporary Europe: A Transnational Agenda." *Conflicted Memories: Europeanizing Contemporary Histories*. Eds. Konrad H. Jarausch and Thomas Lindenberger. New York and Oxford: Berghahn Books. 1–22.

Jestrovic, Silvija. 2012. *Performance, Space, Utopia: Cities of War, Cities of Exile*. Basingstoke: Palgrave Macmillan.

Jones, Amelia. 2011. "'The Artist is Present:' Artistic Re-enactments and the Impossibility of Presence." *TDR: The Drama Review* 55:1: 16–45.

Kaczorowska, Teresa. 2006. *Children of the Katyń Massacre: Accounts of Life after the 1940 Soviet Murder of Polish POWs*. Trans. Frank Kujawinski. Jefferson, NC: McFarland and Co.

Kalb, Jonathan. 2001 [1998]. *The Theatre of Heiner Müller*. New York: Limelight Editions.

Kamiński, Łukasz. 2009. "Warstwy kierownicze należy zlikwidować." (The Management Structures must be Liquidated) *Tygodnik Powszechny* 39 (22 September). http://tygodnik.onet.pl/35,0,33540,8222warstwy_kierownicze_nalezy_zlikwidowac8221,artykul.html [accessed 20 December 2009].

Kantor, Tadeusz. 1983. *Wielopole, Wielopole*. Dir. Andrzej Zajączkowski. OTV Kraków. 70 min.

——. 1984. *Wielopole, Wielopole*. Dir. Adrzej Sapija. W.F.O. Łódź. 70 min.

——. 1990a. *Wielopole Wielopole*. Trans. Mariusz Tchorek and G. M. Hyde. London and New York: Marion Boyars.

——. 1990b. "The Theatre of Death and Love." *Cricot 2 Theatre – Information Guide 1989–1990*. Ed. Anna Halczak. Cracow: Cricoteka.

——. 1993. *A Journey Through Other Spaces: Essays and Manifestos, 1944–1990*. Ed. and trans. Michal Kobialka. Berkeley: University of California Press.

——. 1994. *The Return of Odysseus: The Clandestine Independent Theatre 1944*. Cracow: Cricoteka.

——. 2000. *Metamorfozy: teksty o latach 1938–1974*. Ed. Krzysztof Pleśniarowicz. Cracow: Księg Akademicka.

——. *Theoretical Essays and Programme Notes to "Wielopole, Wielopole."* Cracow: Cricoteka. (Published also in French, German, Italian, Polish, and Spanish; n.d.a).

——. *Let the Artist Croak*. Trans. Charles S. Kraszewski. Cracow: Cricoteka, unpublished manuscript, n.d.b.

——. *I'll Never Come Back Here Again*. Trans. Charles S. Kraszewski. Cracow: Cricoteka, unpublished manuscript, n.d.c.

——. *The Return of Odys. "Partytura" of a Play by Stanisław Wyspiański. Underground Theatre 1944*. Trans. Andrzej and Grażyna Branny. Cracow: Cricoteka, unpublished manuscript, n.d.d.

Kantor, Zdzisław. 2004. *Marian Kantor-Mirski (1884–1942)*. Kraków-Tychy: Teatr Mały and Ośrodek Dokumentacji Sztuki Tadeusza Kantora Cricoteka.

Kaplan, Ann E. 2005. *Trauma Culture: The Politics of Terror and Loss in Media and Literature*. New Brunswick, NJ; London: Rutgers University Press.

Kaplan, Ann E., and Ban Wang, eds. 2004. *Trauma and Cinema: Cross-Cultural Explorations*. Hong Kong: Hong Kong University Press.

Kennedy, Rosanne, and Tikka Jan Wilson. 2003. "Constructing Shared Histories: Stolen Generations Testimony, Narrative Therapy and Address." *World Memory: Personal Trajectories in Global Time*. Eds. Jill Bennett and Rosanne Kennedy. New York: Palgrave Macmillan. 119–39.

Khanna, Ranjana. 2003. *Dark Continents: Psychoanalysis and Colonialism*. Durham, NC: Duke University Press.

Kitowska-Lysiak. Małgorzata. 2002. *Tadeusz Kantor (1915–1990)*. All about Jewish Theatre. http://www.jewish-theatre.com/visitor/article_display.aspx? articleID=478

Klibansky, Raymond, Erwin Panofsky, and Fritz Saxl. 1964. *Saturn and Melancholy: Studies on the History of Natural Philosophy, Religion, and Art*. London: Thomas Nelson and Sons.

Kobialka, Michal. 1993. "The Quest for the Self: Thresholds and Transformations." *A Journey Through Other Spaces: Essays and Manifestos, 1944–1990*. By Tadeusz Kantor. Ed. and trans. Michal Kobialka. Berkeley: University of California Press. 269–310.

——. 2009. *Further On, Nothing: Tadeusz Kantor's Theatre*. Minneapolis and London: University of Minnesota Press.

Kojović, Peđa. 2010. *Sarajevo Theatre Tragedy [Sarajevska pozorišna tragedija]*. Sarajevo: Unpublished English translation.

Koski, Pirkko. 2010. "Kristian Smeds' 'Unknown Soldier': The Destruction of Images and the Construction of Meaning." *Prospero European Review* 1. 15 April 2012. http://www.t-n-b.fr/en/prospero/european-review/fiche. php?id=18&lang=1&edition=8

Kozol, Wendy. 2004. "Domesticating NATO War in Kosovo/a: (In)Visible Bodies and the Dilemma of Photojournalism." *Meridians* 4.2: 1–38.

——. 2008. "Visual Witnessing and Women's Human Rights." *Peace Review* 20.1: 67–75.

Kreikebaum, Marcus. 2003. *Heiner Müllers Gedichte*. Bielefeld: Aisthesis Verlag.

Kristeva, Julia. 1984. *Revolution in Poetic Language*. Trans. Margaret Waller. New York: Columbia University Press.

——.1986. "Stabat Mater." *The Kristeva Reader*. Trans. Leon S. Roudiez. Ed. Toril Moi. New York: Columbia University Press.

——. 1987. *Tales of Love*. Trans. Leon S. Roudiez. New York: Columbia University Press.

——. 1989. *Black Sun: Depression and Melancholia*. Trans. Leon S. Roudiez. New York: Columbia University Press.

——. 1995. *New Maladies of the Soul*. Trans. Ross Guberman. New York: Columbia University Press.

——. 2000. *The Sense and Nonsense of Revolt: The Powers and Limits of Psychoanalysis*. Trans. Jeanine Herman. New York: Columbia University Press.

Kruger, Loren. 2004. *Post-Imperial Brecht: Politics and Performance, East and South*. Cambridge, UK; New York: Cambridge University Press.

Krzemien, Teresa. 1986. "Kantor." *Cricot 2 Theatre Information Guide 1986*. Ed. Anna Halczak. Cracow: Cricoteka.

Kundrus, Birthe. 2011. "German Colonialism: Some Reflections on Representations, Specificities, and Constellations." *German Colonialism: Race, the Holocaust, and Postwar Germany*. Eds. Volker Langbehn and Mohammad Salama. New York: Columbia University Press. 29–47.

Kurkowska-Budzan, Marta. 2004. "My Jedwabne." *The Neighbors Respond: The Controversy over the Jedwabne Massacre in Poland*. Eds. Anthony Polonsky and Joanna B. Michlic. Princeton and Oxford: Princeton University Press. 200–6.

Kushner, Tony. 2006. "Holocaust Testimony, Ethics, and the Problem of Representation." *Poetics Today* 27.2: 288–95.

Labanyi, Jo. 2009. "The Languages of Silence: Historical Memory, Generational Transmission and Witnessing in Contemporary Spain." *Journal of Romance Studies* 9.3: 23–35.

LaCapra, Dominic. 1994. *Representing the Holocaust: History, Theory, Trauma*. Ithaca: Cornell University Press.

——. 1997. "Lanzmann's Shoah: 'Here There Is No Why.'" *Critical Inquiry* 23 (Winter): 231–69.

——. 1998a. "Critical Response II: Equivocations of Autonomous Art", *Critical Inquiry* 24 (Spring): 833–6.

——. 1998b. *History and Memory after Auschwitz*. Ithaca, NY: Cornell University Press.

——. 2001. *Writing History, Writing Trauma*. Baltimore; London: Johns Hopkins University Press.

——. 2004. *History in Transit: Experience, Identity, Critical Theory*. Ithaca, NY: Cornell University Press.

——. 2009. *History and Its Limits: Human, Animal, Violence*. Ithaca, NY: Cornell University Press.

Lachmann, Renate. 1997. *Memory and Literature: Intersexuality in Russian Modernism*. Minneapolis: University of Minnesota Press.

Landsberg, Alison. 2004. *Prosthetic Memory: The Transformation of American Remembrance in the Age of Mass Culture*. New York: Columbia University Press.

Lang, Berel. 2005. *Post-Holocaust: Interpretation, Misinterpretation, and the Claims of History*. Bloomington and Indianapolis: Indiana University Press.

Langbehn, Volker, and Mohammad Salama. 2011. "Introduction: Reconfiguring German Colonialism." *German Colonialism: Race, the Holocaust, and Postwar Germany*. Eds. Volker Langbehn and Mohammad Salama. New York: Columbia University Press. ix–xxxi.

Langenbacher, Eric. 2003. "Changing Memory Regimes in Contemporary Germany." *German Politics and Society* 21.2: 46–68.

——. 2004. "Comprehending Trauma and Its Aftermath." *German Politics and Society* 22.3: 98–106.

——. 2010. "Still Unmasterable Past? The Impact of History and Memory in the Federal Republic of Germany." *German Politics* 19.1: 24–40.

Langley, Lester D. 1996. *The Americas in the Age of Revolution, 1750–1850*. New Haven: Yale University Press.

Lanzmann, Claude. 1985. *Shoah: An Oral History of the Holocaust*. New York: Pantheon Books.

——. 2003 [1985]. Dir. *Shoah*. DVD. Paris: Les Films Aleph; New York: New Yorker Films Artwork.

Laplanche, Jean. 1989. *New Foundations for Psychoanalysis*. Trans. David Macey. Cambridge: Basil Blackwell.

Laplanche, Jean, and J. B. Pontalis. 1985 [1973]. *The Language of Psychoanalysis*. Trans. Donald Nicholson-Smith. New York: W. W. Norton.

Lappin, Elena. 1999. "The Man with Two Heads." *Granata* 66: 7–65.

Laub, Dori. 1992. "An Event without a Witness, Truth, Testimony and Survival." *Testimony: Crisis of Witnessing in Literature, Psychoanalysis, and History*. Eds. Shoshana Felman and Dori Laub. New York: Routledge. 75–92.

——. 1995. "Truth and Testimony: The Process and the Struggle." *Trauma: Explorations in Memory*. Ed. Cathy Caruth. Baltimore: Johns Hopkins University Press. 61–75.

——. 2009. "'On Holocaust Testimony and its 'Reception' within its Own Frame as a Process in its Own Right: A Response to 'Between History and Psychoanalysis' by Thomas Trezise." *History and Memory* 21.1: 127–50.

Lawson, Jeffrey. 1995. *Tadeusz Kantor and Teatr Cricot 2: When Theatrical Art Verged on Death*. Diss. New York University.

Lehmann, Hans-Thies. 1999. *Postdramatisches Theater: Essay*. Frankfurt am Main: Verlag der Autoren.

——. 2006. *Postdramatic Theatre*. Trans. Karen Jürs-Munby. London; New York: Routledge.

Lehmann, Rosa. 2001. *Symbiosis and Ambivalence: Poles and Jews in a Small Galician Town*. New York: Berghahn Books.

Leslie, Esther. 2003. "Absent-Minded Professors: Etch-a-sketching Academic Forgetting." *Regimes of Memory*. Eds. Susannah Radstone and Katherine Hodgkin. London and New York: Routledge. 172–85.

Levi, Primo. 1989. *The Drowned and the Saved*. Trans. Raymond Rosenthal. New York: Vintage Books.

Levy, Daniel, and Natan Sznaider. 2002. "Memory Unbound: The Holocaust and the Formation of Cosmopolitan Memory." *European Journal of Social Theory* 5.1: 87–106.

Levy, Daniel, and Natan Sznaider. 2006. *Holocaust Memory in the Golden Age*. Philadelphia: Temple University Press.

Leys, Ruth. 2000. *Trauma: A Genealogy*. Chicago: University of Chicago Press.

——. 2007. *From Guilt to Shame: Auschwitz and After*. Princeton, NJ: Princeton University Press.

——. 2011. "The Turn to Affect: A Critique." *Critical Inquiry* 37.3: 434–72.

Leydesdorff, Selma. 2009. "When Communism Fell Apart and Neighbours Became Enemies: Stories of Bewilderment in Srebrenica." *Memories of Mass Repression: Narrating Life Stories in the Aftermath of Atrocity*. Eds. Nancy Adler et al. New Brunswick, NJ: Transaction Publishers. 21–39.

Liljeström, Marianne, and Susanna Paasonen, eds. 2010. *Working with Affect in Feminist Readings: Disturbing Differences*. London; New York: Routledge.

Liss, Andrea. 1988. *Trespassing through Shadows: Memory, Photography and the Holocaust.* Minneapolis: University of Minnesota Press.
———. 1991. "Trespassing through Shadows: History, Mourning and Photography in Representation of Holocaust Memory." *Framework* 4.1: 30–9.
Livesey, Jim. 2009. "The Limits of Terror: The French Revolution, Rights and Democratic Transition." *Thesis Eleven* 97.1: 64–80.
Lower, Wendy. 2005. *Nazi Empire-Building and the Holocaust in Ukraine.* Chapel Hill, NC: University of North Carolina Press.
Lowy, Michael. 1992. *Redemption and Utopia: Jewish Libertarian Thought in Central Europe: A Study in Effective Affinity.* Trans. Hope Heaney. London: Athlone Press.
Lukić, Darko. 2009. *Drama ratne traume.* Zagreb: Meandarmedia.
Lužina, Jelena, ed. 2007. *Theatre and Memory.* Skopje: Faculty of Dramatic Arts.
Lyotard, Jean-François. 1984. *The Postmodern Condition: A Report on Knowledge.* Trans. Geoff Bennington and Brian Massumi. Minneapolis: University of Minnesota Press.
Mächler, Stefan. 2001. *The Wilkomirski Affair: A Study in Biographical Truth.* Trans. John E. Woods. New York: Schocken.
Madureira, Luis. 2011. " 'Kalashnikovs, Not Coca-Cola, Bring Self-Determination to Angola' ": The Two Germanys, Lusophone Africa, and the Rhetoric of Colonial Difference." *German Colonialism: Race, the Holocaust, and Postwar Germany.* Eds. Volker Langbehn and Mohammad Salama. New York: Columbia University Press. 294–313.
Malkin, Jeanette R. 1999. *Memory-Theatre and Postmodern Drama.* Ann Arbor: University of Michigan Press.
Mälksoo, Maria. 2009. *The Politics of Becoming European: A Study of Polish and Baltic Post-Cold War Security Imaginaries.* London; New York: Routledge.
Margalit, Gilad. 2010. *Guilt, Suffering, and Memory: Germany Remembers its Dead of World War II.* Trans. Haim Watzman. Bloomington: Indiana University Press.
Markusen, Eric and David Kopf. 1995. *The Holocaust and Strategic Bombing: Genocide and Total War in the Twentieth Century.* Boulder, Colo.: Westview Press.
Maslan, Susan. 2005. *Revolutionary Acts: Theatre, Democracy, and the French Revolution.* Baltimore: Johns Hopkins University Press.
Massumi, Brian. 2002. *Parables for the Virtual: Movement, Affect, Sensation.* Durham, NC: Duke University Press.
Matsuda, Matthew K. 1996. *The Memory of the Modern.* Oxford: Oxford University Press.
Max, Harold. 2003. *Enlightenment Phantasies: Cultural Identity in France and Germany, 1750–1914.* Ithaca and London: Cornell University Press.
Meerzon, Yana. 2011. "Dancing On the X-rays: On the Theatre of Memory, Counter-Memory, and Postmemory in the post-1989 East-European Context." *Modern Drama* 54.4: 475–506.
Melber, Henning. 2011. "The Genocide in 'German South-West Africa' and the Politics of Commemoration: How (Not) to Come to Terms with the

Past." *German Colonialism and National Identity*. Eds. Michael Perraudin and Jürgen Zimmerer. New York: Routledge. 251–64.

Merridale, Catherine. 2010. "Soviet Memories: Patriotism and Trauma." *Memory: Histories, Theories, Debates*. Eds. Susannah Radstone and Bill Schwarz. New York: Fordham University Press. 376–89.

Merritt, Susan Hollis. 2000. "Harold Pinter's *Ashes to Ashes*: Political/Personal Echoes of the Holocaust." *The Pinter Review: Collected Essays 1999 and 2000*. Eds. Francis Gillen and Steven H. Gale. Tampa: University of Tampa Press. 73–84.

Miklaszewski, Krzysztof. 2002. *Encounters with Tadeusz Kantor*. Ed. and trans. George Hyde. London: Routledge.

Miller, Paul B. 2006. "Contested Memories: The Bosnian Genocide in Serb and Muslim Minds. *Journal of Genocide Research* 8.3: 311–24.

Milne, Drew. 2001. "Pinter's Sexual Politics." *Cambridge Companion to Harold Pinter*. Ed. Peter Raby. Cambridge: Cambridge University Press. 195–211.

Mischelis, Michelis. 2001. "Heiner Müllers heitere Therapiegruppe." Rev. of Heiner Müller's *Bildbeschreibung*, dir. Philip Tiedemann. *Die Welt* 23 April.

Möntmann, Nina. 2006. "Community Service." *Frieze* 102 (October): 37–40.

Moeller, Robert. G. 2001. *War Stories*. Berkeley: University of California Press.

——. 2006. "The Politics of the Past in the 1950s: Rhetorics of Victimization in East and West Germany." *Germans as Victims: Remembering the Past in Contemporary Germany*. Ed. Bill Niven. Basingstoke and New York: Palgrave Macmillan. 26–42.

Mommsen, Theodor. 1992. *Romische Kaisergeschichte: Nach den Vorlesungs-Mitschriften von Sebastian und Paul Hansel 1882/86*. Eds. Barbara and Alexander Demandt. Munich: C. H. Beck.

——. 1996. *A History of Rome Under the Emperors*. Trans. Clare Krojzl. Ed. Thomas Wiedemann. London and New York: Routledge.

Morawiec, Elżbieta. 1979. "Wyspiański a 'Teatr Śmierci' Kantora." *Dialog* 2: 141–8.

Morris, Leslie. 2002. "Postmemory, Postmemoir." *Unlikely History: The Changing German-Jewish Symbiosis, 1945–2000*. Eds. Leslie Morris and Jack Zipes. New York: Palgrave – now Palgrave Macmillan. 291–306.

Moses, Dirk A. 2011. "Genocide and the Terror of History." *Parallax* 17.4: 90–108.

Moynihan, Michael C. 2012. "Holocaust Agitprop in Berlin: A Film of Nude People Playing in a Gas Chamber is but One Piece Aiming to Shock at the Berlin Biennale Art Show." *Tablet* 10 June 2012. http://www.tabletmag.com/jewish-news-and-politics/98794/holocaust-agitprop-in-berlin

Müller, Heiner. 1984. *The Task: Hamlet-Machine and Other Texts for the Stage*. Ed. and trans. Carl Weber. New York: Performing Arts Journal Publications. 81–101.

——. 1989. *Explosion of A Memory / Description of A Picture. Explosion of A Memory*. Ed. and trans. Carl Weber. New York: Performing Arts Journal Publications. 93–102.

——. 1990. *Germania*. Trans. Bernard and Caroline Schütze. Ed. Sylvère Lotringer. New York: Semiotext(e).

——. 1992. *Krieg ohne Schlacht: Leben in zwei Diktaturen*. Cologne: Kiepenheuer & Witsch.

——. 1995. "Obituary." *Theatremachine*. Trans. and ed. Marc von Henning. London: Faber and Faber. 24–6.

——. 1999. *Todesanzeige. Stiftung Archiv der Akademie der Künste: Heiner Müller Archiv*. Berlin: Akademie der Künste. 35–9.

——. 1999. *Todesanzeige II. Stiftung Archiv der Akademie der Künste: Heiner Müller Archiv*. Berlin: Akademie der Künste. 41.

——. 1999 [1954]. "Ins Wasser blickend sah ich." *Stiftung Archiv der Akademie der Künste: Heiner Müller Archiv*. Berlin: Akademie der Künste. 30.

——. 2001. *Mommsen's Block: Heiner Müller Reader*. Ed. and trans. Carl Weber. Baltimore; London: Johns Hopkins University Press. 122–9.

——. 2001. "Empty Time." *Heiner Müller Reader*. Ed. and trans. Carl Weber. Baltimore: Johns Hopkins University Press. 237.

——. 2001. "Hapless Angel 2." *Heiner Müller Reader*. Ed. and trans. Carl Weber. Baltimore: Johns Hopkins University Press. 57.

——. 2001. "Self-Portrait Two A.M August 20, 1959." *Heiner Müller Reader*. Ed. and trans. Carl Weber. Baltimore: Johns Hopkins University Press. 49–50.

——. 2001. "Yesterday on a Sunny Afternoon." *Heiner Müller Reader*. Ed. and trans. Carl Weber. Baltimore: Johns Hopkins University Press. 21

Müller, Heiner, and Jan Hoet. 1992. "Insights into the Process of Production: A Conversation." *Documenta IX*. Ed. Jan Hoet. Stuttgart: Edition Cantz. 91–9.

Müller, Herta. 2000. " 'Die Nacht sie hat Pantoffel an:' Der Todesfleck in den Gedichten von Inge Müller." *"Nun breche ich in Stucke . . ."*: *Leben, Schreiben, Suizid: über Sylvia Plath, Virginia Woolf, Marina Zwetajewa, Anne Sexton, Unica Zürn, Inge Müller*. Ed. Ursula Keller. Berlin: Verlag Vorwer. 183–6.

Müller, Inge. 1996. *Irgendwo: noch einmal mocht ich sehn*. Ed. Ines Geipel. Berlin: Aufbau-Verlag GmbH.

——. 1997. "Wer gibt dir ein Recht den Stummen zu spielen"; "Who Gives You a Right to Play Dumb." Trans. Matthew Griffin. *Dimension²* 4.1: 118–19.

——. 1999 [1954]. "Da ist die Brüke." *Stiftung Archiv der Akademie der Künste: Heiner Müller Archiv*. Berlin: Akademie der Künste. 30.

Müller, Jan-Werner. 2002. *Memory and Power in Post-War Europe*. Cambridge: Cambridge University Press.

——. 2010. "On 'European Memory': Some Conceptual and Normative Remarks." *A European Memory?: Contested Histories and Politics of Remembrance*. Eds. Małgorzata Pakier and Bo Stråth. New York: Berghahn Books. 25–37.

——. 2010. *Contesting Democracy: Political Ideas in Twentieth-Century Europe*. New Haven; London: Yale University Press.

Murjas, Teresa. 2011. "'I Suggest a Night at the Theatre, Mr. Cameron': Memory, History and Responsibility in *Our Class (Nasza Klasa, 2009)*." *Contemporary Theatre Review* 21.4: 487–510.

Mytkowska, Joanna, ed. 2005. "Too-True Scenarios." Trans. Marcin Wawrzyńczak. *Artur Żmijewski: If It Happened Only Once It's as if It Never Happened.* Warsaw: Zachęta Narodowa Galeria Sztuki/Hatje Cantz Publishers. 3–17.

Naimark, Norman M. 1995. *The Russians in Germany: A History of the Soviet Zone of Occupation, 1945–1949.* Cambridge, Mass.: Belknap Press of Harvard University Press.

———. 2001. *Fires of Hatred: Ethnic Cleansing in Twentieth-Century Europe.* Cambridge, Mass; London: Harvard University Press.

———. 2009. "Srebrenica in the History of Genocide: A Prologue." *Memories of Mass Repression: Narrating Life Stories in the Aftermath of Atrocity.* Eds. Nancy Adler et al. New Brunswick, NJ: Transaction Publishers. 3–20.

Neiethammer, Lutz. 1992. *Posthistoire: Has History Come to an End?* Trans. Patrick Camiller. London: Verso.

Nesbitt, Nick. 2004. "Troping Toussaint, Reading Revolution." *Research in African Literatures* 35.2: 18–33.

———. 2008. *Universal Emancipation: The Haitian Revolution and the Radical Enlightenment.* Charlottesville: University of Virginia Press.

Nietzsche, Friedrich. 1989. *On the Genealogy of Morals and Ecce Homo.* Ed. Walter Kaufman. Trans. Walter Kaufman and R. J. Hollingdale. New York: Vintage Books.

Nora, Pierre. 1989. "Between History and Memory: Les Lieux de mémoire." *Representations* 26: 7–25.

———. ed. 1996–1998. *Realms of Memory: Rethinking the French Past.* Trans. Arthur Goldhammer. New York: Columbia University Press.

O'Driscoll, Anna. 2011. "Melancholy and Historical Loss: Postunification Portrayals of GDR Writers and Artists." *The GDR Remembered: Representations of the East German State since 1989.* Eds. Nick Hodgin and Caroline Pearce. Rochester; NY: Camden House. 37–53.

Ofer, Dalia, and Weitzman J. Lenore, eds. 1998. *Women in the Holocaust.* New Haven and London: Yale University Press.

Olick, Jeffrey K. 2003. *States of Memory: Continuities, Conflicts, and Transformations in National Retrospection.* Durham: Duke University Press.

Oliver, Kelly. 2001. *Witnessing: Beyond Recognition.* Minneapolis: University of Minnesota Press.

———. 2004. *The Colonization of Psychic Space: A Psychoanalytic Social Theory of Oppression.* Minneapolis: University of Minnesota Press.

———. 2007. *Women as Weapons of War: Iraq, Sex, and the Media.* New York: Columbia University Press.

Orozco, Lourdes. 2007. "Performing the Spanish Civil War in the Catalan Stage: Homage to Catalonia." *Gestos* 22 (Nov.): 55–67.

Ozouf, Mona, and François Furet, eds. 1989. *A Critical Dictionary of the French Revolution.* Trans. Arthur Goldhammer. Cambridge, Mass.: Harvard University Press.

Pakier, Małgorzata, and Bo Stråth, eds. 2010. *A European Memory?: Contested Histories and Politics of Remembrance.* New York: Berghahn Books.

Paperno, Irina. 2001. "Exhuming the Bodies of Soviet Terror." *Representations* 75.1: 89–118.

Passerini, Luisa. 1987. *Fascism in Popular Memory*. Cambridge: Cambridge University Press.

——. ed. 1998. *Identità culturale Europea: Idee, sentimenti, relazioni*. Florence: La Nuova Italia.

——. 2003. "Memories Between Silence and Oblivion." *Contested Pasts: The Politics of Memory*. Eds Katherine Hodgkin and Susannah Radstone. London and New York: Routledge. 238–54.

——. 2007. *Memory and Utopia: The Primacy of Intersubjectivity*. London; Oakville: Equinox.

Perraudin, Michael, and Jürgen Zimmerer, eds. 2011. *German Colonialism and National Identity*. New York: Routledge.

Peter, John. 1996. Review of *Ashes to Ashes* (Royal Court Theatre Upstairs, Ambassadors' Circle). Rpt. in *Theatre Record* 9–22 September: 1188.

Petras, James. 1999. "Aftermath: NATO in Kosova." *Z Magazine* (October): 13–14.

Pinter, Harold. 1996. *Ashes to Ashes*. New York: Grove Press.

Pizer, John. 2011. "Negritude in East German Literature: Anna Seghers, Heiner Müller, and the Haitian Revolution." *The Comparatist* 35: 19–39.

Plath, Sylvia. 1966. *Ariel*. New York: Harper and Row.

Pleśniarowicz, Krzysztof. 1993 ."Polski Teatr Śmierci: Mickiewicz-Wyspiański, Kantor." *Teatr* 12: 17–19.

——. 1994a. *The Dead Memory Machine: Tadeusz Kantor's Theatre of Death*. Trans. William Brand. Cracow: Cricoteka.

——. 1994b. "Odysseus Must Really Return." *The Return of Odysseus: The Clandestine Independent Theatre 1944*. Trans. Paweł Łopatka. Cracow: Cricoteka. 47–63.

——. 2004. *The Dead Memory Machine: Tadeusz Kantor's Theatre of Death*. Trans. William Brand. Aberystwyth, Wales: Black Mountain Press.

Plonowska Ziarek, Ewa. 2006. "Encounters Possible and Impossible: Derrida and Butler on Mourning." *Philosophy Today*: 144–55.

——. 2007. "Melancholic Nationalism and Pathologies of Commemorating the Holocaust in Poland." *Imaginary Neighbours: Mediating Polish-Jewish Relations after the Holocaust*. Eds Dorota Glowacka and Joanna Zylinska. Lincoln, Nebr. and London: University of Nebraska Press. 301–26.

Plunka, Gene A. 2009. *Holocaust Drama: The Theatre of Atrocity*. Cambridge, UK; New York: Cambridge University Press.

Pochoński, Jan, and Reuel K. Wilson. 1986. *Poland's Caribbean Tragedy: A Study of Polish Legions in the Haitian War of Independence, 1802–1803*. New York: Columbia University Press.

Polonsky, Antony, ed. 1990. *"My Brother's Keeper?": Recent Polish Debates on the Holocaust*. London and New York: Routledge.

——. 1992. "'Loving and Hating the Dead': Present-Day Polish Attitudes to the Jews." *Religion, State and Society* 20.1: 69–79.

——. 2000. "Introduction." *Polin* 13: 3–33.

Polonsky, Antony, and Joanna B. Michlic, eds. 2004. *The Neighbours Respond: The Controversy over the Jedwabne Massacre in Poland*. Princeton and Oxford: Princeton University Press.

Probst, Lothar. 2003. "Founding Myths in Europe and the Role of the Holocaust." *New German Critique* 90: 45–58.

Puar, Jasbir K. 2004. "Arguing Against Exceptionalism." *Feminist Studies* 24.2: 522–34.

Puga, Ana Elena. 2008. *Memory, Allegory, and Testimony in South American Theatre: Upstaging Dictatorship.* New York: Routledge.

Quintilian. 1980. *Institutio oratoria.* Ed. and trans. H. E. Butler. 4 vols. [Loeb Classical Library, 1920]; Cambridge: Harvard University Press.

Raack, R. C. 1986. "Nazi Film Propaganda and the Horrors of War." *Historical Journal of Film, Radio and Television* 6.2: 189–95.

Radden, Jennifer. 1987. "Melancholy and Melancholia." *Pathologies of the Modern Self: Postmodern Studies on Narcissism, Schizophrenia, and Depression.* Ed. David Michael Levin. New York: New York University Press.

———. 2003. "Is This Dame Melancholy? Equating Today's Depression and Past Melancholia." *Philosophy, Psychiatry, & Psychology.* 10.1: 37–52.

Radstone, Susannah. 2001. "Social Bonds and Psychical Order: Testimonies." *Cultural Values* 5.1 (Jan.): 59–78.

———. 2007a. "Trauma Theory: Contexts, Politics, Ethics." *Paragraph* 30.1: 9–29.

———. 2007b. "Theory and Affect: Undivided Worlds." *Public Emotions.* Eds. Perri 6, Susannah Radstone, Corinne Squire and Amal Treacher. London: Palgrave Macmillan. 181–201.

———. 2008. "Memory Studies: For and Against." *Journal of Memory Studies* 1.1: 31–9.

———. 2011. "What Place Is This? Transcultural Memory and the Locations of Memory Studies." *Parallax* 17.4: 109–23.

Radstone, Susannah, and Katherine Hodgkin, eds. 2003. *Regimes of Memory.* London; New York: Routledge.

Rainsford, Marcus. 1805. *An Historical Account of the Black Empire of Hayti: Comprehending a View of the Principle Transactions in the Revolution of Saint Domingo, with its Ancient and Modern State.* London: Cunder.

Rajiva, Lila. 2005. *The Language of Empire: Abu Ghraib in the American Media.* New York: Monthly Review.

Ray, Gene. 2003. "Mirroring Evil: Auschwitz, Art, and the 'War on Terror.'" *Third Text* 17.2: 113–25.

Renshaw, Layla. 2011. *Exhuming Loss: Memory, Materiality and Mass Graves of the Spanish Civil War.* Walnut Creek, Calif.: Left Coast Press.

Rhethorica ad Herennium. 1977. Ed. and trans. Harry Caplan. [Loeb Classical Library, 1954]; Cambridge, Mass.: Harvard University Press.

Richards, Sandra L. 2005. "What Is to Be Remembered?: Tourism to Ghana's Slave Castle-Dungeons." *Theatre Journal* 57.4: 617–37.

Richardson, David. 1985. *Abolition and Its Aftermath: The Historical Context, 1790–1916.* London: Frank Cass.

Rokem, Freddie. 2000. *Performing History: Theatrical Representations of the Past in Contemporary Theatre.* Iowa City: University of Iowa Press.

Rothberg, Michael. 2009. *Multidirectional Memory: Remembering the Holocaust in the Age of Decolonization.* Stanford, Calif.: Stanford University Press.

Rosenfeld, Alvin. 1980. *A Double Dying: Reflections on Holocaust Literature.* Indianapolis: Indiana University Press.

Rousso, Henry. 2007. "History of Memory, Politics of the Past: What For?" *Conflicted Memories: Europeanizing Contemporary Histories.* Eds. Konrad H. Jarausch and Thomas Lindenberger. New York; Oxford: Berghahn Books. 23–36.

Roxworthy, Emily. 2008. *The Spectacle of Japanese American Trauma: Racial Performativity and World War II.* Honolulu: University of Hawaii Press.

Rugg, Linda Haverty. 2007. *Picturing Ourselves: Photography and Autobiography.* Chicago: University of Chicago Press.

Rzewiczok, Urszula, and M. Katarzyna Gliwa. 2002. *Drodzy Nieobecni Tadeusza Kantora: Wspomnienie o Tadeuszu Kantorze, Marianie Kantorze-Mirskim i Józefie Kantor.* Katowice: Muzeum Historii Katowic.

Sakellaridou, Elizabeth. 1988. *Study of Female Characters in the Plays of Harold Pinter.* Totowa, NJ: Barnes and Noble.

——. 2003. "A Lover's Discourse – but Whose? Inversions of the Fascist Aesthetic in Howard Barker's *Und* and Other Recent English Plays." *European Journal of English Studies* 7.1: 87–107.

Sanford, George. 2005. *Katyn and the Soviet Massacre of 1940: Truth, Justice and Memory.* London; New York: Routledge.

Sanyal, Debarati. 2002. "A Soccer Match in Auschwitz: Passing Culpability in Holocaust Criticism." *Representations* 79.1: 1–27.

Savran, David. 2000. "The Haunted Houses of Modernity." *Modern Drama* 43.4: 117–28.

Scarpetta, Guy. 2003. "Portrait of the Returning Artist." *Cricot 2 Theatre – Information Guide, 1989–1990.* Ed. Anna Halczak. Cracow: Cricoteka. 189–93.

Schäffner, Wolfgang. 1991. "Der Krieg als Trauma. Zur Psychoanalyse der Kriegsneurose in Alfred Döblins *Hamlet. Hard-War/Soft War.*" *Krieg und Medien 1914 bis 1945.* Eds. M. Stingelin and W. Scherer. Munich: W. Fink. 31–46.

Schaller, Dominik. 2011. "The Struggle for Genocidal Exclusivity: The Perception of the Murder of the Namibian Herero (1904–1908) in the Age of a New International Morality." *German Colonialism and National Identity.* Eds. Michael Perraudin and Jürgen Zimmerer. New York: Routledge. 265–77.

Schama, Simon. 1989. *Citizens: A Chronicle of the French Revolution.* London: Viking.

Schechmer, Richard. 1985. *Between Theater and Anthropology.* Philadelphia: University of Pennsylvania Press.

Schiesari, Juliana. 1992. *The Gendering of Melancholia: Feminism, Psychoanalysis, and the Symbolics of Loss in Renaissance Literature.* Ithaca: Cornell University Press.

Schneider, Rebecca. 2011. *Performing Remains: Art and War in Times of Theatrical Reenactment.* London; New York: Routledge.

Schochet, Simon. 1989. *An Attempt to Identify the Polish-Jewish Officers Who Were Prisoners in Katyn.* New York: Yeshiva University.

Scholem, Gershom. 1971. "Gilgul." *Encyclopedia Judaica Vol. 7*. Jerusalem: Keter. 573–7.

Schumacher, Claude. 1998. *Staging the Holocaust: The Shoah in Drama and Performance*. Cambridge: Cambridge University Press.

Schwartz, Anja. 2007. "'Not This Year!' Reenacting Contested Pasts Aboard The Ship." *Rethinking History* 11.3: 427–46.

Schwartz, Hilleil. 1990. *Century's End: A Cultural History of the Fin de Cycle from the 990s to 1990s*. New York: Doubleday.

Scolnicov, Hanna. 2001. "*Ashes to Ashes*: Pinter's Holocaust Play." *Cycnos* 18.1: 15–24.

Scott, David. 2004. *Conscripts of Modernity: The Tragedy of Colonial Enlightenment*. Durham: Duke University Press.

Scribner, Charity. 2003. *Requiem for Communism*. Cambridge, Mass.; London: MIT.

Sebald, W. G. 2003. *On the Natural History of Destruction*. New York: Random House.

Seidman, Steven. 1991. "The End of Sociological Theory: The Postmodern Hope." *Sociological Theory* 9.2: 131–46.

Shore, Chris. 2000. *Building Europe: The Cultural Politics of European Integration*. London: Routledge.

Shore, Marci. 2005. "Conversing with Ghosts: Jedwabne, Zydokomuna, and Totalitarianism." *Kritika: Explorations in Russian and Eurasian History* 6.2: 345–74.

Sieg, Katrin. 1995. "The Poets and the Power: Heiner Müller, Christa Wolf, and the German *Literaturstreit*." *Contemporary Theatre Review* 4.2: 151–8.

Silverman, Kaja. 1996. *The Threshold of the Visible World*. New York: Routledge.

Silverstein, Marc. 1999. "'Talking about Some Kind of Atrocity': *Ashes to Ashes* in Barcelona." *The Pinter Review: Collected Essays, 1997 and 1998*. Eds. Francis Gillen and Steven H. Gale. Tampa: University of Tampa Press. 74–85.

Sklar, Kathryn Kish, and James Brewer Stewart. 2007. *Women's Rights and Transatlantic Antislavery in the Era of Emancipation*. New Haven: Yale University Press.

Smith, Kathleen E. 1996. *Remembering Stalin's Victims: Popular Memory and the End of the USSR*. New Haven: Yale University Press.

Snyder, Timothy. 2009. "The Historical Reality of Eastern Europe." *East European Politics and Societies* 23.1: 7–12.

Sontag, Susan. 1974. "Fascinating Fascism." *Under the Sign of Saturn*. New York: Anchor. 73–105.

——. 1989 [1977]. *On Photography*. Harmondsworth: Penguin.

——. 2003. *Regarding the Pain of Others*. New York: Farrar, Straus and Giroux.

Staines, Deborah R. 2002. "Auschwitz and the Camera." *Mortality* 7.1: 13–32.

Steinmetz, George. 2006. "Decolonizing German Theory: An Introduction." *Postcolonial Studies* 9.1: 3–13.

Stevens, Edward. 1910. "Letters of Toussaint Louverture and Edward Stevens, 1798–1800." *American Historical Review* 16.1: 64–101.

Stone, Dan. 2010. "Beyond the Auschwitz Syndrome." *History Today* 60.7: 27–33.

——. 2011. "Defending the Plural: Hannah Arendt and Genocide Studies." *New Formations* 71.4: 46–57.

——. 2012. "Memory Wars in the 'New Europe.'" *The Oxford Handbook of Postwar European History*. Oxford: Oxford University Press. 714–31.

——. ed. 2012. "Editor's Introduction: Postwar Europe as History." *The Oxford Handbook of Postwar European History*. Oxford: Oxford University Press. 1–33.

Stott, Tim. 2012. "The Ethics of the Playing Subject." *Culture, Politics, Ethics: Interdisciplinary Perspectives*. Eds. Scott H. Boyd, Ana Cristina Gil, and Baldwin Wong. Oxford: Inter-Disciplinary Press. 1–8. 11 March 2012. http://www.inter-disciplinary.net/wp-ontent/uploads/2009/02/stott-paper.pdf

Suchan, Jaroslaw. 2000. *Tadeusz Kantor: Impossible*. Cracow: Bunkier Sztuki.

Sugiera, Małgorzata. 1999. "Rewriting Homer: Wyspiański's Powrót Odysa and Strauss's Ithaka." *(Dis)Placing Classical Greek Theatre*. Eds. Savas Patsalidis and Elizabeth Sakellaridou. Thessaloniki: University Studio Press.

Suleiman, Susan Rubin. 2000. "Problems of Memory and Factuality in Recent Holocaust Memoirs: Wilkomirski/Wiesel." *Poetics Today* 21.3: 543–59.

——. 2006. *Crises of Memory and the Second World War*. Cambridge Mass.: Harvard University Press.

Szeman, Ioana. 2010. "Collecting Tears: Remembering the Romani Holocaust." *Performance Research* 15.2: 54–9.

Taylor, Diana. 2003. *The Archive and the Repertoire: Performing Cultural Memory in the Americas*. Durham: Duke University Press.

——. 2007. "Double Bind: The Torture Case." *Critical Inquiry* 33 (Summer): 710–33.

——. 2006. Trauma and Performance: Lessons from South America." *PMLA* 121.5: 1674–7.

Taylor, Paul. 1996. "Obscure Objects of Sado-Masochistic Desire." London: *The Independent* 21 September, Weekend, Reviews: 4.

Teraoka, Arlene Akiko. 1985. *The Silence of Entropy or Universal Discourse: The Postmodernist Politics of Heiner Müller*. New York: Peter Lang.

——. 1992. "Heiner Müller's 'Bildbeschreibung.'" *Vom Wort zum Bild: Das Neue Theater in Deutschland und den USA*. Eds. Sigrid Bauschinger and Susan L. Cocalis. Bern: Francke Verlag. 179–98.

Terasaki, Etsuko. 2002. *Figures of Desire: Wordplay, Spirit Possession, Fantasy, Madness, and Mourning in Japanese Noh Plays*. Ann Arbor: University of Michigan Press.

Terdiman, Richard. 1993. *Present Past: Modernity and the Memory Crisis*. Ithaca and London: Cornell University Press.

Terlecki, Tymon. 1983. *Stanisław Wyspiański*. Boston: Twayne Publishers.

Thibaudat, Jean-Pierre. 2003. "Kantor Will Never Return to Wielopole." *Cricot 2 Theatre – Information Guide, 1989–1990*. Ed. Anna Halczak. Cracow: Cricoteka, 183–4.

Thompson, Ewa M. 2005. "Ways of Remembering: The Case of Poland." *Toronto Slavic Quarterly* 23: 1–14.

Thompson, James. 2009. *Performance Affects: Applied Theatre and the End of Effect*. Basingstoke: Palgrave Macmillan.

Thrift, Nigel. 2004. "Intensities of Feeling: Towards a Spatial Politics of Affect." *Geografiska Annaler* 86: 57–78.

Todorov, Tzvetan. 2000. "Letter from Paris." *Salmagundi* 128/129: 3–15.

Todorova, Maria. 2010a. "Introduction: The Process of Remembering Communism." *Remembering Communism: Genres of Representation*. Ed. Maria Todorova. New York: Social Science Research Council. 9–34.

———. 2010b. "Introduction: From Utopia to Propaganda and Back." *Post-Communist Nostalgia*. Eds. Maria Todorova and Zsuzsa Gille. New York: Berghahn Books. 2–13.

———. ed. 2010. *Remembering Communism: Genres of Representation*. New York: Social Science Research Council.

Todorova, Maria, and Zsuzsa Gille. 2010. *Post-Communist Nostalgia*. New York: Berghahn Books.

Tolczyk, Dariusz. 2008. "The Katyn Massacre and the Western Myth of World War II." *American Contributions to the 14th International Congress of Slavists, Ohrid, September 2008. Vol. 2: Literature*. Ed. David M. Bethea and Christina Y. Bethin. Bloomington, Ind.: Slavica Publishers. 1–15.

Trezise, Thomas. 2001. "Unspeakable." *Yale Journal of Criticism* 14.1: 39–66.

———. 2008. "Between History and Psychoanalysis: A Case Study in the Reception of Holocaust Survivor Testimony." *History and Memory* 20.1: 7–47.

Trojanowska, Tamara. 2005. "New Discourses in Drama." *Contemporary Theatre Review* 15.1: 93–104.

Trouillot, Michel-Rolph. 1995. *Silencing the Past: Power and the Production of History*. Boston: Beacon Press.

Tscholakova, Ginka. 1999. "Die Maske des Schweigens." *Stiftung Archiv der Akademie der Künste: Heiner Müller Archiv*. Berlin: Akademie der Künste. 40.

Turner, Charles. 2004. "Jürgen Habermas: European or German?" *European Journal of Political Theory* 3.3: 293–314.

Uerlings, Herbert. 1997. *Poetiken der Interkulturalität: Haiti bei Kleist, Seghers, Müller, Buch und Fichte*. Tübingen: Niemeyer.

Underhill, Karen. 2011. "Next Year in Drohobych: On the Uses of Jewish Absence." *East European Politics and Societies* 25.3: 581–96.

Van Alphen, Ernst. 2005. "Playing the Holocaust." *Art in Mind: How Contemporary Images Shape Thought*. Chicago: Chicago University Press.

Van der Kolk, Bessel A., and Charles P. Ducey. 1989. "The Psychological Processing of Traumatic Experience: Rorschach Patterns in PTSD." *Journal of Traumatic Stress* 2.3: 259–74.

Van der Kolk, Bessell, Alexander C. McFarlane, and Lars Weiseth, eds. 1996. *Traumatic Stress: The Effects of Overwhelming Experience on Mind, Body, and Society*. New York: Guilford Press.

Vaßen, Florian. 1995. "Images Become Text Become Images: Heiner Müller's *Bildbeschreibung* (*Description of a Picture*)." *Heiner Müller: Contexts and History: A Collection of Essays from the Sydney German Studies Symposium 1994 "Heiner Müller, Theatre-History-Performance."* Ed. Gerhard Fischer. Tübingen: Stauffenburg Verlag. 165–87.

Verber, Jason. 2010. "The Conundrum of Colonialism in Postwar Germany." PhD Diss. The University of Iowa.

Verdery, Katherine. 1999. *The Political Lives of Dead Bodies: Reburial and Postsocialist Change.* New York: Columbia University Press.

Verwoert, Jan. 2008. "Game Theory." *Frieze* 114 (April). 11 March 2012. http://www.frieze.com/issue/article/game_theory

Vido-Rzewuska, Marie-Thérèse. 1995. "The Father Figure in Tadeusz Kantor's Work." *Journal of Dramatic Criticism* 10.1: 233–6.

Volkan, Vamik D. 2001. "Transgenerational Transmission and Chosen Traumas: An Aspect of Large-Group Identity." *Group Analysis* 34.1: 79–97.

Volli, Ugo. 1995. "Kantor's Theatre of Exteriority: A Philosophical Approach." *Journal of Dramatic Theory and Criticism* 10.1: 245–9.

Wajda, Andrzej, dir. *Katyń.* DVD. 2009 [2007]. Artificial Eye.

——. 2008. *Katyn.* Trans. Jennifer Zielinska. Warsaw: Prószyński i S-ka.

Walker, Janet. 2003. "The Traumatic Paradox: Autobiographical Documentary and the Psychology of Memory." *Regimes of Memory.* Eds. Susannah Radstone and Katherine Hodgkin. London and New York: Routledge. 104–19.

Weber, Carl. 2001. "Mommsen's Block: A Poem/Performance Text." *Heiner Müller Reader.* Ed. and trans. Carl Weber. Baltimore; London: Johns Hopkins University Press. 122–3.

Weiss, Peter. 1966. *The Persecution and Assassination of Jean-Paul Marat as Performed by the Inmates of Asylum of Charenton under the Direction of the Marquis De Sade.* Trans. Geoffrey Skelton. New York: Atheneum.

Weissman Gary. 2004. *Fantasies of Witnessing: Postwar Efforts to Experience the Holocaust.* Ithaca: Cornell University Press.

Werth, Nicolas. 2008. "The Crimes of the Stalin Regime: Outline for an Inventory and Classification." *The Historiography of Genocide.* Ed. Dan Stone. Basingstoke: Palgrave Macmillan. 400–19.

Wieviorka, Annette. 1994. "On Testimony." *Holocaust Remembrance: The Shapes of Memory.* Ed. Geoffrey Hartman. Oxford: Basil Blackwell. 23–32.

——. 2006. *The Era of Witness.* Trans. Jared Stark. Ithaca, NY: Cornell University Press.

Wilkomirski, Binjamin. 1996. *Fragments: Memories of a Wartime Childhood.* New York: Shocken. [Rpt. in Stefan Mächler. *The Wilkomirski Affair.* New York: Schocken, 2001.] 375–496.

Williams, Linda. 1989. *Hard Core: Power, Pleasure, and the "Frenzy of the Visible".* Berkeley: University of California Press.

Winkel, Roel Vande. 2004. "Nazi Newsreels in Europe, 1939–1945: The Many Faces of Ufa's Foreign Weekly Newsreels (Auslandstonwoche) versus Germany's Weekly Newsreel (Deutsche Wochenschau)." *Historical Journal of Film, Radio and Television* 24.1: 5–34.

Wirth, Andrzej. 1993. "Memory of a Revolution: Sado-Masochistic." *The Mudrooroo/Müller Project: A Theatrical Casebook.* Ed. Gerhard Fischer. Kensington, Australia: New South Wales University Press. 62–6.

Wittkower, Rudolf, and Margot Wittkower. 1963. *Born Under Saturn. The Character and Conduct of Artists: A Documented History from Antiquity to the French Revolution.* New York: Random House.

Witness: Voices from the Holocaust. 1999. Exec. Prod. Marion Learn Swaybill. Prod. Stories to Remember in assn. with The Fortunoff Video Archives for Holocaust Testimonies, Yale University; Joshua M. Green Productions. PBS (CT Public TV). WNET. 1 May 2000.

Wohlfarth, Irving. 1989. "On Some Jewish Motifs in Benjamin." *The Problem of Modernity*. Ed. Andrew Benjamin. London: Routledge. 157–215.

Wolff, Larry. 1994. *Inventing Eastern Europe: The Map of Civilization on the Mind of the Enlightenment.* Stanford: Stanford University Press.

Wyspianski, Stanislaw. 1966. *The Return of Odysseus.* Trans. Howard Clarke. Bloomington: Indiana University Press.

Yaeger, Patricia. 2002. "Consuming Trauma; or, the Pleasures of Merely Circulating." *Extremities: Trauma, Testimony, and Community.* Eds. Nancy K. Miller and Jason Tougaw. Urbana: University of Illinois Press. 25–54.

Yates, Frances A. 1966. *The Art of Memory.* London: Routledge and Kegan Paul.

Young, James E. 1988. *Writing and Rewriting the Holocaust: Narratives and the Consequences of Interpretation.* Bloomington: Indiana University Press.

———. 2009. "Regarding the Pain of Women: Questions of Gender and the Arts of Holocaust Memory." *PMLA* 24.5: 1778–86.

Zarifopol-Johnston, Ilinca. 2009. *Searching for Cioran.* Bloomington: Indiana University Press.

Zaslavsky, Victor. 2008. *Class Cleansing: The Massacre at Katyn.* New York: Telos Press Publishing. 55–6.

Zhurzhenko, Tatiana. 2010. *Borderlands into Bordered Lands: Geopolitics of Identity in Post-Soviet Ukraine.* Stuttgart: Ibidem Verlag.

Zimbardo, Philip. 2007. *The Lucifer Effect: Understanding How Good People Turn Evil.* New York: Random House.

Zimmerer, Jürgen, and Joachim Zeller, eds. 2008. *Genocide in German South-West Africa: The Colonial War (1904–1908) in Namibia and Its Aftermath.* Trans. Edward Neather. Monmouth, Wales: Merlin Press.

Zimmerman, Joshua D. 2003. *Contested Memories: Poles and Jews during the Holocaust and Its Aftermath.* Ed. Joshua D. Zimmerman. New Brunswick: NJ; London: Rutgers University Press.

Żmijewski, Artur, dir. 2004. *80064.* DVD. Duration: 11'05'.

———. 2005a. "80064." *Artur Żmijewski: If It Happened Only Once It's as if It Never Happened.* Ed. Joanna Mytkowska. Warsaw: Zachęta Narodowa Galeria Sztuki/Hatje Cantz Publishers. 23–6.

———. 2005b. "Artur Żmijewski: Komentarz do filmu 80064 (notatki do spotkania z widzami w Brétigny-Sur-Orge 6.01.2005c)." *Obieg* 1. 29 February 20. http://www.obieg.pl/rozmowy/5691

———. 2005c. "The Game of Tag." *Artur Żmijewski: If It Happened Only Once It's as if It Never Happened.* Ed. Joanna Mytkowska. Warsaw: Zachęta Narodowa Galeria Sztuki/Hatje Cantz Publishers. 152.

———. 2008. "Art Must Not Always Speak Meekly: Artur Żmijewski in Conversation with Miklós Erhardt." *IDEA* 29. 11 March 2012. http://idea. ro/revista/?q=en/node/41&articol=535

——. 2010. "Applied Social Arts." *Trembling Bodies: Conversations with Artists.* Eds. Ariane Beyn et al. Trans. Søren Gauger et. al. Bytom: SCSW Kronika/ DAAD. 25–33.

——. 2011. "80064: Transcription of the Subtitles." *Artur Żmijewski: Scenarios of Dissidence.* Eds. Véronique Leblanc and Louise Déry. Montreal: Galerie de l'UQAM / ABC Art Books Canada. 118–21.

Zylinska, Joanna. 2007. "Who Is My Neighbour? Ethics under Duress." *Imaginary Neighbours: Mediating Polish-Jewish Relations after the Holocaust.* Lincoln: University of Nebraska Press. 275–300.

Index